Raising Capital on *Ṣukūk* Markets

Salim Al-Ali

Raising Capital on *Ṣukūk* Markets

Structural, Legal and Regulatory Issues

palgrave
macmillan

Salim Al-Ali
College of Law
United Arab Emirates University
Abu Dhabi, United Arab Emirates

ISBN 978-3-030-14535-4 ISBN 978-3-030-14536-1 (eBook)
https://doi.org/10.1007/978-3-030-14536-1

Library of Congress Control Number: 2019933866

This Palgrave Macmillan imprint is published by the registered company Springer Nature Switzerland AG.
The registered company address is: Gewerbestrasse 11, 6330 Cham, Switzerland

To Ali and Amna
To Maryam, Sahab, and Shamma

Preface

I wrote this book in the hope of making the law and practice of *ṣukūk* (trust investment certificates) markets clearer. *Ṣukūk* is a subject that has gained increasing attention from financial institutions and regulators over the past 28 years. *Ṣukūk* undoubtedly offers great opportunities for investment, liquidity, and trading. However, it is believed that complexity, vagueness, and difficulty surrounds *ṣukūk* due to number of parties involved, underlying transactions, and lengthy documents. The purpose of this book is to offer guidance on the theoretical and practical dimensions of the subject.

The idea for this book started when I was a doctoral student at the University of London. The book advances a scheme for understanding the nature of *ṣukūk* markets that was developed by looking at a set of issues, jurisdictions, and international players.

Acknowledgements

All praise and gratitude are due to Allah, The Most Gracious and The Most Merciful, for endowing me with the health, will, and capability to accomplish this book. Without His bounty and grace, this study would never have come to fruition.

First and foremost, I would like to extend my heartfelt appreciation and gratitude to Professor Barry Rider for his guidance, support, and inspiration. I am immensely grateful to my country, the United Arab Emirates, particularly the United Arab Emirates University for endowing me with scholarship to pursue this study.

I have benefited from discussions with many colleagues and friends. My gratitude goes to all of you and I am sure you know who you are. I also thank the academic, administrative, and library staff at the Institute of Advanced Legal Studies (IALS), University of London.

Very special and most deserved thanks go to my parents, Ali and Amna, for their countless support and prayers for my success. A word of thanks also goes to my siblings for facilitating many things that I needed once I embarked upon this project.

I must take this opportunity to pray for my father-in-law, Saeed, may Allah have mercy upon him, who passed away before the completion of this book.

My wife, Maryam, and my daughters, Sahab and Shamma, are always a constant source of inspiration. I am indebted to you for the time you have given me to work on my book even during the weekends and holidays.

About the Book

Ṣukūk markets are Islamic financial markets in which investment certificates are issued and traded. The modern *ṣukūk* market dates from 1977 with the first issue by Jordan, but they trace their origins back to the Ottoman Empire. *Ṣukūk* markets have witnessed tremendous growth since their humble beginnings. *Ṣukūk* markets offer significant opportunities for raising capital, investment activities, and generating cross-border flows. *Ṣukūk* markets have gained prominence not only in Islamic jurisdictions, but also in conventional jurisdictions. It is evident that *ṣukūk* has evolved over the past years, changing significantly in terms of growth, underlying structure, underlying asset, issuance of currency, *ṣukūk* issuers, target investors, and attached mechanisms. However, the geographical spread of *ṣukūk* does not necessarily mean that the current performance of *ṣukūk* markets is satisfactory. *Ṣukūk* markets in different jurisdictions have come under scrutiny, especially after the global financial crisis. The growth of *sukūk* markets worldwide has highlighted various issues requiring careful attention, particularly the dominance of their nature, the level of controversy, the sources of criticism, the reason behind their existence, and their occurrence in the process of *ṣukūk* structuring. Criticisms have been levelled against *ṣukūk* practices by different *ṣukūk* stakeholders. In addition, there have been legal and regulatory hurdles to the development of *ṣukūk* markets that exist at both national and international levels.

The central question of this book is: what are the most important issues facing *ṣukūk* markets and how can soundness be achieved in the wider context of *ṣukūk* markets? For the purpose of this book, such issues are divided into three categories: structural issues (arising from *ṣukūk* structuring approaches), legal issues (arising from the sharia-compliant nature of transactions), and regulatory issues (arising from national financial regulations concerning the *ṣukūk* market). The first category deals mainly with three issues: asset-backed *ṣukūk*, asset-based *ṣukūk*, and the occurrence of defaults in *ṣukūk*. The second category refers to eight issues that arise due to the sharia-compliant nature of *ṣukūk* transactions. The third category refers to particular issues relating to *ṣukūk* regulation in three jurisdictions, namely Malaysia, the United Arab Emirates, and the Kingdom of Saudi Arabia. After examining structural, legal, and regulatory issues concerning *ṣukūk*, this book proposes remedies and recommends approaches to foster the capacity of *ṣukūk* markets and ensure their soundness in the wider context.

This book consists of eight chapters and a conclusion. Chapter 1 advances a conceptual argument concerning the legal and regulatory hurdles to the development of the Islamic financial markets. It provides a necessary grounding in the fundamental aspects of the law and study of Islamic finance.

Chapter 2 establishes a basic understanding of the term *ṣukūk*, its origins, its features, its economic benefits, its legality, its evolutionary journey, and its classification in the market. It seeks to come to grips with the basic nature of *ṣukūk*, which is noticeably different from conventional bonds.

Chapter 3 deals with the first structural issue in relation to *ṣukūk*, which is asset-backed *ṣukūk*. It contains a discussion on the emergence of a new classification of *ṣukūk* structures in the market. According to this classification, *ṣukūk* structures are either asset backed or asset based. It details the meaning of asset-backed *ṣukūk*, their features, basic structures, advantages, and disadvantages. This chapter explains the choice of asset-backed *ṣukūk* and how a *ṣukūk* structure falls in this particular *ṣukūk* classification.

Chapter 4 addresses the second structural issue pertaining to *ṣukūk*, which is asset-based *ṣukūk*. It explains the concept of asset-based *ṣukūk*, their features, basic structures, advantages, and disadvantages. It looks at the circumstances in which the asset-based *ṣukūk* becomes a preferable choice in the *ṣukūk* structure.

Chapter 5 deals with the third structural issue in *ṣukūk*, which is the occurrence of default events in *ṣukūk* markets. It looks at the consequences of default events in *ṣukūk* markets and draws attention to the differences between asset-backed *ṣukūk* and asset-based *ṣukūk* in the event of default. In particular, the chapter examines seven *ṣukūk* issuances problematised by default, near-default, or financial uncertainty situations.[1] They are as follows:

- East Cameron Gas Company *Ṣukūk* (hereafter East Cameron *Ṣukūk*)
- The Investment Dar *Ṣukūk* (i.e. The Investment Dar *Ṣukūk* Company *Ṣukūk* (hereafter TID *Ṣukūk* 2005) and TID Global *Ṣukūk* I Limited *Ṣukūk* (hereafter TID *Ṣukūk* 2006))
- Nakheel Development Limited *Ṣukūk* (hereafter Nakheel *Ṣukūk*)
- Golden Belt 1 *Ṣukūk* Company B.S.C (c) *Ṣukūk* (hereafter Golden Belt *Ṣukūk*)
- Tamweel PJSC *Ṣukūk* (i.e. Tamweel Residential ABS CI (1) Ltd *Ṣukūk* (hereafter Tamweel Residential *Ṣukūk*) and Tamweel *Ṣukūk* Limited *Ṣukūk* (hereafter Tamweel Limited *Ṣukūk*))

Chapter 6 addresses the second category of *ṣukūk* issues in this book—legal issues. *Ṣukūk* products are required to comply with Islamic law, but some *ṣukūk* applications and practices have been regarded as deviations from Islamic law. Such deviations are caused, in some cases, by the underdeveloped state of legislation regarding certain aspects of *ṣukūk* markets. This chapter explains such issues and looks at the views of Islamic finance-supporting institutions regarding the legality of *ṣukūk* applications and the practices in question.

Chapter 7 examines the legislative and regulatory approaches of Malaysia, the UAE, and the KSA towards *ṣukūk* markets. In this respect, these countries have been selected as case studies for national regulations relating to the *ṣukūk* market. The choice of these countries is motivated by the fact that they are the largest markets for *ṣukūk* issuance and investment. It looks at whether the existing legislation accommodates *ṣukūk* markets in the selected countries. In particular, it examines the legal and regulatory mechanisms for facilitating *ṣukūk* markets in these countries.

Chapter 8 addresses the question of how *ṣukūk* markets can be improved in order to ensure their integrity and efficiency. As the state of *ṣukūk* markets varies across jurisdictions, this chapter constructs a framework which includes a set of legal and regulatory measures which would ensure the soundness of *ṣukūk* markets in a global context.

Chapter 9 concludes this book by summarising its findings. It also raises certain concerns in need of further investigation.

[1] Chapter 8 discussed other disputed *ṣukūk* issued by National *Ṣukūk* Company and Dana Gas *Ṣukūk* Limited. While the discussion of the *ṣukūk* cases in Chap. 5 focuses on default issue, Chap. 8 provides examples of *ṣukūk* cases raising sharia non-compliant risk.

Contents

About the Author

Salim Al-Ali is an assistant professor at College of Law at the United Arab Emirates University (UAEU), having joined the UAEU in November 2006. He was educated at the United Kingdom, where he had received his PhD in Financial Law from University of London. Prior to coming to the United Kingdom, he had completed his master's programme in Malaysia, where he received MSc in Islamic Banking and Finance. He also holds a bachelor's degree in Islamic Law from the University of Sharjah. His research interests are primarily focused on financial law, capital markets, law of Islamic finance, and regulatory and legal aspects of developing Islamic financial markets. Al-Ali was also a part-time lecturer for the LLM programme at the BPP Law School, BPP University based in London, where he lectured on a broad spectrum of jurisprudence including Islamic, English, and comparative laws. Apart from his academic experience and achievements, he is a member of the Fatwa and Sharia Supervisory Board for Al Hilal Group based in Abu Dhabi (Al Hilal Bank, Al Hilal Takaful, and Al Hilal Islamic Bank—Kazakhstan).

Al-Ali has participated in a number of international events and conferences on various areas pertaining to financial services regulation, economic crimes, and the law of Islamic finance, including Tenth Harvard University Forum on Islamic Finance and 2016 Global Islamic Economy Summit. He is a regular speaker at the Cambridge International Symposium on Economic Crime, held annually at the University of Cambridge.

Abbreviations

AAOIFI	Accounting and Auditing Organisation for Islamic Financial Institutions
ABS	Asset-backed securities
AD	Anno Domini
ADCCAC	Abu Dhabi Commercial Conciliation and Arbitration Centre
ADR	Alternative Dispute Resolution
ADX	Abu Dhabi Securities Exchange
AHAB	Ahmad Hamad Al Gosaibi & Brothers
AOSSG	Asian-Oceanian Standards-Setters Group
BBA	*Bayʿ bithaman ʾājil*
BCBS	Basel Committee on Banking Supervision
BMA	Bahrain Monetary Agency
BRV	Bankruptcy-remote vehicle
BSEC	Bemo Securitisation SAL
BNM	Bank Negara Malaysia
CEO	Chief Executive Officer
CMSA	Capital Market Services Act 2007
CRA	Credit rating agency
DCM	Domestic Capital Market
DFM	Dubai Financial Market
DFSA	Dubai Financial Services Authority
DIAC	Dubai International Arbitration Centre
DIEDC	Dubai Islamic Economy Development Centre
DIFC	Dubai International Financial Centre
ECAI	External credit assessment institution
EU	European Union
FAS	Financial Accounting Standards

FCA	Financial Conduct Authority
FSA	Financial Services Authority
FSAP	Financial Sector Assessment Program
GCC	Gulf Cooperation Council
GIC	Government Investment Certificates
GII	Government Investment Issues
HLTF	High-Level Task Force
IAH	Investment account holder(s)
IAIS	International Association of Insurance Supervisors
IASB	International Accounting Standards Board
IBFIM	Islamic Banking and Finance Institute Malaysia
ICM	Islamic Capital Market
ICLIF	International Centre for Leadership in Finance
IDB	Islamic Development Bank
IFIS	Islamic Finance Information Services
IFRS	International Financial Reporting Standards
IFSB	Islamic Financial Services Board
IFSI	Islamic financial services industry
IICRCA	International Islamic Centre for Reconciliation and Commercial Arbitration
IIFM	International Islamic Financial Market
IIFS	Institution(s) offering Islamic financial services
IILM	International Islamic Liquidity Management Corporation
IIRA	Islamic International Rating Agency
IMF	International Monetary Fund
INCEIF	International Centre for Education in Islamic Finance
IOSCO	International Organization of Securities Commissions
IOU	I Owe You
IRTI	Islamic Research and Training Institute
ISDA	International Swaps and Derivatives Association
ISRA	International Sharia Research Academy for Islamic Finance
KLIBOR	Kuala Lumpur Interbank Offer Rate
KLRCA	Kuala Lumpur Regional Centre for Arbitration
KSA	Kingdom of Saudi Arabia
KWD	Kuwaiti Dinar
LFX	Labuan International Financial Exchange
LIBOR	London Interbank Offered Rate
MARC	Malaysian Rating Corporation Berhad
MENA	Middle East and North Africa
MMS	Minerals Management Service
NIDC	Negotiable Islamic Debt Certificate
ORRI	Overriding royalty interest

OTC	Over-the-counter
PRA	Prudential Regulatory Authority
QFCRA	Qatar Financial Centre Regulatory Authority
ROTAS	Roman Transliteration of Arabic Script
SAC	Sharia Advisory Council
SAMA	Saudi Arabian Monetary Agency
SAR	Saudi Arabian Riyal
SC	Securities Commission Malaysia
SCA	Stocks and Commodities Authority
SD	Selective default
SECP	Securities and Exchange Commission of Pakistan
SIBOR	Saudi Interbank Offer Rate
SPC	Special purpose company
SPV	Special purpose vehicle
S&P	Standard and Poor's Ratings Services
SSB	Sharia supervisory board
TMA	*Tahawwut* Master Agreement
TID	The Investment Dar
UAE	United Arab Emirates
UK	United Kingdom
US	United States
USD	United States Dollar
WB	World Bank

List of Figures

List of Tables

List of Cases

Dato' Hj Nik Mahmud bin Daud v. Bank Islam Malaysia Bhd [1998] 3 CLJ 605

Islamic Investment Company of the Gulf (Bahamas) Ltd v Symphony Gems NV QBD Unreported February 13, 2002

Beximco Pharmaceuticals LTD and Others v. Shamil Bank of Bahrain [2004] EWCA Civ 19

Sayyed Mohammed Musawai v. R.E. International (UK) Ltd and others [2007] EWHC

Arab-Malaysian Finance Bhd v. Taman Ihsan Jaya Sdn Bhd and Others [2008] 5 MLJ 631

The Investment Dar Company KSCC v. Blom Development Bank SAL [2009] EWHC 3545 (Ch)

National Ṣukūk Company v. Al-Madina Finance and Investment Company Kuwaiti Court of Cassation, petition no 1895,1932,1933,1937/2011, judgment dated 19 June 2012

Dana Gas PJSC v. Dana Gas Sukuk Limited [2017] EWHC 2340 Comm

Dana Gas PJSC v. Dana Gas Sukuk Limited and Others [2017] EWHC 2928 Comm

Dana Gas PJSC v. Dana Gas Sukuk Limited and Others [2018] EWHC 277 Comm

Dana Gas PJSC v. Dana Gas Sukuk Limited and Others [2018] EWHC 278 Comm

Bank Islam Malaysia Berhad v. Adnan Bin Omar Kuala Lumpur High Court, Unreported Civil Suit No. S3-22-101-91

List of Legislations and International Conventions

Abu Dhabi
Local Law No. 3 of 2000

Bahrain
Central Bank of Bahrain Rulebook

Brunei
Islamic Banking Act (Chapter 168)

Dubai
Local Decree No. 14 of 2000
Dubai Law No. 9 of 2004 in Respect of the Dubai International Financial Centre
Dubai Law No 13 of 2013 Establishment of Dubai Islamic Economy Development Centre

Dubai International Financial Centre
DIFC Law No.1 of 2004 Regulatory Law
DIFC Law No.13 of 2004 Law Regulating Islamic Financial Business
DIFC Law No. 1 of 2012 Markets Law
DFSA Rulebook Modules (Islamic Financial Business Module)
DFSA Rulebook: Glossary Module (GLO)
DFSA Rulebook: Islamic Finance Rules (IFR)
DFSA Rulebook: Markets Rules (MKT)
NASDAQ Dubai Business Rules

European Union
Rome Convention on the Law Applicable to Contractual Obligations 1980
Regulation (EC) No. 593/2008 of the European Parliament and of the Council of 17 June 2008 on the Law Applicable to Contractual Obligations

Gulf Cooperation Council

Convention of Judicial Cooperation between States of the Arab League of 1983

Jordan

Law *nisi* No. 10 for the year 1981

Indonesia

Act of the Republic of Indonesia Number 21 of 2008 Concerning Sharia (Islamic) Banking

International Conventions

New York Convention on the Recognition and Enforcement of Foreign Arbitral Awards of 1958

Convention on the Settlement of Investment Disputes between States and Nationals of Other States 1965

Iran

The Law for Usury (Interest) Free Banking 1983

KSA

Companies Law of 1965
KSA Constitution 1992
New Law of Judiciary 2007
Companies Law 2016
Bankruptcy Law 2018
Capital Market Law
Listing Rules
Offers of Securities Regulations
Royal Decree No. (M/30) dated 2/6/1424H

Kuwait

Central Bank of Kuwait Act 2003
Ministerial Decision 388 of 2007 of Ministry of Commerce and Industry

Labuan

Labuan Financial Services Authority Act 1996
Labuan Islamic Financial Services and Securities Act 2010
LFX Rules

Malaysia

Kelantan Malay Reservations Enactment 1930
Federal Constitution 1957
Companies Act 1965
National Land Code 1965
Islamic Banking Act 1983
Takaful Act 1984

Banking and Financial Institutions Act 1989
Securities Commission Act 1993
Capital Market Services Act 2007
Central Bank of Malaysia Act 2009
Islamic Financial Services Act 2013
Guidelines on *Ṣukūk* 2014
Guidelines on Prospectus
Guidelines on Sales Practices of Unlisted Capital Market Products
Main Market Listing Requirements
Principal Advisor Guidelines
Sharia Governance Framework for Islamic Financial Institutions

Pakistan

Mudarabah Companies and *Mudarabah* Flotation and Control Ordinance of 1980
Guidelines for Sharia Compliance in Islamic Banking Institutions 2008
Instructions for Sharia Compliance in Islamic Banking Institutions 2008
Issue of *Ṣukūk* Regulations 2015

Qatar

QFCRA Islamic Finance Rules 2005
Instructions to Banks 2009

Sudan

Banking Regulation Act 2004

UAE

UAE Constitution 1971
Union Law No. 10 of 1980 Concerning the Central Bank, the Monetary System and Organisation of Banking
Federal Law No. 6 of 1985 regarding Islamic Banks, Financial Institutions and Investment Companies
Federal Law No. 4 of 2000 Concerning the Emirates Securities and Commodities Authority and Market
Decision No. 3 of 2000 Concerning the Regulations as to Disclosure and Transparency
Federal Decree No. 35 of 2004 to Establish Financial Free Zone in Dubai
Federal Law No. 8 of 2004 Regarding the Financial Free Zones
Decision No. (93/r) of 2005 Concerning the Listing of Islamic Bonds
Decision No. 4 of 2010 Takaful Insurance Regulations
Decision No. 16 of 2014 Concerning the Regulation of *Ṣukūk*
Decision No. 26 of 2015 Concerning the Amendment of Certain Rules of Disclosure and Transparency Regulation
Federal Law by Decree No. 9 of 2016 on Bankruptcy

Federal Decree Law No. 9 of 2018 on Public Debt
Federal Decree No. 20 of 2018 on anti-money laundering and countering the financing of terrorism
Decretal Federal Law No. (14) of 2018 Regarding the Central Bank & Organization of Financial Institutions and Activities

UK

Contracts (Applicable Law) Act 1990
English Arbitration Act 1996

USA

Bankruptcy Code

List of *Ṣukūk* Prospectuses

Offering Circular of East Cameron Gas Company
Offering Circular of Nakheel Development Limited
Offering Circular of Golden Belt 1 *Ṣukūk* Company B.S.C. (c)
Offering Circular of Tamweel Residential ABS CI (1) Ltd
Offering Circular of Tamweel *Ṣukūk* Limited
Offering Circular of Dana Gas *Ṣukūk* Limited (2007)
Offering Circular of Dana Gas *Ṣukūk* Limited (2013)

CHAPTER 1

Islamic Financial Markets: Legal and Regulatory Hurdles

1.1 Introduction

It is necessary to first explore the general practice of the Islamic financial services industry (IFSI) before moving into the subject matter of this book. Therefore, this chapter draws attention to matters of particular significance to the progress of the IFSI, which rose to the surface after its great expansion. It highlights some legal and regulatory tensions that exist within the general context of the IFSI. It should also be pointed out that the following discussion of key issues should aid in understanding the main thrust of this book, and serve as an important preamble for any discussion on the IFSI.

1.2 Stability Concern

The willingness of financial regulatory authorities and their professional advisors in both developed and developing markets to ensure soundness and stability within the financial sector has been subject to a sharp increase over the past years. Although there have been many great changes in the financial system arising from the globalisation of financial services and financial innovation, the financial system consists of financial markets and financial institutions at the fundamental level. While financial markets offer opportunities to move funds from the surplus sector (where there are surplus funds) to the deficit sector (where there is a shortage of funds) in the financial system, financial institutions ensure efficient movement of

S. Al-Ali, *Raising Capital on* Ṣukūk *Markets*,
https://doi.org/10.1007/978-3-030-14536-1_1

funds within the financial system.[1] Financial markets are where the demand for and supply of capital meet—for example, in the debt market, stock market, and foreign exchange market. Without the establishment of financial institutions, such as central banks, banks, insurance companies, and mutual funds, financial markets would not be able to operate efficiently.

There is tendency to use the words 'sound' and 'stable' to describe the desired state of financial markets and institutions in recent times; it is therefore necessary to define such terms in the context of the financial sector. Lastra notes that the term 'financial stability' is still vague, and there is a lack of a common definition as to what constitutes financial stability.[2] This is also supported by Čihák, who asserts that there is an absence of an operational definition of financial sector soundness that narrows down possible indictors which could be used to assess the soundness of the financial sector.[3] However, Čihák does provide a general definition of financial sector soundness as the 'smooth functioning of the components of the financial system and resilience to shocks'.[4] Another useful definition is provided by Allen and Wood, who define financial stability as 'a state of affairs in which an episode of financial instability is unlikely to occur, so that fear of financial instability is not a material factor in economic decisions taken by households or businesses'.[5] Besides, Allen asserts that 'financial stability is not merely the absence of crisis, but also the ability to absorb (rather than amplify) shocks'.[6]

The growing interest in enhancing the soundness of financial markets and institutions can be attributed to several factors. The frequency of financial crises, the destructive impact that these have had, the complexity of new financial instruments, and the large amount of financial transactions are among the factors which have increased awareness of the significance

[1] For a comprehensive study of financial markets and institutions, see F Mishkin and S Eakins, *Financial Markets and Institutions* (6th edn, Pearson Prentice Hall 2009).

[2] R Lastra, *International Financial and Monetary Law* (2nd edn, Oxford University Press 2015) 128.

[3] M Čihák, 'IMF Working Paper WP/06/163: How Do Central Banks Write on Financial Stability?' (*IMF*, June 2006) 9. http://www.imf.org/external/pubs/ft/wp/2006/wp06163.pdf. Accessed 10 June 2012.

[4] Ibid. 17.

[5] W Allen and G Wood, 'Special Paper No 160: Defining and Achieving Financial Stability' (*LSE*, April 2005) 13. http://www.lse.ac.uk/fmg/documents/specialPapers/2005/sp160.pdf. Accessed 18 March 2015.

[6] H Allen, 'What is Financial Stability? The Need for Some Common Language in International Financial Regulation' (2014) 45 Georgetown Journal of International Law 929, 943.

of ensuring financial sector soundness.[7] The need for the financial sector to be protected against instability and the importance of preserving its soundness have been well established in the wake of several financial crimes, payment defaults, and insolvency incidents. Developing a sound financial sector is a key requirement for the efficient mobilisation and allocation of resources in any society.[8] The efficiency of financial markets and economic growth are proportionally linked, according to historical evidence.[9] The significance of financial sector stability manifested itself in the launching of the Financial Sector Assessment Program (FSAP) in 1999 by the International Monetary Fund (IMF) and the World Bank (WB), to provide independent analysis for the financial sectors of different countries.[10] After the latest global financial crisis occurred in 2007, a pressing need was recognised for a range of advanced crisis prevention plans to safeguard the financial sector.[11] Thus, efforts need to focus on developing measures to improve the financial sector soundness, taking into consideration the lessons that have been learnt from the crisis.[12]

Financial markets and institutions operate at national, regional, and global levels. At all levels, the prevailing structure and regulations of the financial sector are based on 'conventional finance'.[13] As a result of its existence in major economies and developed countries such as North America and the European Union (EU), conventional finance has shaped the financial sectors of other parts of the world. However, 1963 saw a key development and transformation of the structure and regulation of financial markets and institutions, when a new type of finance emerged that was

[7] M Čihák, *supra* note 3, 4.

[8] IDB, IFSB and IRTI, 'Islamic Financial Services Industry Development: Ten-Year Framework and Strategies' (*IFSB*, May 2007) 1. http://www.ifsb.org/docs/10_yr_framework.pdf. Accessed 15 September 2012.

[9] Ibid.

[10] IMF, 'The Financial Sector Assessment Program (FSAP)' (*IMF*, 2012). http://www.imf.org/external/np/exr/facts/pdf/fsap.pdf. Accessed 15 August 2012.

[11] H Alamsyah, 'Lender of Last Resort in Islamic Banking' (Fourth Islamic Financial Stability Forum: Strengthening Financial Safety Nets in the Islamic Financial Services Industry, Malaysia, November 2011) 1.

[12] V Nienhaus, 'Capacity Building in the Financial Sector: Strategies for Strengthening Financial Institutions' (Inaugural Islamic Financial Stability Forum: Developing Capacity Building to Enhance Financial Stability in the Islamic Financial Services Industry, Sudan, April 2010) 1.

[13] The term 'conventional finance' or 'conventional financial industry' is used throughout this book to refer to the form of finance in which its practices and products are interest-based.

completely different from conventional finance—this was Islamic finance. The establishment of Mit Ghamr Bank in Egypt in 1963 undoubtedly formed the official starting point of the Islamic financial services industry (IFSI).[14] The modern era of conducting financial activities in accordance with Islamic law is better described as the transformational effect of Islamic law on global financial markets.[15]

The IFSI has made steady progress over the last five decades. Three elements constitute the IFSI—namely Islamic banking, *takāful* (Islamic insurance), and the Islamic capital market (ICM). As of 2016, the total assets of the IFSI around the world were believed to be around USD 1.89 trillion.[16] It is estimated that the total assets of the IFSI grew at a compound annual growth rate of 17.4% for the period 2009–2013.[17] While Islamic banking represents the largest segment of the IFSI, with 80% of the total IFSI assets,[18] *takāful* is considered the smallest segment of the IFSI, with 1.1% of the total IFSI assets.[19] So far, the IFSI has operated in more than 70 jurisdictions, including Australia, Algeria, Azerbaijan, Bahrain, Bangladesh, Brunei, Egypt, France, Germany, Indonesia, Iran, Jordan, Kuwait, Lebanon, Malaysia, Mauritius, Oman, Pakistan, the Philippines, Qatar, the Kingdom of Saudi Arabia (KSA), South Africa, Sudan, Switzerland, Thailand, Turkey, the United Arab Emirates (UAE), the United Kingdom (UK), the United States of America (USA) and Yemen.[20] Thus, the IFSI is not confined to Islamic countries since its operation has extended to non-

[14] D Abdullah and K Chee, *Islamic Finance: Why it Makes Sense* (Marshall Cavendish Business 2010) 8. Some consider that the Dubai Islamic Bank founded in 1975 is the first Islamic bank in the world since Mit Ghamr Bank was closed later. See M Mohsin, 'The Practice of Islamic Banking System in Sudan' (2005) 26 Journal of Economic Coorperation 27, 29. For more discussion on the development and growth of the IFSI, see H Greuning and Z Iqbal, *Risk Analysis for Islamic Banks* (The International Bank for Reconstruction and Development and the WB 2008) 10–15; H Askari, Z Iqbal and A Mirakhor, *New Issues in Islamic Finance and Economics: Progress and Challenges* (John Wiley & Sons 2009) 1–45.

[15] See J Ercanbrack, *The Transformation of Islamic Law in Global Financial Markets* (Cambridge University Press 2015).

[16] IFSB, 'Islamic Financial Services Industry: Stability Report 2017' (*IFSB*, 2017) 7. https://www.ifsb.org/docs/IFSB%20IFSI%20Stability%20Report%202017.pdf. Accessed 25 December 2018.

[17] IFSB, 'Islamic Financial Services Industry: Stability Report 2014' (*IFSB*, 2014) 3. http://www.ifsb.org/docs/2014-05-06_IFSI%20Stability%20Report%202014%20(Final).pdf. Accessed 22 March 2015.

[18] Ibid. 11.

[19] Ibid. 34.

[20] H Dar, R Rahman and R Malik (eds), *Global Islamic Finance Report* (Ebdiz Consulting 2014) 71, 74.

Islamic countries (hereafter referred to as conventional countries). It is worth noting that the total assets of the IFSI are mostly concentrated in the Middle East and Asia.[21] While the financial system operates entirely based on the IFSI in Iran and Sudan, a dual financial system (the IFSI alongside conventional finance) operates in other countries.[22]

This book is mainly concerned with the second fastest growing segment of the IFSI, after Islamic banking, which is the *ṣukūk* (trust investment certificates) market.[23] At this stage, it is sufficient to note that *ṣukūk* is an ICM instrument that is issued and traded in international and domestic capital markets for the purpose of investment, liquidity, and trading. The increasing popularity of the IFSI does not mean its activities are immune to criticism. In this respect, Robbins[24] and Ahmed[25] assert that the IFSI is currently at a crossroads owing to some questionable practices and worrying cases in different jurisdictions. Although issues related to the IFSI have been widely addressed in recent debates and literature, these tend to focus on 'what many see as the more positive and constructive aspects of creating wealth'.[26] Rider suggests that the emphasis should be on issues relating to regulatory, governance, and legal risks of the IFSI.[27] The following discussion addresses this approach, discussing the tensions from legal and regulatory perspective.

1.3 Sharia, Islamic Law, and Islamic Finance: Unresolved Definitional Issues

It is common for the term 'Islamic finance' to be linked with sharia and Islamic law in existing literature and public debates. This is because Islamic finance is derived from the teachings of sharia and Islamic law. Abdullah and Chee define Islamic finance as 'a form of finance that is based on sharia, or the body of Islamic law'.[28] Therefore, it is important to understand what

[21] IFSB, *supra* note 17, 9.

[22] Ibid.

[23] Ibid. 3.

[24] H Robbins, 'Soul Searching and Profit Seeking: Reconciling the Competing Goals of Islamic Finance' (2010) 88 Texas Law Review 1125, 1138.

[25] H Ahmed, 'Islamic Finance at a Crossroads: The Dominance of the Asset-Based Sukuk' (2010) 6 Journal of International Banking and Financial Law 366.

[26] B Rider, 'Islamic Financial Law: Back to Basics' in IFSB (ed), *The Changing Landscape of Islamic Finance: Imminent Challenges and Future Directions* (IFSB 2010) 103.

[27] Ibid.

[28] D Abdullah and K Chee, *supra* note 14, 4.

constitutes sharia, Islamic law, and Islamic finance, and whether they convey the same meaning. Without proper understanding of the terms 'sharia', 'Islamic law', and 'Islamic finance', the nature of the IFSI operation cannot be fully comprehended.

One might expect that such basic terms are well clarified in existing literature, given the increasing body of Islamic finance scholarship. However, there remains confusion about their precise meaning within the IFSI, even after more than 50 years since its establishment. Some tend to use the terms sharia and Islamic law interchangeably. For example, Crane states 'Islamic law, known as the sharia, is the framework of ultimate reality and the ethical guidance that Muslim scholars have derived from the direct Revelation of Allah to man'.[29] In addition, Bakar says 'Islamic law as a divinely revealed law is best represented by the term sharia'.[30] Others tend to make a distinction between the terms sharia and Islamic law; Edge defines sharia as 'the traditional rules of Islamic law which Muslims follow and apply in the various Sunni and Shia schools of Islamic jurists',[31] and Islamic law as 'those rules of Islamic law which Muslims follow and apply in the contemporary world'.[32] The ensuing discussion shows that using the terms sharia and Islamic law interchangeably in the context of Islamic finance causes confusion, as they are different things. It also demonstrates that Edge's approach to defining the terms sharia and Islamic law is inaccurate.

The approach of this book to the definition of such terms reflects practical aspects rather than philosophical analysis. Sharia and Islamic law are not, of course, the same thing. Sharia[33] refers to the divine revelations found in the Quran and Sunna. Islamic law refers to the understanding of the sharia, which is represented by the term Islamic jurisprudence or fiqh.[34]

[29] R Crane, 'The Essence of Islamic law' (1998) 3 The Journal of Islamic Law 185.

[30] M Bakar, 'Developing Modern Islamic Financial System via Ijtihad: an Overview' in M Bakar and E Ali (eds), *Essential Readings in Islamic Finance* (CERT Publications 2008) 27.

[31] I Edge, 'Islamic finance, alternative dispute resolution and family law: developments towards legal pluralism?' in R Griffith-Jones (ed), *Islam and English Law: Rights, Responsibilities and the Place of Shari'a* (Cambridge University Press 2013) 116.

[32] Ibid.

[33] It is an Arabic term which is used in the Quran. It literally means the path to the watering place or the straight road. See M Laldin, *Introduction to Shari'ah & Islamic Juridprudence* (CERT Publications 2008) 2–3.

[34] Fiqh is an Arabic term which literally means an understanding.

One can infer from the Sunna, *Ṣaḥīḥ Muslim* (19:4294),[35] that it recognises the distinction between the lawgiver's opinion, represented by divine revelation, and human understanding, represented by fiqh. According to Kamali, this distinction between sharia (divine revelation) and Islamic law (fiqh) has been proposed by many writers in the twentieth century.[36]

The distinction between the sharia and Islamic law serves different purposes, as shall be seen below. Divine revelation refers to the Quran and Sunna, and these constitute the sharia. The Quran is defined by Kamali as 'the book containing the speech of God revealed to the Prophet Muḥammad in Arabic and transmitted to us by continuous testimony'.[37] The Sunna refers to 'all that is narrated from the Prophet, his acts, his sayings and whatever he has tacitly approved, plus all the reports which describe his physical attributes and character'.[38] In the Quran (4:59), Allah (God) instructed the followers of the religion of Islam to obey the divine revelation.[39] In order to avoid misunderstanding and misinterpretation of the divine revelation, Allah gave people who are capable, known as jurists or scholars, the authority to explain the sharia to the public. The Quran (21:7) instructs Muslims to refer to the jurists when they are uncertain.[40] Therefore, jurists in this capacity have explained the sharia and answered Muslims' questions, based on their understanding of the sharia. The jurists' interpretations of the divine revelation are what constitute Islamic law. It has been found that the jurists follow particular methods and techniques that enable them to understand the sharia and express their own views about any unresolved questions. Such methods vary and are represented by the four main schools of Islamic law—namely the *ḥanafī*, *mālikī*, *shāafiʿī*, and *ḥanbali*

[35] It is one of the six canonical collections of Hadith. The Prophet Muḥammad was reported to have said: 'When you besiege a fort and the besieged want you to let them out in accordance with Allah's Command, do not let them come out in accordance with His Command, but do so at your (own) command, for you do not know whether or not you will be able to carry out Allah's behest with regard to them'.

[36] M Kamali, *Shari'ah Law: An Introduction* (Oneworld Publications 2008) 16.

[37] M Kamali, *Principles of Islamic Jurisprudence* (3rd edn, The Islamic Texts Society 2003) 16.

[38] Ibid. 58.

[39] The Quran (4:59) is translated thus: 'O you who believe! Obey Allah and obey the Messenger, and those of you who are in authority'.

[40] The Quran (21:7) is translated thus: 'And we sent not before you but men to whom we revealed. So ask the people of the reminder if you do not know'.

schools.[41] Each school has its own approach to interpreting the divine revelation, and this is what has led to divergent views within Islamic law. Methods developed by different legal schools to understand the sharia include *ijmāʿ* (consensus), *qiyās* (analogical reasoning), *istiṣḥāb* (presumption of continuity), *istiḥsān* (equity or juristic preference), *maṣlaḥah mursalah* (considerations of public interest), *sad al-dhārāʾiʿ* (blocking the means), *ʿurf* (custom), *aqwāl al-ṣaḥābah* (sayings of the companions), and *sharʿ man qablanā* (revealed laws preceding the sharia). These have been described as non-revealed or secondary sources of Islamic law.[42]

Based on the above discussion, one can state that Islamic law has been developed based on jurists' understanding of the sharia, and therefore jurists regard Islamic law as 'an understanding of the sharia, and not the sharia itself'.[43] To illustrate, a jurist's view represents an opinion within Islamic law, and not the sharia per se. Defining Islamic law as jurists' understanding of the divine revelation implies that the final authority is the lawgiver's (Allah's) and not a particular legal school's view or a jurist's opinion. In addition, the distinction between the sharia and Islamic law provides legal grounds for the existence of divergent opinions in Islamic law. The above proposed definition of Islamic law should be used for the purpose of comparing Islamic law with other legal systems, such as common law.[44]

[41] The *ḥanafī* school is the school of Islamic law whose origins are attributed to Abū Ḥanīfah Al-Nuʿmān in Kufa, Iraq, in the eighth century. The *mālikī* school is the school of Islamic law attributed to Mālik Bin Anas in the eighth century in the Arabian Peninsula. The *shāafiʿī* school is the school of Islamic law founded by Muḥammad Al-Shāfiʿi in the eighth century in Iraq and Egypt. The origins of the *ḥanbali* school of Islamic law are attributed to Aḥmad Bin Ḥanbal in ninth-century Baghdad. For general discussion on legal schools of Islamic law, see D Zacharias, 'Fundamentals of the Sunnī Schools of Law' (2006) 66 ZaöRV 491; G Makdisi, 'The Significance of the Sunni Schools of Law in Islamic Religious History' (1979) 10 International Journal of Middle East Studies 1.

[42] For more discussion about sources of Islamic law, see M Kamali, *supra* note 36, 19; W Hallaq, *The Origins and Evolution of Islamic Law* (Cambridge University Press 2005) 134–149.

[43] M Kamali, *supra* note 36, 16.

[44] For more discussion on Islamic Law in comparison with other legal systems, see G Badr, 'Islamic Law: Its Relation to Other Legal Systems' (1978) 26 The American Journal of Comparative Law 187. For more discussion on Islamic law in general, see A Souaiaia, 'On the Sources of Islamic Law and Practices' (2004–2005) 20 Journal of Law and Religion 123; C Melchert, 'Traditionist-Jurisprudents and the Framing of Islamic Law' (2001) 8 Islamic Law and Society 383; M Zahraa, 'Characteristic Features of Islamic Law: Perceptions and Misconceptions' (2000) 15 Arab Law Quarterly 168; D Bonderman, 'Modernization and Changing Perceptions of Islamic law' (1968) 81 Harvard Law Review 1169.

Having defined the sharia and Islamic law, we should next consider the concept of Islamic finance. Islamic law has great influence on all aspects of Muslim life, including finance and commerce. The widespread definition of Islamic finance is a mode of finance which complies with Islamic law and particularly *fiqh al-muʿāmalāt* (Islamic financial law). The latter is a branch within Islamic law which provides rules and guidance regarding financial matters. However, this definition is still very broad, given that Islamic financial law is a set of divergent juristic views. In this respect, Bakar argues that while the notion of Islamic finance is quite clear, its substance is not.[45] Rider also notes that the reference to Islamic law in the IFSI means a set of interpretations and views which form Islamic financial law.[46] The vagueness surrounding the essence of Islamic finance is justified by the availability of different juristic opinions regarding a single matter in many cases under Islamic financial law. Therefore, efforts should be focused on determining what constitutes Islamic financial law for the purpose of stability and integrity of the IFSI.

There have been some legal cases in the IFSI which have raised definitional concerns about the nature of sharia, Islamic law and Islamic finance. The case of *Beximco Pharmaceuticals Ltd and Others v Shamil Bank of Bahrain*,[47] which was an appeal heard in the English Court of Appeal, among others, demonstrates how a Western court has understood the nature of Islamic financial law and its applicability to the IFSI. The Court of Appeal had to consider the nature of sharia in order to rule on the construction and effect of the governing law clause included in the financing agreement. The court's position on the sharia as a governing law of the contract will be discussed later. At this stage it is important to highlight two relevant points made by the court in regard to the nature of sharia: (1) Islamic financial law is based on divergent views of earlier jurists rather than rules or law[48] and (2) the difficulty of referring to Islamic financial law in the context of the IFSI because of the controversy as to what juristic view should be applied.[49]

[45] Bakar, 'Shari'ah Approaches to Product Development and Product Enhancement in Islamic Banking and Finance: An Appraisal' in M Bakar and E Ali (eds), *Essential Readings in Islamic Finance* (CERT Publications) 113.

[46] B Rider, *supra* note 26, 103.

[47] [2004] EWCA Civ 19.

[48] Ibid. [30].

[49] Ibid. [40].

The case of *Arab-Malaysian Finance Bhd v Taman Ihsan Jaya Sdn Bhd and Others*[50] further highlights that the definition of Islamic financial law remains a problem in the IFSI. The Malaysian High Court had to consider the definition of Islamic financial transaction to rule on what amount a defaulted customer should pay under *bayʿ bithaman ʾājil* (deferred payment sale, BBA). The judge asserted that 'unless the financing facility is plainly stated to be offered as specific to a particular *madhhab*, then the fact it is offered generally to all Muslims means that it must not contain any element not approved by any of the recognised *madhhabs*'.[51] According to this description, in order to rule that a particular Islamic financial transaction is in compliance with Islamic law, all of its elements must comply with all legal schools. Consequently, if it contains an element which is only approved by one legal school, it will not be deemed acceptable under Islamic law. In practice, offering an Islamic financial transaction whereby all elements involved are justified by all legal schools is highly impractical. The issue of whether the views of an individual legal school, all legal schools, or the majority of legal schools should represent Islamic finance remains uncertain.

1.4 IFSI: Back to Basics

The IFSI is built upon four principles that govern all its transactions and practices. The significance of these principles lies in that they distinguish the IFSI from its conventional counterpart. At the heart of the IFSI is the prohibition of *ribā* (usury), prohibition of *gharar* (uncertainty), prohibition of *qimār* (gambling), and the prohibition of dealing with prohibited activities. While there is no controversy in Islamic financial law regarding the importance of observing the above basics, there is debate about their meanings and applications in the IFSI. *Ribā* is generally defined as unjustified increase in capital arising from deferment in the time of exchange or excess in the quantity of one of the countervalues.[52] It should be pointed out that the Sunna (*Ṣaḥīḥ Muslim* 10:3853) specified six items with which *ribā* can transpire—namely gold, silver, wheat, barley, dates, and salt. If an exchange is made between the same items, parity and spot transaction

[50] [2008] 5 MLJ 631 [59].

[51] Ibid.

[52] For a detailed discussion on *ribā*, see R Nawawi, *Islamic law on Commercial Transaction* (CERT Publications 2009) 149–181; M Bakar, 'Riba and Islamic Banking and Finance' in M Bakar and E Ali (eds), *Essentail Readings in Islamic Finance* (CERT Publications 2008).

must be ensured. If an exchange is made between different items, only the requirement of spot transaction must be met. As for *gharar*, it is described as 'uncertainty or hazard caused by lack of clarity regarding the subject matter or the price in a contract or exchange'.[53] Therefore, *gharar* arises in the event of the absence of necessary information or a lack of information disclosed to the buyer about the transaction. Avoiding all aspects of uncertainty is impractical in commercial activities, and thus the *gharar* that is prohibited by jurists is excessive *gharar* rather than nominal *gharar*. With regard to *qimār*, this generally refers to gaining wealth by chance, making a profit at the cost of others, without paying equivalent compensation.[54] As for prohibition of dealing with prohibited activities, Islamic financial law prohibits investing in, or getting returns from, business activities which involve, amongst others, alcohol, pork, and pornography.

The issue of whether the basics of the IFSI have been observed in practice requires careful attention. In this context, Rider stresses the point that 'unless those advancing the cause of financial services and products can give proper emphasis to the core values of Islamic law, then a significant opportunity will be missed'.[55] However, there have been arguments for permitting some applications which contradict the basics of the IFSI. For example, Al-Sālim claims that *ribā* does not occur or apply with modern currency notes.[56] Al-Sālim's opinion implies that it is permitted to impose an additional amount on the borrower in a loan transaction. In addition, Ṭanṭāwī argues that *ribā* does not occur or apply when account holders get interest from the conventional banks.[57] It goes without saying that if the above two views are considered in practice, then the IFSI would not be needed at all. Further, Al-ʿuthmānī's view that 85% of *ṣukūk* issuances are not sharia-compliant because of some *ribā* and *gharar* elements questions the level of adherence of the IFSI to the basic values.[58]

[53] M Ayub, *Understanding Islamic Finance* (John Wily & Sons Ltd 2007) 57.

[54] Ibid. 61–62.

[55] B Rider, *supra* note 26, 104.

[56] See Alarabiya, 'Al-Sālim Yarud ʿalā Al-Muṣliḥ: Al-Ribā Lā Yajrī Fī Al-Wrāq Al-Naqdiyyah ʿind Al-Madhāhib Al-Arbaʿah' (*Alarabiya*, 2011). http://www.alarabiya.net/articles/2011/08/20/163226.html. Accessed 30 March 2015.

[57] Aljazeera, 'Majmaʿ Al-Fiqh Al-Islāmī Yastankir Fatwā Jawāz Fawāid Al-Bunūk' (*Aljazeera*, 2003). www.aljazeera.net/News/archive/archive?ArchiveId=46677. Accessed 30 March 2015.

[58] Reuters, 'Most Sukuk "not Islamic": Body Claims' (*Arabianbusiness*, 2007). http://www.arabianbusiness.com/most-sukuk-not-islamic-body-claims-197156.html#.VRm73fldXHU. Accessed 30 March 2015.

The above declarations have triggered concerns regarding the clarity of the basic principles of the IFSI at both theoretical and practical levels. As institutions offering Islamic financial services (IIFS) strive to fulfil the desires of different types of clients and market segments, their operations and services should reflect the core principles. Failure to uphold the basics of the IFSI jeopardises its reputation, market confidence, and future progress.

1.5 Sharia Governance: A Mechanism for Sharia Compliance

The transactions, products, and practices of the IFSI are generally described as sharia-compliant. The concept of sharia compliance is unique to the IFSI and a major distinguishing feature between the IFSI and its conventional counterpart. Sharia compliance simply means the state of complying with the requirements of Islamic law. Sharia compliance is not a recommended practice, but rather it is an obligation imposed on the IIFS. The significance of sharia compliance is reflected in the inclusion of so-called sharia governance in the corporate governance of IIFS.[59] The term 'sharia governance' refers to 'the set of institutional and organisational arrangements through which an IIFS ensures that there is effective independent oversight of sharia compliance'.[60] The sharia compliance of the IFSI is entrusted to individuals with specialised knowledge of Islamic law and the current practices of the IFSI, known as sharia jurists, sharia scholars, or sharia experts. In practice, they are usually represented by a sharia supervisory board (SSB). This is also known by other names, such as a sharia advisory council, sharia committee, or sharia board.

Therefore, understanding the nature and role of an SSB is very important in the context of the IFSI. In many countries the obligation of ensuring sharia compliance has been achieved by issuing special legislation on sharia governance. Countries can be divided into two categories in terms of existing laws that promote and ensure the compliance of the IFSI. The first category comprises countries that have not promulgated any legislation on

[59] See generally A Haqqi, 'Shariah Governance in Islamic Financial Institution: An Appraisal' (2014) 11 US-China Law Review 112.

[60] IFSB, 'Guiding Principles on Sharīʿah Governance Systems for Institutions offering Islamic Financial Services' (*IFSB*, December 2009) 2. http://www.ifsb.org/standard/IFSB-10%20Shariah%20Governance.pdf. Accessed 17 April 2015.

sharia governance—namely Egypt, Iran,[61] the KSA, the UK and Turkey.[62] The second category includes countries that have issued legislation concerning sharia governance, including Bahrain, Brunei, Indonesia, Kuwait, Malaysia, the UAE, Pakistan, Qatar, and Sudan.[63]

Examining the regulations concerning SSBs in different countries reveals that they differ on many aspects, and so far, there is no standardised regulation of sharia governance. The bulk of regulations regarding SSBs concentrate on the establishment of an SSB, functions of the SSB, appointment of the SSB members, and conditions of qualified SSB members. There are several possible models for the operation of SSBs and sharia scholars within the IFSI, which include an internal SSB in all IIFS, an individual sharia scholar for each institution, a periodic forum for sharia advisors, consultancy services by an independent SSB in the private sector,

[61] Although the Central Bank of the Islamic Republic of Iran issued The Law for Usury (Interest) Free Banking in 1983, there are no provisions concerning sharia governance or sharia boards.

[62] See Z Hasan, 'Shariah Governance in Islamic Financial Institutions in Malaysia, GCC Countries and the UK' (PhD Thesis, Durham University 2011) 3; A Alkhamees, 'The Impact of Shari'ah Governance Practices on Shari'ah Compliance in Contemporary Islamic Finance' (2012) Journal of Banking Regulation 1.

[63] See generally N Muhamed and R Radzi, 'An International Comparative Study on Shariah Governance Supervision of Sukuk Defaults' (2012) 8 Journal of Islamic Economics, Banking and Finance 20. Important regulations concerning sharia governance in these countries are listed as follows:

- Bahrain: Central Bank of Bahrain Rule Book (Volume 2, Part A, High Level Standards, High Level Controls, The Principles of Islamic Sharia').
- Brunei: Islamic Banking Act (Chapter 168).
- Indonesia: Act of the Republic of Indonesia Number 21 of 2008 Concerning Sharia (Islamic) Banking.
- Kuwait: Central Bank of Kuwait Act 2003.
- Malaysia: Central Bank of Malaysia Act 2009; Islamic Financial Services Act 2013; Capital Markets and Services Act 2007; Sharia Governance Framework for Islamic Financial Institutions; Guidelines on *Ṣukūk*.
- UAE: Decretal Federal Law No. (14) of 2018 Regarding the Central Bank & Organization of Financial Institutions and Activities; Federal Law No. 6 of 1985 regarding Islamic Banks, Financial Institutions and Investment Companies; Takaful Insurance Regulations 2010, DIFC Law No.13 of 2004 Law Regulating Islamic Financial Business; DFSA Rulebook Modules (Islamic Financial Business Module).
- Pakistan: Instructions for Sharia Compliance in Islamic Banking Institutions 2008; Guidelines for Sharia Compliance in Islamic Banking Institutions 2008.
- Qatar: Instructions to Banks 2009; QFCRA Islamic Finance Rules 2005.
- Sudan: Banking Regulation Act 2004.

and a central SSB operating at a national level.[64] While the first four models are examples of sharia governance at micro-level, the last model is an example of sharia governance at the macro-level. So far, an SSB exists in the central bank or at a regulatory level in five countries—Malaysia, Indonesia, Brunei, Pakistan, Sudan,[65] Oman,[66] and the UAE.[67]

The responsibility of sharia boards to promote integrity and stewardship in the IFSI and their role in auditing compliance cannot be overlooked.[68] However, existing regulations on sharia governance and current practices of SSBs have raised some concerns about the integrity of the IFSI. Although the purpose of establishing an SSB is quite clear, there is ambiguity about SSB's roles and responsibilities.[69] In this respect, Rider states '[t]here is ambiguity in practice as to the obligations of sharia boards to concern themselves with monitoring and compliance. The focus tends to be on the making of particular and often specific decisions'.[70] It is also uncertain in many countries whether decisions made by an SSB are binding or advisory in nature for the IIFS.[71] For example, the Financial Services Authority (FSA) in the UK considers the role of the SSB to be solely advisory in nature.[72] Furthermore, the issue of whether SSB members are

[64] M Ayub, *supra* note 53, 472.

[65] Z Hasan, *supra* note 62, 81.

[66] B Vizcaino, 'Oman sets up central Sharia Board in Move to Boost Islamic Finance' (*Reuters*, 2014). https://www.reuters.com/article/oman-islam-financing/oman-sets-up-central-sharia-board-in-move-to-boost-islamic-finance-idUSL6N0S305J20141008. Accessed 25 December 2018.

[67] Although the Federal Law No. 6 of 1985 regarding Islamic Banks, Financial Institutions and Investment Companies mentions the establishment of the Higher Sharia Authority under the Central Bank of the UAE, it did not come into existence until 2018. See generally E Chand, 'Islamic Banking: New Higher Sharia Authority set up' (*emiratesnews247*, 2018). http://www.emiratesnews247.com/islamic-banking-new-higher-sharia-authority-set/. Accessed 25 December 2018.

[68] See generally M Laldin and H Furqani, 'Meeting Expectations: The Roles and Resposibilities of Sharia Scholars in Islamic Finance' in K Hassan and M Lewis (eds), *Handbook on Islam and Economic Life* (Edward Elgar 2014).

[69] A Alkhamees, *supra* note 62, 4.

[70] B Rider, 'Legal Aspects of Islamic Asset Securitisation' in IFSB (ed), *Strategies for the Development of Islamic Capital Markets: Infrastructures and Legal Aspects of Islamic Asset Securitisation* (IFSB 2011) 132.

[71] A Alkhamees, *supra* note 62, 6.

[72] M Ainley and others, 'Islamic Finance in the UK: Regulation and Challenges' (*FSA*, 2007) 13. http://www.fsa.gov.uk/pubs/other/islamic_finance.pdf. Accessed 7 April 2015. In April 2013, the responsibilities of the FSA have been split between two newly formed authorities: Prudential Regulation Authority (PRA) and the Financial Conduct Authority (FCA).

deemed accountable and liable has not been well addressed, even in countries with advanced sharia governance, such as Malaysia.[73] This is of particular significance in the event an incorrect pronouncement or poor sharia advice is made by an SSB member.[74] In addition, it has been argued that SSB practices lack transparency in areas such as the process of sharia supervision, disposal of non-sharia-compliant returns, and sharia rulings.[75] Furthermore, the independence of SSBs has been questioned owing to elements of their make-up that may put them under pressure to certify certain products, including appointment of SSB members, hefty payments for SSB members, providing credit facilities to members, or offering shares or executive positions in the IIFS.[76] Another concern is the conflict of interest and duties of SSB members that occurs if they have multiple board memberships and receive high remuneration from the IIFS.[77] Also, it has been found that some SSB members lack competence, and there has been undue leniency in selecting SSB members.[78] The issue of whether a member of an SSB must be qualified as a sharia scholar is a matter of debate.

1.6 Governing Law of the IFSI: An English Law Perspective

The IFSI is subject to the national legal systems of operating countries, and therefore it is important to ensure that the sharia compliance of the IFSI is not compromised under different legal systems. The term 'governing law' generally refers to the law or legal system that has the authority to interpret financial transactions and govern disputed matters amongst contractual parties. In the context of the IFSI, the governing law must ensure the sharia compliance of Islamic financial transactions. Ideally, Islamic law would serve the purpose of ensuring sharia compliance of the IFSI, given

[73] A Alkhamees, *supra* note 62, 8.

[74] In this case, an important question is raised, which is: is it possible to sue the SSB member? For more discussion, see S Abdul Jabbar, 'Investor Protection in the Islamic Financial Services Industry' (PhD Thesis, University of London 2010) 156–158.

[75] A Alkhamees, *supra* note 62, 10.

[76] Ibid. 11–12.

[77] Ibid. 16–17.

[78] Ibid. 20. The requirements of SSB members vary from one jurisdiction to another. For example, the Central Bank of Malaysia Act 2009 requires members to have a qualification in Islamic law, or knowledge or experience in Islamic law and other related disciplines, such as law, finance and banking.

that its transactions and products have been designed based on Islamic law. Applying non-Islamic law in the context of the IFSI may compromise the concept of sharia compliance.

Choosing Islamic law as the governing law for the IFSI is challenging in practice. This is because of three elements: (1) the presence of the IFSI in conventional jurisdictions, (2) conflicting positions taken by the contractual parties regarding the governing law,[79] and (3) uncertainty about whether the national legal system of a country recognises Islamic law as a legitimate choice of law in contracts. These elements constitute the so-called conflict of laws situation in the IFSI. This refers to the uncertainty regarding the governing law and whether Islamic law, the national legal system, or a combined legal system will be applied.[80] The conflict of laws situation poses a serious question as to what will be the applicable law in the event of disputes involving Islamic financial transactions.

The above discussion poses a crucial question as to whether Islamic law is regarded as a choice of law in countries in which the IFSI operates. This question is equally important for Islamic countries and conventional countries, given that the position of Islamic law as a sovereign law in the Islamic world is a matter of great complexity. In the IFSI, the governing law issue arises when there is a dispute between contracting parties. Such a dispute is either resolved outside the courts or inside the courts: while the common form of the former is arbitration, the latter refers to litigation. The ensuing discussion shall focus on the applicability of Islamic law for the IFSI in arbitration and litigation in the UK. The choice of the UK is motivated by two facts: English law is the most oft-chosen law for international Islamic financial transactions[81] and its influence on other legal systems and countries.

The choice of Islamic law as a governing law in arbitration is legitimate from an English law perspective. Firstly, the nature and salient features of arbitration as an alternative dispute resolution (ADR) facilitate the choice of Islamic law.[82] According to Lew, Mistelis, and Kroll, there are four

[79] K Djaraouane and C Serhal, 'Choice of Governing Law in Islamic Finance Agreements' (2009) 2 International Business Law Journal 115.

[80] See A Junius, 'Islamic Finance: Issues Surrounding Islamic Law as a Choice of Law under German Conflict of Laws Principles' (2007) 7 Chicago Journal of International Law 537, 543.

[81] J Colon, 'Choice of Law and Islamic Finance' (2011) 46 Texas International Law Journal, 425.

[82] For more discussion on arbitration in the context of the IFSI, see A Nadar, 'Islamic Finance and Dispute Resolution: Part 1' (2009) 23 Arab Law Quarterly 1; A Nadar, 'Islamic Finance and Dispute Resolution: Part 2' (2009) 23 Arab Law Quarterly 181.

fundamental features of arbitration—it is an alternative to national court, it is a private tool for dispute resolution, it can be chosen by the contractual parties, and it provides final and binding determination of contractual parties' rights and obligations.[83] Secondly, the English Arbitration Act 1996 considers Islamic law as a valid governing law in arbitration.[84] Section 46 (1) (b) of the English Arbitration Act 1996 states: 'The arbitral tribunal shall decide the dispute—... (b) if the parties so agree, in accordance with such other considerations as are agreed by them or determined by the tribunal'. The best illustration of this point is the decision in the case of *Sayyed Mohammed Musawi v. R.E. International (UK) Ltd and Others*.[85] The issue in this case was whether Islamic law is regarded as a legitimate choice of law in arbitration under the English Arbitration Act 1996.[86] The dispute in this case occurred between parties who had entered into a ***muḍārabah*** (investment partnership) agreement in 1987 for the acquisition and development of some land in London, and subsequently disagreed about their respective rights.[87] In order to resolve the dispute, they entered into an arbitration agreement in 2003, to be governed in accordance with Islamic law.[88] In 2004, the arbitrator issued an award in favour of the claimant and the defendants challenged this award.[89] The court held that the award was enforceable.[90]

The issue of whether Islamic law is a legitimate choice of law in litigation, from the perspective of English law, requires careful consideration. Before 2008, it was commonly said that Islamic law could not be a governing law of disputes involving Islamic financial transactions in the UK. In other words, English law would govern disputes related to the IFSI. This position in litigation was confirmed by the decision in *Islamic Investment*

[83] J Lew, L Mistelis and S Kroll, *Comparative International Commercial Arbitration* (Kluwer Law International 2003) 3.

[84] See Section 46 (1) (b) of the English Arbitration Act 1996.

[85] [2007] EWHC 2981.

[86] H Abdelhady, 'Islamic Law in Secular Courts (Agian)' (2010) 27 GPSOLO Magazine, 36.

[87] H Abdelhady, 'Islamic Law in Secular Courts (Agian): Teachable Moments from the Journey' (2009) 4 International Law News.

[88] Ibid.

[89] Ibid.

[90] *Sayyed Mohammed Musawi v. R.E. International (UK) Ltd and Others* [2007] EWHC 2981 [115].

Company of the Gulf (Bahamas) Ltd v. Symphony Gems NV[91] and *Beximco Pharmaceuticals Ltd and Others v. Shamil Bank of Bahrain*.[92]

One of the issues in the case of *Islamic Investment Company of the Gulf (Bahamas) Ltd v Symphony Gems NV*[93] regarded the legality of the associated *murābaḥah* (a sale with a mark-up) agreement.[94] The defendant (Symphony Gems NV) argued that the agreement violated the tenants of Islamic law.[95] The court was aware of the sharia non-compliant nature of the agreement according to expert evidence.[96] However, the court rejected the sharia non-compliance argument for two reasons: (1) that English law was chosen to govern the contract and (2) the agreement was not applied in a country where Islamic law is the law of the land.[97]

The main issue in *Beximco Pharmaceuticals Ltd and Others v. Shamil Bank of Bahrain*[98] was whether the governing law clause contained in the financing agreements was recognised under the English judicial system. The governing law clause read: 'Subject to the principles of the Glorious sharia, this Agreement shall be governed by and construed in accordance with the laws of England'.[99] The Court of Appeal held that it was not binding and rejected giving any legal effect to the governing law clause: notwithstanding the fact the contract in question was sharia-compliant in nature.[100] The court's position was justified by the Rome Convention on the Law Applicable to Contractual Obligations 1980 (hereafter referred to as the Rome Convention), which has force of law in the UK, according to Section 2 (1) of the Contracts (Applicable Law) Act 1990.[101] The following Articles of the Rome Convention read together provide an answer regarding whether Islamic law can be chosen as a governing law of a contract in the EU: Article 1 (1): 'The rules of this Convention shall apply to

[91] QBD Unreported 13 February 2002.

[92] [2004] EWCA Civ 19. For more discussion on this court case, see Junius; N Foster, 'Islamic Finance Law as an Emergent Legal System' (2007) 21 Arab Law Quarterly 170.

[93] QBD Unreported 13 February 2002.

[94] A Aldohni, 'The Challenge of Islamic Banking Disputes in the English Courts: The Applied Law' (2009) 24 Journal of International Banking & Financial Law 350.

[95] Ibid.

[96] Ibid.

[97] Ibid.

[98] [2004] EWCA Civ 19 [1].

[99] Ibid.

[100] Ibid. [52].

[101] Ibid. [40]. Signed between all member states of The EU, the Rome Convention provides a common choice of law system in contracts.

contractual obligations in any situation involving a choice between the laws of different countries' and Article 3 (1): 'A contract shall be governed by the law chosen by the parties'. The Articles assert that the law chosen by the parties will be recognised only if it is a law of a country. According to the court, Islamic law is not a national system of law and therefore it cannot be a legitimate choice of law in contracts.[102] Some argue that such a conclusion is likely to be made even outside the EU, in other common law and civil law jurisdictions.[103]

However, the above often-quoted position regarding the legitimacy of Islamic law as a governing law of contracts in the UK should be revisited after 2007. This is because of the adoption of Regulation (EC) No. 593/2008 of the European Parliament and of the Council of 17 June 2008 on the Law Applicable to Contractual Obligations (hereafter referred to as the Rome I Regulation) that has replaced the Rome Convention.[104] Paragraph (13) of the Preamble to the Rome I Regulation says '[t]his Regulation does not preclude parties from incorporating by reference into their contract a non-State body of law or an international convention'. This position is not to be confused with Article (3) (3) of the Rome I Regulation which 'has apparently retained the Rome Convention position with respect to applicable law under Article 3'.[105] In this respect, Zahid and Ali state:

> [Rome I Regulation] has maintained the status of State law as the principal choice of law. At the same time, it has recognised the international practice of choosing any non-State law as the applicable law by laying down a guiding principle in Paragraph (13).[106]

Therefore, Rome I Regulation removes the limitation of the Rome Convention regarding applicable law.[107] The Rome I Regulation does not require a state law to be the applicable law, and hence it allows Islamic law to be applied as a governing law in its jurisdictions.

[102] Ibid.

[103] See J Colon, *supra* note 81, 425.

[104] See A Zahid and H Ali, 'Shari'ah as a Choice of Law in International Islamic Financial Contracts: Shamil Bank of Bahrain Case Revisited' (2013) 10 US-China Law Review 27.

[105] Ibid. 31. Article 3 (3) of the Rome I Regulation states: 'Where all other elements relevant to the situation at the time of the choice are located in a country other than the country whose law has been chosen, the choice of the parties shall not prejudice the application of provisions of the law of that other country which cannot be derogated from by agreement'.

[106] Ibid.

[107] Ibid. 30.

1.7 Liquidity in the IFSI

In the financial sector, the term liquidity concerns two areas: (1) the liquidity of financial markets and instruments and (2) the solvency of financial institutions.[108] While the former is concerned with the number of buyers and sellers who are willing to trade,[109] the latter is related to the ability of financial institutions to meet financial obligations to third parties.[110] These areas are of course interrelated and they pose serious challenges for developing a sound IFSI. Grewal asserts that the lack of liquidity in the IFSI is no secret, and it is one of the most oft-challenges encountered by the IFSI.[111] Liquidity has been viewed as one of the risks facing the IFSI; liquidity risk means 'potential loss to IIFS arising from their inability either to meet their obligations or to fund increases in assets as they fall due without incurring unacceptable costs or losses'.[112]

The significance of liquidity for those who regulate, invest, and are actively involved in the IFSI cannot be overstated. The global financial crisis in 2007 has been described as a liquidity crisis,[113] a label which highlights the importance of liquidity in the financial sector. When one imagines the ramifications of the occurrence of a liquidity crisis for a single financial institution, liquidity management becomes extremely important.[114] A liquidity crisis in a financial institution causes increasing uncertainty about the liquidity situation of other financial institutions, the drying up of money market liquidity, bank runs, uncertainty about future cash flows, and uncertainty about market conditions.[115] A lack of liquidity

[108] I Rifke, 'The Management of Liquidity Risk in Islamic Banks: The Case of Indonesia' (PhD Thesis, Durham University 2010) 36.

[109] Y Mersch, 'About the Role of Central Banks in Financial Stability and Prudential Liquidity Supervision, and the Attractiveness of Islamic Finance' (IFSB 2nd Public Lecture on financial policy and Stability, Kuala Lumpur, 2009) 8.

[110] I Rifke, *supra* note 108, 36.

[111] B Grewal, 'Constraints on Growth in Islamic Finance' (IFSB 4th Public Lecture on Financial Policy and Stability, Jordan, 2011) 10.

[112] IFSB, 'Guiding Principles of Risk Management for Institutions (Other Than Insurance Institutions) Offering Only Islamic Financial Services' (*IFSB*, December 2005) 19. http://www.ifsb.org/standard/ifsb1.pdf. Accessed 9 April 2015.

[113] Y Mersch, *supra* note 109, 9.

[114] See generally A Campbell and P Cartwright, *Banks in Crisis: The Legal Response* (Ashgate Publishing 2002).

[115] Y Mersch, *supra* note 109, 4.

in financial markets also results in investors being discouraged from entering the market because of the fear that exit will be difficult or at least without fair prices.[116]

IIFS face liquidity problems under several circumstances. For example, a liquidity problem arises for Islamic banks when their investment account holders (IAHs) and depositors withdraw their money unexpectedly or carry out fund transfers for one reason or another.[117] In addition, IIFS also encounter funding pressure and liquidity problems in the event of a price drop of assets held for trading because of the nature of their investment portfolios.[118] Furthermore, a strain on funding for IIFS can occur owing to the lack of liquid markets for holdings Islamic financial instruments.[119] In addition, IIFS are exposed to liquidity problems arising from late payment or non-payment of money due, caused by failures in applicable payment and settlement systems.[120]

The IFSI is at a competitive disadvantage compared to the conventional financial industry when it comes to the current state of its liquidity infrastructure. Liquidity infrastructure is defined as follows:

> [A] set of key institutional and operational arrangements which in any jurisdiction can provide a facilitating environment to financial institutions in that jurisdiction for managing their liquidity in normal and stressed times, as well as supporting market liquidity in the system.[121]

There are several reasons that increase the difficulty of tackling liquidity problems in the IFSI. There is a lack of Islamic financial instruments that can be utilised to manage liquidity problems,[122] and the traditional approaches of

[116] J Board, 'Development of Islamic Capital Markets' in IFSB (ed), *Strategies for the Development of Islamic Capital Markets: Infrastructures and Legal Aspects of Islamic Asset Securitisation* (IFSB 2011) 23.

[117] IFSB, 'Guiding Principles on Liquidity Risk Management for Institutions Offering Islamic Financial Services [Excluding Islamic Insurance (*Takāful*) Institutions And Islamic Collective Investment Schemes]' (*IFSB*, March 2012) 5. http://www.ifsb.org/standard/eng_IFSB-12%20Guiding%20Principles%20on%20Liquidity%20Risk%20Mgmt%20_(March2012).pdf. Accessed 23 January 2015.

[118] Ibid.

[119] Ibid.

[120] Ibid.

[121] Ibid.

[122] B Grewal, *supra* note 111, 10.

conventional financial institutions to resolve liquidity problems are not available to the IIFS, because of Islamic law constraints.[123] These include interest-based loans from the interbank market, debt transfers, and a lender of last resort.[124] Although the replication of conventional liquidity instruments might help in the short term, enhancing liquidity in the IFSI requires developing innovative Islamic financial instruments for liquidity purposes.

There have been some initiatives in Bahrain, Malaysia, Indonesia, and the UAE aimed at establishing short-term liquidity management schemes or Islamic money markets.[125] However, Abdullah notes that 'Islamic money markets are not well integrated into the overall money markets in most jurisdictions'.[126] This is explained by two aspects of the current structure of Islamic money markets in most jurisdictions: (1) the dominance of transactions among IIFS and (2) special transactions with conventional banks.[127] The current Islamic liquidity products are limited and differ from one jurisdiction to another, including the commodity *murābaḥah*, interbank *muḍārabah*, Islamic repurchase agreements, and short-term *ijārah ṣukūk*.[128] The liquidity problems and concerns in the IFSI have motivated the Islamic Financial Services Board (IFSB) to establish a High-Level Task Force (HLTF) on liquidity management which aims to develop a liquidity management framework for IIFS.[129] Another initiative at the international level is the establishment of the International Islamic Liquidity Management Corporation (IILM) in 2010, founded to deal with liquidity management problems in the IFSI.

[123] S Cox, 'The Role of Capital Markets in Ensuring Islamic Financial Liquidity' in S Archer and R Abdel Karim (eds), *Islamic Finance: The Regulatory Challenge* (John Wiley & Sons 2007) 271.

[124] IFSB, 'Guiding Principles on Liquidity Risk Management for Institutions Offering Islamic Financial Services [Excluding Islamic Insurance (*Takāful*) Institutions And Islamic Collective Investment Schemes]' (*IFSB*, March 2012) 5. http://www.ifsb.org/standard/eng_IFSB-12%20Guiding%20Principles%20on%20Liquidity%20Risk%20Mgmt%20_(March2012).pdf. Accessed 23 January 2015; S Cox, *supra* note 123, 271.

[125] See D Abdullah, 'Liquidity Management in Institutions Offering Islamic Financial Services' (Addressing Liquidity Management Challenges to Enhance the Financial Stability of the Islamic Financial Services Industry, KSA, December 2010) 3, 4.

[126] Ibid. 3.

[127] IFSB, 'Technical Note on Issues in Strengthening Liquidity Management of Institutions Offering Islamic Financial Services: The Development of Islamic Money Markets' (*IFSB*, March 2008) 1. http://www.ifsb.org/docs/mar2008_liquidity.pdf. Accessed 10 April 2015.

[128] D Abdullah, *supra* note 125, 5.

[129] IFSB, IDB and IRTI, 'Islamic Financial and Global Financial Stability' (*IFSB*, 2010) 43. http://www.ifsb.org/docs/IFSB-IRTI-IDB2010.pdf. Accessed 10 April 2015.

1.8 Investor Protection in the IFSI

Investor protection in the IFSI has become a crucial issue because of the IFSI's expansion into new markets, the growth of investors' base, and the development of new sharia-compliant transactions. Given that it is relatively small and new compared to its conventional counterpart, it is worth looking at important aspects of investor protection in the IFSI. The term 'investor protection' refers to the state of investors' rights and claims being safeguarded against fraud and dishonest practices through a set of regulatory mechanisms. This definition is best illustrated by the following quote from La Porta et al.:

> When investors finance firms, they typically obtain certain rights or powers that are generally protected through the enforcement of regulations and laws. Some of these rights include disclosure and accounting rules, which provide investors with the information they need to exercise other rights.[130]

Investor protection is of particular significance in the financial sector because of its impact on, among other things, the development of financial markets and allocation of real resources.[131] It is well recognised that the bulk of financial regulations are concerned with offering protection for various categories of investors, including retail, institutional, professional, and foreign investors and speculators.[132] Dishonesty, information problems, and the risk of systemic failure are traditionally identified as principal areas of investor protection legislation.[133] In the financial sector, investors are protected by various regulatory tools which are divided into specific regulatory tools and general regulatory tools.[134] Examples of the former are 'entry controls, anti-fraud legislation, mandatory disclosure obligations and capital adequacy requirements'.[135] The latter refers to important applications of the general law towards investor protection that are found under law of agency, law of trust, law of tort, criminal law, and civil law.[136]

[130] R La Porta and others, 'Investor Protection and Corporate Governance' (2000) 58 Journal of Financial Economics 3, 6.

[131] See ibid. 13–17.

[132] See S Abdul Jabbar, *supra* note 74, 45–46.

[133] See A Page and R Ferguson, *Invetor Protection* (Weidenfeld and Nicolson 1992) 35–39.

[134] S Abdul Jabbar, *supra* note 74, 75.

[135] Ibid.

[136] See ibid. See also Page and Ferguson 15–31; J Fisher and M Waters, *The Law of Investor Protection* (2 edn, Sweet & Maxwell 2003) 5–6.

In the context of the IFSI, the issue of investor protection has not been adequately addressed in related literature. In this respect, Abdul Jabbar states that there are 'laws relating to investor protection issues in the Islamic financial services industry that have not received adequate attention, namely conflicts of interest and duties, insider dealing, fraud and money laundering'.[137] The specificities of the IFSI and the sharia-compliant nature of its transactions require special consideration of the issues associated with investor protection from an Islamic law point of view. The question of whether the current body of Islamic law is able to address the above-mentioned concerns regarding investor protection in the IFSI requires careful attention. Rider argues '[i]t is certainly the case that a jurisdiction that attempted to rely solely on the sharia to afford investors and depositors protection would not meet the expectations of the international financial community'.[138]

One should not infer from the above discussion that Islamic law plays no significant role with regard to investor protection. From the Islamic law perspective, investor protection falls within sharia objectives, particularly the objective of preserving wealth or protection of property. Under Islamic law, investors are protected through rules relating to, inter alia, contracting parties, subject matter of the contract, prohibition of fraud, and sale options. Rider stresses the vital role played by Islamic law in ensuring investor protection, as it places great emphasis on good faith and fair dealing.[139] However, the main concern regards the 'underdeveloped state of Islamic law on certain aspects of investor protection'.[140] This can be attributed to the absence of organisational law, corporate law, and the notion of corporation in the traditional corpus of Islamic law.[141] As a result, details about shareholders' rights and creditors' rights, as have been addressed under modern laws such as securities law and bankruptcy law, do not appear in the classical body of Islamic law.[142] This is compounded by the debate in Islamic law about the legality of the limited liability feature of a corporation, as 'it could be used as a basis for avoiding legal liability or even perpetrating a fraud'.[143] Apart

[137] S Abdul Jabbar, *supra* note 74, 42.

[138] B Rider, *supra* note 70, 219.

[139] Ibid.

[140] Ibid.

[141] H Ahmed, 'Islamic Law, Investors' Rights and Corporate Finance' (2012) 12 Journal of Corporate Law Studies 367, 384–385.

[142] Ibid. 385.

[143] S Wong and J Seward, 'Insolvency Regimes: Developing an Analytical Framework for Meeting Legal and Regulatory Challenges for Islamic Finance' in IFSB and WB (eds), *Effective Insolvency Regimes: Institutional, Regulatory, and Legal Issues Relating to Islamic Finance* (IFSB & WB 2011) 107.

from the above concerns relating to the current state of Islamic law, the level of investor protection in the IFSI has been affected in practice by disproportionate concern from large British and American law firms regarding issues associated with the development of the IFSI.[144] This emanates from the concerns of their clients, who tend to focus on transactional issues rather than broader issues.[145]

1.9 Relevance of the Book

The primary purpose of this study is to examine the contemporary issues encountered in the foundation and operation of sound *ṣukūk* markets. *Ṣukūk* are sharia-compliant instruments offered in the domestic and international capital markets for the purpose of investment, trading, and fund generation.[146] *Ṣukūk* markets have grown significantly worldwide since their emergence. *Ṣukūk* have been issued in Islamic jurisdictions as well as conventional jurisdictions including the USA, the UK, Germany, China, France, and Singapore. A good illustration of the economic role is that they can provide funds for large infrastructure projects such as airports, academic cities and hospitals.

However, the practices of *ṣukūk* markets have come under close scrutiny. From legal and regulatory perspectives, *ṣukūk* markets present a challenging subject because of the complexity of *ṣukūk* arrangements, the number of parties involved, and the variety of deals. In order to imagine the complexity of *ṣukūk*, one should read the following description of one *ṣukūk* issuance:

> This Nakheel *Ṣukūk* structure involved 17 different transaction documents, 19 if you count multiple copies of the same document, and the offering circular ran to 254 pages. 6 separate companies in the Nakheel group were involved; two of them in dual roles. The *ṣukūk* had some other interesting features, including being based on a 50-year lease of land some of which had yet to be reclaimed from the sea'.[147]

[144] B Rider, *supra* note 70, 137.

[145] Ibid.

[146] The term *ṣukūk* and its meaning in the IFSI will be explained in further detail in Chap. 2.

[147] P Casey, 'Emerging Issues From Inadequate Disclosure Requirements for Islamic Capital Market Products' in IFSB, IOSCO and SC (eds), *Disclosure Requirements for Islamic Capital Market Products* (IFSB, IOSCO, SC 2013) 35.

This enormous variety of deals inevitably causes issues in *ṣukūk* markets requiring a high level of intellectual rigour. This is compounded by the fact that *ṣukūk* markets operate in different countries that all have different regulations concerning *ṣukūk*. Apart from this, concerns over *ṣukūk* have been triggered off by other factors. In this respect, Laldin states:

> [T]here was call for re-examination of *ṣukūk* structure particularly after the famous remarks made by the Chairman of the AAOIFI's Sharia Board. Defaults in several *ṣukūk* in 2009 also triggered the need to re-examine the *ṣukūk* structure and the industry as a whole.[148]

In 2007, Al-ʿuthmānī, a leading sharia scholar, declared that 85% of *ṣukūk* existing in the market were not sharia-compliant.[149] Such a declaration certainly raises doubt about the credibility and integrity of *ṣukūk* markets. Furthermore, the need to investigate *ṣukūk* markets is caused by some events that have had an impact on the level of investor protection in *ṣukūk* markets. Lin, Lahsasna and Ahmed argue that '[t]he restructuring process of landmark deals continues to highlight areas that have been overlooked by investors, particularly sharia risks which may affect investors' protection'.[150] The fact that certain types of *ṣukūk* are subject to sharia criticism is well established. In this context, Dusuki and Mokhtar state 'there are many contentious sharia issues arising in asset-based *ṣukūk*'.[151]

Therefore, the urgent need to analyse the issues arising in *ṣukūk* markets is apparent. The topic of *ṣukūk* has been subject to extensive research and academic discussion from different perspectives.[152] However, the existing literature has not adequately addressed issues associated with *ṣukūk* markets. An example of an important issue that has not been profoundly analysed is the distinction between asset-backed *ṣukūk* versus asset-based *ṣukūk*. There has also been little examination of investors' rights under different *ṣukūk* structures, markets, and regulations that vary

[148] M Laldin, 'Sukuk in Various Juridictions: Shariah and Legal Issues' (2012) 2 Journal of Islamic Business and Management 15, 17.

[149] Reuters.

[150] L Lin, A Lahsasna and R Ahmed, 'Sharīʿah Issues in Islamic Capital Markets: Ṣukūk' (2013) 5 ISRA International Journal of Islamic Finance 99, 100.

[151] A Dusuki and S Mokhtar, *Critical Appraisal of Shariah Issues on Ownership in Asset-Based Sukuk as Implemented in the Islamic Debt Market* (ISRA 2010) 29.

[152] See U Idris, 'Evaluation of Research Developments on the Islamic Securities (Sukuk)' (7th International Conference on Islamic Economics, Jeddah, March 2008).

from one jurisdiction to another. Furthermore, there has been little interest in drawing attention to matters outside Islamic law which have considerable impact on *ṣukūk* markets, and existing literature stops short of examining *ṣukūk* markets under different legal environments. The legal and regulatory risks thrown up by the existing general legal environment and their impact on those investing and trading in *ṣukūk* markets have not received adequate attention. This harks back to Rider's comments pertaining to the areas of focus in the existing literature on Islamic finance[153]; Rider argues that there is little interest in learning about issues related to governance, regulation, and institutional aspects of the IFSI,[154] clearly stating '[i]n the context of Islamic financial business there has been little debate and almost no legal analysis'.[155]

The above discussion demonstrates a huge research gap in the study of *ṣukūk* markets, which provides strong motivation to conduct further research. This thesis provides in-depth discussion of the issues facing *ṣukūk* markets from legal and regulatory perspectives, and focuses attention on how soundness can be ensured in the wider context of *ṣukūk* markets. These issues go to the heart of what the *ṣukūk* market is really about, as recent debate has recognised in *ṣukūk* the replication of conventional bonds in ways that are considered unsatisfactory from an Islamic law point of view.

1.10 Conclusion

The above discussion seeks to illuminate issues of particular significance in the general practice of the IFSI for those who have a substantive interest in the IFSI. In this respect, some tend to overstate the positive figures pertaining to the asset growth of the IFSI, and overlook serious facts affecting its operations. It has been a common approach in the current academic debate and literature to concentrate on the positive aspects of creating wealth in accordance with the instructions of Islamic economy and finance. Such approach is needed, to some extent, to convince the international financial community of the appearance of a different financing mode, and it has played a vital role in the early stages of IFSI growth. Illuminating the hurdles to the development of the IFSI would position it

[153] B Rider, *supra* note 26, 103.
[154] Ibid.
[155] Ibid. 105.

in a right place compared to its conventional counterpart. It also would partially put away the blame concerning many negative aspects of the IFSI practices that are repeatedly highlighted by the press and media. The fact that IFSI is not currently operating up to its great potential cannot be overlooked. This is justified by its small size and age compared to its conventional counterpart and its involuntary connection with the international financial system. Having set out issues of particular significance in the general practice of the IFSI, the primary subject of this book needs to be considered in the next chapter.

CHAPTER 2

An Overview of *Ṣukūk*

2.1 Introduction

The emergence of *ṣukūk* (trust investment certificates) in international capital markets and increased interest in *ṣukūk* has been followed by a set of questions about the theory and origins of such structures. The tremendous expansion of *ṣukūk* has surprised observers; there is curiosity to know more about the basics of *ṣukūk* and its historical development, especially in the Western world. This chapter deals with the nature of *ṣukūk* and how it has evolved over the years into a well-known industry. It explains the purpose of dealing with *ṣukūk* and how *ṣukūk* contributes to the economic development of a country. The basis of *ṣukūk* in Islamic law and various *ṣukūk* structures in the market are outlined in this chapter. By the end of this chapter, it is hoped that the reader will be familiar with the general concept of *ṣukūk* before moving on to the issues of particular significance in this book.

2.2 Definition of *Ṣukūk*

Linguistically, *ṣukūk* is an Arabic term. *Ṣukūk* is plural of *ṣak*, and it has other two plural forms: *ṣikāk* and *aṣuk*.[1] For the purpose of simplicity, the term *ṣukūk* is used throughout this book to denote both the plural and singular form depending on the context. In common market parlance, the term *ṣukūk* is used to refer to a financial instrument that is structured based on the unique

[1] M Bin Manẓūr, *Lisān Al-ʿarab*, vol 10 (1 edn, Dār Ṣādir Undated) 457.

S. Al-Ali, *Raising Capital on* Ṣukūk *Markets*,
https://doi.org/10.1007/978-3-030-14536-1_2

features of Islamic finance and mainly utilised for the purpose of funding, investment, and liquidity management. *Ṣukūk* are also known by other names in academic literature such as investment certificates, investment trust certificates, *ṣukūk* securities, Islamic bonds, and Islamic securities. However, using the term *ṣukūk* interchangeably with the last two terms is misleading; appending the word 'Islamic' in front of the terms 'bonds' and 'securities' does not assist in defining the nature of *ṣukūk*. Safari, Ariff, and Mohamad have criticised the tendency of modern Islamic finance press to use the term Islamic bond.[2] They argue that the crucial features of *ṣukūk* are lost when the term Islamic bond is used instead.[3] Also, Ali and Mufti argue that it is a misnomer to refer to *ṣukūk* as Islamic bonds since the former are not IOUs.[4]

Despite its increasing popularity, *ṣukūk* has no collective definition or standardised description adopted by all industry stakeholders. For an institutional definition, one can look at Sharia Standard No. 17 of the Accounting and Auditing Organization for Islamic Financial Institutions (AAOIFI) which defines *ṣukūk*, with preference of 'investment *ṣukūk*' designation, as follows:

> [C]ertificates of equal value representing undivided shares in ownership of tangible assets, usufruct and services or (in the ownership of) the assets of particular projects or special investment activity, however, this is true after receipt of the value of the *ṣukūk*, the closing of subscription and the employment of funds received for the purpose for which the *ṣukūk* were issued.[5]

Another example of an institutional definition of *ṣukūk* is from the IFSB:

> *Ṣukūk* (plural of *ṣak*), frequently referred to as Islamic bonds, are certificates with each *ṣak* representing a proportional undivided ownership right in tangible assets, or a pool of predominantly tangible assets, or a business venture (such as a *muḍārabah*). These assets may be in a specific project or investment activity in accordance with sharia rules and principles.[6]

[2] M Safari, M Ariff and S Mohamad, *Sukuk Securities: New Ways of Debt Contracting* (Wiley & Sons 2014) 22.

[3] Ibid.

[4] R Ali and I Mufti, 'Legal and Structural Anatomy of a Sukuk' in R Ali (ed), *Sukuk and Islamic Capital Markets* (Globe Business Publishing 2011) 51.

[5] AAOIFI, *Shari'a Standards for Islamic Financial Institutions* (AAOIFI 2010) 307.

[6] IFSB, 'Capital Adequacy Requirements for Ṣukūk, Securitisations and Real Estate investment' (*IFSB*, January 2009) 3. http://www.ifsb.org/standard/eng_%20IFSB-7%20Capital%20Adequacy%20Requirements%20for%20Sukuk,%20Securitasations%20and%20Real%20Estate%20investment%20(Jan2009).pdf. Accessed 4 March 2015.

A further institutional definition for *ṣukūk* is provided by the International Islamic Financial Market (IIFM) as follows: '[A] commercial paper that provides an investor with ownership in an underlying asset. It is asset-backed trust certificates evidencing ownership of an asset or its usufruct (earnings or fruits)'.[7] From a regulatory perspective, Securities Commission (SC) Malaysia has defined *ṣukūk* as 'certificates of equal value which evidence undivided ownership or investment in the assets using sharia principles and concepts endorsed by the SAC'.[8] Another regulatory definition is provided by Kuwaiti Ministerial Decision 388 of 2007, which defines *ṣukūk* as:

> The instruments that have equal value issued by companies under certain types of contracts which comply with the Islamic sharia such as *mushāraka*, *muḍārabah*, *ijāra* or an investment agency in certain investment project or activity, subject to the provisions of the relevant laws.[9]

The Stocks and Commodities Authority (SCA) in the UAE has defined *ṣukūk* as '[t]radable financial instruments of equal value which represent a share of ownership of an asset or a group of assets and are issued in accordance with sharia'.[10] Furthermore, a formal meaning of *ṣukūk* can be found in the Issue of *Ṣukūk* Regulations 2015 of the Securities and Exchange Commission of Pakistan (SECP) as follows:

> [I]nstrument of equal value representing investment of the *ṣukūk* holders in the capital of the issuer to the extent of undivided share in ownership of the identified tangible assets, usufruct and services or in the ownership of the assets of particular projects or special investment activity based on characteristics and structures including participatory mode approved by the sharia Advisor.[11]

Ṣukūk have also been described in conventional regimes, for example, the Board of Taxation of Australian government has published the following description:

[7] IIFM, 'IIFM Ṣukūk Report 1st Edition' (*IIFM*, 2010) 3. http://www.iifm.net/documents/iifm-sukuk-report-1st-edition. Accessed 4 March 2015.

[8] Guidelines on *Ṣukūk*, Part A, Chapter 2.

[9] Ministerial Decision 388 of 2007 of Ministry of Commerce and Industry, Article 2.

[10] SCA's Decision No 16 of 2014 Concerning the Regulation of *Ṣukūk*, Chapter 1, Article 1.

[11] Issue of *Ṣukūk* Regulations 2015, Chapter I.

> *Ṣukūk* is the Islamic finance equivalent of conventional tradable notes or bonds, which represents the ownership (actual or beneficial) by the *ṣukūk* holders in an underlying sharia-compliant asset or financing arrangement. Returns are paid to the investors in line with their proportional ownership in that asset and investment, and vary according to asset performance rather than the time elapsed.[12]

Further, *ṣukūk* are defined in the circular concerning Islamic finance issued by the Luxembourg Tax Director on 12 January 2010 as 'securities representing entitlement to a claim or share where both the income and capital are indexed to the performance of one or more assets held by the issuer, the income stream from which is used to remunerate and reimburse the *ṣukūk*'.[13]

From the above definitions, it can be seen that understanding of the term *ṣukūk* oscillates between broad and narrow definitions. *Ṣukūk* definitions provided by Islamic finance standard-setting bodies such as the AAOIFI and IFSB have not been considered by the regulatory regimes in countries such as Kuwait, Malaysia, the UAE, and Pakistan. The definition of *ṣukūk* has found a place in either relevant statutes or guidelines in several countries. The above-mentioned definitions place more emphasis on the particular aspect of *ṣukūk* as representative of ownership. While all of these definitions seek to describe precisely what *ṣukūk* is, they fail to agree on the very essence of *ṣukūk*. On the one hand, AAOIFI's definition confines the asset underlying *ṣukūk* to tangible assets; in this respect, Dusuki notes that the AAOIFI's definition does not consider financial assets or financial receivables as potential assets in *ṣukūk* because the AAOIFI prohibits the sale of debt.[14] On the other hand, SC's definition includes all types of assets and does not exclude financial receivables. The substance of *ṣukūk* shall become clearer in the discussion that follows on the main features of such instruments.

[12] The Board of Taxation, 'Review of the Taxation Treatment of Islamic Finance: Discussion Paper' (*Taxboard*, 2010) 5. http://www.taxboard.gov.au/content/reviews_and_consultations/islamic_finance_products/discussion_paper/downloads/Islamic_Finance_Discussion_Paper.pdf. Accessed 23 April 2015.

[13] The Tax Director, 'Circular of the Tax Director' (*Luxembourgforfinance*, 2010) 4. http://www.luxembourgforfinance.lu/sites/luxembourgforfinance/files/taxcirc_2010_12jan_islamfin_en.pdf. Accessed 27 November 2012.

[14] A Dusuki, 'Challenges of Realizing Maqasid al-Shariah (Objectives of Shariah) in Islamic Capital Market: Special Focus on Equity-Based Sukuk' (International Islamic Management Conference on Islamic Capital Market, Penang, October 2009) 10.

2.3 Essential Features of *Ṣukūk*

Several essential features of *ṣukūk* aid understanding of the conceptual thrust of *ṣukūk* in the area of financial innovation and investment, and serve as a yardstick to assess whether or not the resultant structure complies with such thrust. They do not only aim at providing investors with all the necessary information about the essence of *ṣukūk* but also help them to differentiate *ṣukūk* from other financial products and reach a proper investment decision. A good illustration of this is the East Cameron *Ṣukūk* for which Campbell Evans, the chief executive officer (CEO) of East Cameron Partners LP, had received several financing proposals from hedge funds and major investment banks in the USA in order to raise funds.[15] Issuing *ṣukūk* was among the financing solutions proposed to the CEO.[16] In this situation, the CEO needed to understand how *ṣukūk* actually works and compare such a proposal with other proposed standard financing alternatives including conventional bonds, bank loans, and equity.[17] This highlights the significance of understanding the characteristics of *ṣukūk* in order to make an informed decision.

One can speak of two types of *ṣukūk* features. The first type refers to general features which are relevant to all financial instruments in IFSI. In this context, there is no difference between *ṣukūk* and other Islamic financial products when it comes to the key Islamic financial principles: prohibition of *ribā* (usury), *gharar* (uncertainty), gambling, and investing in assets and activities that are prohibited in Islamic law. These are four features inherent in all *ṣukūk* structures.

The second type refers to features which are specifically relevant to *ṣukūk*. These features can be inferred from the above-mentioned definitions of *ṣukūk*. While most of the specific features are related to the sharia-compliant nature of *ṣukūk*, few of them reflect the market practice. The first distinguishing feature of *ṣukūk* is that it represents an ownership interest over the underlying asset, and not a debt owed by the issuer or another method of borrowing money; this makes the *ṣukūk* holder an owner, and not a lender. It also implies that *ṣukūk* establishes the claim of its holder over the financial rights represented by such *ṣukūk*.[18] Second, *ṣukūk* are

[15] S Sapp, *East Cameron Partners: The Sukuk Bond* (Ivey School of Business Foundation 2010) 2.

[16] Ibid.

[17] Ibid. 3.

[18] AAOIFI, *supra* note 5, 309.

issued on an equal value basis. To illustrate, the price of each *ṣukūk* will be the same as all other *ṣukūk*, and there is no difference in their value in order to facilitate the purchase and tradability process of *ṣukūk*.[19] If USD 1,000,000 *ṣukūk* issuance is allocated for ten investors, each investor will receive a certificate of USD 100,000. Third, the ownership that is represented by each *ṣukūk* is a common or undivided share in the ownership. This means, inter alia that ownership in *ṣukūk* exists as a whole, and not in separate parts. A common ownership implies that each *ṣukūk* represents a share in the whole, and each *ṣukūk* bearer has an equal right to enjoy the whole *ṣukūk* project. It also means that individual *ṣukūk* cannot be divided amongst a group in the event of ownership transfer. Fourth, there is a wide range of assets that can be chosen to underlay *ṣukūk* structure, including tangible assets, usufructs, and services; buildings, cars, and machines are examples of potential assets, whether they are available now or to be developed in the future. Fifth, *ṣukūk* is a tradable financial instrument; tradability of *ṣukūk* means that the *ṣukūk* holder can sell certain types of *ṣukūk* in the secondary market. Sixth, *ṣukūk* are designed based on a number of sharia contracts, each offering different *ṣukūk* structures.[20] These sharia contracts govern issuance, trading, and profit and loss situations of the *ṣukūk* structure in question. Seventh, *ṣukūk* are offered through a subscription whereby all relevant information is accessible such as issue price, maturity date, rating, periodic distribution, and governing law.

Having elucidated the meaning of *ṣukūk* and its primary characteristics, it is possible to identify the key differences between *ṣukūk* and standard alternatives for raising funds in the capital market, namely debt securities (bonds or notes) and equity securities (ordinary shares, common shares or common stock). Understanding the distinction between these three financing instruments is significant for an entity wishing to raise funds. The key differences include[21]:

[19] See Z Al-Damāgh, *Al-Ṣukūk Al-Islāmiah wa Dawrahā fī Al-Tanmiyah Al-Iqtiṣādiah* (Dār Al-Thaqāfah Lil-Nashr 2012) 71.

[20] AAOIFI, *supra* note 5, 310.

[21] On the differences between *ṣukūk*, debt securities, and equity securities, see G Fuller, *The Law and Practice of International Capital Markets* (3 edn, LexisNexis 2012) 10; N Adam and A Thomas (eds), *Islamic Bonds: Your Guide to Issuing, Structuring and Investing in Sukuk* (Euromoney Books 2004) 54.

1. *Ṣukūk*, by its nature, is an undivided ownership share in assets or business ventures. Debt security is a debt of the issuer. Equity security is ownership share in a corporation.
2. The income on *ṣukūk* is referred to as profit, which is only payable when the underlying project is profitable and does not incur losses. The income on debt securities is known as interest, which must be paid irrespective of profits. The income on equity securities is called dividends, which is only paid when there are adequate distributable profits.
3. While *ṣukūk* and debt securities have a specified date for repayment, equity securities do not provide for repayment on a specified date.
4. While *ṣukūk* is issued only for sharia-compliant purposes, debt securities and equity securities are not.
5. The value of *ṣukūk* and equity securities can increase. However, the value of debt securities does not.

The above discussion reveals that *ṣukūk* have similarities and differences with debt securities as well as with equity securities. This has led some commentators to view *ṣukūk* as a hybrid of debt security and equity security because it provides for both ownership interest in the underlying asset and ownership interest in the cash flows generated by the asset.[22]

2.4 Historical Origins of *Ṣukūk*

When discussing the contemporary *ṣukūk* trend gaining momentum in the international financial arena, questions arise about the origins of the product. In this respect, there are three potential origin answers for *ṣukūk*: (1) an early Islamic financial product that can be traced back to the early period of Islam, (2) a new product invented by modern IFSI, and (3) a product borrowed from conventional finance. Some discussion of the historical development of *ṣukūk* is needed to clarify how *ṣukūk* started and came into practice; such discussion is relevant to the sharia-compliant nature of *ṣukūk*.

[22] See M Graham, 'Islamic Finance and the United States Bankruptcy Courts: The Future of Sukuk Certificate Holders' Rights and the Importance of Considering Shari'ah Precepts in the Bankruptcy Process' (2012) 20 Tulane Journal of International and Company Law 327, 334; A Abdel-Khaleq and C Richardson, 'New Horizons for Islamic Securities: Emerging Trends in Sukuk Offerings' (2007) 7 Chicago Journal of International Law 409, 412.

As *ṣukūk* is an Arabic word, examination of *ṣukūk* origins should start by looking at the contexts in which this word has been used in the Arabic language. It is evidenced that Arab people used this word during the classical period in two denotations. The first is to strike, to hit, or to touch.[23] In this respect, it is used when two things meet or touch each other, sometimes strongly and with intensity, in various situations, for example, putting the knees closer, closing the door, giving a slap, and shooting an arrow.[24] The Quran (51:29) uses this word as a verb, which is translated thus: 'Then his wife came forward with a loud voice: she smote her face…'. Also, the verb form of the word *ṣak* can be found in Hadith in *Ṣaḥīḥ Muslim* (one of the six canonical collections of Hadith) (19:4450) where the *ṣaḥābi* (companion) said: '…shoot at him an arrow…'. The second meaning of the word *ṣukūk* is a book or written document that records and acknowledges debt, property, commercial transactions, or financial rights.[25] In this respect, it has the connotation of *dhikru al-ḥaq* (right mentioning).[26] One should note that the term *ṣukūk* in the current Islamic finance press is originated from the second meaning of the *ṣukūk* in Arabic language.

A good illustration of the second meaning of the word *ṣukūk* is the practice of allocating grants and allowances by rulers.[27] History records that the Umayyad Caliphate practised the institution of *ṣukūk* as a way of paying troops in the late first century of Islam (corresponding to the seventh century AD).[28] These grants were sent to eligible people in the form of *ṣukūk* in order to enable them to enjoy it after receiving this kind of book. In practice, however, they used to sell these *ṣukūk* to other people in advance to obtain their financial rights before taking possession of them.[29] It seems that the main reason for such practice was that the *ṣukūk* were sent from distant destinations, and people who were in need could not wait for the *ṣukūk* to be delivered. Therefore, they sold them on before taking delivery.

[23] M Bin Manẓūr, *supra* note 1, 457.

[24] Ibid.

[25] Ibid.

[26] Ibid.

[27] Ibid.

[28] See A Hassan, *Sales and Contracts in Early Islamic Commerical Law* (The Other Press 2007) 119; A Khorshid, 'Sukuk and Securitization' in A Khorshid (ed), *Euromoney Encyclopedia of Islamic Finance* (Euromoney Institutional Investor PLC 2009) 281.

[29] M Bin Manẓūr, *supra* note 1, 457.

It is worth mentioning that the validity of the practice of *ṣukūk* selling is a topic of juristic debate due to different interpretations of the Hadith in *Ṣaḥīḥ Muslim* (10:3652), which is translated as follows:

> Abū Hurayrah (Allah be pleased with him) is reported to have said to Marwān: Have you made lawful the transactions involving interest? Thereupon Marwān said: I have not done that. Thereupon Abū Hurayrah (may peace be upon him) said: You have made lawful the transactions with the help of documents only, whereas Allah's Messenger (may peace be upon him) forbade the transaction of foodgrains until full possession is taken of them. Marwan then addressed the people and forbade them to enter into such transactions (as are done with the help of documents). Sulaymān said: I saw the sentinels snatching (these documents) from the people.

The first view prohibits the practice of *ṣukūk* selling based on the above clear text of the Hadith.[30] According to this view, the practice of *ṣukūk* selling amounts to selling something which is not yet owned. The second view validates the practice of *ṣukūk* selling[31] by providing an alternative interpretation of the above Hadith. Proponents of this view argue that the practice of *ṣukūk* selling is permissible for the original recipient of *ṣukūk*, and not permissible for the party who purchases the *ṣukūk* from the original recipient of *ṣukūk*.[32]

One cannot trace the modern *ṣukūk* directly back to the practice of *ṣukūk* as a rights-enforcing document as described above. The fact that they carry the same name in the literature does not mean that they are the same thing, or that the modern *ṣukūk* is a manifestation of the classical form of *ṣukūk* used during the early period of Islam. There are major differences between them: the classic use of *ṣukūk* was not meant for investment purposes and was not structured based on Islamic commercial contracts. It was used as a payment method and for recording people's rights. In addition, the validity of selling classic *ṣukūk* has been questioned by scholars. Thus, reliance on the classical usage of *ṣukūk* does not provide a historical perspective of contemporary *ṣukūk* development.

The literature does not provide an exact date for the origin of modern *ṣukūk*, and there is no clear consensus on this matter. Arrif, Safari, and

[30] Y Al-Nawawī, *Ṣaḥīḥ Muslim Bisharḥ Al-Nawawī*, vol 10 (Dār Iḥyāʾ Al-Turāth Al-ʿaraby 1392) 171.

[31] Ibid.

[32] Ibid.

Mohammed claim that the first recorded use of modern *ṣukūk* goes back to AD 1285, when the Ottoman Empire obtained a large amount of money by setting aside part of the treasury assets to be owned by a lending public to reconstruct and improve the infrastructure of the Empire after the devastation of crusades.[33] Cizakca is of the view that the roots of modern *ṣukūk* can be traced back to the eighteenth or even the fifteenth century.[34] According to Cizakca, the structure of every modern *ṣukūk* involves three distinct elements: generation of revenue, securitisation of this revenue, and creation of a special purpose vehicle (SPV).[35] The ensuing discussion examines whether Islamic law contains practices that forebear Cizakca's aforementioned three elements of modern *ṣukūk*, borrowed from conventional finance.

Regarding the revenue-generation element, Cizakca notes that its origin can be traced back to the fifteenth century in the form of cash *waqf* (known as *istighlāl*) practised by the Ottoman Empire.[36] Cizakca argues that the very essence of modern *ijārah ṣukūk* is found in the cash *waqf* in which the endowed capital is invested to raise funds for a charitable purpose, which is the main reason for the establishment of *waqf* (charitable endowment).[37] This process involves a sale and leaseback transaction between the *waqf* administration and the borrower in which the house of the latter is sold and then bought back.[38] The latter occupies the house and pays a rental amount for a certain time until the house is bought back.[39]

Regarding the securitisation of revenue element, Cizakca notes that this can be found in the *ishām* system introduced by the Ottoman Empire in 1775.[40] *Ishām* refers to a system of securitisation of a ready stream of revenue belonging to the Empire.[41] The revenue generation found in modern *ṣukūk* was not needed as the *ishām* notion was based on an existing source of revenue.[42]

[33] M Safari, M Ariff and S Mohamad, 'Sukuk Securities, their Definitions, Classification and Pricing Issues' in M Arrif, M Iqbal and S Mohamad (eds), *The Islamic Debt Market for Sukuk Securities: The Theory and Practice of Profit Sharing Investment* (Edward Elgar) 20.

[34] M Cizakca, 'Domestic Borrowing without the Rate of Interest: Gharar and the Origins of Sukuk' (Symposium on Sukuk Financial Instruments, Dubai, May 2010) 2.

[35] See ibid. 15, 16.

[36] Ibid.

[37] Ibid.

[38] Ibid.

[39] Ibid. 16.

[40] Ibid. 15.

[41] Ibid.

[42] Ibid.

Regarding the SPV element, Cizakca argues that its origin can be traced back to the *waqf* since the SPV bears all the essential features of *waqf*.[43] Both the SPV process and *waqf* involve the creation of a trust entity that holds the asset in question for the benefit of the beneficiaries.[44] In this respect, Cizakca states:

> This remarkable similarity between the SPVs of a modern *ṣukūk* and *waqfs* should not surprise us. This is because, the modern SPVs are established as common law trusts. But the English trusts were originally borrowed from the Islamic world during the crusades.[45]

The above statement stresses the point that the trust concept found in English Law was borrowed from Islamic law. The incorporation of Merton College of Oxford University in 1274 based on the *waqf* concept forms a good illustration of the influence of *waqf* on the development of trust under English Law.[46] As Gaudiosi states '[y]et, in its early phases of development, Oxford may have owed much to the Islamic legal institutions of *waqf* (pl. *awqaf*) charitable trust'.[47] It has been argued that the modern *ṣukūk* has resulted from borrowing in two cycles: borrowing of the *waqf* by the English in the thirteenth century, and borrowing of the trust concept from English law by developers of the modern *ṣukūk*.[48]

Thus, some commentators claim that the Western community refined and expanded the above-mentioned notions related to *ṣukūk* origins and then introduced new concepts such as trust, SPV, and securitisation.[49] This argument is supported by Schacht:

> Several institutions of this customary commercial law of Islam were transmitted to medieval Europe through the intermediary of the law merchant, the customary law of international trade, as is attested by [...] the term cheque, from Arabic *al-ṣak* which means a written document.[50]

[43] Ibid. 16.

[44] On *waqf*, see M Abbasi, 'The Classical Islamic Law of Waqf: A Concise Introduction' (2012) 26 Arab Law Quarterly 121.

[45] M Cizakca, *supra* note 34, 17.

[46] See M Gaudiosi, 'The Influence of the Islamic Law of Waqf on the Development of the Trust in England: The Case of Merton College' (1988) 136 University of Pennsylvania Law Review 1231.

[47] Ibid.

[48] M Cizakca, *supra* note 34, 18.

[49] See R Haneef, 'Recent Trends and Innovations in Islamic Debt Securities: Prospects for Islamic Profit and Loss Sharing Securities' in S Ali (ed), *Islamic Finance: Current Legal and Regulatory Issues* (Islamic Finance Project 2005) 30.

[50] J Schacht, *An Introduction to Islamic Law* (Oxford University Press 1982) 78.

From the above discussion, it can be seen that there is a tendency in the literature to relate the modern *ṣukūk* with earlier practices, namely cash *waqf*, *ishām*, and classical *waqf*. Therefore, the modern *ṣukūk* is seen as a product derived from earlier practices of Muslims rather than an invention of the modern IFSI or even its conventional counterpart.[51] Having said this, the question arises as to when *ṣukūk* in its modern guise arose and how it has evolved.

2.5 Growth and Evolution of *Ṣukūk*

Opinions vary in the literature concerning the origins of modern *ṣukūk* and their initial issuances.[52] However, one can identify four main stages of *ṣukūk* development, with considerably varying levels of number of issuances, capitalisation, geographical spread, and structural innovation. Arranged on the basis of activities and sophistication that took place in the market, these phases are as follows:

1. Introductory period (1977–1999)
2. Growth of the *ṣukūk* market (2000–2007)
3. Decline in the *ṣukūk* market (2008–2009)
4. *Ṣukūk*: back on track (2010–2018)

These phases of *ṣukūk* development and growth are detailed below.

2.5.1 Introductory Period (1977–1999)

The first phase (1977–1999) is better described as the theoretical foundation of modern *ṣukūk* in the Islamic world after the emergence of securitisation in the USA in the 1970s.[53] The first use of *ṣukūk* was in Jordan, when the Ministry of Awqaf, Islamic Affairs and Holy Places needed to

[51] See A Hanif and J Johansen, 'Sukuk' in C Nethercott and D Eisenberg (eds), *Finance: Law and Practice* (1 edn, Oxford University Press 2012) 255; Khorshid 281.

[52] See, for example, I Khan, 'Preface' in A Thomas (ed), *Sukuk* (Sweet & Maxwell Asia 2009) x; Z Al-Damāgh, *supra* note 19, 65–66.

[53] For the history of securitisation in the USA, see D Barbour, J Norton and T Slover, 'Asset Securitisation in Emerging Market Economics: Fundamentals Considerations' (1997) Yearbook of International Financial and Financial Law 281, 294; R Diaz-Granados, 'A Comparative Approach to Securitization in the United States, Japan, Germany, and France' (1996) 4 Willamette Bulletin of International Law and Policy 1, 11.

renovate the *waqf* properties in the absence of sufficient funds and suitable Islamic financing instrument.[54] Under the name of Law *nisi* No.10 for the year 1981, a *Muqaradah* Bonds Law was approved (following four years of preparation beginning in 1977).[55] Further, the Federal Government of Pakistan promulgated the *Mudarabah* Companies and *Mudarabah* Flotation and Control Ordinance of 1980[56]; however, neither of these two legislative moves led to any significant *ṣukūk* activities owing to insufficient infrastructure in the market.[57] In 1983, the Malaysian Parliament felt it necessary to develop a funding facility that was not an interest-bearing instrument, following the establishment of the first Islamic bank in Malaysia.[58] Such an instrument was needed to start operation of an IFSI in the region as well as to meet statutory liquidity requirements.[59] The Government Investment Act 1983 (now known as the Government Funding Act 1983) was enacted resulting in the issue of Government Investment Certificates (GIC) (now known as the Government Investment Issues—GII).[60] As this instrument was based on the *qarḍ ḥasan* (interest-free loan) concept, it had drawbacks in that it could not be traded in the secondary market.[61] Although this Malaysian attempt did not represent a proper *ṣukūk* structure, it motivated further activity towards the creation of the *ṣukūk* market.

[54] W Khayrullah, 'Al-Muqaradah Bonds as the Basis of Profit Sharing' (*Irti*, Undated) 3. http://www.irti.org/English/Research/Documents/IES/157.pdf. Accessed 30 April 2015.

[55] This law defines the *muḍārabah* (investment partnership) bond and limits the institutions that can issue this bond. The law allowed only specified organisations to issue this particular kind of *ṣukūk*. It also demonstrates the basic elements for issuing process and points out that the capital will be guaranteed by the Government. For further information, see ibid.

[56] This law promotes *muḍārabah* as a mode of investment, providing conditions and operation of *muḍārabah* raising through *muḍārabah* fund. It states that the owners of *muḍārabah* fund are the certificate holders. Also, *muḍārabah* fund has its own legal status and is a separate entity by law. See T Rahman, *Mudarabah and the Pakistan Perspective* (IDB 2000) 16–17.

[57] Z Iqbal and A Mirakhor, *An Introduction to Islamic Finance* (2 edn, John Wiley & Sons 2011) 184.

[58] BNM, 'Information: About IIMM' (*BNM*, Undated). http://iimm.bnm.gov.my/index.php?ch=4&pg=4&ac=22#3. Accessed 12 December 2012.

[59] Ibid.

[60] Ibid.

[61] To address this concern, Bank Negara Malaysia (BNM) opened a window that facilitates selling and the purchasing process among the players with determination of the price by BNM. See ibid.

The Malaysian attempt was followed by the issuance of a USD 200 billion *mushārakah ṣukūk* in 1984 by Turkey to fund the construction of the *Al-Būsfūr Al-Thānī* Bridge (*Muḥamad Al-Fātiḥ* Bridge).[62] Another far-reaching effort in this period was the issue of a sharia resolution concerning *ṣukūk* called '*al-muqāraḍah* bonds and investment certificates' in 1988 by the International Islamic Fiqh Academy (IIFA).[63] This resolution reflected the increasing interest at that time for such instrument and the necessity for a sharia view on *ṣukūk*. Another pioneering effort in this introductory period was the issuance of RM 150 million *bayʿ bithaman ʾājil* (deferred payment sale, BBA) *ṣukūk* in 1990 by Shell Group Malaysia.[64] This was the first ever corporate ringgit-denominated *ṣukūk* issued by a foreign-owned company in Malaysia.[65] Although this phase had only a small number of *ṣukūk* issuances issued on an isolated basis, it formed the basis of the future *ṣukūk* market.

2.5.2 Growth of the Ṣukūk *Market (2000–2007)*

The second phase of the *ṣukūk* market began in 2000, ten years after the last private issue of *ṣukūk*. In 2000, the Sudanese government issued 'Government *Mushārakah* Certificates' which constituted a transformative stage in *ṣukūk* market development.[66] Then, in June 2001, the Bahrain Monetary Agency (BMA) issued USD 25 million *salam ṣukūk*, as short-term government bills.[67] This was closely followed by issuance of USD 100 million *ijārah ṣukūk* in August 2001 by the BMA, the world's first issued by a central bank.[68] In December of the same year, the first global-rated corporate USD 150 million *ijārah ṣukūk* were issued by Kumpulan Guthrie Berhad, a corporation in Malaysia.[69] This US dollar-dominated *ṣukūk* represented a significant milestone for the development of the *ṣukūk* market, since it opened the door for international investors in Asia and the

[62] Z Al-Damāgh, *supra* note 19, 66.

[63] See IIFA, *Resolutions and Recommendations of the Council of Islamic Fiqh Academy* (1 edn, IDB 2000) 61–66.

[64] BNM and SC, *Malaysian Debt Securities and Sukuk Market: A Guide for Issuers and Investors* (BNM and SC 2009) 4.

[65] Ibid.

[66] IIFM, *supra* note 7, 8.

[67] Bahrain Monetary Agency (ed) *Islamic Banking and Finance in the Kingdom of Bahrain* (Bahrain Monetary Agency 2002) 72.

[68] Ibid.

[69] BNM and SC, *supra* note 64, 136.

Middle East to become involved in *ṣukūk*.[70] This period also witnessed a breakthrough issuance, namely the USD 600 million first global sovereign *ṣukūk* offered by the Malaysian government in 2002.[71]

This phase is described as the growth phase in the *ṣukūk* market for two reasons: (1) it witnessed issuances of landmark *ṣukūk* and (2) it witnessed strong interest from several jurisdictions to tap *ṣukūk*. Apart from the early entrants (Sudan, Bahrain, and Malaysia), other entrants to the *ṣukūk* market in this period were as follows[72]:

- Singapore in 2001 (a quasi-sovereign *ṣukūk*)
- Pakistan in 2002
- Indonesia in 2002
- Qatar in 2003 (sovereign *ṣukūk*)
- The German Federal State of Saxony-Anhalt in 2004 (sovereign *ṣukūk*, the first ever *ṣukūk* in Europe)
- The KSA in 2004 (Munshaat Real Estate Company *Ṣukūk*)
- The UAE in 2004 (The National Central Cooling Company 'Tabreed')
- The UK in 2005 (Sanctuary Building *Ṣukūk*, the first corporate *ṣukūk* in Europe)
- Brunei in 2006 (Brunei Liquefied Natural Gas *Ṣukūk*)
- The USA in 2006 (East Cameroon Gas Company *Ṣukūk*)

It can be seen that the above list includes three *ṣukūk* issuances from conventional jurisdictions. This period not only witnessed *ṣukūk* issuances by governments and corporates, but also *ṣukūk* issuances by international institutions. For example, the Islamic Development Bank (IDB) issued its first international *ṣukūk* in 2003.[73] Another example is the issuance of RM 760 million *ṣukūk* by the WB in 2005 in Malaysia.[74]

[70] See R Wedderburn-Day, 'Sovereign Sukuk: Adaption and Innovation' (2010) 73 Law and Contemporary Problems 325.

[71] BNM and SC, *supra* note 64, 136.

[72] See IIFM, 'IIFM Study on Indonesian Sukuk Market & Global Sukuk Issuances' (*IIFM*, August 2010). http://www.iifm.net/documents/iifm-study-indonesian-sukuk-market-global-sukuk-issuances. Accessed 4 March 2015; IIFM, *supra* note 7.

[73] Islamic Development Bank Group, *Islamic Development Bank Group in Brief* (IDB 2013) 21.

[74] M Bennett and Z Iqbal, 'The Role of Sukuk in Meeting Global Development Challenges' in S Jaffer (ed), *Global Growth, Opportunities and Challenges in the Sukuk Market* (1 edn, Euromoney Trading Inc) 69.

According to a study evaluating *ṣukūk* growth and development for the period 2001–2007, the total value of *ṣukūk* worldwide reached USD 39 billion by October 2007.[75] It is also estimated that 360 *ṣukūk* were offered throughout the world during these six years.[76] *Ṣukūk* issuances, both corporate and sovereign, expanded rapidly; the total world value of *ṣukūk* issued in 2001 amounted to USD 250 million, compared to USD 12,210 million *ṣukūk* issued in 2007.[77] This study also shows that the total value of corporate *ṣukūk* amounted to USD 22,385 million for the period 2001–2007, as opposed to USD 9130 million of sovereign *ṣukūk*[78]; corporate *ṣukūk* achieved more growth, demonstrating the strong interest from corporations to tap *ṣukūk*. The UAE and Malaysia came first and second, respectively, in terms of issues' size of the total world *ṣukūk* issuance: arranged based on issues' size, the UAE contributed 36.2%, Malaysia 32.1%, the KSA 15.7%, Bahrain 5.3%, Kuwait 3.0%, Pakistan 2.3%, Qatar 2.0%, Brunei 1.1%, the USA 0.2%, Germany 0.2%, and Indonesia 0.1%.[79] However, Malaysia and the UAE were first and second, respectively, in terms of number of issues: the total number of issues was 137 in Malaysia and 29 in the UAE.[80] The study reveals that 62.1% of the total world *ṣukūk* value originated in the Gulf Cooperation Council (GCC), as opposed to 36% in Asia (primarily Malaysia, Pakistan, and Brunei).[81] An important aspect of this period is the variety of *ṣukūk* types, including *ijārah ṣukūk* (43.6%), *mushārakah ṣukūk* (27.5%), *muḍārabah ṣukūk* (18.4%), *murābaḥah ṣukūk* (5.0%), *istiṣnāʿ ṣukūk* (2.4%), *manāfiʿ ṣukūk* (2.2%), *ijārah* (lease) securitisation (0.7%), and *salam ṣukūk* (0.3%).[82] It can be seen that *ijārah ṣukūk* was the most common structure used in this period.

The above paragraph provides the key facts about the main players in the *ṣukūk* market, common *ṣukūk* structures, and growth rates for the period 2001–2007. The sizable and diverse *ṣukūk* of this period has been attributed to several factors which are, of course, interrelated. The first and

[75] Global Investment House, 'Sukuks – A New Dawn of Islamic Finance Era' (*Global Investment House*, January 2008) 7. http://www.menafn.com/updates/research_center/regional/special_ed/gih0108.pdf. Accessed 12 December 2012.

[76] Ibid. 20.

[77] Ibid. 18.

[78] Ibid.

[79] Ibid. 17.

[80] Ibid. 1.

[81] Ibid.

[82] Ibid. 19.

foremost factor is the increasing demand for infrastructure megaprojects in a number of emerging countries that have been financed through *ṣukūk*.[83] The availability of funding capital and reserves, especially in the GCC region, had the effect of spurring the *ṣukūk* market to faster growth.[84] These two elements have increased the interest of issuers who are looking for investment opportunities to tap the *ṣukūk* market.

2.5.3 Decline in the Ṣukūk *Market (2008–2009)*

After the initial expansion of the *ṣukūk* market, the value of *ṣukūk* offerings was the subject of unexpected downturn worldwide. According to a study by Kuwait Finance House Research, the value of *ṣukūk* dropped across all issuing countries in 2008 with the exception of Qatar and Indonesia.[85] Although the composition of offering countries was the same in 2007 and 2008, the total value of issues raised in 2008 was USD 15,464 million compared to USD 34,300 million in 2007, showing a marked decrease in value.[86] Malaysia and the UAE were first and second in 2008, respectively, in terms of *ṣukūk* issue size.[87] By the end of 2009, the total global *ṣukūk* issued (domestic and international) reached USD 24,555 million, compared to USD 15,464 million in 2008.[88] Malaysia also dominated the market in 2009 with the total value of *ṣukūk* amounting to 54.2%.[89]

There were three primary reasons for the decline of the *ṣukūk* market in this period. First, the spread of the credit crunch worldwide through 2008 and 2009 affected demand in the *ṣukūk* market.[90] Many new offerings were delayed and/or priced slightly higher, reflecting the unstable market conditions.[91] Second, a drop in investor demand for *ṣukūk* in this period was caused by troubled *ṣukūk* and the default of several *ṣukūk* which had been thought to be healthy. These included the East Cameron *Ṣukūk*

[83] J Zaidi, 'Nature of Risks Present in Sukuk Structures: Rating Agency Perspective' in A Thomas (ed), *Sukuk* (Sweet & Maxwell Asia 2009) 320.

[84] I Khan, *supra* note 52, xi.

[85] Kuwait Finance House Research, *Sukuk: Back on Track* (Kuwait Finance House Research 2010) 13.

[86] Ibid.

[87] Ibid.

[88] Ibid.

[89] Ibid. 12.

[90] Ibid. 13.

[91] Ibid.

default in October 2008, the 'D' rating for the New Allied Electronics Industries Ltd *Ṣukūk* in January 2009, and the Investment Dar (TID) *Ṣukūk* 2005 default in May 2009.[92] It has been argued that the defective structure of *ṣukūk* was not the cause of these defaults but rather the deteriorating credit situation of *ṣukūk* issuers.[93] Third, Al-ʿuthmānī's criticism of *ṣukūk* structures in late 2007 created a wave of controversy which affected the interest of issuers and investors in *ṣukūk* markets.

2.5.4 Ṣukūk *Market: Continuing Opportunities and Challenges (2010–2018)*

The year 2010 can be described as a year of optimism, with the global *ṣukūk* market showing signs of recovery after facing several serious problems. According to the Thomson Reuters, *Ṣukūk* Market Outlook 2018, the global *ṣukūk* market saw 431 issues in 2010, 546 issues in 2011, 763 issues in 2012, 834 issues in 2013, 809 issues in 2014, 729 issues in 2015, 538 issues in 2016, and 661 issues up to the third quarter of 2017.[94] The total amount issued hit a record USD 51.24 billion in 2010, USD 84.40 billion in 2011, USD 137.14 billion in 2012, USD 116.93 billion in 2013, USD 101.75 billion in 2014, USD 65.43 billion in 2015, USD 62.21 billion in 2016, and USD 79.51 billion up to the third quarter of 2017.[95] The future growth of global *ṣukūk* looks bright, constituting 14.3% of total global Islamic financial assets by the third quarter of 2011.[96]

One can see that 2012 recorded the highest value of *ṣukūk* issued from 2010 up to the third quarter of 2017. Also, 2013 recorded the highest number of issuances for the same mentioned period. The year 2016 witnessed a noticeable drop on the *ṣukūk* market in terms of number and value of issuances. This has been attributed to low oil prices and appeal of the conventional bonds.[97] Also, 2016 drop is attributable to the Bank Negara Malaysia (BNM) decision in 2015 to stop issuing short-term

[92] Ibid. 15.

[93] Ibid.

[94] R Al Ansari and S Mohamed, 'Thomson Reuters *Ṣukūk* Market Outlook 2018' (Thomson Reuters 2018) 2.

[95] Ibid.

[96] Kuwait Finance House Research, *Global Sukuk Report 3Q2011* (Kuwait Finance House Research 2011) 2.

[97] R Al Ansari and Others, 'Sukuk Perceptions & Forecast Study 2017' (Thomson Reuters 2017) 4.

ṣukūk.[98] The year 2017 witnessed strong contribution by the KSA in the global *ṣukūk* market after issuing over USD 25 billion worth of *ṣukūk* which has taken the market to a new level.[99] Such great *ṣukūk* issuance has been attributed to the KSA Vision 2030 announced in April 2016 that aims to diversify the economy by reducing the dependence on oil and attracting foreign investors to tap into the market.[100] In addition, the world's first ever *ṣukūk* amounting to USD 58.4 million came in 2017 by the Tadua Energy to finance a major solar power project in Malaysian Sabah State.[101] The first half of 2018 experienced 15% slowdown in total *ṣukūk* issuance compared to the same period of 2017, amounting to USD 44.2 billion compared with USD 52.2 billion in the first half of 2017.[102] This drop has been justified by the absence of major *ṣukūk* issuances from the GCC found in 2017.[103]

According to the Stability Report 2014 authored by the IFSB, the *ṣukūk* market grew at an average rate of 41.6% per annum between 2005 and 2012.[104] Table 2.1 demonstrates the total volume and value of *ṣukūk* by country for the period January 1996–September 2013.

It can be seen from this table that Malaysia took the lead in both volume and value of *ṣukūk* from January 1996 to September 2013. The UK is the number one issuing country in Europe. By September 2013, there were 23 countries in which *ṣukūk* markets operated. Bahrain was the first country in the GCC region to tap *ṣukūk*. In addition, these figures show that there has been increasing interest in *ṣukūk* markets from sovereigns and corporations in both Islamic and conventional jurisdictions. The reasons for such strong interest in *ṣukūk* become clear when one considers the potential benefits and functions of *ṣukūk*.

[98] Ibid. 26.

[99] R Al Ansari and S Mohamed, *supra* note 94, 3.

[100] Ibid. 4.

[101] Ibid. 6.

[102] S&P Global Ratings, 'Islamic Finance Outlook 2019 Edition' (S&P Global Ratings 2018) 13.

[103] S&P Global Ratings, 'Islamic Finance Outlook 2019 Edition' (S&P Global Ratings 2018) 13.

[104] IFSB, 'Islamic Financial Services Industry: Stability Report 2014' (*IFSB*, 2014) 21. http://www.ifsb.org/docs/2014-05-06_IFSI%20Stability%20Report%202014%20(Final).pdf. Accessed 22 March 2015.

Table 2.1 Global aggregate of *ṣukūk* issued—breakdown by country (January 1996 to September 2013)[a]

No.	*Country*	*Number of issues*	*Value of issues ($ m)*	*No.*	*Country*	*Number of issues*	*Value of issues ($ m)*
1	Malaysia	2438	324,576.9	13	UK	5	279.1
2	UAE	73	47,876.4	14	China	3	274.7
3	KSA	64	39,296.0	15	Yemen	2	251.5
4	Indonesia	216	19,924.1	16	Sudan	3	220.9
5	Qatar	19	19,245.6	17	Germany	2	190.9
6	Bahrain	273	13,918.5	18	Gambia	242	149.2
7	Pakistan	57	6348.9	19	Iran	4	132.8
8	Turkey	9	5469.7	20	Jordan	1	120.3
9	Brunei	95	4980.7	21	Japan	1	100.0
10	Kuwait	22	2992.4	22	Kazakhstan	1	73.3
11	Singapore	9	984.2	23	France	1	0.7
12	USA	3	765.7	Grand total		3543	488,172

[a]E Alim (ed), ***Ṣukūk Perceptions and Forecast Study 2014*** (Thomson Reuters 2013) 16

2.6 Economic Benefits and Importance of Ṣukūk

The literature is overwhelmingly in favour of *ṣukūk* due to the beneficial role they play in national economies. Although *ṣukūk* are fundamentally different from conventional debt securities, there are several close affinities between the two instruments in terms of their economic role. In general, the *ṣukūk* market aims to bridge the prohibition of the conventional bond market[105] and offer similar or even better economic functions without breaching Islamic Law rules. Common arguments in support of *ṣukūk* can be categorised into their benefits for economic development, IFSI, and being an efficient and effective financial instrument.

Ṣukūk play a favourable role in economic development, in ensuring the soundness and stability of the economy. This is clear when one looks at the nature of *ṣukūk* issuances and investments, and the consequences of choosing *ṣukūk* to raise funds in the financial sector. *Ṣukūk* channels funds into real sector activities[106] and therefore avoids the speculative movement of

[105] A Tariq and H Dar, 'Risks of Sukuk Structures: Implications for Resource Mobilization' (2007) 49 Thunderbrid International Business Review 203, 215; B Kettell, *Islamic Capital Markets* (Brian Kettell 2009) 212.

[106] B Kettell, *Islamic Capital Markets* (Brian Kettell 2009), 215.

monies and threat of future financial crises that are connected with conventional debt securities.[107] This is also supported by the fact that *ṣukūk* issuers can only seek further financing within an affordable ratio of assets to the funds borrowed because of the asset transfer requirement to be placed in escrow.[108] Further, the risk involved in *ṣukūk* structures is based on a productive project that must demonstrate real economic benefits and not on uncertain businesses.[109] In addition, *ṣukūk* contributes to the wider economy because it results from a genuine transaction that is based on a real and identifiable asset.[110] Another important aspect of *ṣukūk*'s contribution to an economy is its equal distribution of wealth amongst the community, resulting from the loss- and profit-sharing feature of *ṣukūk*.[111]

In addition to its role in the stability of a country's economy, *ṣukūk* provide great investment opportunities and facilitates cash generation for all types of investors. As the demand for *ṣukūk* issuance from public authorities increases, the role of *ṣukūk* in public finance by way of sharing the income streams of public assets cannot be overlooked.[112] The *ṣukūk* market is also an ideal solution for inefficiency in many markets, particularly in the GCC area, arising from large surplus liquidity because of increased oil prices and increase in trade activities.[113] The *ṣukūk* market also links issuers and investors in emerging markets and enables them to participate in various economic projects.[114] Further, the *ṣukūk* market is seen as a credible substitute for other financing instruments since it provides the required funds for unprecedented infrastructure projects in many

[107] S Vishwanath and S Azmi, 'An Overview of Islamic Sukuk Bonds' (2009) The Journal of Structured Finance 58, 60.

[108] A Saeed and O Salah, 'History of Sukuk: Pragmatic and Idealist Approaches to Structuring Sukuk' in M Ariff, M Iqbal and S Mohamad (eds), *The Islamic Debt Market for Sukuk Securities: The Theory and Practice of Profit Sharing Investment* (Edward Elgar 2012) 95.

[109] S Vishwanath and S Azmi, 'An Overview of Islamic Sukuk Bonds' (2009) The Journal of Structured Finance 58, 60.

[110] M Azhar and J Haider, 'Islamic Capital Market: Sukuk and its Risk Management in the Current Scenario' (Master Thesis, Umea University 2010) 32.

[111] Ibid. 32.

[112] A Saeed and O Salah, 'History of Sukuk: Pragmatic and Idealist Approaches to Structuring Sukuk' in Ariff M, Iqbal M and Mohamad S (eds), *The Islamic Debt Market for Sukuk Securities: The Theory and Practice of Profit Sharing Investment* (Edward Elgar 2012) 94.

[113] A Khorshid, 'Sukuk and Securitization' in Khorshid A (ed), *Euromoney Encyclopedia of Islamic Finance* (Euromoney Institutional Investor PLC 2009) 279.

[114] Ibid. 297.

countries that need trillions of dollars.[115] In fact, *ṣukūk* is one of the main avenues to satisfy increasing demand for capital and huge liquidity pool in many countries witnessing various economic activities.[116] These include airports, bridges, hospitals, schools, roads, railways, medical districts, and commercial cities. This is especially relevant in the Middle East and North Africa (MENA) and Asian regions where infrastructure development no longer depends on oil and gas revenues.[117] This is compounded by the current domestic and international banking situation, struggling to lend large amounts of money and concentrating on rebuilding balance sheets.[118]

Regarding the function of *ṣukūk* within the IFSI, empirical evidence has especially pointed to the *ṣukūk* markets' significant role in promoting the IFSI, attracting interest from the business community worldwide, and placing the industry in a better position within the international financial market.[119] Undoubtedly, *ṣukūk* is a major factor in the remarkable growth of Islamic capital markets and the popularity of Islamic financial transactions.[120] In its role as facilitator strengthening Islamic financial products, the *ṣukūk* market contributes to the integration of sharia-compliant services into international markets.[121] Further, the *ṣukūk* market is relevant to liquidity management for the IIFS[122]; *ṣukūk* can be utilised to manage and provide liquidity for Islamic banks on a short-term basis. Islamic banks can utilise *ṣukūk* as a tool to mobilise savings.[123] *Ṣukūk* offers an investment opportunity for Islamic financers, and therefore it solves the inefficiency

[115] M Al-Amine, *Global Sukuk and Islamic Securitization Market: Financial Engineering and Product Innovation* (Brill 2012) 2.

[116] Ibid. 45; S Cakir and F Raei, 'IMF Working Paper WP/07/237: Sukuk vs. Eurobonds: Is There a Difference in Value-at-Risk?' (2007) 3. https://www.imf.org/external/pubs/ft/wp/2007/wp07237.pdf. Accessed 1 December 2012.

[117] M Al-Amine, *supra* note 115, 26.

[118] Ibid.

[119] Ibid. 1.

[120] A Ahmad, 'Islamic Modes of Finance and the Role of Sukuk' in Qatar Financial Centre Authority (ed), *Islamic Finance: Instruments and Markets* (Bloomsbury Information Ltd 2010) 9.

[121] N Saidi, 'Islamic Finance is Coming of Age: IFC Lists Sukuk on DIFC' (*Khaleej Times*, 2009). http://www.khaleejtimes.com/biz/inside.asp?xfile=/data/business/2009/November/business_November183.xml&section=business. Accessed 20 January 2013.

[122] M Al-Amine, *supra* note 115, 29.

[123] F Al-Salem, 'Islamic Financial Product Innovation' (2009) 2 International Journal of Islamic and Middle Eastern Finance and Management 187, 191.

problem, increasing the level of liquidity in the market.[124] Given the lack of sharia-compliant products and reliance on limited instruments in the IFSI, the development of *ṣukūk* is regarded as an important achievement in the local markets.[125] It has also been argued that the *ṣukūk* market increases market growth capacity since its growth relies very much on *ṣukūk* issuance resulting from asset securitisation, as opposed to institution size and ability to borrow.[126] Issuance of *ṣukūk* improves financial returns for the issuing entity, improves the credit rating of the issuing and financing entity, and spreads the risks involved in raising large amounts of capital.[127] Utilising the *ṣukūk* mechanism, the IIFS are able to put in place a wider pool of assets which was previously difficult and ineffective.[128] This results in improving the capability and efficiency of financing for such institutions.

With regard to the efficiency and effectiveness of *ṣukūk* as a financial instrument, for Muslim investors, who are prohibited from dealing with conventional debt securities, *ṣukūk* particularly can provide alternative investment avenues. To illustrate, Muslim investors are not allowed to invest by way of purchasing conventional bonds issued by a company seeking refinancing.[129] In addition, investing in *ṣukūk* for non-Muslim investors represents a new asset class and brings further diversity of investment, reducing risk.[130] Compared to, for instance, bank deposits, the *ṣukūk* market looks like a very attractive investment avenue, owing to the existence of secondary markets, and generation of extra returns.[131] *Ṣukūk* provides investors with the opportunity to enjoy either medium- or long-term periodic income.[132] As a result of their flexibility and tradability features, *ṣukūk* allow investors to exit the project at any time before maturity of the investment period.[133] For investors, *ṣukūk* are considered a relatively secure form

[124] A Khorshid, *supra* note 113, 279.

[125] F Al-Salem, 'Islamic Financial Product Innovation' (2009) 2 International Journal of Islamic and Middle Eastern Finance and Management 187, 191.

[126] Ibid.

[127] Ibid.

[128] A Tariq and H Dar, 'Risks of Sukuk Structures: Implications for Resource Mobilization' (2007) 49 Thunderbrid International Business Review 203, 206.

[129] B Kettell, *supra* note 106, 216–217.

[130] Ibid. 213.

[131] F Al-Salem, *supra* note 125, 192.

[132] B Kettell, *supra* note 106, 213.

[133] Ibid.

of investment due to an asset underlying the value of the certificates.[134] Given different structures that *ṣukūk* can be based on, they are able to meet the special needs of venture cash flows.[135] For some governments, issuing *ṣukūk* represents a significant alternative to IMF financing.[136] The essential advantage of *ṣukūk* lies in their great ability to translate the future cash flow of an asset into present cash flow.[137] The *ṣukūk* market is an ideal fit to meet the various needs of local and international investors, offering a risk diversification choice for their portfolios.[138] Current available funding sources such as customer deposits and interbank lending cannot compete with *ṣukūk*, especially since the change in financial regulatory requirements, following the global financial crisis.[139]

However, although much of the literature has highlighted their advantages in several ways, a few studies have also briefly alluded to some drawbacks of *ṣukūk*. Disadvantages are considered mainly in terms of the failure of certain *ṣukūk* structures to meet sharia rules, the mimicking of conventional bonds, and the higher upfront costs of the required documentation and legal advice.[140] However, such drawbacks should be seen in light of the fact that the *ṣukūk* market is still in relative infancy. Such issues relate to the product development and enhancement of *ṣukūk*. The central advantage of the *ṣukūk* market is that it cannot lead to consequences that harm national economies, such as financial bubbles due to the underlying asset requirement.

2.7 The Legality of *Ṣukūk* in Islamic Law

Any discussion of the *ṣukūk* market is incomplete without addressing its basis from the sharia point of view. There is no specific reference to modern-style *ṣukūk* in the Quran, Sunna, and other sources of sharia. It is therefore important to attain a wider understanding of the position of *ṣukūk* within Islamic financial law. A question legitimately asked is why have *ṣukūk* been allowed in the modern context of capital markets? Additionally, what is the rationale for permitting modern *ṣukūk*? Indeed,

[134] Ibid. 215.

[135] M Safari, M Ariff and S Mohamad, *supra* note 33, 18.

[136] This was a statement by the Pakistani Prime Minister in 2005. See ibid. 33.

[137] B Kettell, *supra* note 106, 212.

[138] See F Al-Salem, *supra* note 125, 191; K Alsaeed, 'Sukuk Issuance in Saudi Arabia: Recent Trends and Positive Expectations' (PhD Thesis, Durham University 2012) 10.

[139] See K Alsaeed, *supra* note 138, 149.

[140] See ibid.; Al-Amine, *supra* note 115, 115–133.

given the prohibition on conventional bonds, the grounds that allow investing and trading in the current *ṣukūk* market need to be elucidated.

In its formal resolution No. 60 (11/6) concerning *sanadāt* (bonds), the IIFA in 1990 prohibited the issuing, purchasing, and trading of bonds that represent loans generating interest or other conditional benefit regardless of the issuer type and name given to the bonds.[141] This sharia opinion was confirmed by the IIFA in 1998 by resolution No. 101 (4/11) 'Sale of Debt and Loan Debentures and their Islamic Substitutes in Public and Private Sectors'.[142] More importantly, resolution No. 60 (11/6) introduces *ṣukūk* based on *muḍārabah* or another investment activity as an alternative to conventional bonds, providing a sharia basis for the issuing, purchasing, and trading of such instruments.

However, the above resolutions did not elaborate specific proofs supporting the legality of *ṣukūk* from the sharia perspective. One may question the allowance of modern *ṣukūk* in the IFSI on the grounds that they constitute simply a re-engineering of conventional bonds with some required adjustments. Having discussed the historical roots of modern *ṣukūk*, this argument cannot be taken for granted as opinions vary concerning their origin. From an Islamic law standpoint, the legality of *ṣukūk* can be derived from the Quran (2:275) which is translated thus: 'Allah has permitted trading and forbidden *ribā*'. In short, the *ṣukūk* structure involves sale and trade, which is explicitly approved in the main source of sharia. A basis of *ṣukūk* also can be found in the *qā'idah fiqhyah* (legal maxim) which states that 'the norm in regard to things is that of permissibility',[143] opening the door for further innovative products and sophisticated structures in Islamic finance. Given the economic contributions of *ṣukūk*, they are also advised to be used based on the public interest doctrine. *Ijtihād* (scholarly endeavour) plays a vital role in determining a proper sharia rule concerning the basis of any new product in Islamic law.

2.8 *Ṣukūk* Structures and Classification

The term '*ṣukūk* structure' refers to a sharia-compliant arrangement designed to raise funds by way of certificate issuances resulting from securitisation. Therefore, the concept of securitisation is relevant to the way

[141] IIFA, *supra* note 63, 119–120.
[142] Ibid. 234–235.
[143] See Kamali, *Shari'ah Law: An Introduction* (Oneworld Publications 2008) 146.

ṣukūk are structured. There are various definitions of securitisation, and it is used to refer to different things[144]; in this context, securitisation refers to 'a process of dividing ownership of tangible assets, usufructs or both into units of equal value and issue securities as per their value'.[145] *Ṣukūk* structure varies significantly in practice, and therefore it is misleading to envisage a monolithic *ṣukūk* structure dominating the market. In other words, it is inaccurate to assume that there is a standard format which is adopted for all issues of *ṣukūk*. The project nature, the financing needs of issuers, the desire of investors, underlying sharia contracts, and the underlying asset are among the key factors that lead to the existence of different *ṣukūk* arrangements. Therefore, it is more productive to look at features common to all *ṣukūk* structures rather than outlining a hypothetical standard structure of *ṣukūk*. *Ṣukūk* structures typically involve the following steps: (1) identifying the underlying assets or project; (2) identifying the sharia contract; (3) establishing the SPV; (4) the issuance of certificates, (5) creating an income stream, and (6) the maturity of the *ṣukūk*.[146]

The above stages are not straightforward in practice, and several parties must be involved in order to accomplish one issuance. Some or all of the following parties are involved in a *ṣukūk* issuance: (1) the sponsor or originator who is the initial owner of the asset to be securitised; (2) the issuer (usually the SPV) who issues the certificates; (3) the trustee who declares a trust over the underlying asset and protects the interests of *ṣukūk* holders; (4) the agent(s) who is appointed by the issuer to conduct various administrative duties (such as a paying agent); (5) the rating agency that assigns a credit rating for the issue; (6) the credit enhancer who ensures the payments due on *ṣukūk*; (7) legal counsel who provide legal opinions about the issuance and may participate in *ṣukūk* arrangement; (8) sharia scholars who confirm the sharia compliance of the issuance; and (9) *ṣukūk* holders who become the investors and owners during the life of the

[144] J Shenker and A Colletta, 'Asset Securitiszation: Evolution, Current Issues and New Frontiers' (1991) 69 Texas Law Review 1369, 1373.

[145] AAOIFI, *supra* note 5, 322.

[146] See Z Iqbal and A Mirakhor, *An Introduction to Islamic Finance* (2 edn, John Wiley & Sons 2011) 185–187. There are two main relationships in a *ṣukūk* structure. First, there is a relationship between *ṣukūk* holders and the SPV, which is based on trust or agency depending on the jurisdiction. Second, there is a relationship between *ṣukūk* holders (or the SPV) and the originator, which is based on the sharia contract underlying the structure.

ṣukūk.[147] The process of structuring *ṣukūk* bears some parallels to the structuring process of conventional debt securities. It has been stated that '[t]he legal structure and format of *ṣukūk* certificates frequently take the format of global certificates, which like bonds may be listed, rated and easily cleared'.[148] The possibility of implementing the above-mentioned steps in different ways leads to a variety of *ṣukūk* structures in practice. *Ṣukūk* structures can be viewed from different perspectives, and therefore there are many different ways of classifying *ṣukūk*. The main classifications of *ṣukūk* are as follows:

- *Ṣukūk* issuer: *ṣukūk* are thus divided into four types according to the issuing entity: (1) sovereign *ṣukūk*, (2) government *ṣukūk*, (3) corporate *ṣukūk*, and (4) quasi-sovereign *ṣukūk*.[149] While the first type refers to *ṣukūk* issued by a national government in a foreign currency, the second type refers to *ṣukūk* issued by a national government in the county's own currency.[150] The third type refers to *ṣukūk* issued by a corporation, as opposed to a national government. The fourth type refers to '*ṣukūk* issued by a public sector entity that is like sovereign *ṣukūk*. It may carry explicit or implicit government guarantee'.[151]
- Target investors: in this respect, *ṣukūk* are divided into three types: (1) international *ṣukūk*, (2) domestic or local *ṣukūk*, and (3) global *ṣukūk*. While international investors are the target investors in the first type, domestic investors are the target investors in the second type. The third type combines international and domestic investors as target investors. It also refers to total *ṣukūk* issued in the world which includes international and domestic *ṣukūk*.
- Issuing market: in this respect, *ṣukūk* are classified as (1) primary *ṣukūk* and (2) secondary *ṣukūk*. While the former refers to new issues that are offered to initial investors in the primary market, the latter refers to previously issued offerings that are resold and traded in the secondary market.

[147] See generally AAOIFI, *supra* note 5, 322–323; G Fuller, *The Law and Practice of International Capital Markets* (3 edn, LexisNexis 2012) 247; J Shenker and A Colletta, *supra* note 144, 1376.

[148] S Mokhtar and others, 'Sukuk and the Capital Markets' in A Thomas (ed), *Sukuk* (Sweet & Maxwell Asia 2009) 21.

[149] See IIFM, *supra* note 7, 36.

[150] Ibid.

[151] Ibid.

- Underlying sharia contract: *ṣukūk* can be structured based on a number of contracts under Islamic law. In this respect, 14 types of *ṣukūk* structures are identified by the AAOIFI which are: (1) *ṣukūk* of ownership in leased assets, (2) *ṣukūk* of ownership of usufructs of existing assets, (3) *ṣukūk* of ownership of usufructs of described future assets, (4) *ṣukūk* of ownership of services of a specified party, (5) *ṣukūk* of ownership of described future services, (6) *salam* (a forward sale (fungible commodity)) *ṣukūk*, (7) *istiṣnāʿ* (contract of manufacture) *ṣukūk*, (8) *murābaḥah* (sale with a mark-up) *ṣukūk*, (9) *mushārakah* (participation financing) *ṣukūk*, (10) *muḍārabah* (investment partnership) *ṣukūk*, (11) investment agency *ṣukūk*, (12) *muzāraʿah* (sharecropping) *ṣukūk*, (13) *musāqāh* (irrigation) *ṣukūk*, and (14) *mughārasah* (agricultural) *ṣukūk*.[152]

  The above-mentioned structures serve different financing and investment purposes. The first five types come under the concept of *ijārah* (lease), and therefore they are considered *ijārah ṣukūk*. *Ṣukūk* types (1)–(11) are the most common structures in practice. Another classification system based on the underlying sharia contract is as follows[153]: (1) sale-based *ṣukūk* such as *murābaḥah ṣukūk*; (2) lease-based *ṣukūk* such as *ijārah ṣukūk*; (3) partnership or equity-based *ṣukūk* such as *mushārakah ṣukūk*; (4) agency-based *ṣukūk* such as investment agency *ṣukūk*, and (5) hybrid *ṣukūk* combining two or more sharia contracts.
- Tradability: *ṣukūk* are divided into two categories here according to whether they can be traded in the secondary market, which are: (1) tradable *ṣukūk* and (2) non-tradable *ṣukūk*. The former refers to structures representing tangible assets or ownership of an investment venture such as *mushārakah ṣukūk* and *muḍārabah ṣukūk*. The latter refers to structures representing receivables of cash or goods such as *salam ṣukūk* and *murābaḥah ṣukūk*.
- Cash flows[154]: *ṣukūk* are divided into six categories, namely (1) profit-shared *ṣukūk*, (2) discount *ṣukūk*, (3) fixed pay-off *ṣukūk*, (4) constant growth pay-off *ṣukūk*, (5) variable pay-off *ṣukūk*, and (6) actual pay-off *ṣukūk*.

[152] For description of these types, see AAOIFI, *supra* note 5, 307–309. See also M Mcmillen, 'Asset Securitisation Sukuk and Islamic Capital Markets: Structural Issues in these Formative Years' (2008) 25 Wisconsin International Law Journal 703.

[153] Laldin, 'Sukuk in Various Juridictions: Shariah and Legal Issues' (2012) 2 Journal of Islamic Business and Management 15, 18.

[154] See M Safari, M Ariff and A Mohamad, *supra* note 33, 24–26.

Profit-shared *ṣukūk* can be seen in *mushārakah ṣukūk*. This is also applied in diminishing *mushārakah ṣukūk*, but with diminishing rate payments including rewards and principal amounts over a finite period. Discount *ṣukūk* is another type wherein no cash flow is paid in the intermediate periods but rather at the end of the period. It is important here to generate regular returns to ensure that the end value is more than the principal amount. This is seen in, for example, treasury bills based on *murābaḥah*. An example of fixed pay-off *ṣukūk* is *ijārah ṣukūk*. Constant growth pay-off is found in BBA *ṣukūk*, where the payment for each period increases at a constant growth rate. In the event that income exceeds the agreed amount, the pay-off will remain at the agreed rate. In variable pay-off *ṣukūk*, the pay-off varies in each period according to a profit ratio. The actual pay-off for each period is made based on a benchmark such as London Interbank Offer Rate (LIBOR).

- Redemption features: some features have been added to *ṣukūk* in order to provide both issuers and investors more flexibility to redeem *ṣukūk* or end the whole project. Such features have resulted in the development of distinct *ṣukūk* in the market. The best examples of these *ṣukūk* are (1) callable *ṣukūk*, (2) puttable *ṣukūk*, (3) convertible *ṣukūk*, and (4) exchangeable *ṣukūk*. Callable *ṣukūk* contain a call provision, allowing the issuer to redeem or buy back *ṣukūk* issued prior to maturity.[155] Puttable *ṣukūk* contain a put provision, allowing the *ṣukūk* holders to redeem or sell back *ṣukūk* issued prior to maturity.[156] Convertible *ṣukūk* enable *ṣukūk* holders to convert their *ṣukūk* to another security (often shares) issued by the same issuer prior to maturity.[157] Exchangeable *ṣukūk* enable *ṣukūk* holders to exchange the *ṣukūk* for a security issued by another party prior to maturity.[158]

The above discussion presents different types of *ṣukūk* as perceived in the *ṣukūk* market. It does not necessarily mean such classifications and types are recognised from an Islamic law point of view. Each classification regards *ṣukūk* from a particular perspective, and *ṣukūk* are not limited to

[155] A Tariq, 'Managing Financial Risks of Sukuk Structures' (Master Thesis, Loughborough University 2004) 65.

[156] Ibid.

[157] H Abdullah and R Ismail, 'Sukuk under Development' (*IFLR*, 2009). http://www.iflr.com/Article/2283704/Sukuk-under-development.html. Accessed 6 January 2013.

[158] Ibid.

the above-mentioned classifications. One *ṣukūk* issuance can fall into a number of the above-mentioned classifications; for instance, a *mushārakah ṣukūk* issued by a Malaysian corporation targeting international investors can be described as a corporate *ṣukūk*, an international *ṣukūk*, tradable *ṣukūk*, and profit-shared *ṣukūk*.

2.9 Pricing and Valuation of *Ṣukūk*

Another general concern in the context of *ṣukūk* is related to how *ṣukūk* is priced, especially considering the differences between *ṣukūk* and conventional debt securities. It has been said that '[p]ricing is a main concern for *ṣukūk* since it is new to the market and has yet to develop any suitable mechanism to determine its price'.[159] Identifying the valuation process of *ṣukūk* is an important step in establishing its fair price, discovering its true worth, and estimating its actual performance.[160] Islamic finance theory suggests that the pricing mechanism of Islamic financial products is governed by the following key principles: profit sharing, risk sharing, and asset backing.[161] One can generally speak of four different stages of pricing involved in *ṣukūk*, namely issuing price (principal amount), returns, selling price of secondary *ṣukūk*, and sale of *ṣukūk* in the event of total loss.

The issuing price refers to the total cash needed by the issuer which is collected by issuance of *ṣukūk* to the investors. The determination of issuing price is straightforward since it simply depends on how much capital is needed by the issuing entity. Thus, an oil company seeking to buy machines costing USD 100 billion will issue *ṣukūk* of USD 100 billion to meet its financing need. In this example, the issuing price of the *ṣukūk* is determined by reference to the actual value (market value) of the underlying asset or project. The underlying sharia contract generates and justifies the earning of the principal amount by the issuer. For example, in *ijārah ṣukūk* and *murābaḥah ṣukūk*, both used for asset acquisition, the issuing price amounts to the price paid by the SPV to purchase the asset in question from the supplier. In *mushārakah ṣukūk* and *muḍārabah ṣukūk*, the capital contribution by the investors amounts to the principal amount.

[159] E Ahmed, A Islam and T Alabdullah, 'Islamic Sukuk: Pricing Mechanism and Rating' (2014) 4 Journal of Asian Scientific Research 640, 644.

[160] M Safari, M Ariff and A Mohamad, *supra* note 33, 27.

[161] M Ariff, M Iqbal and S Mohamad (eds), *The Islamic Debt Market for Sukuk Securities: The Theory and Practice of Profit Sharing Investment* (Edward Elgar 2012) xiv.

Returns on *ṣukūk* refers to the profit and earnings made to the investors by the issuer. In *murābaḥah ṣukūk*, the mark-up price generates the returns to *ṣukūk* holders. In *ijārah ṣukūk*, the rental payments arising from the lease transaction generate the returns to *ṣukūk* holders. In *mushārakah ṣukūk* and *muḍārabah ṣukūk*, the profits produced by the underlying venture amount to returns to *ṣukūk* holders. In this respect, Ahmed, Islam, and Alabdullah state:

> *Ṣukūk* returns are derived from leases, profit or sales of assets such as property, equipment or joint venture business. Technically, these leases, profits or sales are structured to deliver the equivalent of a fixed annual interest rate since they are not considered as the forbidden 'interest' payments.[162]

Regarding the selling price of secondary *ṣukūk*, a distinction should be made between *ṣukūk* representing assets or projects and *ṣukūk* representing future financial receivables. While the selling price of the former must represent the market value as opposed to face value, the selling price of the latter is subject to the rules concerning the sale of debt under Islamic law. This is also applicable in the event of asset loss, destruction, or unfit use resulting in a total loss where asset valuation becomes more serious.[163]

However, the above discussion does not accurately reflect the pricing of *ṣukūk* in practice. Currently, *ṣukūk* values are determined based on payoffs, followed by identifying their nature (fixed, variable, or growing), and then finding the present value of the promised cash flows by adopting a suitable discount rate.[164] As currently practised in the market, returns on *ṣukūk* are priced through conventional benchmarks[165] such as the Kuala Lumpur Interbank Offer Rate (KLIBOR), London Interbank Offer Rate (LIBOR), and Saudi Interbank Offer Rate (SIBOR). The differences between bid and asking prices and trading volume have both been used in determining the price of *ṣukūk*.[166] This means that the current pricing

[162] E Ahmed, A Islam and T Alabdullah, 'Islamic Sukuk: Pricing Mechanism and Rating' (2014) 4 Journal of Asian Scientific Research 640, 645.

[163] B Rider, 'Legal Aspects of Islamic Asset Securitisation' in IFSB (ed), *Strategies for the Development of Islamic Capital Markets: Infrastructures and Legal Aspects of Islamic Asset Securitisation* (IFSB 2011) 163.

[164] M Safari, M Ariff and A Mohamad, *supra* note 33, 27.

[165] E Ahmed, A Islam and T Alabdullah, *supra* note 162, 645.

[166] K Alsaeed, *supra* note 138, 59.

mechanisms for *ṣukūk* do not actually differ from those used for conventional debt securities.

Therefore, the current market price of *ṣukūk* is not a true indication and reflection of its theoretical value in Islamic finance due to the absence of valid pricing models.[167] While it is possible to compare the market-revealed prices of conventional bonds with their theoretical values, this is not applicable to *ṣukūk*.[168] Further, it has been argued that estimating the theoretical value of *ṣukūk* by applying conventional valuation formulae is misleading since the nature and risk sharing of cash flows are different.[169] Therefore, one finds that *ṣukūk* and conventional debt securities share pricing risk features, and this is explained by the issuer's desire to facilitate understanding and risk assessment of this new asset class in the market.[170]

This discussion has identified three problems deterring an efficient pricing mechanism of *ṣukūk*—first, the *ṣukūk* market currently relies on conventional market benchmarks, interest-based benchmarks, as proxies to determine the price of *ṣukūk* profit or rental return.[171] This practice is justified by the absence of a collective Islamic benchmark. Another justification makes returns on *ṣukūk* competitive with conventional bonds by using interest rate proxies.[172] As a result, this causes a *ṣukūk* overpricing concern driven by market considerations.[173] The situation is further compounded when it comes to *ijārah ṣukūk* since each benchmark indicator offers a different return on this type of *ṣukūk*.[174] Second, the lack of market depth in the form of number of issuances and participants in some juris-

[167] M Arrif, M Iqbal and S Mohamad, 'Introduction to Sukuk Debt Securities Markets' in M Arrif, M Iqbal and S Mohamad (eds), *The Islamic Debt Market for Sukuk Securities: The Theory and Practice of Profit Sharing Investment* (Edward Elgar 2012) 3.

[168] M Amri, 'Bond Pricing Practices in the Sukuk Market' in M Arrif, M Iqbal and S Mohamad (eds), *The Islamic Debt Market for Sukuk Securities: The Theory and Practice of Profit Sharing Investment* (Edward Elgar) 164.

[169] Ibid.

[170] R Wilson, 'Innovation in the Structuring of Islamic Sukuk Securities' (2008) 24 Humanomics 170, 177.

[171] J Zaidi, 'Overcoming Barriers to Liquidity: Commoditization, Sukuk, Promoting Issuance and a Secondary Market' (*Iirating*, 2007) 4. http://www.iirating.com/Documents/PresentationSpeeches/speeches/Islamic%20Finance%20and%20Investment%20World%20Europe%202007.pdf. Accessed 11 May 2015.

[172] R Wilson, 'Islamic Capital Markets: the Role of Sukuk' in Qatar Financial Center Authority (ed) (Bloomsbury Information Ltd 2010) 59.

[173] Ibid. 58.

[174] R Wilson, 'How Expansive are the Frontiers' in A Thomas (ed), *Sukuk* (Sweet & Maxwell Asia 2009) 354.

dictions reduces the efficiency of *ṣukūk* pricing.[175] Third, there is difficulty in the valuation of underlying physical assets in any commercial sense due to a limited market or its complete absence in some circumstances,[176] for instance, legal restrictions may prevent the sale of buildings owned by a government.[177]

2.10 Conclusion

This chapter has presented the history and recent background of *ṣukūk* in order to facilitate a proper understanding of the subject. It argues that a collective term and definition should be considered when addressing *ṣukūk*. In their simple form, *ṣukūk* are certificates which represent proportionate ownership in an undivided part of the asset in question and entitle their holders to the returns. From a historical perspective, it concludes that such instruments did not exist in the classical period of Islam. However, claims have been made that the roots of modern *ṣukūk* can be found in some earlier Islamic practices and transactions. Nevertheless, there are strong signs that modern *ṣukūk* emerged in the market after the introduction of conventional securitisation in the 1970s. The issue of whether conventional securitisation originated from the concept of *waqf* has been subject to debate.

By pointing out its unique features, this discussion clearly differentiates between *ṣukūk* and other products in the market, particularly conventional debt securities. National governments, municipalities, corporations, financial institutions, and institutional investors benefit from different advantages offered by *ṣukūk*. Although *ṣukūk* received little attention in the early stages and faced a number of subsequent hindrances, they have proved their capability to change behaviour in the market. Islamic law welcomes further innovations and keeps the door open for new products in Islamic finance, and *ṣukūk* has found its place as a permissible instrument.

Despite stressing the fundamental differences between *ṣukūk* and conventional debt securities, it can be seen that current market practice applies the same valuation and pricing mechanisms for both. The *ṣukūk* structure forms the basis for issuance of certificates, and therefore understanding the underlying structure is significant. Due to continuing market innova-

[175] J Zaidi, *supra* note 171, 4.
[176] B Rider, *supra* note 163, 163.
[177] Ibid.

tions, *ṣukūk* takes various forms resulting in different classification methods for *ṣukūk*. Each classification aims to be inclusive; however, it seems that they do not reflect the most important aspects of existing *ṣukūk* structures. Therefore, a new classification of *ṣukūk* has recently been adopted by some institutions and experts in the market. According to this new classification, *ṣukūk* are seen as either asset backed or asset based. While other classical classifications of *ṣukūk* are straightforward, if inconclusive, there is much vagueness in this new classification. This has raised some questions about the effectiveness of such a classification and how it addresses contemporary *ṣukūk* application.

The next question to be addressed relates to structural issues resulting from dividing *ṣukūk* into asset-backed and asset-based categories. Chapters 3 and 4 examine this in detail.

CHAPTER 3

Asset-Backed *Ṣukūk*

3.1 Introduction

Any analysis of *ṣukūk* (trust investment certificates) markets would be incomplete without addressing the structure of the *ṣukūk* product. As mentioned in Chap. 2, the *ṣukūk* structure forms the basis of all issuance and investment activities. It is therefore important to attain a deeper understanding of how the structure of *ṣukūk* works. The *ṣukūk* market does not operate in a vacuum; it is influenced by a set of legal and regulatory tools, all of which impact the structure of *ṣukūk* products. This chapter examines the question of classifying *ṣukūk* into asset-backed and asset-based types, and looks at how such classification reflects the current *ṣukūk* in the market. Categorising *ṣukūk* as asset backed or asset based is an approach to examining the recent application of *ṣukūk*. As shall be seen below, the essence of this classification lies in exploring some structural issues related to contemporary *ṣukūk*.

This chapter first investigates the reasons behind the emergence of asset-backed and asset-based *ṣukūk*. It then considers the first type under this classification, asset-backed *ṣukūk*. It defines asset-backed *ṣukūk* and explains how a *ṣukūk* structure fits into the asset-backed *ṣukūk* category. It presents both the advantages and disadvantages that arise from the choice of asset-backed *ṣukūk*. It concludes by looking at the present standing and future prospects of this *ṣukūk* type.

S. Al-Ali, *Raising Capital on* Ṣukūk *Markets*,
https://doi.org/10.1007/978-3-030-14536-1_3

3.2 The Dawn of a New Area in the *Ṣukūk* Market: Division of *Ṣukūk* into Asset Backed and Asset Based

The need to understand the essence of asset-backed *ṣukūk* and asset-based *ṣukūk* has been well identified; Haneef states that 'one needs to understand a distinction that is becoming increasingly popular in the market: asset-backed *ṣukūk* versus asset-based *ṣukūk*'.[1] Further, Al-Amine notes '[o]ne important classification of *ṣukūk* that has dominated discussion recently is the division of *ṣukūk* into asset-backed and asset-based'.[2] A discussion of asset-backed *ṣukūk* and asset-based *ṣukūk* is of particular importance because there is some vagueness about the substance of these particular types of *ṣukūk* in the market. As Maurer noted 'the main difficulty with *ṣukūk*, however, has to do with whether they are in fact asset-backed, or whether they are asset-based'.[3] This point is confirmed by a report that was published by Kuwait Finance House Research in 2010, which states '[m]any people often confuse the two and cannot differentiate between the features of the different types of *ṣukūk*'.[4] The use of the terms 'asset-backed' and 'asset-based' *ṣukūk* is often a source of confusion and appears to be misleading.[5] Furthermore, there is a pressing need to comprehend the two structures in order to understand how they are viewed in different jurisdictions and whether such distinction relates to the sharia-compliant nature of *ṣukūk*.[6] Indeed, Maurer argues that the division of *ṣukūk* into asset backed and asset based is relevant to the debate on their permissibility under Islamic law.[7] Another compelling argument for discussing *ṣukūk* catego-

[1] R Haneef, 'From Asset-Backed to Asset-Light Structures: The Intricate History of Sukuk' (2009) 1 ISRA International Journal of Islamic Finance 103.

[2] M Al-Amine, 'Unresolved Sharī'ah Issues in Ṣukūk' in M Kamali and A Abdullah (eds), *Islamic Finance: Issues in Ṣukūk and Proposals for Reform* (International Intitute of Advanced Islamic Studies and Islamic Foundation 2014) 35.

[3] B Maurer, 'Form Versus Substance: AAOIFI Projects and Islamic Fundamentals in the Case of Sukuk' (2010) 1 Journal of Islamic Accounting and Business Research 32, 36.

[4] Kuwait Finance House Research, *Sukuk: Back on Track* (Kuwait Finance House Research 2010) 10.

[5] A Hassoune, K Howladar and S Harris, 'The Meaning of Ratings for Islamic Financial Institutions and Sharī'ah -Compliant Instruments' in IFSB (ed), *The Changing Landscape of Islamic Finance: Imminent Challenges and Future Directions* (IFSB 2010) 148.

[6] Kuwait Finance House Research, *supra* note 4, 10.

[7] B Maurer, 'Form Versus Substance: AAOIFI Projects and Islamic Fundamentals in the Case of Sukuk' (2010) 1 Journal of Islamic Accounting and Business Research 32, 36.

rised as asset backed or asset based is the relevance of this distinction to making an informed investment decision for the originators as well as *ṣukūk* holders. As noted by Hassoune, Howladar, and Harris, 'investors therefore need to look at each structure individually to understand its risk/return differences. Asset-backed and asset-based are semantically similar descriptions but mask significant risk/return differences'.[8]

One here looks at the genesis of two types of *ṣukūk*: asset-backed *ṣukūk* and asset-based *ṣukūk*. Before presenting a studied definition of these types of *ṣukūk*, it is important to shed light on how this new classification of *ṣukūk* has emerged in the market. Identifying the factors that have led to the emergence of these types of *ṣukūk* helps in understanding the basis of this classification. The ensuing discussion elaborates on this.

3.2.1 The Shift in Ṣukūk *Classification: From the Traditional to a New Approach*

Given the recent significant interest in asset-backed *ṣukūk* and asset-based *ṣukūk*, it is of growing importance to understand the reasons for the birth of these structures of *ṣukūk* in the market. An understanding of the forces that have shaped this new classification is relevant for a number of reasons. The first reason is that there are aspects of the current *ṣukūk* market regimes that make little sense without special reference to this kind of *ṣukūk*. The second reason for discussing the introduction of this *ṣukūk* classification is to provide a greater depth of understanding for some of the principles and conditions incorporated into present *ṣukūk* structures and legislations. Third, it is not surprising that contemporary concerns surrounding the *ṣukūk* market have arisen due to lack of awareness of the development of the said *ṣukūk* category. It is with these perceptions in mind that the following discussion on the origins of asset-backed *ṣukūk* and asset-based *ṣukūk* is provided.

Asset-backed *ṣukūk* and asset-based *ṣukūk* were, until relatively recently, not considered as discrete classifications that warranted analysis in their own right. One of the essential issues generated by academic debate is concerned with the birth of asset-backed *ṣukūk* and asset-based *ṣukūk*: should existing *ṣukūk* in the market be categorised as asset backed or asset based? What are the main elements that contributed to the existence of this new classification of *ṣukūk*? How is it to be distinguished from

[8] A Hassoune, K Howladar and S Harris, *supra* note 5, 148.

traditional classifications of *ṣukūk*? These questions arise as preliminary issues in the broader discussion of the nature of asset-backed *ṣukūk* and asset-based *ṣukūk*.

The classification of *ṣukūk*, either by regulatory or by institutional bodies, essentially draws upon variations and sometimes combinations of pre-existing concepts. Examples of traditional *ṣukūk* classifications are presented in some detail in Chap. 2, but for the present purpose it is sufficient to mention the broad bases of *ṣukūk* classification. In this respect, Dusuki and Mokhtar identify three bases: the underlying contract of *ṣukūk* structure, the asset type represented by the *ṣukūk*, and the technical and commercial features of the *ṣukūk* arrangement.[9]

The difference between asset-backed and asset-based *ṣukūk* has been recognised by rating agencies in recent years. In 2006, Moody's Investors Service (hereafter Moody's) issued a report 'Shari'ah and Sukuk: A Moody's Primer' which categorised *ṣukūk* structures existing in the market into asset-backed *ṣukūk* and unsecured (repurchase) *ṣukūk*.[10] The latter form is also known as asset-based *ṣukūk*, as elaborated in Chap. 4. This is arguably the first mention of asset-backed and asset-based *ṣukūk* classification in the rating literature. This approach to classifying *ṣukūk* via the separation between asset-backed and asset-based structure is also supported by Malaysian Rating Corporation Berhad (MARC)[11] and RAM Rating Services Berhad.[12] In addition to rating agencies, this method of *ṣukūk* categorisation is acknowledged by the IFSB.[13] The AAOIFI, however, does not recognise the distinction between asset-backed and asset-based structures. Regarding this, Ali states '[t]he terminology of asset-based and

[9] A Dusuki and S Mokhtar, *Critical Appraisal of Shariah Issues on Ownership in Asset-Based Sukuk as Implemented in the Islamic Debt Market* (ISRA 2010) 5.

[10] K Howladar, *Shari'ah and Sukuk: A Moody's Primer* (Moody's Investors Service 2006) 5; K Howladar, *The Future of Sukuk: Substance Over Form? Understanding Islamic Securitisation, Asset-Backed and AAOIFI Principles* (Moody's Investor Service 2009) 4.

[11] MARC, 'Rating Approach to Sukuk: A Marc Perspective' (*MARC*, 2008) 2. http://www.marc.com.my/home/userfiles/file/Methodologies/Rating%20Approach%20to%20Sukuk%20-%20A%20MARC%20Perspective.pdf. Accessed 18 March 2013.

[12] L Noor, 'Sukuk Rating-General Approach, Criteria and Methodology' in RAM Rating Services Berhad (ed), *Malaysian Sukuk Market Handbook: Your Guide to the Malaysian Islamic Capital Market* (RAM Rating Services Berhad undated) 150–154.

[13] See IFSB, 'Capital Adequacy Requirements for Ṣukūk, Securitisations and Real Estate investment' (*IFSB*, January 2009) 3–4. http://www.ifsb.org/standard/eng_%20IFSB-7%20Capital%20Adequacy%20Requirements%20for%20Sukuk,%20Securitasations%20and%20Real%20Estate%20investment%20(Jan2009).pdf. Accessed 4 March 2015.

asset-backed is not present in the AAOIFI standards'.[14] SC, a capital market regulator in Malaysia, differentiates between asset-backed and asset-based structures.[15] In 2011, Paris Europlace published the 'French Sukuk Guidebook' which recognises the distinction between asset-backed and asset-based *ṣukūk*.[16]

Each *ṣukūk* classification, a traditional or a new approach, provides a particular description and touches upon different aspects of various structures. It has been argued that classifying *ṣukūk* as either an asset-backed or asset-based structure provides the clearest picture with regard to the risk and returns of the underlying structure. Much debate has taken place over the emergence of this new classification and how it has evolved in the market.

3.2.2 Factors Contributing to the Emergence of the New Ṣukūk *Classification*

The shift in *ṣukūk* classification away from the traditional approach towards one based on asset-backed or asset-based structure is motivated by several factors that have also generated controversy and debate. According to the Islamic Finance Information Services (IFIS), the default of several major *ṣukūk* in various jurisdictions led to the distinction between two types of *ṣukūk* in the market (i.e. asset-backed and asset-based structures).[17] In this respect, the market realised that certain *ṣukūk* behaved differently in the event of default. Mohammad states that '[a] significant question which has arisen as a result of *ṣukūk* defaults is whether a *ṣukūk* is asset based, as opposed to being asset-backed'.[18] Further, the AAOIFI pronouncement in 2008 made it increasingly likely that there would be a new classification

[14] M Ali, 'Ṣukūk: Perception, Innovation and Challenges' in M Kamali and A Abdullah (eds), *Islamic Finance: Issues in Sukuk and Proposals for Reform* (International Institute of Advanced Islamic Studies and Islamic Foundation 2014) 64.

[15] SC, *The Islamic Securities (Sukuk) Market* (LexisNexis Malaysia 2009) 48.

[16] Paris Europlace is an independent body representing the Paris financial centre which is in charge of Islamic finance development in France. See Paris Europlace, 'French Sukuk Guidebook' (*Paris-europlace*, 2011) 41. http://www.paris-europlace.net/files/French_Sukuk_Guidebook_Nov_2011.pdf. Accessed 18 March 2013.

[17] IFIS, 'IFIS Global Sukuk Market H2-2010 Report' (*IFIS*, 2010) 11. http://www.kantakji.com/media/8073/mn100.pdf. Accessed 17 January 2013.

[18] F Mohammad, 'Greater Disclosure Required in the Sukuk Industry' (2010) Butterworths Journal of International Banking and Financial Law 258.

of *ṣukūk* in the market.[19] In addition, the discussion of a new classification of *ṣukūk* was promoted by underdeveloped regulations in a number of jurisdictions. The existing regulations imposed enormous strains on *ṣukūk* structures, which struggled to deal with the legal restrictions requiring changes in structuring processes. A good illustration of this is the USD 600 million 'Malaysian Global *Ṣukūk*' issued in 2002 in which the original structure was revised and a new structure was introduced with a beneficial ownership notion, on the grounds that the previously proposed offer was considered a direct break of the negative pledge clause required for all international bonds.[20]

The industry felt that not all *ṣukūk* were the same in the structuring process and therefore there was a need for a practical distinction between them due to the different implications of the underlying structures of *ṣukūk* that may arise in a variety of contexts. Several elements incorporated into *ṣukūk* structures have led to different performances of *ṣukūk* as financial instruments. There have been some signs in the market warranting the need for an accurate and precise classification of the existing structures. For example, it was found that most *ṣukūk* structures do not fulfil the requirement of representing true ownership.[21] Also, examining the commercial terms and legal documents of *ṣukūk* issues proves that not all *ṣukūk* have real assets underlying their structures.[22] One of the expected reasons behind this is the insolvency of the originators and uncertain procedures resulting from this situation.[23] The different risk profiles associated with the same structure, for example *ijārah ṣukūk* in the event of default and liquidation, are among the factors that necessitate a real and new distinction between *ṣukūk* structures industry wide.[24] Furthermore, it was found that the status of *ṣukūk*, whether classified as asset backed or asset based, is

[19] See Kuwait Finance House Research, *supra* note 4, 10.

[20] R Haneef, *supra* note 1, 108–110.

[21] A Dusuki and S Mokhtar, *supra* note 9, 6.

[22] IFSB, 'Capital Adequacy Requirements for Ṣukūk, Securitisations and Real Estate investment', *supra* note 13, 3.

[23] B Rider, 'Legal Aspects of Islamic Asset Securitisation' in IFSB (ed), *Strategies for the Development of Islamic Capital Markets: Infrastructures and Legal Aspects of Islamic Asset Securitisation* (IFSB 2011) 97.

[24] N Muhamed and R Radzi, 'Implication of Sukuk Structuring: The Comparison on the Structure of Asset Based and Asset Backed Ijarah Sukuk' (Second International Conference on Business and Economic Research, Malaysia, March 2011) 2452.

closely linked with the issuer's obligations and investors' rights.[25] Another important factor is noted by Muhamad and Radzi who say that '[t]he debate on asset-based versus asset-backed structure ha[d] also surfaced, particularly over the comparative treatment of *ṣukūk* holders'.[26] For instance, it was realised that the rights of *ṣukūk* holders in the situation of default differ from one structure to another.[27] The fact that *ṣukūk* structures are rated differently by rating agencies has contributed to the distinction between asset-backed and asset-based structures.[28]

Due to the above-mentioned reasons, the new classification ultimately was seen as a significant area of study in its own right. While it is desirable for those who are responsible for the development of the *ṣukūk* market to offer increasingly innovative structures, it is equally important for them to increase awareness of the differences between structures in terms of asset, risk, and return. It is believed that a clear understanding of the asset-backed/asset-based distinction of *ṣukūk* structures will bring further growth and stability to the IFSI.[29]

Having pointed out the importance of differentiation between asset-backed and asset-based structures to the *ṣukūk* market, the discussion now considers the first type, asset-backed *ṣukūk*, in more detail.

3.3 Definition of Asset-Backed *Ṣukūk*

For the purpose of this book, the term 'asset-backed *ṣukūk*' refers to a very specific *ṣukūk* arrangement, as opposed to an asset-based arrangement. The term 'asset-backed *ṣukūk*' is not used interchangeably with other terms in the context of *ṣukūk*, whether *ṣukūk* or asset-based *ṣukūk*. For a regulatory definition of asset-backed *ṣukūk* one can look at IFSB's standard 'Capital Adequacy Requirements for *Ṣukūk*, Securitisations and Real Estate Investment', hereafter IFSB-7, which provides the following definition:

> [A]n asset-backed *ṣukūk* structure that meets the requirements for being an asset-backed structure as assessed by a recognised external credit assessment institution (ECAI): this structure would leave the holders of *ṣukūk* to bear

[25] Ibid.
[26] Ibid. 2451.
[27] Ibid. 2458.
[28] See generally ibid. 2456.
[29] RAM Rating Services Berhad, 'Dubai Sukuk Defaults: Does One Bad Apple Spoil the Entire Barrel' (2009) 26 Islamic Finance Bulletin 10, 11.

> any losses in case of the impairment of the assets. The applicable risks are those of the underlying assets, and these will in principle be reflected in any credit rating issued by a recognised ECAI.[30]

An example of an institutional definition would be Moody's definition, where asset-backed *ṣukūk* are described as follows:

> Where investors enjoy asset-backing, they benefit over some form of security or lien over the assets, and are therefore in a preferential position over other, unsecured creditors. In other words, in the event the issuer were to default or become insolvent, the noteholders would be able to recover their exposure by taking control of and ultimately realising the value from the asset(s). In this event, the transaction may achieve ratings that are higher than the unsecured issuer rating of the originator.[31]

Another definition of asset-backed *ṣukūk* is provided by RAM Rating Services Berhad:

> Asset-backed *ṣukūk* are characteristically non-recourse *ṣukūk*, with the underlying assets forming the lone source of profit and capital payments. True to form, the credit risk of this type of *ṣukūk* will be solely determined by the performance and credit quality of the underlying asset, i.e. the asset's cash flow and, in some situations, expected value at maturity given various stress situations and scenarios. *Ṣukūk* investors generally do not have access to the asset owner; likewise, they are safeguarded from the latter's financial plights, made certain by the transaction's structural and legal make-up.[32]

It is also appropriate to look at the definition provided by a legal practitioner who, under the name of Islamic asset securitisation structure, defined asset-backed *ṣukūk* as structures that 'involve asset transfers from an originator into a trust or similar special purpose vehicle (SPV), with *ṣukūk* issuance by that SPV and payments on the *ṣukūk* derived from the payments received in respect of those transferred assets'.[33]

[30] IFSB, *supra* note 13, 3.

[31] P Lotter, *Understanding Moody's Approach to Unsecured Corporate Sukuk* (Moody's Investors Service 2007) 5.

[32] L Noor, *supra* note 12, 150.

[33] M Mcmillen, 'Contractual Enforceability Issues: Sukuk and Capital Markets Development' (2007) 7 Chicago Journal of International Law 427, 428.

From the above definitions, it can be seen that asset-backed *ṣukūk* is also known by other names such as Islamic asset securitisation structure and non-recourse *ṣukūk*. Further, the IFSB makes a reference to rating agencies when pinning down asset-backed *ṣukūk*, which is attributed to the fact that it is a relatively new and inherently practical concept within the *ṣukūk* industry. The overwhelming majority of *ṣukūk* including asset-backed structures is vetted by rating agencies and therefore they are arguably in a better position to provide an accurate definition. Yet, most laws and regulations concerning *ṣukūk*, whether at a national or international level, do not provide a definition for the term 'asset-backed *ṣukūk*'. They rather define *ṣukūk* in general terms, assuming that all arrangements bear the same structural elements. The meaning of asset-backed *ṣukūk* shall become clearer after examining its basic structure and elements over the course of this chapter.

3.4 Structure of Asset-Backed *Ṣukūk*

A comprehension of conventional securitisation is a prerequisite to understanding the structure of asset-backed *ṣukūk*. This is due to the similarities between them in practice. From a rating agency's perspective, it is stated that 'Moody's will only consider them to be asset-backed or asset-secured if the key securitisation elements are in place'.[34] The parallels between the two are highlighted by Dusuki and Mokhtar: '[a]sset-backed *ṣukūk* mirror securitization practice in the conventional space'.[35] Thus, one can explain the structure of asset-backed *ṣukūk* by looking at conventional securitisation, and then identifying the principal features that need to be present in asset-backed *ṣukūk*.

3.4.1 Defining Conventional Securitisation

Although securitisation is commonly used in capital markets and widely explained in the literature, there is no single standard definition of securitisation.[36] Shenker and Colletta give the following description of securitisation:

[34] K Howladar, *supra* note 10, 5.

[35] A Dusuki and S Mokhtar, *supra* note 9, 10.

[36] J Shenker and A Colletta, 'Asset Securitiszation: Evolution, Current Issues and New Frontiers' (1991) 69 Texas Law Review 1369, 1373.

> [T]he sale of equity or debt instruments, representing ownership interests in, or secured by, a segregated, income-producing asset or pool of assets, in a transaction structured to reduce or reallocate certain risks inherent in owning or lending against underlying assets and to ensure that such interests are more readily marketable and, thus, more liquid than ownership interests in and loans against the underlying assets.[37]

The end product of the above securitisation process is known as asset-backed securities. Fuller describes the basic form of asset-backed securities as

> [A] special purpose vehicle company ('SPV') issuing bonds or notes ('asset-backed securities' or 'ABS'), using the proceeds of the issue to acquire assets or debts (which are often referred to as 'receivables'), and using the cash-flows arising from receivables to fund the cash flows payable on the ABS.[38]

The above-mentioned structure is a traditional form of ABS, and it is better known as 'true sale structure' because it involves the SPV purchasing the receivables. In essence, asset-backed *ṣukūk* is structured to be a true sale structure and, in this sense, it is similar to the asset-backed securities of conventional finance. ABS have the main following features: (1) ABS have security over the SPV's assets backing the transaction; (2) ABS are 'limited recourse' instruments, meaning that the SPV only pays in accordance with the returns generated by the assets backing the arrangement; (3) there is no recourse to the sponsor or originator (the entity selling the receivables to the SPV); and (4) the insolvency or bankruptcy remoteness of the SPV.[39]

The previously mentioned definitions of asset-backed *ṣukūk* indicate the principal features that are normally present in asset-backed *ṣukūk*: (1) the actual owners of the underlying asset are the *ṣukūk* holders; (2) the returns on *ṣukūk* depend on the performance of the asset backing the deal; (3) the performance of the underlying asset is not affected by the insolvency of the originator or sponsor; and (4) the asset backing the deal is subject to both market and credit risk.[40] Although they can be seen to be very similar in make-up, the differences

[37] Ibid. 1374–1375.

[38] G Fuller, *The Law and Practice of International Capital Markets* (3 edn, LexisNexis 2012) 178.

[39] Ibid. 178–179.

[40] See A Dusuki and S Mokhtar, *supra* note 9, 10.

between asset-backed *ṣukūk* and conventional ABS arise from the sharia-compliant nature of the former; the assets underlying asset-backed *ṣukūk* must comply with Islamic law rules. To illustrate, the assets securitised in conventional practice could be interest-bearing loans, prohibited items, or involving prohibited activities. However, such assets are not allowed to be securitised in asset-backed *ṣukūk*. Another important difference between asset-backed *ṣukūk* and conventional ABS is in terms of the nature of rights. While the former involves ownership rights, the latter takes the form of collateral rights.[41]

3.4.2 *Essential Pillars of Asset-Backed* Ṣukūk

For a *ṣukūk* structure to be categorised as asset backed, key elements of securitisation must be ensured in the structure, namely (1) bankruptcy remoteness of the SPV; (2) true sale; (3) enforceability of security; and (4) the generation of independent cash flows.[42] If all or some of these elements do not exist in the *ṣukūk* structure in question, it is not viewed as an asset-backed structure. Therefore, it is important to understand how such securitisation elements work in asset-backed *ṣukūk*.

Bankruptcy remoteness of the SPV relates to the way the SPV is structured in asset-backed *ṣukūk*. As mentioned earlier, the SPV is the issuer of *ṣukūk*, also sometimes referred to as special purpose company (SPC), special purpose entity (SPE), or bankruptcy-remote vehicle (BRV).[43] In asset-backed *ṣukūk*, the SPV is structured in such a way that reduces 'the risk of it being declared bankrupt or insolvent'.[44] A set of elements is introduced so as to achieve the insolvency remoteness of the SPV which includes the following[45]:

[41] IFSB, *supra* note 13, 3.

[42] See K Howladar, *supra* note 10, 7; P Lotter, *supra* note 31, 6.

[43] K Baudistel, 'Bankruptcy-Remote Special Purpose Entities: An Opportunity for Investors to Maximize The Value of Their Returns While Undergoing More Careful dnd Realistic Risk Analysis' (2013) 86 Southern California Law Review 1309, 1313–1314; G Fuller, *supra* note 38, 195.

[44] G Fuller, *supra* note 38, 195.

[45] See ibid. 195–196; J Pearce and I Lipin, 'Special Purpose Vehicles in Bankruptcy Litigation' (2011) 44 Hofstra Law Review 177, 178–179; R Ali, 'Legal Certainty for Sukuk' in A Thomas (ed), *Sukuk* (Sweet & Maxwell Asia 2009) 101–102.

- Setting up the SPV in a tax-free or low-tax jurisdiction, such as the Cayman Islands, Jersey, or Guernsey, so as to minimise the danger of winding up the SPV for non-payment of tax.
- Preventing the SPV from being involved in any other activities or incurring any liabilities outside the deal.
- Preventing the SPV from merging with any other entities or having any employees.
- Seeking an approval from all the SPV creditors with regard to limited recourse (i.e. recourse only to the returns generated by the asset backing the deal).
- Requiring all SPV creditors to waive their rights or not take any enforcement action against the SPV in the event of a shortfall in earnings. Such a practice is known as 'non-petition'.
- Ensuring that the first-ranking security over the asset backing the deal is for SPV creditors.
- Appointing independent directors for the SPV. Thus, the directorship of the SPV is independent of the originator or sponsor.
- The SPV usually takes the form of an orphan company with its shares held in a charitable trust.

The above characteristics are desirable for the SPV of asset-backed *ṣukūk* for two main reasons: to ensure that the SPV is not under the control of the originator and to prevent the courts from consolidating the SPV's assets with the originator's assets in any insolvency proceedings brought against the latter.[46]

The true sale element refers to the way in which the asset underlying the *ṣukūk* is transferred from the originator to the SPV. In asset-backed *ṣukūk*, the SPV acquires the underlying asset from the originator by way of a true sale. The presence of a true sale in asset-backed *ṣukūk* also means that the legal title to the asset backing the deal passes from the originator to the SPV.[47] In this regard, it is important to ensure that the transfer of the asset is viewed as a true sale that is adequate under insolvency law to remove the asset backing the deal from the originator's assets and balance sheet.[48] Ensuring that the transfer of assets is designed to constitute a true

[46] R Ali, *supra* note 45, 102.

[47] M Al-Amine, *supra* note 2, 36.

[48] P Rajapakse, R Copp and J Gardner, 'Assessment of Insolvency Issues for the Mortgage Originator and Trustee-Issuer in Securitisation Programs' (2008) 34 Monash University Law Review 370.

sale is significant to avoid 'claw back risk' and re-categorisation of the transaction as a loan.[49] The former refers to the possibility of the underlying assets being re-acquired by the originator or insolvency practitioner in the event of the originator's insolvency.[50] In this regard, Al-Amine identifies five requirements for a true sale in *ṣukūk*: (1) a legal transfer of ownership of the asset backing the deal from the originator to the SPV; (2) the removal of the assets sold from the originator's balance sheet; (3) the absence of any condition prohibiting the SPV from the sale or disposable right; (4) the return on *ṣukūk* is derived from the underlying asset; and (5) the SPV is entitled to direct recourse to the asset backing the deal in the event of insolvency.[51]

Enforceability of security is concerned with the parties' rights and obligations in relation to *ṣukūk* as an asset-backed structure. In this regard, all documents related to the asset-backed *ṣukūk* should be valid, binding, and enforceable.[52] As mentioned earlier, an asset-backed *ṣukūk* involves transfer of asset, true sale, and *ṣukūk* holders' ownership or interest over the asset backing the deal. Therefore, the applicable or chosen law should have an appropriate asset transfer mechanism for the arrangement.[53] This is usually facilitated by the choice of English Law and New York Law.[54] In particular, the former dominates in the *ṣukūk* market because it features a trust concept which provides *ṣukūk* holders with direct ownership or interest over the asset in question.[55]

[49] R Ali, *supra* note 45, 100. See also K Klee and B Butler, 'Asset-Backed Securitization, Special Purpose Vehicles and Other Securtization Issues' (2002) 35 Uniform Commercial Code Law Journal 23, 49.

[50] K Howladar, *supra* note 10, 7.

[51] M Al-Amine, *supra* note 2, 34. Statement of Financial Accounting Standards No. 140 (Accounting for Transfers and Servicing of Financial Assets and Extinguishments of Liabilities) issued in 2000 provides a three-part test to determine whether a transfer is accounted as a true sale: (1) isolation of the transferred assets from the originator and thus they are beyond the reach of the originator and its creditors; (2) there is no constraints on the SPV's right to pledge or exchange the transferred assets; and (3) there is no control over the transferred assets by the originator, whether by an agreement entitling the originator to repurchase or redeem the transferred assets before the maturity or the originator's ability to get back specific assets unilaterally.

[52] K Howladar, *supra* note 10, 7.

[53] R Ali, *supra* note 45, 94.

[54] K Howladar, *supra* note 10, 7.

[55] R Ali, *supra* note 45, 93.

The element of the generation of independent cash flows is concerned with the source of payments in asset-backed *ṣukūk*. It has been already stressed that the performance of asset-backed *ṣukūk* is driven by the asset backing the deal, and is not connected with the credit risk of the originator or the sponsor. This is facilitated by the nature of the securitised asset, which is an income-producing asset. Therefore, it is unlikely that a non-income-producing asset such as raw land would be used for asset-backed *ṣukūk*.[56] It is conceivable that the cash flow coming from the asset will not be adequate or is less than what is expected by investors. While certain processes are applied to ensure that principal and interest are paid on time in conventional securitisation, this is an area where further consideration from an Islamic law perspective is required. Assets selected for securitisation generally satisfy certain criteria in order to fulfil the purpose of an income-producing asset. These include assets with standardised terms (homogeneous), loss or profit experience, and servicing processes acceptable to rating agencies and investors.[57] Also, the suitability of these assets relies on displaying specific characteristics, particularly regular payment streams, low default experience, and ease of pooling them together.[58]

Having presented the primary features of asset-backed *ṣukūk*, an example of such a structure under the concept of *ijārah* (lease) is provided in Fig. 3.1. The structure demonstrates the following: (1) the originator sells leased assets (an income-generating asset) to the SPV; (2) the SPV issues *ṣukūk* to raise funds; (3) holders of *ṣukūk* pay the purchase price; and (4) the SPV distributes rental payments to *ṣukūk* holders that are paid by the obligor.[59]

3.5 Asset-Backed *Ṣukūk*: Structural Motivation and Pitfalls

While asset-backed *ṣukūk* is seen as a preferable structural option by some market participants, others do not consider it as such for several reasons. To fully appreciate asset-backed *ṣukūk*, one must look at the advantages

[56] J Shenker and A Colletta, *supra* note 36, 1376.

[57] Ibid. 1377.

[58] G Giglio, 'Asset Securitisation in Argentina' (2005) 10 Journal of International Banking Law and Regulation 514.

[59] See S Mokhtar and A Thomas, 'Ijarah Sukuk' in A Thomas (ed), *Sukuk* (Sweet & Maxwell Asia 2009) 156.

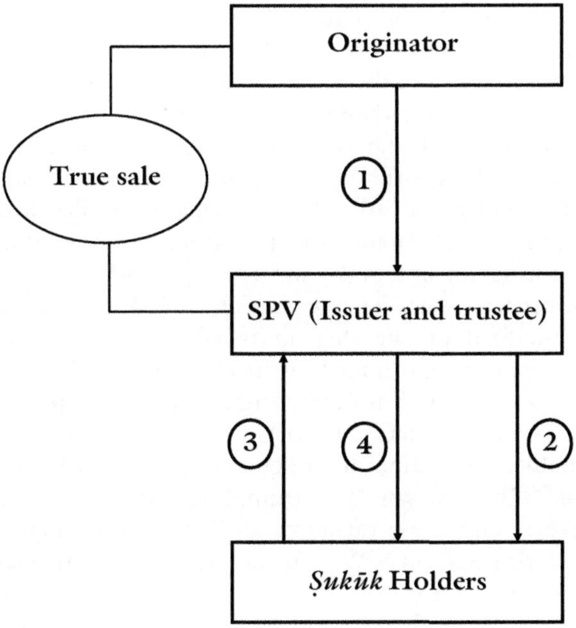

Fig. 3.1 The concept of *ṣukūk* as an asset-backed structure using *ijārah*. Source: Author

and disadvantages that such structures bring to different market participants, particularly originators and investors.

3.5.1 Advantages

The choice of asset-backed *ṣukūk* is made by investors looking for the creditworthiness of the asset itself, and not the creditworthiness of the originator or sponsor.[60] This is due to the bankruptcy remoteness of the SPV that facilitates the achievement of creditworthiness independent of the originator.[61] Another reason why investors and originators may consider an asset-backed *ṣukūk* is its marketability feature.[62] In this

[60] D Barbour, J Norton and T Slover, 'Asset Securitisation in Emerging Market Economics: Fundamentals Considerations' (1997) Yearbook of International Financial and Financial Law 281, 284.

[61] Ibid.

[62] Ibid. 285.

regard, the originator's ability to attract investors is not affected by any adverse conditions encountered by the originator because the primary interest of the investors is the credit quality of the asset.[63] As an added benefit, an asset-backed *ṣukūk* allows the originator to transform several risks associated with the assets into one single risk, by transferring the assets to investors, offering an opportunity of risk simplification, diversification, and reallocation.[64] This separation also leads to a low cost of funding and off-balance sheet funding.[65] This can be referred to as the accounting advantage of asset-backed *ṣukūk*. For illustration, when the originator issues an asset-backed *ṣukūk*, the transaction is not recorded in the form of a liability on its balance sheet because it is considered a sale rather than financing from an accounting perspective.[66] Thus, capital is raised without affecting the debt-to-equity ratio on the originator's balance sheet.[67] In other words, the off-balance sheet structure enables an originator to generate income without locking up their capital.[68] In addition, an originator that has not achieved the required investment-grade rating can still take advantage of an asset-backed *ṣukūk* through an SPV that has obtained an investment-grade rating.[69] Another motivation for an originator to choose an asset-backed *ṣukūk* is the enhancement of its overall credit rating that is achieved via removing risky and illiquid assets from its portfolio.[70] The enhancement of capital structure is another benefit that encourages originators to use asset-backed *ṣukūk*.[71] In this regard, the capital structure is enhanced due to the accounting treatment of the sale that removes the securitised assets and associated liabilities from the originator's balance sheet.[72] Associated with this previously mentioned benefit is that asset-backed *ṣukūk* liberates capital for the purpose of

[63] Ibid.

[64] See S Cosentino, 'Swimming in New Waters-Bank Participation in Securitized Loan Pools' (1997) 65 UMKC Law Review 543, 547.

[65] S Schwarcz, 'The Alchemy of Asset Securitization' (1994) 1 Stanford Journal of Law, Business and Finance 133, 142; G Giglio, *supra* note 58.

[66] S Schwarcz, *supra* note 65, 142; G Giglio, *supra* note 58.

[67] S Schwarcz, *supra* note 65, 143.

[68] F Oditah, 'Great Britain' in T Baums and E Wymeersch (eds), *Asset-Backed Securitization in Europe* (Kluwer Law International 1996) 106.

[69] S Schwarcz, *supra* note 65, 137.

[70] D Barbour, J Norton and T Slover, *supra* note 60, 285–286.

[71] Ibid. 286.

[72] Ibid.; E Park, 'Allowing Japanese Banks to Engage in Securitization: Potential Benefits, Regulatory Obstacles and Theories for Reform' (1996) 17 University of Pennsylvania Journal of International Economic Law 723, 729.

productive use which had been reserved and maintained against the risk of underlying securitised assets.[73] For originators, issuing asset-backed *ṣukūk* not only enhances their financial ratios, but also enables them to comply with capital adequacy requirements. Improving the originator's liquidity by issuing asset-backed *ṣukūk* is mentioned as one of its advantages. In this respect, illiquid assets are converted to tradable certificates and this enhances the liquidity of the originator's portfolio.[74] However, one should here differentiate between the restructuring of assets and securitisation; carrying out securitisation internally by converting one asset to another type is considered asset restructuring rather than securitisation, whereby securities are retained on the originator's balance sheet.[75]

It is important to distinguish between the advantages of asset-backed *ṣukūk* and conventional asset-backed securities. The latter has other advantages that are either irrelevant to the IFSI or require further considerations from the Islamic law perspective. For example, conventional securitisation brings a lower interest rate for the originator compared to a conventional loan arising from a credit rating received for these securities that is higher than the originator.[76] Also, it facilitates obtaining lower interest rates through traditional funding sources as a result of an improvement in the originator's credit rating.[77] Another advantage is an additional fee income received by the originator in its capacity as a servicer in the securitisation process.[78]

3.5.2 Disadvantages

Disadvantages of an asset-backed *ṣukūk* can be seen in the effort required in the structuring process and the difficulty encountered when implementing its structural terms and conditions. For instance, it is possible that the true sale mechanism may fail to be achieved owing to a lack of care in ensuring the complete separation of securitised assets.[79] Given that the asset is the only object of recourse in an asset-backed structure, any

[73] D Barbour, J Norton and T Slover, *supra* note 60, 286.
[74] Ibid.
[75] B Rider, *supra* note 23, 142.
[76] D Barbour, J Norton and T Slover, *supra* note 60, 285.
[77] Ibid. 285–286.
[78] Ibid. 287.
[79] Basel Committee on Banking and Supervision, 'Asset Transfers and Securitisation' (*BIS*, 1992) 2. http://www.bis.org/publ/bcbs10a.pdf. Accessed 14 May 2013.

destruction or non-performance of the asset will considerably affect the value of the *ṣukūk*.[80] In obtaining a satisfactory market reception of securitised assets, the remaining portfolio of the originator is exposed to further risk arising from the sale of the highest quality assets.[81] Due to the laws governing the securitisation process in emerging economies, the range of assets available to be securitised is limited.[82] This issue is of particular interest to the IFSI as the asset range is further limited in the case of asset-backed *ṣukūk* owing to Islamic law restrictions relating to the sale of debt or securitising loans. Furthermore, the accumulation of a substantial number of suitable assets in the originator's portfolio for the securitisation process may take a lengthy period, delaying the issue of asset-backed *ṣukūk* when it is highly needed.[83] Obtaining an investment-grade rating for asset-backed *ṣukūk* is another obstacle, requiring sufficiently additional credit support in order to create securitisation.[84] Although some techniques, such as credit enhancement, are used to eliminate the investor's exposure to risk,[85] the transfer of risk to investors in asset-backed *ṣukūk* might be seen as a disadvantage from investors' viewpoint. The expensive initial cost of structuring asset-backed *ṣukūk* is a problem facing originators that arises from several transaction costs including placement underwriter, credit enhancement, legal advice, accounting consultancy, and due diligence.[86] Over-collateralisation forms a further cost to the originator since the amount of securitised assets sold to the SPV must be higher than the amount paid for the asset-backed *ṣukūk* to avoid losses arising from defaults or delayed collection.[87] Also, there is a risk of payments not being received on time, and risk-averse investors dislike and avoid this kind of transaction.[88] When there is a low ratio of the average size of assets to the largest assets, the default of the latter will have a serious impact on the entire pool.[89] Additionally, asset-backed *ṣukūk* may face a lower invest-

[80] P Wouters, 'Asset-Backed Sukuk: Islamic Finance Going its Own Way' (*Islamic Finance News*, 2011). http://www.fimm.com.my/%5Cpdf%5CProduct%20Knowledge%5C30Mac11_Asset-backed%20Sukuk.pdf. Accessed 12 March 2013.

[81] Basel Committee on Banking and Supervision, *supra* note 79, 6.

[82] D Barbour, J Norton and T Slover, *supra* note 60, 294.

[83] Ibid. 295.

[84] Ibid.

[85] Ibid. 285.

[86] Ibid. 297.

[87] S Schwarcz, *supra* note 65, 141.

[88] Ibid. 137.

[89] D Barbour, J Norton and T Slover, *supra* note 60, 299.

ment rating if the securitisation pool lacks assets (that are either diversified or insufficient).[90] The limited information concerning the assets used in the securitisation process is another hurdle in asset-backed *ṣukūk* since investors often lack knowledge about asset quality or performance.[91] There should be caution regarding the issuing of asset-backed *ṣukūk* by riskier companies, despite the benefits of the asset-backed *ṣukūk* structure. In this situation securitisation is less of a benefit and risk-averse investors will likely avoid these arrangements.[92]

It is appropriate here to state some of the pitfalls of conventional securitisation that are not applicable to asset-backed *ṣukūk*. For example, the pressure of generating the necessary volume of loans to meet a continuing securitisation programme may lead the originator to lower credit standards and reduce the credit risk assessment of loan assets.[93] In addition, loans with balloon maturities and infrequent payments that impede conventional securitisation[94] have no effect on asset-backed *ṣukūk* as the latter avoids the selling of debts. Furthermore, the retained responsibility for serving the assets by the originator is identified as a disadvantage since this will affect the rating of conventional asset-backed securities arising from an inexperienced servicer.[95] Whether the originator can be the servicer in the securitisation process is another concern which needs to be addressed in asset-backed *ṣukūk*.

3.6 Market Perspectives on Asset-Backed *Ṣukūk*

Given the above discussion of the advantages of asset-backed *ṣukūk*, one might assume that they constitute a large portion of existing *ṣukūk* in the market. However, according to the *ṣukūk* database of IFIS, asset-backed *ṣukūk* offered in the global market accounted for only 11 transactions out of 560 or 2% of the total number of *ṣukuk* as of August 2009.[96] Seven of them were Malaysian issuances, and the remaining four were global offerings. Seven of them were issued based on the *ijārah* contract (see Table 3.1).

[90] Ibid.

[91] Ibid.

[92] S Schwarcz, *supra* note 65, 137.

[93] D Barbour, J Norton and T Slover, *supra* note 60, 288.

[94] Ibid. 299.

[95] Ibid.

[96] A Dusuki and S Mokhtar, *supra* note 9, 8; H Ahmed, 'Islamic Finance at a Crossroads: The Dominance of the Asset-Based Sukuk' (2010) 6 Journal of International Banking and Financial Law 366.

Table 3.1 Asset-backed *ṣukūk* issuances in the global *ṣukūk* market[a]

No.	*Concept*	*Issuer*	*Date issued*	*Issued amount*	*Underlying asset*
1	BBA	ABS Plantation Asset	September 2005	175 (RM `000)	Plantation asset
2	*Ijārah*	Golden Crop Return	November 2005	442 (RM `000)	Plantation asset
3		Dura Palms	June 2006	284 (RM `000)	Plantation land
4		ABS Logistic	May 2007	300 (RM `000)	Warehouse
5		Menara ABS	January 2008	1100 (RM `000)	Office buildings
6		Caravan I (Hanco)	February 2004	98 (SAR million)	Leased vehicles
7		Tamweel	July 2007	220 (USD million)	Leased properties
8	*Muḍārabah*	Sun Finance (Sorouh)	August 2008	5020 (AED million)	Land plots
9	*Mushārakah*	Musyarakah One Capital	April 2005	2500 (RM `000)	Debt
10		Cagamas MBS	August 2005	2050 (RM `000)	Debt
11		East Cameron Gas	July 2006	166 (USD million)	Hydrocarbon

[a]A Dusuki and S Mokhtar, *supra* note 9, 9

Although asset-backed *ṣukūk* apparently comply with Islamic law, they form a very small portion of the overall market. The lack of asset-backed *ṣukūk* can be blamed on the disadvantages pointed out in the previous section; in particular, the fact that very few countries have specific securitisation laws supporting the establishment of the SPV leads to fewer issues of asset-backed *ṣukūk*.[97] It seems that the structuring of asset-backed *ṣukūk* is still problematic, even in jurisdictions with clear securitisation laws. In this regard, Al-Amine states that '[e]ven in countries with securitisation laws such Malaysia, which has a clear guidelines on a true sale, asset-backed securitisation has not taken off'.[98] Apart from the underdeveloped regulatory framework in relation to securitisation in many jurisdictions, Al-Amine mentions two other obstacles to securitisation or asset-backed

[97] K Howladar, *supra* note 10, 7.
[98] M Al-Amine, *supra* note 2, 49.

ṣukūk: (1) foreigners are restricted from owning particular assets in the GCC and (2) the insolvency law is not yet developed.[99]

Nevertheless, there is hope that asset-backed *ṣukūk* has the potential to dominate the future market.[100] Howladar asserts that although asset-backed *ṣukūk* are currently in minority, it is most likely that such types will increase due to its closeness to Islamic law and popularity in the legal profession.[101]

3.7 Conclusion

A closer analysis of *ṣukūk* markets' development reveals two distinct types of *ṣukūk*, namely asset-backed and asset-based *ṣukūk*. However, despite the differences between asset-backed and asset-based *ṣukūk*, investors and the industry generally fail to distinguish between them. This can be potentially problematic particularly when a default or an insolvency situation arises in Islamic jurisdictions, let alone Western jurisdictions. This shall be discussed in more detail in Chap. 5.

The fundamental structure of asset-backed *ṣukūk* aims to segregate the securitised assets from the originator, vesting them in the SPV. This structure has great implications on the *ṣukūk* issued and the rights of *ṣukūk* holders in an insolvency context. In order to assess asset-backed *ṣukūk*, courts and legal advisors should focus on the perfection of the essential pillars rather than labels on the legal documents. Yet, there is little-to-no guidance available to market participants as to what exactly asset-backed *ṣukūk* should look like and what would happen to investors in the event of insolvency. This chapter has aimed to clarify the understanding of asset-backed *ṣukūk*, the advantages and disadvantages of adopting asset-backed *ṣukūk*, and the current market status.

Having discussed the concept of *ṣukūk* as an asset-backed structure, the next chapter looks at the concept of *ṣukūk* as an asset-based structure.

[99] Ibid.
[100] P Wouters, *supra* note 80.
[101] K Howladar, *supra* note 10, 7.

CHAPTER 4

Asset-Based *Ṣukūk*

4.1 Introduction

This chapter continues the underlying debate about the division of *ṣukūk* (trust investment certificates) into asset-backed and asset-based structure. Beginning by looking at the meaning and structure of asset-based *ṣukūk*, it then puts in place the standards of such a structure. The chapter equally addresses the question of why asset-based *ṣukūk* dominates the current market, as well as looking at the reasons behind the remarkable preference investors have for this structure. While drawing a neat dividing line between asset-backed and asset-based *ṣukūk* is difficult in some situations, this chapter clarifies the division.

4.2 Definition of Asset-Based *Ṣukūk*

Before defining asset-based *ṣukūk*, one should mention that this is the most common term used in the academic literature for the structure. However, such a structure is also referred to as normal *ṣukūk*,[1] unsecured *ṣukūk*,[2] repurchase *ṣukūk*,[3] Islamic bond,[4] and credit-backed securities.[5]

[1] SC, *The Islamic Securities (Sukuk) Market* (LexisNexis Malaysia 2009) 48.

[2] K Howladar, *Shari'ah and Sukuk: A Moody's Primer* (Moody's Investors Service 2006) 5.

[3] Ibid.

[4] M Mcmillen, 'Contractual Enforceability Issues: Sukuk and Capital Markets Development' (2007) 7 Chicago Journal of International Law 427, 428.

[5] N Muhamed and R Radzi, 'Implication of Sukuk Structuring: The Comparison on the Structure of Asset Based and Asset Backed Ijarah Sukuk' (2nd International Conference on

S. Al-Ali, *Raising Capital on* Ṣukūk *Markets*,
https://doi.org/10.1007/978-3-030-14536-1_4

For the purpose of this book, the term asset-based *ṣukūk* is used. This is also a practice of a number of institutions, including IFSB, RAM Rating Services Berhad, and Moody's that adopt this name in its publications and reports as shall be seen in this chapter.

According to RAM Rating Services Berhad, asset-based *ṣukūk* is of two types: debt securitisation and financial *ijārah* (lease).[6] The former type is defined as *ṣukūk* that:

> evidences the indebtedness originating from the contracts of exchanges of *murābaḥah*, *bayʿ bithaman ʾājil* or *istiṣnāʿ*, arising from back-to-back sales of the issuer's assets. Such *ṣukūk* gives the holders the rights to the obligations attached to the indebtedness.[7]

The latter type is defined as *ṣukūk* 'arising from *ijārah* contracts, through the sale and leaseback or lease of third-party held acquired assets, with purchase-option obligations (financial lease)'.[8] Besides, Moody's defines asset-based *ṣukūk* as that for which 'the originator undertakes to repurchase the assets from the issuer at maturity of the *ṣukūk*, or upon a predefined early termination event, for an amount equal to the principle repayment'.[9]

Aside from the above definitions provided by the rating agencies, asset-based *ṣukūk*, under the name of Islamic bonds, is defined as structures that 'are based, ultimately, upon the credit of an entity—issuer, guarantor, or other credit support provider—that is participating in the transaction, rather than on specific assets and cash flows derived from those specific assets'.[10] Further, asset-based *ṣukūk* is described as a structure:

> [W]here the initial sale of the original assets by the originator to the SPV does not take place, so the ownership (title) of assets remains with the originator of the *ṣukūk* ... An undertaking is also made by the originator to buy back the *ṣukūk* at their face value on the maturity date of *ṣukūk*.[11]

Business and Economic Research, Malaysia, March 2011) 2456.

[6] W Kamil, 'Introduction to Sukuk' in RAM Rating Services Berhad (ed), *Malaysian Sukuk Market Handbook: Your Guide to the Malaysian Islamic Capital Market* (RAM Rating Services Berhad undated) 29.

[7] Ibid.

[8] Ibid.

[9] P Lotter, *Understanding Moody's Approach to Unsecured Corporate Sukuk* (Moody's Investors Service 2007) 5.

[10] M Mcmillen, *supra* note 4, 428.

[11] S Zaheer and S Wijnbergen, 'Sukuk Defaults: on Distress Resolution in Islamic Finance' (*Tinbergen*, 2013) 8. http://papers.tinbergen.nl/13087.pdf. Accessed 26 May 2015.

Another useful working definition by Akhtar is as follows:

> The asset based *ṣukūk* operates so that the investors have a beneficial interest in the cash flows generated by the underlying assets and there are sold by the originator to a SPV in the form of a trust. The trustee issues certificates representing the investor's ownership interest, while the proceeds are used to purchase the assets. The *ṣukūk* acts as a conventional unsecured bond without recourse to the asset and rates the investors according to the obligor's credit worthiness and not their rights of ownership.[12]

According to the above-mentioned definitions, a rather more working definition for asset-based *ṣukūk* can be formulated which is *ṣukūk* each of which represents the holder's beneficial ownership over the underlying asset where the holder assumes some ownership rights to such an asset and relies on the creditworthiness of the originator rather than the cash flows derived from the asset in question. The following discussion has been devoted to look at the IFSB's definition, owing to its unique position towards the term asset-based *ṣukūk*.

4.2.1 A Turning Point in Asset-Based Ṣukūk *Definition: IFSB Perspective*

IFSB's definition of and position towards the concept of asset-based *ṣukūk* has varied considerably and therefore requires special attention. This is significant so as to avoid the confusion about the term asset-based *ṣukūk* that may arise from reading its different standards. IFSB initially defined asset-based *ṣukūk* 'where the underlying assets offer fairly predictable returns to the *sukūk* holders, such as in the case of *salam*, *istiṣnāʿ* and *ijārah*'.[13] This definition appeared on its 'Capital Adequacy Standard for Institutions (Other than Insurance Institutions) Offering Only Islamic Financial Services' issued in December 2005—hereafter IFSB-2. This was the first usage of the term asset-based *ṣukūk* by the IFSB. In this context, IFSB has divided *ṣukūk* into asset-based *ṣukūk* and equity-based *ṣukūk*. IFSB has made it clear that the *ṣukūk* discussed in IFSB-2, which is called

[12] Z Akhtar, 'Stakeholding in Sharia Compliant Assets and Investor Protection' (2011) 7 Journal of International Banking and Regulation 362.

[13] IFSB, 'Capital Adequacy Standard for Institutions (other than Insurance Institutions) Offering Only Islamic Financial Services (IIFS)' (*IFSB*, December 2005) 47. http://www.ifsb.org/standard/ifsb2.pdf. Accessed 4 March 2015.

later asset-based *ṣukūk* in the same published standard, is one whereby *ṣukūk* holders assume all rights and obligations of the underlying assets. Such description is applicable only to asset-backed *ṣukūk* that has been discussed in detail in Chap. 3. Therefore, IFSB-2 essentially focuses on asset-backed *ṣukūk*, despite the term asset-based *ṣukūk* being used instead. For illustration, IFSB in its first position towards the *ṣukūk* market assumed that all *ṣukūk* structures include complete ownership transfer to *ṣukūk* holders and called them asset-based *ṣukūk*.[14] Although IFSB in IFSB-2 recognised that there are *ṣukūk* without full ownership transfer, IFSB tended to disregard this *ṣukūk* structure from a purely practical perspective, assuming that they do not exist on the *ṣukūk* market.[15] Since then, IFSB has altered its previous definition of asset-based *ṣukūk* and its previous *ṣukūk* classification which seems to ignore or overlook the actual terms and documents of *ṣukūk* structures as being practised in the market.

The new definition of asset-based *ṣukūk* came in January 2009 in IFSB-7 in the context of dividing *ṣukūk* into asset-backed and asset-based structure.[16] Two types of asset-based *ṣukūk* are described in IFSB-7—pay-through asset-based *ṣukūk* and pass-through asset-based *ṣukūk*. The former type is described as follows:

> [T]he issuer purchases the assets, leases them on behalf of the investors and issues the *ṣukūk*. Normally, the assets are leased back to the originator in a sale-and-leaseback type of transaction. The applicable credit risk is that of the originator, subject to any sharia-compliant credit enhancement by the issuer. The recognised ECAI will put weight, in determining the rating, on

[14] Indeed, IFSB-2 is prepared to focus on this type of *ṣukūk*. IFSB-2 clearly states: 'This section is applicable only to *sukūk* or certificates that represent the holder's proportionate ownership in an undivided part of an underlying asset where the holder assumes all rights and obligations to such asset'. See ibid. 47. See also A Dusuki and S Mokhtar, *Critical Appraisal of Shariah Issues on Ownership in Asset-Based Sukuk as Implemented in the Islamic Debt Market* (ISRA 2010) 6.

[15] This stand of IFSB can be understood from both IFSB-2 and IFSB-7. According to IFSB-2: 'This section does not cover certificates that give the holders the entitlement to receive returns on an asset of which the ownership is not transferred to the sukūk holders'. See IFSB, *supra* note 13, 47. However, IFSB-7 asserted that not all *ṣukūk* have real assets in their core. See IFSB, 'Capital Adequacy Requirements for Ṣukūk, Securitisations and Real Estate investment' (*IFSB*, January 2009) 3. http://www.ifsb.org/standard/eng_%20IFSB-7%20Capital%20Adequacy%20Requirements%20for%20Sukuk,%20Securitasations%20and%20Real%20Estate%20investment%20(Jan2009).pdf. Accessed 4 March 2015.

[16] IFSB, *supra* note 15, 3–4.

> the payment schedule of the repurchase undertaking and the capability of the originator to make the scheduled payments to the issuer ... Such structures are sometimes referred to as "pay-through" structures, since the income from the assets is paid to the investors through the issuer.[17]

The second type is described as follows:

> [A] separate issuing entity purchases the underlying assets from the originator, packages them into a pool and acts as the issuer of the *ṣukūk*. This issuing entity requires the originator to give the holders recourse, but provides sharia-compliant credit enhancement by guaranteeing repayment in case of default by the originator.[18]

It seems that IFSB in its new attempt to define asset-based *ṣukūk* has categorised them into two groups after further looking at how assets are transferred and owned in line with conventional finance terminologies and concepts. Given that the terms 'pay-through' and 'pass-through' are conventional terms used to refer to specific types of mortgage-backed securities,[19] one may wonder on what grounds IFSB provided such terms. In this regard, Rider states '[i]t should be noted that, notwithstanding the underlying assets, returns paid to the investors may not be associated with the actual performance of those assets, as the securitisation may be done under a "pay-through" or "pass-through" *sukūk* structure'.[20]

It is probably fair to say that the above definitions do not provide sufficient description of asset-based *ṣukūk*. They vary, and each definition touches upon some elements of asset-based *ṣukūk*. The picture around asset-based *ṣukūk* becomes clearer in the following discussion on its basic structures and primary features.

4.3 Structure of Asset-Based *Ṣukūk*

In order to understand the structure of asset-based *ṣukūk*, it is worth highlighting that it resembles bond issuance in conventional finance. The similarity between asset-based *ṣukūk* and unsecured conventional bonds is

[17] Ibid.

[18] Ibid. 4.

[19] See E Ferran, *Mortgage Securitisation-Legal Aspects* (Butterworths 1992) 23.

[20] B Rider, 'Legal Aspects of Islamic Asset Securitisation' in IFSB (ed), *Strategies for the Development of Islamic Capital Markets: Infrastructures and Legal Aspects of Islamic Asset Securitisation* (IFSB 2011) 145.

confirmed by many commentators such as Dusuki and Mokhtar,[21] Ahmed,[22] and Haneef.[23] Each issue of asset-based *ṣukūk* tends to have its own specific variations and attributes. Therefore, it would be inappropriate to assume that all issues of asset-based *ṣukūk* fall under a standard format. However, following are four main structures in which the performance of *ṣukūk* is linked to the credit risk of the originator, and not driven by the asset backing the deal. This is essentially the basic theme of all asset-based *ṣukūk*. These are as follows:

1. A *ṣukūk* structure involving incomplete transfer of ownership or beneficial ownership
2. A *ṣukūk* structure involving creation of indebtedness
3. A *ṣukūk* structure involving a sale and buy-back transaction
4. A *ṣukūk* structure involving an originator's undertaking

A *ṣukūk* structure is described as asset based when it involves beneficial ownership or incomplete transfer of the underlying asset from the originator to the SPV. In this regard, Al-Amine states that:

> [I]t is asset-based when mere beneficial ownership has been transferred to investors … the transfer of ownership in such a sale/purchase agreement between the issuer and the originator would be only beneficial ownership and would not involve full legal title.[24]

While there is a true sale or complete transfer of ownership in asset-backed *ṣukūk* as demonstrated in Chap. 3 (see Fig. 3.1), the asset transfer in this form of asset-based structure is not legally completed. It is asset based because *ṣukūk* holders do not enjoy all rights associated with the ownership. For example, the beneficial ownership does not provide them with the right to dispose of the assets in the event of default. Therefore, they

[21] A Dusuki and S Mokhtar, *supra* note 14, 11.

[22] H Ahmed, 'Islamic Finance at a Crossroads: The Dominance of the Asset-Based Sukuk' (2010) 6 Journal of International Banking and Financial Law 366.

[23] R Haneef, 'From Asset-Backed to Asset-Light Structures: The Intricate History of Sukuk' (2009) 1 ISRA International Journal of Islamic Finance 103, 110.

[24] M Al-Amine, 'Unresolved Sharīʿah Issues in Ṣukūk' in Kamali M and Abdullah A (eds), *Islamic Finance: Issues in Ṣukūk and Proposals for Reform* (International Intitute of Advanced Islamic Studies and Islamic Foundation 2014) 35.

rely very much on the originator rather than the asset in question. In other words, the notion of beneficial ownership in asset-based structure links the economic performance of *ṣukūk* with the credit risk of the originator.

As for a *ṣukūk* structure involving creation of indebtedness, a best illustration of such structure is *murābaḥah ṣukūk* for asset acquisition. In such structure, the underlying asset is not income generating, and the returns on *ṣukūk* are created by way of selling the underlying asset by the SPV to the originator. In essence, the originator is in need of the underlying asset, but the originator does not have the sufficient liquidity to buy it. The SPV buys the asset in question from the supplier or dealer and then sells it to the originator. The difference between the purchase price and sale price forms the source of income to *ṣukūk* holders. Such structure is an asset-based *ṣukūk* because *ṣukūk* holders rely on the ability of the originator to make payments on *ṣukūk* (see Fig. 4.1). It is the transaction between the SPV (seller) and the originator (buyer) that creates the income stream rather than the asset in question. The structure shows (1) the SPV issues *ṣukūk* to raise funds; (2) the SPV buys the asset from the supplier; (3) the SPV sells the asset to the originator at a mark-up for a deferred price;

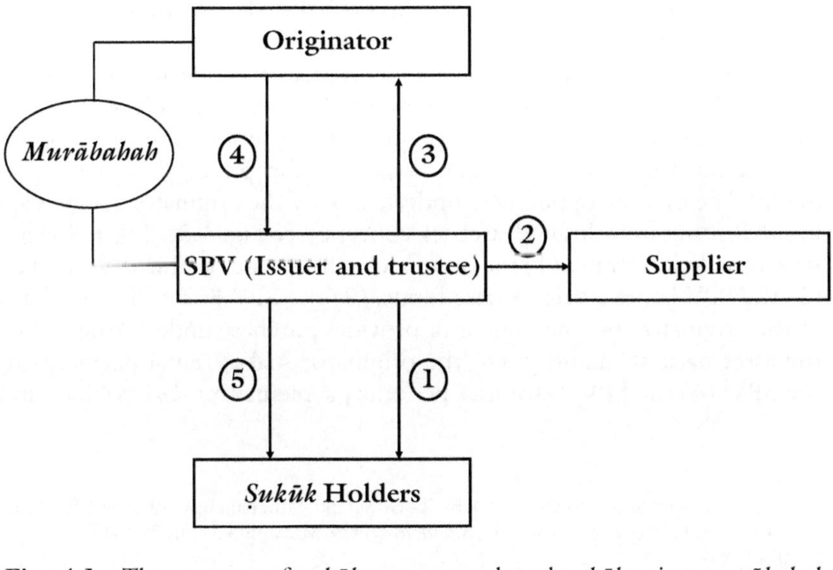

Fig. 4.1 The concept of *ṣukūk* as an asset-based *ṣukūk* using *murābaḥah*. Source: Author

(4) the originator makes periodic payments to the SPV, and (5) the SPV distributes periodic payments to *ṣukūk* holders.[25]

Pertaining to a *ṣukūk* structure involving a sale and buy-back transaction, a best example of such type is *bayʿ al-ʿīnah ṣukūk* (sale and buy-back transaction). This is also referred to as two-party *murābaḥah ṣukūk*; the former name is the accurate term. In such a structure, the originator has the asset at the time of issuance, as opposed to the first type of asset-based structure (*murābaḥah ṣukūk* for asset acquisition). The structure involves sell and buy-back transaction between the originator and the SPV. There is no supplier or dealer involved in this structure. The underlying asset moves between two parties and eventually stays with the originator (the original owner). The returns on *ṣukūk* are created by the difference between the sale price (spot and lower) and purchase price (deferred and higher). This structure is an asset-based *ṣukūk* because the returns on *ṣukūk* depend on the credit quality of the originator, and the asset in question does not play an effective role. In essence, the underlying asset used is not the purpose of the whole arrangement (see Fig. 4.2). The figure demonstrates (1) the originator sells its asset to the SPV for cash; (2) the SPV issues *ṣukūk* to raise funds; (3) the SPV sells the asset back to the originator at a mark-up price for a deferred price; (4) the originator makes periodic payments of the sale price; and (5) the SPV distributes periodic payments to *ṣukūk* holders.[26]

As for a *ṣukūk* structure involving an originator's undertaking, an illustration of this is a structure that involves 'a "purchase undertaking" from the originator or an affiliate to repurchase the asset at maturity (or upon early termination) for an amount equal to the principal repayment(s) due'.[27] The exercise of purchase undertaking by the originator can be seen in *ṣukūk* using the sale and leaseback concept (see Fig. 4.3). The following structure demonstrates (1) the originator sells its asset to the SPV for cash; (2) the SPV issues *ṣukūk* to raise funds; (3) the SPV leases the asset back to the originator; (4) the originator provides purchase undertaking to buy the asset back at maturity; (5) the originator makes rental payments to the SPV; (6) the SPV distributes periodic payments to *ṣukūk* holders; and

[25] See A Thomas and S Mokhtar, 'Debt-Based Sukuk: Murabahah, Istisna' and Istithmar (Tawarruq) Sukuk' in A Thomas (ed), *Sukuk* (Sweet & Maxwell Asia 2009) 131.

[26] Ibid. 132.

[27] K Howladar, *supra* note 2, 8.

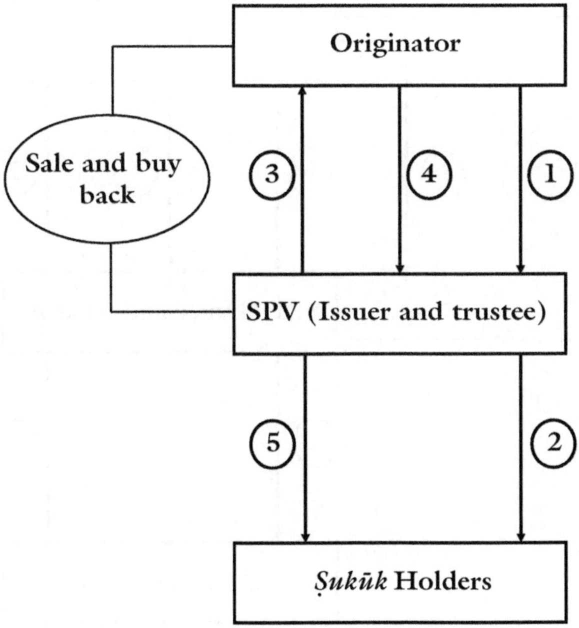

Fig. 4.2 The concept of *ṣukūk* as an asset-based *ṣukūk* using *bayʿ al-ʿīnah*. Source: Author

(7) the originator buys that asset back at maturity by exercising the purchase undertaking.[28]

Careful consideration needs to be taken when looking at the *ṣukūk* structure involving sale and leaseback transaction (known as sale and leaseback *ṣukūk* or *ijārah ṣukūk* sale and leaseback). In this structure, the originator is essentially in need of liquidity and therefore sells the asset that it owns to the SPV. Then the SPV leases back the asset in question to the originator (the original owner). The income stream in this structure is generated by way of leasing the asset back to the originator. In order to be considered an asset-based structure, it should involve purchase undertaking as described above. It is considered an asset-backed structure when it does not involve purchase undertaking (for an amount equal to the issuance price) because the income stream depends on the performance of the

[28] S Mokhtar and A Thomas, 'Ijarah Sukuk' in Thomas A (ed), *Sukuk* (Sweet & Maxwell Asia 2009) 153.

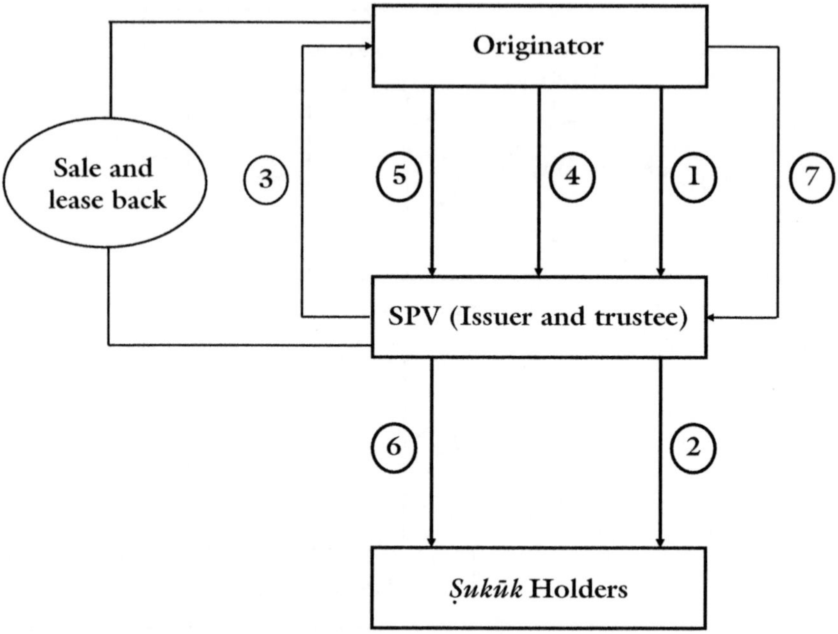

Fig. 4.3 The concept of *ṣukūk* as an asset-based *ṣukūk* using sale and leaseback. Source: Author

asset. For those who consider sale and leaseback transaction as a form of *bayʿ al-ʿīnah*, the sale and leaseback *ṣukūk* is viewed as an asset-based *ṣukūk*. This is explained in Chap. 6. Another example for a *ṣukūk* structure involving an originator's undertaking is a *mushārakah ṣukūk*, in which 'the income stream may actually be directly funded by the purchase undertaking, without preliminary recourse to profit distribution'.[29]

Before leaving the discussion on how asset-based *ṣukūk* are structured in the market, it is interesting to look at the perspective of SC in this area and assess whether it is meaningful. SC divides asset-based *ṣukūk* into four groups[30]:

1. Sales-based *ṣukūk*: BBA, *murābaḥah* (a sale with a mark-up), *salam* (a forward sale (fungible commodity)), and *istiṣnāʿ* (contract of manufacture).

[29] K Howladar, *supra* note 2, 9.
[30] SC, *supra* note 1, 48.

2. Lease-based *ṣukūk*: *ijārah*, *ijārah muntahiyah biāltamlīk* (operating lease of property), and *ijārah mawṣūfah fī al-dhimah* (lease of described future assets or services).
3. Partnership-based *ṣukūk*: *muḍārabah* (investment partnership) and *mushārakah* (participation financing).
4. Agency-based *ṣukūk*: *wakālah biālistithmār* (investment agency).

Looking at the above classification of asset-based *ṣukūk*, one can say that it is misleading and does not make sense. SC's perspective on asset-based *ṣukūk* does not help in understanding how asset-based *ṣukūk* are designed in the market. It includes structures that can be classified as asset backed or asset based. As Muhamed and Radzi noted, '*ṣukūk ijārah* may be asset-based or asset-backed, yielding a wholly different risk profile in the event of default and liquidation'.[31] Therefore, one cannot describe a particular structure as asset backed or asset based by looking at the name or label of the sharia contract used. It is an asset-backed *ṣukūk* if all securitisation elements are achieved, and it is asset based if any securitisation element is missed. The substance of the asset-based structure shall be more obvious with further explanation below of the primary features of such *ṣukūk*.

4.4 Essential Pillars of Asset-Based *Ṣukūk*

The absence of securitisation elements is the distinguishing feature of asset-based *ṣukūk*. From the above-mentioned asset-based structures, one identifies four primary features of the concept of *ṣukūk* as an asset-based structure. These are as follows: (1) dependence on the creditworthiness of the originator; (2) ineffective role of the underlying asset, and (3) originator's undertaking (purchase undertaking and make-up for shortfall on returns). If all or some of these elements exist in the *ṣukūk* structure, it is described as an asset-based structure.

As for the dependence on the creditworthiness of the originator, this element means that *ṣukūk* holders in asset-based structure depend on the ability of the originator to make payments on *ṣukūk*. In other words, the originator in an asset-based structure is responsible for the *ṣukūk* payments, and not the asset in question. The economic performance of asset-based structure is linked to the creditworthiness of the originator.[32] The dependence on the originator in asset-based structure implies that there is

[31] N Muhamed and R Radzi, *supra* note 5, 2452.
[32] P Lotter, *supra* note 9, 5.

a credit connection between the originator and the underlying asset.[33] Hence, the credit risk in asset-based structures is that of originator, and not the underlying asset. This explains why the disclosure of *ṣukūk* documents and circulars focuses very much on the performance profile and balance sheet of the originator rather than the underlying asset.[34]

The reasons for the reliance on the originator in asset-based *ṣukūk* vary. One of the reasons is related to the way the asset is transferred to the SPV. In this regard, asset-based *ṣukūk* does not involve real transfer of the underlying asset but rather a beneficial ownership transfer.[35] As noted by Hassoune, Howladar, and Harris, the 'asset transfer is essentially in form rather than in substance'.[36] A good illustration of this point is when the asset transfer is not legally completed due to absence of the registration.[37] In such a situation, ownership title and risks associated with underlying assets do not move to *ṣukūk* holders.

Pertaining to the ineffective role of the underlying asset, this element is concerned with the key role of the asset in asset-based *ṣukūk*. The underlying asset is the backbone of every *ṣukūk* structure. While the asset exists at the core of the asset-based *ṣukūk*, this asset does not play a genuine function for several reasons. The underlying asset in asset-based *ṣukūk* is typically not income generating. Further, the transaction between *ṣukūk* originator and SPV is the one that generates returns for *ṣukūk* holders, as opposed to the underlying asset. The asset in asset-based structures remains on the books of the originators from an accounting perspective.[38] In addition, the primary role of the underlying asset is to facilitate and strengthen the structure's sharia compliance rather than serving as a source of return and principal payments.[39] Although the underlying assets can be seen in the *ṣukūk* structure, the credit reliance or connection to originator remains.[40] The securitised assets in asset-based *ṣukūk* are not qualified for derecognition, owing to the exclusive recourse to the originator.[41] The

[33] Ibid. 6.

[34] D Dey and S Ure, 'Islamic Securitisation' in R Ali (ed), *Sukuk and Islamic Capital Markets* (Globe Business Publishing 2011) 147.

[35] Z Akhtar, *supra* note 12; IIFM, 'IIFM Ṣukūk Report 1st Edition' (*IIFM*, 2010) 18. http://www.iifm.net/documents/iifm-sukuk-report-1st-edition. Accessed 4 March 2015.

[36] A Hassoune, K Howladar and S Harris, 'The Meaning of Ratings for Islamic Financial Institutions and Sharīʿah -Compliant Instruments' in IFSB (ed), *The Changing Landscape of Islamic Finance: Imminent Challenges and Future Directions* (IFSB 2010) 153.

[37] B Rider, *supra* note 20, 162.

[38] A Dusuki and S Mokhtar, *supra* note 14, 28.

[39] Ibid. 28; M Al-Amine, *supra* note 24, 36–37.

[40] K Howladar, *supra* note 2, 10.

[41] IFSB, *supra* note 15, 8.

originator in asset-based *ṣukūk* cannot exclude the underlying assets from the calculation of its risk-weighted assets, as opposed to in asset-backed *ṣukūk*.[42] This clearly proves the ineffectiveness of the asset in question in asset-based *ṣukūk*.

With regard to the third determining feature of asset-based *ṣukūk*, originator's undertaking refers to two types of undertaking provided by the originator: purchase undertaking and undertaking to make up for shortfall on returns. According to the Moody's, purchase undertaking is a key feature of an asset-based *ṣukūk*.[43] Purchase undertaking exists in most *ṣukūk* issued from 2001 to 2009 as provided by IIFM *Ṣukūk* Report 1st Edition.[44] Briefly, purchase undertaking means that the originator will purchase the assets from the issuer for an amount equal to the principal value in particular eventualities, namely maturity, dissolution of trust, pre-defined early termination, and default of the transaction.[45] Repurchase undertaking aims to separate the arrangement from a negative performance of the underlying asset.[46] In this respect, Moody's notes that purchase undertaking is exercised by originators for the purpose of supporting the credit quality of the *ṣukūk*.[47] Where purchase undertaking exists within the structure, it is deemed one of the payment sources for *ṣukūk* holders.[48] In other words, it is a tool that facilitates the creation of an amount owed to *ṣukūk* holders.[49]

Understanding the consequences of having purchase undertaking in a *ṣukūk* structure is of particular significance. As a result of the presence of purchase undertaking in asset-based structure, *ṣukūk* holders do not encounter asset risk in the form of asset price fluctuation.[50] The existence of purchase undertaking fundamentally changes the credit risk of the

[42] Ibid.

[43] P Lotter, *supra* note 9, 1. See also A Hassoune, K Howladar and S Harris, *supra* note 36, 160.

[44] IIFM, *supra* note 35, 18.

[45] P Lotter, *supra* note 9, 4; A Hassoune, K Howladar and S Harris, *supra* note 36, 160.

[46] A Jobst, 'IMF Working Paper WP/07/117: The Economics of Islamic Finance and Securitization' (*IMF*, 2007) 20. http://www.imf.org/external/pubs/ft/wp/2007/wp07117.pdf. Accessed 20 August 2013.

[47] K Howladar, *supra* note 2, 10.

[48] A Dusuki and S Mokhtar, *supra* note 14, 26.

[49] B Rider, *supra* note 20, 191.

[50] A Dusuki and S Mokhtar, *supra* note 14, 26.

ṣukūk transaction.[51] For instance, credit risk exposure of *ṣukūk* holders will be for the corporation or sovereign that provided purchase undertaking.[52] Also, the market value of the underlying assets becomes unimportant from the *ṣukūk* holders standpoint since the amount is already identified to be equal to the issuance price.[53] Further, it is important to understand that the purchase undertaking is ranked *pari passu* with any other senior unsecured obligations of the originator.[54] For instance, in the event that the originator fails to meet its obligation to purchase the assets, the *ṣukūk* holders are in neither a better nor weaker place than other creditors.[55] In addition, purchase undertaking makes the issue of whether the asset is able to generate adequate returns on *ṣukūk* is irrelevant to *ṣukūk* holders because they are assured their returns by the originator's purchase undertaking.[56]

In relation to the undertaking to make up for shortfall on returns, there is a possibility that a *ṣukūk* asset or venture generates less than periodic distribution amounts, forming a worrying mismatch. According to the Moody's, the originator's liability to make up for shortfall on returns constitutes a primary feature of an asset-based *ṣukūk*.[57] This is normally solved in the form of compensation against any deficit by the originator or guarantor, giving this structure the fixed-income feature of a conventional bond.[58] Meeting any shortfall in the transaction indicates that profit payment is the crucial responsibility of the originator, not the asset in question.[59]

Although the above-mentioned elements vary considerably, they share in restricting the effective function of underlying assets and contributing to further reliance on the originator. Inevitably, the above discussion reveals worrying sharia and legal issues that are beyond the scope of this chapter. What we seek here is understanding the nature of asset-based *ṣukūk*, and not exploring the varieties of sharia threats that arise.

[51] K Howladar, *supra* note 2, 10.
[52] Ibid.
[53] P Lotter, *supra* note 9, 5.
[54] Ibid. 4.
[55] Ibid. 5–6.
[56] A Dusuki and S Mokhtar, *supra* note 14, 26.
[57] A Hassoune, K Howladar and S Harris, *supra* note 36, 160.
[58] Ibid. 152.
[59] P Lotter, *supra* note 9, 4.

4.5 Asset-Based *Ṣukūk*: Structural Motivations and Pitfalls

Having explored how asset-based *ṣukūk* are designed and structured, the focus of discussion shifts to the pros and cons of such structure in view of market practice.

4.5.1 Advantages

Given the benefits of asset-backed *ṣukūk* as mentioned in Chap. 3, what justifications can there be for asset-based *ṣukūk*? Some advocates of asset-based *ṣukūk* argue that it is an appropriate structure and preferable choice in many legal environments in which setting up a proper SPV that meets the fiduciary responsibilities is difficult from a legal point of view.[60] For instance, the requirement of transferring beneficial title of the assets to *ṣukūk* holders is not possible in such jurisdictions.[61] Asset-based *ṣukūk* is a feasible structure in jurisdictions where there is uncertainty in relation to whether *ṣukūk* holders have the ability to use their rights and repossess the underlying asset in the event of default.[62] For illustration, if an effective right of possession in the event of default cannot be exercised by *ṣukūk* holders because of the nature of ownership rights concerning the underlying asset in an applicable legal environment, recourse moves to the originator. *Ṣukūk* holders prefer asset-based *ṣukūk* because they will not encounter any volatility of the value of the underlying asset due to predetermination of purchase price via purchase undertaking.[63] Given the presence of purchase undertaking in asset-based structures, *ṣukūk* holders not only avoid risk of loss, but also benefit from cash flow and principal guarantee.[64] Additionally, a standard argument used to justify asset-based *ṣukūk* is that it offers to some extent less risky investment prospects for *ṣukūk* holders because they face only the credit risk of the originator.[65] Given that the credit risk in asset-based *ṣukūk* is that of the originator, the

[60] IFSB, *supra* note 15, 4.

[61] Ibid.

[62] Ibid.

[63] P Lotter, *supra* note 9, 3.

[64] A Dusuki and S Mokhtar, *supra* note 14, 29.

[65] IIFM, 'IIFM Ṣukūk Report 2nd Edition: A Comprehensive Study of the Global Sukuk Market' (*IIFM*, 2011) 38. http://www.iifm.net/documents/iifm-sukuk-report-2nd-edition-comprehensive-study-global-sukuk-market. Accessed 4 March 2015.

structure will take advantage of an investment-grade credit rating of a highly rated sovereign.[66] Another perceived advantage is the credit enhancement provided by the originator in a pass-through structure, which enables the issuance to achieve an investment-grade credit rating.[67] Asset-based *ṣukūk* provide originators with unsecured funding since they do not have to give up their asset to obtain money.[68] Furthermore, the originators in asset-based *ṣukūk* are at liberty to use the money obtained from *ṣukūk* issuance for any object.[69] Another potential benefit is that payments to *ṣukūk* holders are made from originator's whole operations, and not necessarily from returns produced by the asset.[70] Asset-based structure contains a liquidity facility which is provided by the originator in the event of shortfall of cash flow.[71] An additional argument in favour of asset-based *ṣukūk* is that it lets originators enjoy little or no cost arising from disclosure obligations on the assets.[72] Neither legal nor financial due diligence on asset transfer is practised in asset-based *ṣukūk*, and therefore this reduces structural costs from an originator's perspective.[73] It is also argued that *ṣukūk* holders do not have to worry about their periodic returns and capital amount in asset-based structure since they are already guaranteed.[74]

4.5.2 *Disadvantages*

The opinions outlined above might seem to suggest that *ṣukūk* originators and investors should opt for asset-based *ṣukūk*. However, this structure may cause several legal uncertainties and threats to all *ṣukūk* parties, particularly the *ṣukūk* holders, owing to the absence of a true sale transaction.[75] A familiar criticism is that *ṣukūk* holders of asset-based *ṣukūk* are unsecured investors and have no reference to the underlying asset.[76]

[66] IFSB, *supra* note 15, 5.

[67] Ibid.

[68] A Dusuki and S Mokhtar, *supra* note 14, 27.

[69] Ibid.

[70] Ibid. 27–28.

[71] IIFM, *supra* note 65, 37.

[72] Ibid.

[73] Ibid. 38.

[74] Ibid.

[75] J Nazar, 'Regulatory and Financial Implications of Sukuk's Legal Challenges for Sustainable Sukuk Development in Islamic Capital Market' (8th International Conference on Islamic Economics and Finance, Qatar, December 2011) 12.

[76] IIFM, *supra* note 65, 38.

Therefore, they are not in a different position from an originator's unsecured creditors.[77] Even if the asset is secured in asset-based structure, the amount arising from selling the asset will be used to pay liabilities only and *ṣukūk* holders will not enjoy the balance amount.[78] Also, the presence of purchase undertaking makes the structure equal to a pure debt instrument.[79] When a security is provided to *ṣukūk* holders by the originator, this is not necessarily linked to the underlying assets.[80] Another disadvantage of asset-based *ṣukūk* is the legal risk caused via a purchase undertaking in some jurisdictions. It is open to debate to what extent such purchase undertaking is enforceable or applicable under various legal environments.[81] Furthermore, it is uncertain how asset-based *ṣukūk* is ranked or prioritised within the whole capital structure of the originator.[82] Another argument against asset-based *ṣukūk* is that there is a possibility that it obtains lower rating when senior claims impair *ṣukūk* holders' claims; this also can be seen in a subordinated conventional bond.[83] When the originator is from a private sector, reaching satisfactory investment-grade credit rating will be difficult and problematic.[84] Moreover, sharia concerns surrounding asset-based *ṣukūk*[85] make such a structure less attractive for those seeking strict compliance with Islamic law. For example, asset-based *ṣukūk* incorporates several forms of capital protection that require further consideration from an Islamic law perspective.[86] Chapter 6 is devoted to the discussion of such issues. The indebtedness created through purchase undertaking is another burden on the originator.[87] Misconception arises from asset-based *ṣukūk*, for example, assuming that they provide investors with absolute propriety rights.[88]

[77] Ibid.
[78] Ibid.
[79] Ibid.
[80] Ibid.
[81] IFSB, *supra* note 15, 5.
[82] Ibid.
[83] P Lotter, *supra* note 9, 4.
[84] IFSB, *supra* note 15, 5.
[85] A Dusuki and S Mokhtar, *supra* note 14, 29.
[86] IIFM, *supra* note 65, 40.
[87] Ibid.
[88] B Rider, *supra* note 20, 191.

4.6 Asset-Based *Ṣukūk*: Is It a Staging Post to Asset-Backed Structure?

As of August 2009, asset-based *ṣukūk* forms around 98% of the *ṣukūk* structures in the global market.[89] In this regard, SC states that 'more than 90% of all global *ṣukūk* issues in the market are on-balance sheet issues which are asset based'.[90] One may ask why asset-based *ṣukūk* is more common than asset-backed *ṣukūk*. The above-mentioned advantages of asset-based *ṣukūk* explain the increasing popularity and issuances of this particular type of *ṣukūk*. In particular, investor appetite factor helps to explain the overwhelming percentage of asset-based *ṣukūk*, since sovereign risk tends to drive the structure more than the underlying asset risk.[91] Essentially, the risk related to the issuer is the one that investors are interested in when they purchase *ṣukūk*, and not risk of the project undertaken.[92] This is partially attributed to the current practice of rating agencies where the approach of rating is similar for both *ṣukūk* and conventional bonds.[93] This is compounded by the absence of a rating agency that is primarily established to deal with the *ṣukūk* industry (independent *ṣukūk* rating agency).[94] Also, the number of asset-based *ṣukūk* has increased because originators tend to avoid a common law true sale 'by entering into what appeared to be a sale, but was not a perfect sale at all'.[95] Moreover, financial institutions contributed to increasing number of asset-based structures by offering structures akin to conventional bonds with which investors have experience and familiarity.[96]

Exploring some issues that exist in the general legal environment may provide more understanding of the popularity of asset-based *ṣukūk*. This harks back to the reasons for lack of asset-backed *ṣukūk* as discussed in

[89] H Ahmed, *supra* note 22; A Dusuki and S Mokhtar, *supra* note 14, 8.

[90] SC, *supra* note 1, 48–49.

[91] A Jobst and others, 'Islamic Bond Issuance: What Sovereign Debt Managers Need to Know' (2008) 1 International Journal of Islamic and Middle Eastern Finance and Management 330, 333.

[92] J Nazar, *supra* note 75, 10.

[93] Ibid.

[94] Ibid.

[95] P Wouters, 'Asset-Backed Sukuk—Islamic Finance Going its Own Way' (*Islamic Finance News*, 2011). http://www.fimm.com.my/%5Cpdf%5CProduct%20Knowledge%5C30Mac11_Asset-backed%20Sukuk.pdf. Accessed 12 March 2013, 23.

[96] D Dey and S Ure, *supra* note 34, 147.

Chap. 3. The currently inadequate legal infrastructure increased the investor desire for asset-based *ṣukūk*, particularly underdeveloped insolvency laws.[97] The securitisation system is underdeveloped in many countries and lacks components addressing important concerns, such as a foreign ownership.[98] For instance, it is uncertain whether an offshore SPV is legally allowed to own assets in these jurisdictions.[99] Therefore, IFSB states that:

> Asset-based structures in Islamic finance are found in cases where, given the applicable legal environment, the ownership rights over the underlying asset may not reliably result in an effective right of possession in case of default, and in consequence, the *ṣukūk* holders need to have a right of recourse to the originator in case of default.[100]

After discussing the concept of *ṣukūk* as either asset backed or asset based, one may ask about the optimal *ṣukūk* structure, particularly after the emphasis that is currently being put on the soundness and stability of IFSI. There is a clear preference for asset-backed *ṣukūk* in the academic literature, as opposed to asset-based *ṣukūk*. In this respect, Dusuki and Mokhtar say 'asset-backed *ṣukūk* clearly fulfil the sharia requirement and dispel all the contentious fundamental issues ... Hence, there is a need to move towards more asset-backed *ṣukūk* in the market'.[101] However, this point can be challenged and turned around. There are asset-based *ṣukūk* that do not contradict with Islamic law; a good illustration of this is the concept of *ṣukūk* as an asset-based *ṣukūk* using *murābaḥah*. Therefore, one cannot give a general ruling about asset-based *ṣukūk*, negatively or positively. In a contemporary business environment, particularly against the background of financial crises, it is evident that there is an important need for asset-backed financing. However, this discussion should not be simply taken as a proof for preference of asset-backed over asset-based arrangements or vice versa. Bearing in mind its commercial nature, one may think that asset-based *ṣukūk* is an IOU document.[102] Although its economic

[97] A Dusuki and S Mokhtar, *supra* note 14, 11.
[98] Ibid.
[99] Ibid.
[100] IFSB, *supra* note 15, 4.
[101] A Dusuki and S Mokhtar, *supra* note 14, 29.
[102] R Ali, 'An Overview of the Sukuk Market' in R Ali (ed), *Sukuk and Islamic Capital Markets: A Practical Guide* (Globe Business Publishing 2011) 8.

benefits are similar to conventional bond, the means by which it is formed is totally different.[103] Whether an asset-backed or asset-based structure is more effective will depend crucially on the market development and country's legal framework. Therefore, asset-based *ṣukūk* is not a post staging towards asset-backed *ṣukūk* because the concept of *ṣukūk* lies on both of them.

4.7 Conclusion

The main question that has been dealt with in the literature is whether *ṣukūk* should be asset backed or asset based. This question seems to ignore the fact that *ṣukūk* structure takes two forms, which are asset backed or asset based. It also assumes that one of the *ṣukūk* forms should dominate the market. Therefore, the discussion of the division of *ṣukūk* into asset backed or asset based has concentrated on the sharia compliance issues rather than the birth of this new classification. This question has shifted the focus of relevant studies from understanding the substance of the subject matter. Many discussions have been made based on the assumption that one of them is not sharia-compliant, and thus it should discontinue in the market. This has led to the conclusion that asset-based *ṣukūk* is not sharia-compliant. Such a statement has ignored that fact that some forms of asset-based *ṣukūk* are acceptable in Islamic law. Thus, it is the source and substance of this division that should have been tackled, and not only the form of this division.

Having discussed the concept of *ṣukūk* as both asset backed and asset based, one can draw some differences between them. The role of the underlying asset within both structures is the starting point to distinguish between asset-backed and asset-based structures. While the asset exists in both structures, its role varies depending on the underlying structure. The role of the underlying asset in asset-backed *ṣukūk* is genuine, meaning it plays a vital role in the profitability of the *ṣukūk*. The asset in an asset-backed structure is the main source for returns on *ṣukūk*. In contrast, the asset in asset-based structure does not play a significant role in *ṣukūk* profitability. Rather, the transaction between the originator and the SPV, that facilitates the asset transfer, produces the profit in asset-based *ṣukūk*. Another important difference is related to the use of the *ṣukūk* proceeds. While the capital amount in asset-backed arrangements is directly invested

[103] Ibid.

in a portfolio of assets that generate cash flows, the capital amounts in asset-based structure are utilised to purchase the assets that is then sold or leased back to the original seller. As a result, the returns come from the underlying asset in the former. Although the earning occurs effectively in the latter because of the asset, it comes actually from the seller or lessor in the form of purchase price plus profit or rental payments. When looking at the asset-based structure, one sees that it is entirely based on *ṣukūk* originator. The techniques involved in asset-based structures, such as purchase undertaking, result in less reference to the underlying asset. As seen in this chapter, asset-based *ṣukūk* was designed in response to less devolved Islamic financial markets and legal infrastructure in particular. This has brought structural changes as well as a trend towards originator's recourse *ṣukūk*. The difference between asset-backed and asset-based structures cannot be comprehended without reference to the way the asset transfer is perfected. While there is a complete ownership in the former, incomplete ownership exists in the latter. Complete ownership results from a true sale transaction between the originator and the SPV. This leads to the transfer of the asset along with all associated rights. In contrast, incomplete ownership results from the absence of a true sale transaction. Certain rights associated with ownership are only transferred via incomplete ownership. The notion of legal ownership vis-à-vis beneficial ownership that originates from the English Common Law system has influenced the construction of ownership in both asset-backed and asset based *ṣukūk*.

The above can potentially be problematic, since the investors' understanding of *ṣukūk* structure still does not exclude the effective role of the asset within the entire operation. An area that needs further explanation in asset-backed and asset-based *ṣukūk* is the impact of these structures on investor protection, given the different regimes in which *sukūk* is offered as well as issued. It is crucial to form a comparative overview on the various impacts of both structures on investor protection, not only to develop the *ṣukūk* market but, more importantly, to ensure the soundness of the IFSI. Added to all the above is a serious oversight that there is no equal guidance as to how investors make an informed decision regarding selection of *ṣukūk*, let alone what exactly would happen to investors in the event of defaults. The next chapter examines the consequences of default in *ṣukūk* markets and whether the impacts of default events vary depending on the *ṣukūk* structure, whether asset backed or asset based.

CHAPTER 5

Default in the *Ṣukūk* Market: A Case Study of Default and Near-Default *Ṣukūk* Issuances

5.1 Introduction

The primary focus of this chapter is an examination of default and near-default in the *ṣukūk* (trust investment certificates) market; at a fundamental level, the issue of default and its implications in *ṣukūk* markets relates to the underlying structure of *ṣukūk*. Again, the significance of the division of *ṣukūk* between asset backed and asset based manifests in the event of default. This chapter shall explore the consequences of default scenario on different *ṣukūk* structures, and look at the behaviour of asset-backed and asset-based *ṣukūk* in the default event. This is of particular significance in order to understand whether the two structures react differently in the default situation. This analysis of default in the *ṣukūk* market contributes towards further understanding of *ṣukūk* structure, particularly the distinction between asset-backed and asset-based *ṣukūk*.

Further, there is pressing need to discuss default in the context of *ṣukūk* markets because several *ṣukūk* issuances were subject to default over the past few years. This chapter shall outline how such default or near-default cases have been dealt with in different jurisdictions, and examine the reasons behind *ṣukūk* defaults. This discussion shall lead to several questions that arise in the context of *ṣukūk* defaults, particularly in relation to legal resolutions of *ṣukūk* defaults and the relevance of Islamic law of insolvency.

As a prelude to the more detailed discussion that follows later, this chapter begins by outlining the concept of default within the IFSI. It then

S. Al-Ali, *Raising Capital on* Ṣukūk *Markets*,
https://doi.org/10.1007/978-3-030-14536-1_5

considers Islamic law of insolvency and its applicability in the event of *ṣukūk* defaults, given the sharia-compliant nature of *ṣukūk* transactions. This chapter examines seven problematic *ṣukūk* that were subject to default, near-default, or financial uncertainty. Legal concerns arising from default and near-default events of these *ṣukūk* and how regulators have responded to such problematic cases are among the issues considered in this chapter.

5.2 Theoretical Investigation of the Nature of Default in the IFSI

This section considers, in a rudimentary way, the nature of default in the IFSI and outlines key concerns that are associated with the occurrence of default in the *ṣukūk* market. A good grasp of the default notion in the IFSI is significant before addressing default or near-default cases in *ṣukūk* markets.

5.2.1 The Concept of Default in the IFSI

In spite of a number of recent default cases of Islamic financial products, particularly *ṣukūk* and home financing, the concept of default has not received adequate attention in the existing academic literature. Sundararajan argues that the definition of default in the context of different Islamic financial instruments requires further analysis.[1] There is less agreement on what the concept of default is, let alone the events that actually constitute default. Indeed, the consensus of whether the concept of default exists in the IFSI is not absolute, and there is debate as to the possibility of considering default in respect of Islamic financial transactions. Some people do not see the default scenario as possible, clearly rejecting the idea that considers default an issue in the IFSI. This view is justified by the key specificities of Islamic financial transactions, particularly profit-sharing and risk-avoidance nature.[2] Another justification for the opponents of default occurrence in the IFSI is the interpretation of default under Islamic law.

[1] V Sundararajan, 'Profit Sharing Investment Accounts: Measurement and Control of Displaced Commercial Risk (DCR) In Islamic Finance' (undated) 19 Islamic Economic Studies 41, 47.

[2] RAM Rating Services Berhad, *Sukuk Focus May 2010* (RAM Rating Services Berhad 2010) 1.

They argue that 'sharia law doesn't even contemplate a default, because you can't default if all you're ever giving is a profit share. If there are no profits, then you aren't defaulting. You are just deferring, or sitting around the table to discuss'.[3] However, Ahmad and Wahab acknowledged that default can happen in Islamic finance and considered a default-free argument as a misconception.[4] The fact that *ṣukūk* are structured based on the principles of Islamic financial law does not make such structures default-free.[5] Nevertheless, one can say that, from an Islamic law perspective, the default scenario occurs in the context of certain Islamic financial transactions arising from payment default. A good illustration of this point is that Islamic law asks for more flexibility with the defaulting party and extending further time for settlement of debts.

However, careful attention needs to be provided post-default situation and how such an event is dealt with under different transactions from an Islamic law point of view. In this regard, it is argued that '[p]ayment default is contemplated by Islamic finance ... Perhaps what is not contemplated is the unintended consequences of a default in relation to the sharia contract'.[6] Therefore, of particular significance in practical terms will be defining efficiently and effectively the concept of default and its consequences under the laws and standards governing the IFSI. While it is desirable for those responsible for regulating the IFSI to set standards, it is equally important for them to provide a standard definition of default that would facilitate the implementation of such standards.[7] Having in place a standardised and harmonised definition of default will ensure efficient measurement of the probability of default, facilitating informed decisions in relation to rating and risk weights.[8] The absence of a clear description of the default event constitutes a major deterrent to investors

[3] D O'Neill, 'Sukuk Market on Trial as Islamic Bonds Default' (2009) 40 Euromoney 45.

[4] N Ahmad and N Wahab, 'Estimates of Distance-To-Default (DTD) Risk Indicator for Selected Sukuk in Malaysia' (3rd International Conference on Business and Economic Research, Indonesia, March 2012) 2635.

[5] Ibid.

[6] Kadir Andri & Partners, 'Payment Default in Islamic Finance' (*IFLR*). http://www.iflr.com/Article/2452811/Payment-default-in-Islamic-finance.html. Accessed 18 November 2013.

[7] V Sundararajan, *supra* note 1, 46.

[8] Ibid.

in the IFSI. As far as *ṣukūk* default is concerned, it is believed that 'until a *ṣukūk* default is satisfactorily settled, uncertainty will cloud the market'.[9]

Before defining default in the context of *ṣukūk*, it is worth providing a linguistic and conventional finance perspective of the term default. The word 'default' literally means the '[f]ailure to do something required by law, usually failure to comply with mandatory rules of procedure'.[10] In the common financial parlance, the word default refers to the failure to pay an amount due, such as default on loan or mortgage repayment. In this respect, it is useful to refer to rating agencies' definitions of default, as they are critical in assessing default events. According to Standard and Poor's Ratings Services (S&P), the term default means 'the failure to meet a principal or interest payment on the due date (or within the specified grace period) contained in the original terms of the debt issue'.[11] Moody's identifies four events that constitute default for debt or debt-like instruments which are: (1) missed or delayed payment of interest or principal amount; (2) bankruptcy filing against debt issuer or obligor; (3) distressed exchange offered by the obligor to creditors to cover the diminished financial obligation (i.e. restructured debt, new package of securities, and cash or asset); and (4) change in the payment terms of credit agreement.[12] While the definition of S&P is narrower, focusing on the payment default, the definition of Moody's is broader, considering events that may result in future default. Such definitions, however, may raise questions as to whether they are appropriate in the context of IFSI, owing to the primary features of Islamic financial transactions.

For an Islamic finance perspective on *ṣukūk* default, one can look at IFSB-7. Servicer default and issuer default are two events of default that have been described in the IFSB-7 in the context of risk exposure to *ṣukūk*. While the former refers to the originator default in its capacity as a servicer, the latter concerns with the originator failing to pay coupon

[9] R Wigglesworth, 'Fears Rise Over Islamic Bonds' (*Financial Times*, 2009). http://www.ft.com/cms/s/0/7e73fb0a-dac5-11de-933d-00144feabdc0.html#axzz2l0eYFI00. Accessed 18 November 2013.

[10] G Cooch and M Williams, *Oxford Dictionary of Law Enforcement* (Oxford University Press 2007) 160.

[11] S&P, *Ratings Performance 2002: Default, Transition, Recovery, and Spreads* (S&P 2003) 86.

[12] Moody's Investros Service, *Rating Symbols and Definitions* (Moody's Investors Service 2012) 33.

payments and principal amount at the maturity.[13] Besides, it is worth looking at *Tahawwut* (Hedging) Master Agreement (TMA) issued by the IIFM and the International Swaps and Derivatives Association (ISDA) in 2010.[14] To illustrate, a cross-default event of default clause of TMA is concerned with defaults of transactions that have the commercial effect of a borrowing.[15] It is stated that 'defaults under Islamic Financing transactions such as *ṣukūk* would be caught by the cross-default Event of Default clause'.[16] AAOIFI does not have any clause worth mentioning that focuses on default that is relevant in the context of *ṣukūk*. Although AAOIFI issued Sharia Standard No. 3 entitled 'Default in Payment by A Debtor', AAOIFI made it clear that this standard is for solvent debtors, and not for insolvent or bankrupt debtors.[17] This standard is therefore not particularly relevant to defaults under *ṣukūk* since such events occur on the market because of the defaulting party being insolvent.

From the prior discussion, one can clearly see that the default concept in the IFSI, and *ṣukūk* in particular, lacks clarity. This is an area of potential

[13] IFSB, 'Capital Adequacy Requirements for Ṣukūk, Securitisations and Real Estate investment' (*IFSB*, January 2009) 7. http://www.ifsb.org/standard/eng_%20IFSB-7%20Capital%20Adequacy%20Requirements%20for%20Sukuk,%20Securitasations%20and%20Real%20Estate%20investment%20(Jan2009).pdf. Accessed 4 March 2015.

[14] This is the first standardised document for cross-border transactions concerned with hedging products in Islamic finance. For more information, see IIFM and ISDA, 'IFM and ISDA Launch Tahawwut (Hedging) Master Agreement' (*ISDA*, 2010). http://www.isda.org/media/press/2010/press030110.html. Accessed 18 November 2013.

[15] Section (1) of the cross-default clause states 'a default, event of default or other similar condition or event (however described) in respect of such party, any Credit Support Provider of such party or any applicable Specified Entity of such party under one or more agreements or instruments relating to Specified Obligations of any of them (individually or collectively) where the aggregate of the principal and amount equivalent to principal of such agreements or instruments, either alone or together with the amount, if any, referred to in clause (2) below, is not less than the applicable Threshold Amount (as specified in the Schedule) which has resulted in such Specified Obligations becoming, or becoming capable at such time of being declared, due and payable under such agreements or instruments before it would otherwise have been due and payable'. In the TMA, the meaning of specified obligations covers 'any amount raised under any transaction including any Islamic Financing having the commercial effect of a borrowing'. See IIFM and ISDA, *ISDA/IIFM Tahawwut Master Agreement* (IIFM and ISDA 2010).

[16] White & Case LLP, 'ISDA/IIFM Launch Tahawwut Master Agreement' (*White & Case LLP*, 2010) 11. http://www.whitecase.com/files/Publication/9446775f-ab73-45e4-9431-fc8ca9765529/Presentation/PublicationAttachment/378e2415-b4ab-49c3-9c3f-02a221de1d18/alert_ISDAIIFM_Launch.pdf. Accessed 19 November 2013.

[17] AAOIFI, *Shari'a Standards for Islamic Financial Institutions* (AAOIFI 2010) 29–42.

concern in the case of regulating the IFSI since the focus of international standard-setting organisations so far tends to be more on the default-affecting institutions rather than the one affecting the customers and investors. Perhaps a rather more useful definition of default in the *ṣukūk* scenario is provided by Bakar, who divides *ṣukūk* default into actual and technical default: the former refers to an 'inability of the issuer to make timely payment of any financial obligation to the *ṣukūk* investors',[18] the latter is defined as 'the failure of the issuer to meet certain financial ratios during the tenure of the *ṣukūk*'.[19] Nevertheless, in purely practical terms, reviewing *ṣukūk* arrangements is necessary to ensure the occurrence of a default and what acts would actually lead to such event. In this regard, Majid, Shahimi, and Abdulla say 'default occurs due to the breach of any binding obligations under the original terms of the agreement between the issuer and the *ṣukūk* holders'.[20] Further, Mahmood and Kamil note that acts leading to default could be in the form of failure to settle payments or change in the contract structure signed between the parties.[21]

5.2.2 *Potential Sources of* Ṣukūk *Defaults*

What fuels further debate, after the default period in the *ṣukūk* market, is the key causes leading to defaults. There is some degree of disagreement as to whether the incidence of default in the *ṣukūk* market is driven by the market risk or by structural deficiencies of *ṣukūk*. As shall be seen below, some people tried to pin the blame for defaults on a single reason. However, it is believed that each reason is a potential source for the default problem and contributed to certain degree to the market distress.

The first possible source of *ṣukūk* defaults is the credit risk. Muhamed and Radzi opine that '[m]ostly, *ṣukūk* defaults are the result of market and

[18] M Bakar, 'Restructuring Of Sukuk: A Shariah Perspective' (*Amanie i-Connect*, 16 May 2012). http://www.amanie-iconnect.com/component/k2/item/10-restructuring-of-sukuk-a-shariah-perspective. Accessed 10 November 2014.

[19] Ibid.

[20] H Majid, S Shahimi and M Abdullah, 'Sukuk Defaults and Its Implication: A Case Study of Malaysian Capital Market' (8th International Conference on Islamic Economics and Finance, Qatar, December 2011) 2.

[21] N Mahmood and W Kamil, 'Islamic Finance and the Impact of Insolvency' in *Effective Insolvency Regimes: Institutional, Regulatory, and Legal Issues Relating to Islamic Finance* (IFSB and WB 2011) 51.

credit risk rather than structural problems or sharia compliancy shortfalls'.[22] Some commentators report that '[t]he occurrence of *ṣukūk* defaults is driven by credit risk and has nothing to do with the validity of the *ṣukūk* methodology'.[23] The market will still force these structures to fall in a default situation regardless of the structure type.[24] The assumption that if the deals were financed based on conventional structures, the default situation would have been avoided is not necessarily accurate. Indeed, threats, failures, and defaults in *ṣukūk* markets were attributed to the inevitable effects of the global financial crisis.[25] By tracing the roots of market risk that led to default cases in this particular period, it was found that they did not fundamentally differ from the core causes of the sub-prime crisis in the USA, particularly property bubbles, large single exposure to a single group, and reliance on foreign liquidity.[26] The effect of credit risk on the performance of *ṣukūk* markets was very clear during the crisis, causing a 50% drop by the end of 2008.[27]

Another avenue of blame for the series of *ṣukūk* defaults has been the structural deficiencies of the offerings. Several structures triggered off sharia concerns contributing to intense debate about the sharia compliance of such arrangements.[28] It has been argued that the sharia advisors were driven by market demands into showing leniency towards large *ṣukūk* deals.[29] Therefore, *ṣukūk* defaults have been attributed to failure by the sharia advisors to fulfil the moral aspects of their duties.[30]

[22] N Muhamed and R Radzi, 'An International Comparative Study on Shariah Governance Supervision of Sukuk Defaults' (2012) 8 Journal of Islamic Economics, Banking and Finance 20, 24.

[23] K Remo-Listana, 'Market, Not Methodology, Drives Sukuk Defaults' (*Emirates 247*, 15 June 2010). http://www.emirates247.com/eb247/banking-finance/islamic-finance/market-not-methodology-drives-sukuk-defaults-2010-06-15-1.255596. Accessed 20 November 2013.

[24] Ibid.

[25] J Admas, 'Opening Remarks to the Roundtable Discussion' in IFSB and WB (eds), *Effective Insolvency Regimes: Institutional, Regulatory, and Legal Issues Relating to Islamic Finance* (IFSB and WB 2011) 1.

[26] SC, 'Mega Sukuk Defaults – Acid Test for Islamic Finance' (2009) 4 Quarterly Bulletin of Malaysian Islamic Capital Market 1, 4.

[27] N Muhamed and R Radzi, *supra* note 22, 22.

[28] RAM Rating Services Berhad, *supra* note 2, 1.

[29] M Saleem, 'Sukuk Default: Questions About Shari'ah Supervision' (2010) 174 NewHorizon, 22.

[30] Ibid.

Even though several problems and issues have already been identified in relation to *ṣukūk* structures, the possibility to explore further concerns remains, owing to the fact that most of them have not been tested in the courts yet.[31] Another underlying concern related to *ṣukūk* deficiencies is the practice of preparing the legal documents of *ṣukūk*. Legal conditions and terms of *ṣukūk* circulars have added ambiguity instead of certainty arising from the cutting and pasting of conventional bond provisions. The familiarity of international investors with conventional provisions has been put forward as a justification of law firms' practice. In fact, there have been instances where the default provisions of bond structures have been incorporated into *ṣukūk* contracts.[32] In addition, the different implications of asset-based and asset-backed structures in the event of default are viewed as real deficiencies in *ṣukūk*. Another important deficiency can be seen in the practice of the *ṣukūk* originators where they 'spent a lot of time on the matter of credit enhancements (protecting banks) and very little time on protecting investors' rights'.[33]

5.2.3 *Legal Resolutions of* Ṣukūk *Defaults*

Having established the basis of *ṣukūk* defaults, the next question to determine is how default scenarios are typically resolved. It is perhaps in regard to the IFSI and *ṣukūk* markets in particular where the regulation of default resolution is least manifest. Marinescu argues that 'one complicating factor to growth in the *ṣukūk* space is the lack of legal clarity around default mechanisms'.[34] IFSB-7 mentions two possible resolutions available to *ṣukūk* holders when the originator fails to pay the principal amount equal to issue price at maturity. *Ṣukūk* holders have the right to take legal action against the defaulting originator and of selling or foreclosing on the underlying asset.[35] Associated with this issue is an understanding of the distinction between asset-backed and asset-based structures to ensure clearer recognition of the different default mechanisms that are accessible. While the resolution of default in case of an asset-backed structure would come

[31] N Muhamed and R Radzi, *supra* note 22, 25.

[32] H Majid, S Shahimi and M Abdullah, *supra* note 20, 2.

[33] M Khnifer, 'When Sukuk Default – Asset Priority of Certificate-holders vis a vis Creditors' (2010) 11 Opalesque Islamic Finance Intelligence 9, 14.

[34] I Marinescs, 'Where Does the Dirham Stop in a Sukuk Default?' (2012) 35 Hastings International and Comparative Law Review 451, 452.

[35] IFSB, *supra* note 13, 7.

in the form of selling the *ṣukūk* asset, waiting for purchase undertaking exercised by the originator or joining the list of originator creditors would be the default solutions available for asset-based *ṣukūk* holders.

There is a lack of clarity as to which dispute resolution form should be opted in a *ṣukūk* default scenario. While many parties may choose arbitration or restructuring on the brink of default or post-default, litigation is the likely approach in large *ṣukūk* arrangements with disparate parties involved.[36] Chapter 6 shall address restructuring approaches from an Islamic law perspective. At this point, it is enough to understand that the choice of restructuring *ṣukūk* in the case of default raises different sharia concerns.

In the context of default resolutions, risk of re-categorisation of the defaulted *ṣukūk* structure remains one of the main concerns for *ṣukūk* holders since asset-backed structure may by re-categorised as asset-based structure in the event of litigation in Islamic jurisdictions, let alone Western jurisdictions.[37] This situation is compounded by the existence of less developed bankruptcy regimes in most jurisdictions in which the IFSI operates.[38] Here, how Islamic and Western jurisdictions would interpret consequences of default in the IFSI is an issue warranting considerable attention.[39] In this respect, the legal advice obtained from law firms plays a vital role in expecting how the law would probably operate in such a situation.[40] While it is well established that normal entitlements under default situations would be resolved by making the payments due, this matter requires careful attention in practice. Mahmood and Kamil therefore argue that 'the settlement amount needs to be defined and decided and the settlement mechanism must be transparent'.[41] The application of different sharia contracts as financing facilities gives rise to disputes between contracting parties in regard to determination of the settlement amount. For example, whether the defaulter should pay the entire sale price or financing amount in contract of sales used for financing purpose is subject to confusion and dispute.[42]

[36] I Marinescs, *supra* note 34, 463–464.

[37] Ibid. 462.

[38] Ibid. 465.

[39] H Yunis, 'Islamic Finance Transactions and the Impact of Insolvency' in IFSB and WB (eds), *Effective Insolvency Regimes: Institutional, Regulatory, and Legal Issues Relating to Islamic Finance* (IFSB and WB 2011) 21.

[40] K Howladar, *The Future of Sukuk: Substance Over Form? Understanding Islamic Securitisation, Asset-Backed and AAOIFI Principles* (Moody's Investor Service 2009) 5.

[41] N Mahmood and W Kamil, *supra* note 21, 53.

[42] Ibid. 51.

5.3 Islamic Law of Insolvency

Having investigated the nature of default in the context of *ṣukūk*, one should look at the law that governs the default situation. There are several impacts of *ṣukūk* default, and therefore it is important to know how the law deals with the consequences of *ṣukūk* default. The law that governs instances of *ṣukūk* default is the corporate insolvency[43] law. Given the sharia-compliant nature of *ṣukūk* transactions, one may assume that the event of *ṣukūk* default shall be governed by the rules relating to insolvency under Islamic law. The following discussion provides a brief assessment of the extent to which this so-called Islamic law of insolvency resolves the consequences of *ṣukūk* defaults.

5.3.1 The Relevance of Insolvency Law to **Ṣukūk**

Before directly addressing the applicability of Islamic law of insolvency in the event of *ṣukūk* defaults, it is worth highlighting the importance of the law relating to insolvency of companies in the context of *ṣukūk*. At a fundamental level, corporate insolvency law is applied when companies become insolvent or fall into a default situation. The default case poses a primary question as to how such a case will be dealt with under the law relating to the insolvency of companies. In the context of *ṣukūk* structures, two parties in the form of a corporation may trigger off the default situation, namely the originator and the SPV. In this regard, the default situation creates a clear difference between the asset-backed *ṣukūk* and asset-based *ṣukūk*. The issue of default and the law regulating the financial difficulties of *ṣukūk* is of particular significance in the context of asset-based *ṣukūk* for several reasons. First, asset-based *ṣukūk* is the more likely structure to be affected by the insolvency of the originator due to the dependence of the structure on the economic performance of the originator. Second, most *ṣukūk* structures in the market have been subject to default fall within the category of an asset-based structure. Third, the securitisation elements incorporated in asset-backed *ṣukūk* eliminate the risk of insolvency of the originator and make the originator's insolvency irrelevant to the underlying structure.

Therefore, the insolvency law is relevant when the originators and the SPV in asset-based *ṣukūk* are under certain circumstances that cause insol-

[43] For the purpose of this book, the words 'insolvency' and bankruptcy' are synonyms.

vency such as 'under-capitalisation, over-trading, over-leveraging, failure to keep pace with changing markets, lack of adequate management and financial controls, failure to take remedial measure in due time, in the case of banks, sub-prime lending'.[44] The importance of insolvency law in the event of *ṣukūk* default and originator's insolvency cannot be overlooked. It addresses, among others, the possibility of avoiding liquidation, the ranking of claims, distribution of assets among creditors, and rules governing cross-border insolvencies.[45] The significance of insolvency law in this discussion does not arise mainly from its importance as work-out provisions,[46] or indeed from its role in the creation, continuation, and development of sharia-compliant products and the markets that accommodate them.[47] It is most significant to draw clear insolvency procedures that inform contractual parties what will occur in the event of investment failure and positively contribute towards fresh ventures.[48] There is a particularly close relationship between financing and regulations relating to insolvency and loss since ventures do occasionally fail.[49]

Insolvency law is generally defined as the law that is concerned with the process of repayment to creditors from debtors' remaining assets and outlines other alternative procedures when there is not enough to meet all claims.[50] Insolvency and bankruptcy laws offer for investors a predictable legal environment.[51] In this regard, Goode identifies three objectives for corporate insolvency law: (1) maximising return to creditors, (2) establishing a fair and equitable system for the ranking of claims, and (3) providing mechanisms by which the causes of the company's failure are identified and mismanagement is minimised.[52] One stresses that the significance of bankruptcy law arises from the fact that it has a great impact on liquidity, a

[44] R Goode, *Principles of Corporate Insolvency Law* (4th edn, Sweet & Maxwell 2011) 9.

[45] Ibid. 1.

[46] J Board, 'Development of Islamic Capital Markets' in IFSB (ed), *Strategies for the Development of Islamic Capital Markets: Infrastructures and Legal Aspects of Islamic Asset Securitisation* (IFSB 2011) 14.

[47] B Rider, 'Legal Aspects of Islamic Asset Securitisation' in IFSB (ed), *Strategies for the Development of Islamic Capital Markets: Infrastructures and Legal Aspects of Islamic Asset Securitisation* (IFSB 2011) 81.

[48] J Board, *supra* note 46, 10.

[49] H Hamoudi, 'The Surprising Irrelevance of Islamic Bankruptcy' (2011) 19 American Bankruptcy Institute Law Review 505, 506.

[50] J Duns, *Insolvecny: Law and Policy* (1st edn, Oxford University Press 2002) 2.

[51] B Rider, *supra* note 47, 50–51.

[52] R Goode, *supra* note 44, 58.

common issue across Islamic and conventional financial markets. Although market regulations are important for the development of Islamic financial markets, laws relating to insolvency have a greater significance for further continuous growth from a legal point of view.[53] Insolvency law, among other applicable laws, may affect the enforcement of creditors' rights which in one way or another will cause certain limitations for *ṣukūk* investors.[54]

5.3.2 Assessment of Existing Insolvency Rules in Islamic Law

Practitioners and lawyers care very much about insolvency matters[55] and wonder whether Islamic law properly addresses them in the modern sense. As to the problems facing developing a sustainable IFSI, one argues that law relating to insolvency is one of the largest remaining concerns,[56] and therefore there is need to address insolvency matters from an Islamic law perspective. There are hardly any studies that provide a road map for laws relating to insolvency in the contemporary context of the IFSI. While there is remarkable scholarly attention on various areas of IFSI, the subject of insolvency in sharia has not received the same level of exposition.[57] In this respect, one cannot speak of a significant literature in Arabic, let alone English. Most literature on insolvency from an Islamic perspective is concerned with insolvent individuals rather than business entities. Indeed it has even been argued that there is no corporate insolvency law in Islamic law since it has only several rules related to insolvent individuals.[58] Many issues in the context of corporate insolvency that worry modern lawyers are notably not well addressed by sharia scholars compared to modern regimes, for example, the scenario of insufficient assets to satisfy all claims in the event of asset distribution.[59]

Islamic law has put in place certain rules related to insolvency which are primarily concerned with insolvent individuals. In this regard, Islamic law

[53] B Rider, *supra* note 47, 81.

[54] Ibid. 207.

[55] H Hamoudi, *supra* note 49, 515.

[56] J Board, *supra* note 46, 10.

[57] A Awad and R Michael, 'Iflas and Chapter 11: Classical Islamic Law and Modren Bankruptcy' (2010) 44 The International Lawyer 975, 976.

[58] N Foster, 'Islamic Perspectives on the Law of Business Organisations: Part 1: an Overview of the Classical Sharia and a Brief Comparison of the Sharia Regimes with Western-Style Law' (2010) 11 European Business Organization Law Review 3, 13.

[59] Ibid.

defines insolvency as a situation in which the debt exceeds the debtor's assets, and therefore there is no ability to repay the debt amount.[60] There are several texts in sharia sources grounding fundamentals and establishing principles of a fair insolvency system. Examples of these principles that provide balanced treatment for both debtor and creditor include moral dealing with the debtor who is in difficulty, time extension or forgiveness, social responsibility, charity, payment obligation of all debts, and fulfilment of all obligations.[61] One of the important concepts in the context of bankruptcy procedures is that interest cannot be imposed on the delay of debt payment.[62] The bankruptcy proceeding in Islamic law is referred to as an involuntary proceeding, commenced by one or more creditors rather than a debtor.[63] Islamic jurists have pointed out some rules related to insolvency, including interdiction of the bankrupt, the need for a court order, creditor rights, selling of debtor's property, and prevention of bankrupt debtors from travelling.[64]

As mentioned above, the system of administrating insolvency proceedings established by classical jurists is entirely concerned with individuals. It is open to debate how far these laws concerning insolvent individuals are applicable or appropriate to modern corporations and Islamic finance practice. There is no so-called Islamic bankruptcy law of companies since all types of partnerships in Islamic law are based on liability of the individual or partners in the business enterprise, which had neither legal personality nor limited liability.[65] To give a general idea of the width of such discussion, traditional forms of partnership in Islamic law include contrac-

[60] There are a number of terms related to bankruptcy that have been used by jurists including insolvency (*taflīs*), difficulty (*ʿsār*), interdiction (*ḥajr*), clearness (*taṣfiyah*), damage (*halāk*), loss (*khasārah*). They have different implications and meanings in the context of bankruptcy. For more discussion, see A Al-Manṣūr, *Iflāsu Al-Sharikāti wa Atharuhu fī Al-Fiqhi wa Al-Niẓām*, vol 1 (1st edn, Dār Kunūz Ishbīlā Lil-Nashr Wa Al-Tawzīʿ 2012) 31–60.

[61] J Kilborn, 'Foundations of Forgiveness in Islamic Bankruptcy Law: Sources, Methodology, Diversity' (*SSRN*, undated). http://papers.ssrn.com/sol3/papers.cfm?abstractid=1908896. Accessed 6 April 2013.

[62] M Mcmillen, 'Sharīʿah Considerations in The Bankruptcy Context and The First Bankruptcy (East Cameron)' in IFSB and WB (eds), *Effective Insolvecny Regimes: Institutional, Regulatory and Legal Issues Relating to Islamic Finance* (IFSB and WB 2011) 28.

[63] Ibid.

[64] For more information, see W Al-Zuhayli, *Financial Transactions in Islamic Jurisprudence* (M El-Gamal tr, 2nd edn, Dar Al-Fikr 2007) 383–407.

[65] See N Foster, *supra* note 58, 12; A Awad and R Michael, *supra* note 57, 985.

tual partnership (*sharikah al-ʿinān*), partnership in creditworthiness, partnerships for undertaking work, and *muḍārabah* (investment partnership).[66] In this respect, Islamic law established several rules concerning loss of the business enterprise, loss of responsibility, partner's loss share, and termination of the partnerships without literal mention of bankruptcy.[67]

5.3.3 Problems Related to Insolvency Law in IFSI

From various works which expound upon the regime of partnerships in Islamic law, one observes the divergence in insolvency approach between classical Islamic law and modern regimes. Applying bankruptcy rules related to individuals as developed in Islamic law to the present practice of the IFSI is not appropriate, owing to major differences between the nature of bankruptcy of individuals and that of modern corporations.[68] The absence of the concept of the modern corporation and related concepts such as limited liability and legal personality under Islamic law[69] are central to the discussion of an Islamic corporate law of insolvency. The remainder of Islamic juristic schools did not draw a distinction between commercial and non-commercial entities in insolvency cases. This is because '[c]lassical Islamic law recognises only natural persons; it does not grant standing to corporation'.[70] Attempts have been made to link the concept of corporation and legal liability to some notions in Islamic law such as *waqf*, *baytu al-māl* (State Treasury), wealth of a deceased person, and *muḍārabah* contract.[71] The issue of whether the concept of corporation is found on such notions is subject to debate.

This impacts how classical Islamic law governs certain issues in the context of corporate insolvency; for instance, details of shareholders' and creditors' rights thrown up by modern bankruptcy laws and other laws do not appear in the Islamic law due to the absence of organisational law in classical Islamic jurisprudence.[72] Perhaps a rather more important issue in

[66] AAOIFI, *supra* note 17, 203, 235.

[67] A Al-Manṣūr, *supra* note 60, 61.

[68] For more discussion, see ibid. 65–71.

[69] N Foster, *supra* note 58, 12; H Ahmed, 'Islamic Law, Investors' Rights and Corporate Finance' (2012) 12 Journal of Corporate Law Studies 367, 385.

[70] T Kuran, 'The Absence of the Corporation in Islamic Law: Origins and Persistence' (2005) 53 The American Juornal of Comparative Law 785.

[71] H Ahmed, *supra* note 69, 385–386.

[72] Ibid. 391.

regard to bankruptcy law that has not been addressed in Islamic law is the priority of claims in the case of corporations[73]; while secular bankruptcy regimes divide creditors in groups and treat them differently, Islamic law, as a general statement, treats all creditors equally.[74] Another important issue is related to the solutions provided by conventional laws for insolvent corporations which need careful consideration from Islamic law perspective. For instance, liquidation, reorganisation, and repayment plans are solutions provided by the Bankruptcy Code under Chapter 7, Chapter 11, and Chapter 13, respectively. In this respect, Awad and Michael note, 'strictly speaking the simple Chapter 11 solution of a debt discharge through a Plan of Reorganization is not permitted, because a Muslim is obligated to repay his or her debts'.[75]

Given the less developed markets where the IFSI is mostly practised, one can state that insolvency process in IFSI is not only less clear but also the implementation of these procedures is less rigorous. This is compounded when it comes to Islamic assets compared to conventional assets that have special features, presenting particular problems in a number of Islamic jurisdictions that apply, for example, UK law to transactions.[76] An illustration of this is the Dubai World Debt and Nakheel *Ṣukūk* where creditors have expressed preference for a direct restructuring deal with Dubai World over taking a legal action in an uncertain environment due to the absence of equivalent law to the US bankruptcy discussed in Chapter 11 or the administration procedures in the UK.[77] Given the absence of Islamic bankruptcy law in legislation, there are very limited recorded resolutions of insolvency cases since most of them are resolved out of court.[78] It is even argued that avoidance of full insolvency in most jurisdictions is far less likely, owing to the failure of applicable laws to intervene on an efficient and timely basis, for example, before the insolvency or bankruptcy is already in place.[79]

[73] Ibid.

[74] A Al-Manṣūr, *supra* note 60, 431–437.

[75] A Awad and R Michael, *supra* note 57, 999.

[76] J Board, *supra* note 46, 26.

[77] B Rider, *supra* note 47, 207.

[78] M Al-Sheaibi, 'Insolvency Regimes: Regulatory, Institutional and Legal Challenges in Islamic Finance in Saudi Arabia' in IFSB and WB (eds), *Effective Insolvency Regimes: Institutional, Regulatory, and Legal Issues Relating to Islamic Finance* (IFSB and WB 2011) 92–93.

[79] B Rider, *supra* note 47, 216.

What is clear is that there is a discrepancy in regard to interest between development of the IFSI and Islamic law of insolvency[80] as the latter has not been well perceived, let alone undertaken. Evaluation of the suitability of Islamic law of insolvency is vital in terms of fostering the development of efficient Islamic financial markets. The earlier discussion of the deficiencies of Islamic law on insolvency is not a criticism, but rather an attempt to understand its current state and its applicability to the IFSI. In this regard, Hamoudi states:

> [M]y belief that Islamic insolvency is not well suited to be the national law of modern Muslim nation states is not meant as criticism of the system of administering bankruptcy proceedings as developed by the medieval jurists who established rules not entirely dissimilar to those of modernity in order to handle problems of insolvency.[81]

Recent efforts have been made to develop Islamic law of bankruptcy and increase the awareness level about potential weaknesses in comparison with secular bankruptcy laws.[82] What is desirable is further development of an Islamic framework for bankruptcy that tackles the serious issues of insolvency and caters for growth in Islamic financial markets. This must include the impact of bankruptcy on various types of modern corporations, on the legal personality of a corporation, on its subsidiaries, on its creditors, and on investment deposits.

5.4 Case Studies of Default and Near-Default *Ṣukūk*

While it was previously unheard of for the *ṣukūk* market to have defaults, the industry has in recent years experienced a string of defaults on offerings anticipated to be healthier and praised as breakthroughs in the IFSI. It is useful to know at what time *ṣukūk* defaults started to take place in the market. It is often difficult to obtain data in relation to defaulted *ṣukūk* due to the fact that some *ṣukūk* were traded over-the-counter (OTC) and the underdeveloped records system in some jurisdictions. In this respect, developing a standardised record of *ṣukūk* defaults will not only enable investors

[80] H Hamoudi, *supra* note 49, 510.
[81] Ibid. 511.
[82] See, for example, Al-Manṣūr.

to make informed decisions but will also facilitate the establishment of a mature market.[83] According to a study conducted by RAM Rating Services Berhad, there were 42 Malaysian *ṣukūk* issued for the period 1997–2011 that have defaulted, with the first default case listed in June 2002.[84] The total number of defaults in the *ṣukūk* market will be definitely greater if one adds up global defaulted issuances with the Malaysian figures. Therefore, one can say that there had been no *ṣukūk* default prior to 2002 in Malaysia and, perhaps, worldwide. *Ṣukūk* defaults took place in several jurisdictions with a different market share of defaults, namely, Malaysia, the UAE, Kuwait, Pakistan, the KSA, the USA, and Indonesia.[85] It is apparent from the defaulted issuances that all types of *ṣukūk* structure are potentially subject to a default eventuality.

For the purpose of this book, certain high-profile default cases have been chosen, mostly from the Middle East region. These particular *ṣukūk* provide the best illustration for the discussion of asset-backed and based structures and associated concerns in the default scenario. In addition, these *ṣukūk* defaults have attracted the most attention in the global market, owing to the reputation of the originators, the consequences of default, and size issues. Majid, Shahimi, and Abdullah claim that '[u]nlike the high-profile default cases in the Middle East, Malaysia's *ṣukūk* defaults have received less criticism and scrutiny from global industry players'.[86] Arranged in issuance date order, the following subsections present key information about the originators, associated parties, and *ṣukūk* structure of the selected cases.

5.4.1 *East Cameron* Ṣukūk[87]

Perhaps one of the most interesting *ṣukūk* issuance so far is the East Cameron *Ṣukūk*. East Cameron Partners LP is an independent Texas-based company specialising in exploration and production of oil and gas.

[83] S&P, 'Islamic Finance Outlook 2012' (*S&P*, September 2012) 56. http://www.standardandpoors.com/spf/upload/Ratings_EMEA/2012-09-01_IslamicFinanceOutlook.pdf. Accessed 4 December 2013.

[84] See RAM Rating Services Berhad, *supra* note 2, 12; N Ahmad and N Wahab, *supra* note 4, 2647–2649.

[85] See Kuwait Finance House Research, *Sukuk: Back on Track* (Kuwait Finance House Research 2010) 15; D Siswantoro, 'Analysis of the First Ijarah Sukuk Default In Indonesia: How Could It Be?' (2013) 3 International Journal of Islamic Banking & Finance 1.

[86] H Majid, S Shahimi and M Abdullah, *supra* note 20, 10.

[87] The main source of information is the Offering Circular of East Cameron Gas Company.

According to a government lease obtained in early 2000 from Conoco Phillips (integrated energy and refining company), the company holds the right of exploration and exploitation of two gas properties located in the shallow waters off of Louisiana; Block 71, East Cameron Area (EC 71) and Block 72, East Cameron Area (EC 72).[88] East Cameron Partners believed that some development work needed to be done at the two sites, with an approximate cost of USD 45 million.[89] Macquarie (an Australian Bank) provided the outside funds needed for the sites' development with two conditions: (1) 15% loan interest per annum and (2) a 50% equity stake.[90] Later, East Cameron Partners wanted more funds to finance further exploration on the sites, but its partner (i.e. Macquarie) was unwilling to invest more in this business.[91] The option of *ṣukūk* issuance was well received by East Cameron Partners because this deal would facilitate purchasing its partner share, enjoying more cash flow from gas exploration, and the exploration needed on the properties.[92] In addition, East Cameron Partners obtained these outside funds without any interest being paid to the lender. This demonstrated the issuance purpose and why East Cameron Partners preferred *ṣukūk* to other financial arrangements available on the market.

The East Cameron *Ṣukūk* was issued on 5 July 2006 that amounted to USD 165.67 million due in July 2019. The structure of the *ṣukūk* is as follows. Designed as a two-tier structure, the *ṣukūk* involves two SPVs, which are the East Cameron Gas Company (a Cayman Island exempted limited liability company, Issuer SPV) and Louisiana Offshore Holding (a Delaware limited liability company, Purchaser SPV).[93] Under the Funding Agreement, the Issuer SPV will issue *ṣukūk* and advance the offering proceeds to the Purchaser SPV. The Purchaser SPV, among others, will use the funds received to purchase the overriding royalty interest (ORRI) over the properties from the originator. The originator, among others, will use the proceeds to re-acquire its partner share (Macquarie) and pay some fees

[88] S Sapp, *East Cameron Partners: The Sukuk Bond* (Ivey School of Business Foundation 2010) 2.

[89] Ibid.

[90] Ibid.

[91] Ibid.

[92] Ibid.

[93] The main reason for the creation of two SPVs in this structure is that oil rights must be sold to a US corporation only since the US government has given these rights to East Cameron Partners.

related to the transaction.[94] This was a ***mushārakah*** (participation financing) structure whereby the originator (East Cameron Partners) and Issuer SPV (the Trustee) co-own the *ṣukūk* asset (ORRI).[95] Therefore, ***ṣukūk*** holders share in any rewards and risks arising from the sale of oil and gas in the open market.

5.4.2 The Investment Dar Ṣukūk: *TID* Ṣukūk *2005 and TID* Ṣukūk *2006*[96]

Listed on the Kuwait Stock Exchange (KSE) since April 1999, The Investment Dar (TID) is a holding company incorporated in Kuwait in 1994 with the aim of carrying out different business activities, including consumer financing and real estate development in accordance with Islamic finance principles. As part of its business deals, there are two *ṣukūk* offered by TID (the originator). The first issuance was issued by The Investment Dar *Ṣukūk* Company B.S.C.(c) (a shareholding company incorporated in Bahrain, the issuer, the trustee) on 27 October 2005 amounting to USD 100 million in *mushārakah ṣukūk* with the maturity date of 26 October 2010, that is, TID *Ṣukūk* 2005.

The second issuance was issued on 20 September 2006 amounting to USD 150 million of *mushārakah ṣukūk*, maturing after five years from the issuance date, that is TID *Ṣukūk* 2006. According to the *mushārakah* agreement, TID Global *Ṣukūk* I Limited (incorporated in the Cayman Islands, the issuer, the trustee) will contribute *ṣukūk* proceeds constituting 48.78% of *mushārakah* capital. Also, the originator will contribute all rights and benefits to TID vehicles and property worth USD 157.5 million

[94] At the time of *ṣukūk* issuance, there was more than USD 27 million in outstanding conventional debt because of credit facility provided by Merrill Lynch Credit Products, LLC, to finance the originator's operations in 2005 and 2006. Portions of the proceeds amount are used to pay the full amount outstanding under this facility so as to ensure acceptable equity ratio from an Islamic law perspective. This case clearly defines how company's outstanding conventional debt could be eliminated in practice as this would probably face most originators in Western jurisdictions. See Offering Circular of East Cameron Gas Company 1, 42. See also A Abdel-Khaleq and C Richardson, 'New Horizons for Islamic Securities: Emerging Trends in Sukuk Offerings' (2007) 7 Chicago Journal of International Law 409, 423.

[95] *Ijārah* (lease) structure was initially proposed whereby oil rigs and drilling equipment would be used as *ṣukūk* asset. However, these assets were worth less than the amount required (i.e. USD 150–170 million).

[96] Source of information: S Zaheer and S Wijnbergen, 'Sukuk Defaults: on Distress Resolution in Islamic Finance' (*Tinbergen*, 2013) 8. http://papers.tinbergen.nl/13087.pdf. Accessed 26 May 2015.

constituting a 52.22% *mushārakah* share. A total of USD 305.7 million will be invested and any returns will be distributed between the TID and the issuer. The structure also contained purchase undertaking provided by the originator and management agreement.

5.4.3 *Nakheel* Ṣukūk[97]

Nakheel Holdings-1 LLC was the originator in this structure: a subsidiary of Nakheel World LLC together with Nakheel Holdings-2 LLC and Nakheel Holdings-3 LLC. These three holding companies own Nakheel PJSC, a joint stock company since 2006, operating in the real estate sector. This issuance was offered on 14 December 2006 amounting to USD 3520 million of *ijārah ṣukūk* maturing on 14 December 2009. Nakheel Development Limited (incorporated in Jabel Ali as a free zone company, the issuer, the trustee) purchased the *ṣukūk* assets from Nakheel Holdings-1 LLC pursuant to a purchase agreement. The *ṣukūk* assets consisted of leasehold rights for a period of 50 years of specific land, buildings, and other property located at Dubai Waterfront. According to a 3-year lease agreement, the issuer (the lessor) leased the *ṣukūk* assets to Nakheel Holdings 2 (the lessee). Issuance proceeds were used by the issuer to pay for the *ṣukūk* assets purchased according to the purchase agreement terms. The deal involved several mechanisms, including servicing agency agreement, purchase agreement, purchase undertaking, lease agreement, the *ṣukūk* assets sale undertaking, security agency agreement, guarantee, and share pledges.

5.4.4 *Golden Belt* Ṣukūk[98]

The originator in this structure was Saad Trading, Contracting and Financial Services Company, a limited partnership company incorporated in the KSA in 1991. The company is part of Saad Group, a privately owned group of companies founded in 1980 in the KSA. The company invests mainly in three sectors, namely real estate, equity securities, and construction. The Golden Belt *Ṣukūk* was issued on 15 May 2007 priced at USD 650 million maturing on 15 May 2012. The Offering Circular of Golden Belt 1 *Ṣukūk* Company B.S.C.(c) called the structure as *ṣukūk al-manāfiʿ*

[97] Source of information: Offering Circular of Nakheel Development Limited.

[98] Source of information: Offering Circular of Golden Belt 1 *Ṣukūk* Company B.S.C.(c).

(lease-and-leaseback). According to a head lease agreement for a period covering 25 years, Saad Trading, Contracting, and Financial Services Company (a Saudi a limited partnership company, Head Lessor) will lease designated areas of land to the Golden Belt 1 *Ṣukūk* Company B.S.C.(c) (SPV incorporated in Bahrain, the Issuer, Head Lessee) with advance rental payments made by the Issuer. According to a sub-lease agreement equal to the *ṣukūk* period, the issuer as sub-lessor will sub-lease the specific lands to the originator (sub-lessee). The sub-lessee will make rental payments to the issuer, constituting the principal issuer's source of funds.

5.4.5 Tamweel PJSC **Ṣukūk***: Tamweel Residential* **Ṣukūk** *and Tamweel Limited* **Ṣukūk**[99]

Established in 2004, Tamweel PJSC, a private joint stock company, is a large provider of real estate finance in the UAE and a subsidiary of Dubai Islamic Bank since Q4 2010. The company primarily engages in Islamic financing and property development. In its capacity as originator, Tamweel PJSC is involved with structuring of two substantive issuances (detailed below).

The first issuance is called Tamweel Residential *Ṣukūk*. This was issued on 25 July 2007 amounting to USD 210 million due in 2037. It was an *ijārah ṣukūk* comprising four classes A, B, C, and D. The underlying asset consisted of residential properties located in Dubai, registered under the name of the originator (Tamweel PJSC) at the Dubai Land Department. Consisting of two SPVs, the Tamweel Properties (1) Limited (TPL) (a Dubai International Financial Centre limited liability company, the SPV) would purchase the *ṣukūk* assets from the originator and then sell some of them to the Tamweel Residential ABS CI (1) Ltd (a Cayman Islands limited liability company, the Issuer). The principal source of payment for *ṣukūk* holders was rental payments and sale proceeds of the properties. The structure contained several techniques such as the acquisition agreements, servicing agreement, issuer security deed, paying agency agreement, liquidity facility agreement, purchase undertaking, and sale undertaking.

The other issuance is Tamweel Limited *Ṣukūk* issued on 21 July 2008 amounting to AED 1100 million due in 2013. Tamweel *Ṣukūk* Limited (a

[99] Source of information: Offering Circular of Tamweel Residential ABS CI (1) Ltd and Offering Circular of Tamweel *Ṣukūk* Limited.

Cayman Islands limited liability company, the issuer, the trustee) will pay the originator's rights, interest, and title to a portfolio of leased assets as well as a portfolio of *istiṣnāʿ* (contract of manufacture) assets. These two portfolios (Portfolio Assets) form the underlying asset of the structure. Essentially, Tamweel Limited *Ṣukūk* contains two types of *ṣukūk* (*ijārah* and *istiṣnāʿ*) issued by the issuer (SPV) to purchase a pool of assets from the originator. The transaction involved mechanisms such as purchase agreement, *istiṣnāʿ* agreement, service agency agreement, purchase undertaking, and sale undertaking.

5.5 Issues in the Event of *Ṣukūk* Default and Financial Difficulty

Having shed light on the background information of the above-mentioned *ṣukūk*, this section now looks at the significant concerns related to them. The relevance of issues discussed below varies from one issuance to another.

5.5.1 The Issue of Asset-Backed Ṣukūk *Versus Asset-Based* Ṣukūk

Among the above-mentioned examples of *ṣukūk*, only two structures are considered asset-backed *ṣukūk*, while the remaining five issuances are asset-based structures. There is a widespread agreement in the market that East Cameron *Ṣukūk* and Tamweel Residential *Ṣukūk* are true examples of asset-backed structure. The arranger of East Cameron *Ṣukūk*, Bemo Securitisation SAL (BSEC), asserted that the structure is an Islamic true-sale securitisation.[100] This shall be explored further with analysis of the property rights associated with East Cameron *Ṣukūk* in the following subsection.

The two *ṣukūk* issuances by Tamweel PJSC provide illustration for the ongoing discussion of asset-backed versus asset-based structures. Albeit offered by the same originator, the underlying structures of each *ṣukūk* are fundamentally different. In regard to Tamweel Residential *Ṣukūk*, Moody's indicated that '[f]rom an Islamic perspective, the deal was important as it was the first true-sale, globally rated, asset-backed *ṣukūk* in the region and "complies" with the recent sharia recommendations issued by AAOIFI'.[101]

[100] Bemo Securitisation SAL, 'East Cameron Gas Sukuk: A New Sukuk Innovation Comes to Market' (*Securitization*, 19 June 2006). http://www.securitization.net/pdf/content/BSEC_19Jun06.pdf. Accessed 9 December 2013.

[101] K Howladar, *supra* note 40, 11.

While provisions of the Offering Circular of Tamweel Residential ABS CI (1) Ltd illustrate certain features of an asset-backed structure in relation to source of payments[102] and the value of *ṣukūk* assets,[103] the Offering Circular of Tamweel *Ṣukūk* Limited, on the other hand, provides clear signs of an asset-based structure, especially terms related to payments on the certificates,[104] bankruptcy remoteness, and risk exposures.[105]

If the originator was to become insolvent in both cases, different consequences would have occurred. In regard to the Tamweel Residential *Ṣukūk*; (1) the legal ownership will reside with *ṣukūk* holders and any losses will be passed to the *ṣukūk* holders, (2) the underlying assets will continue making payments to the *ṣukūk* holders, and (3) the *ṣukūk* will survive and will not be affected upon the insolvency of the originator.[106] However, assuming that the same consequences can be applied in the case of Tamweel Limited *Ṣukūk* is incorrect. This transaction will not survive when the originator goes bust. Here, one can clearly see how *ṣukūk* holders take very different positions and are exposed to different types of risk, depending on the underlying structure, whether asset backed or asset based.

5.5.2 *Property Rights*

Careful analysis of property rights has particular significance to the default scenario in relation to East Cameron *Ṣukūk* and Nakheel *Ṣukūk*. Since it was the first of its kind backed by energy sources, the East Cameron *Ṣukūk* required careful consideration of both sharia rules and the US oil and gas

[102] 'The ability of the Issuer to meet its obligations under the Notes, including following the occurrence of any Event of Default … will primarily depend upon the receipt by it of Rental Payments and other payments relating to the Leases and the Properties'. See Offering Circular of Tamweel Residential ABS CI (1) Ltd 22.

[103] 'The value of the Security may be affected by, among other things, a decline in property values. No assurance can be given that the values of the Properties have remained or will remain at the level at which they were on the dates the related Leases were entered into'. See Offering Circular of Tamweel Residential ABS CI (1) Ltd 30.

[104] 'Certificateholders should note that … the ability of the Issuer to pay amounts due under the Certificates will depend on payments made by the Service Agent and payments made by the Obligor'. See Offering Circular of Tamweel *Ṣukūk* Limited 3.

[105] '[T]he Issuer is subject to all the risks to which Tamweel is subject, to the extent that such risks could limit Tamweel's ability to satisfy in full and on a timely basis its obligations under the Transaction Documents to which it is a party'. See Offering Circular of Tamweel *Ṣukūk* Limited 11.

[106] K Howladar, *supra* note 40, 9.

laws affecting characterisation of the property. The originator, an independent gas and oil exploration and production company, holds leasehold interest in the properties as the lessee and the US government is the lessor.[107] The oil and gas properties in question are actually federal properties administrated by the Minerals Management Service (MMS) in the USA.[108] It was unsettled as to whether the applicable law regards the offshore federal oil and gas leases as an ownership interest in real property.[109] But, before discussing this, one should understand what has actually been sold to *ṣukūk* holders in this structure. As mentioned, the underlying asset is the rights to the revenue from the oil and gas reserves; *ṣukūk* holders were therefore sold the rights to the stream of returns generated from oil and gas sales.[110] East Cameron *Ṣukūk* represents beneficial ownership in the oil and gas properties.[111] This may raise sharia concerns related to prohibition of debt trading since what is actually sold in the case of this structure is the royalty interest and not the oil fields. This is compounded by the fact that the two properties are leases by the US government. However, under Louisiana law—the de facto law governing oil and gas leases—the rights to the cash flows of oil and gas are regarded as real property.[112] These laws effectively give the Issuer SPV the right to receive a portion of oil and gas productions which can be sold later in the market.

While the leasehold is viewed as real property in East Cameron *Ṣukūk*, this is not necessarily applicable in every case. According to the Offering Circular of Nakheel Development Limited, *ijārah* was chosen to be the underlying structure in which the *ṣukūk* asset had been sold and leased back (a sale-and-leaseback transaction).[113] One can therefore assume that *ṣukūk* holders have proprietary rights in relation to the underlying asset arising from the first phase of the transaction (i.e. sale). However, this assumption is inaccurate because what has been actually transferred is the leasehold rights, and not an underlying tangible asset. In the case of the Nakheel

[107] Offering Circular of East Cameron Gas Company 46.

[108] Ibid.

[109] Ibid. 24.

[110] S Sapp, *supra* note 88, 5.

[111] Offering Circular of East Cameron Gas Company 17.

[112] B Goud, 'Description of a Sukuk Fatwa' (*Zawya*, 15 February 2009). http://www.zawya.com/blogs/blakegoud/090215215223/. Accessed 11 December 2013.

[113] Offering Circular of Nakheel Development Limited 1. See also O Salah, 'Dubai Debt Crisis: A Legal Analysis of the Nakheel Sukuk' (2010) 4 The Berkeley Journal of International Law 19, 28.

Ṣukūk, an accurate description of the arrangement is *ṣukūk ijārah al-manāfiʿ* in which the structure involves lease-and-leaseback transaction.[114] In this context, it is relevant to look at how the laws of UAE as applicable to the Emirate of Dubai view real property ownership. According to the Offering Circular of Nakheel Development Limited, '[t]raditionally leases have not been viewed as real or property rights in Dubai. Instead they have been viewed as unregistered personal contractual rights binding as between the parties as opposed to being attached to the land in question'.[115] However, the law may view leasehold rights as real property rights if the leases are registered in the Dubai Land Department, although this could not be achieved in this case due to the absence of formal regulations related to the registration process at the inception of the Nakheel *Ṣukūk*.[116]

5.5.3 *Default: Remedies and Process*

Although all the above issuances have encountered financial difficulty and uncertainty, not all of them have defaulted in the market. Only four issuances can be described as defaulted *ṣukūk*, namely East Cameron *Ṣukūk*, The Investment Dar *Ṣukūk*, and Golden Belt *Ṣukūk*. Nakheel *Ṣukūk* is better described as a near-default case. Arranged according to date of default order, they are as follows:

1. October 2008: East Cameron *Ṣukūk*
2. May 2009: The Investment Dar *Ṣukūk*
3. November 2009: Golden Belt 1 *Ṣukūk*
4. November 2009: Nakheel *Ṣukūk*

Before moving into default and near-default cases, the situation of the Tamweel PJSC *Ṣukūk* will be explained. *Ṣukūk* issued by Tamweel PJSC (i.e. Tamweel Residential *Ṣukūk* and Tamweel Limited *Ṣukūk*) were not a matter of default but rather of financial uncertainty; these two *ṣukūk* have been watched closely after announcing a merger plan in November 2008.[117] As announced, Tamweel PJSC and Amlak Finance, the first

[114] Ibid.

[115] Offering Circular of Nakheel Development Limited 130.

[116] Ibid.

[117] T Atkins, 'Amlak, Tamweel to Merge into Real Estate Bank' (*Reuters*, 22 November 2008). http://www.reuters.com/article/2008/11/23/amlak-tamweel-idUSLN39638820081123. Accessed 22 December 2013.

Islamic home finance provider in the UAE, would come together in October 2008 under the Real Estate Bank creating the largest real estate financial institution in the UAE.[118] This announcement has affected the rating of Tamweel Limited *Ṣukūk* as shall be seen in the following subsection. However, the merger of the two Islamic finance lenders did not take place as they are still operating independently so far.

The following subsections look closely at the reasons behind each problematic structure and inquire how each situation has been remedied.

5.5.3.1 Formal Bankruptcy Case

This case is considered the first ever *ṣukūk* default instigated and resolved under formal bankruptcy procedures. After almost two years of good performance from the East Cameron *Ṣukūk*, the originator defaulted on the periodic payments to the *ṣukūk* holders. Neither deficiency on the *ṣukūk* structure nor the market risk was the reason behind the default; a number of oil and gas sites have been destroyed, causing shortfall in oil and gas production when Hurricane Ike hit the Gulf of Mexico in September 2008.[119] This default event affected *ṣukūk* holders as they needed to address several operational issues, including payments to unsecured creditors, payments to the MMS, arranging a new operator, and how to keep the sites operating.[120]

The originator filed for bankruptcy under Chapter 11 in the US Bankruptcy Court for the Western District of Louisiana on 16 October 2008.[121] The originator also, on the same date, filed a complaint asking for injunctive relief against the Purchaser SPV, Issuer SPV, and Collateral Agent to stop selling, transferring, and liquidating the ORRI.[122] Most importantly, the originator requested re-categorisation of the current *ṣukūk* as a secured loan facility.[123] One wonders about the motivation of the originator to seek to re-categorise the structure as a secured loan trans-

[118] Ibid.

[119] The United States Securities and Exchange Commission, 'Form 10-K' (*Wikinvest*, 31 December 2008). http://www.wikinvest.com/stock/TEL_Offshore_Trust_(TELOZ)/Filing/10-K/2009/F3243816. Accessed 11 December 2013.

[120] Mcmillen, 'Sharīʿah Considerations in The Bankruptcy Context and The First Bankruptcy (East Cameron)' 42.

[121] Ibid. 40.

[122] Ibid. 41.

[123] Ibid.

action at this particular time. The originator claimed that no true sale took place in the transaction in relation to the ORRI.[124] It seems that the originator attempted to include the ORRI into the bankruptcy estate in order to deny *ṣukūk* holders the proprietary rights related to the *ṣukūk* asset and enable other creditors to share with them the royalties in the event of liquidation.[125]

As a significant precedent in the bankruptcy area of the *ṣukūk* market, the market was anxiously awaiting the resolution of this case since it would probably encourage or deter future *ṣukūk*, especially in new markets such as the USA. The central issue in the case was whether *ṣukūk* holders own the ORRI[126]; Judge Robert Summerhays rejected the re-categorisation request by the originator and viewed the *ṣukūk* structure as a true-sale securitisation.[127] The Judge asked the parties to transfer the lease titles to the *ṣukūk* holders, thus acknowledging their ownership over the ORRI.[128] The Judge has effectively understood the content of the *ṣukūk*, even though there were previously no formal bankruptcy cases in the *ṣukūk* market. The originator has been asked for further arguments supporting the case, which is still pending in the Court.[129]

5.5.3.2 Originators Restructuring Cases

Another interesting default case is TID's default on its two *ṣukūk* issuances, constituting the first default case in the Arabic Gulf region. On 12 May 2009, The Investment Dar *Ṣukūk* Company (SPV) announced a delay in the periodic distribution payments for more than 14 days in relation to the USD 100 *ṣukūk* million (TID *Ṣukūk* 2005).[130] As of September 2008, TID had a total of USD 3.73 billion debt outstanding, based on

[124] Z Hasan and M Asutay, 'An Analysis of the Courts' Decisions on Islamic Finance Disputes' (2011) 3 ISRA International Journal of Islamic Finance 41, 61.

[125] Ibid.

[126] Ibid.

[127] See Al-Amine, 'Unresolved Sharīʿah Issues in Ṣukūk' 47.

[128] F Ossa, 'Sovereign Sukuk Are Back, but Asset-Backeds Still Sidelined' (*Structured Finance News*, 1 April 2011). http://www.structuredfinancenews.com/issues/11_4/sovereign-sukuk-are-back-but-asset-backeds-still-sidelined-218081-1.html. Accessed 11 December 2013.

[129] Hasan and Asutay 61.

[130] R El Gamal, 'Update 1-Kuwait's Dar Defaults on $100 mln Sukuk' (*Reuters*, 12 May 2009). http://uk.reuters.com/article/2009/05/12/dar-sukuk-idUKLC28153620090512. Accessed 20 December 2013.

Bloomberg data.[131] As part of its debt restructuring plan arranged with Credit Suisse Group AG, TID later announced that the default event will be solved through borrowing up to USD 1 billion and potentially selling off some of its assets.[132] The main reason behind TID's failure to meet its financial obligations was the effects of the global financial crisis. The company stated that the 'year 2009 was a very hard and difficult year in all the sense of the word … the Company encountered increasing pressures in relation to cash flow and depreciation of assets'.[133] As a justification of the default, TID stated that the intention was to put *ṣukūk* holders in the same level with other creditors based on the restructuring plan of its overall debt.[134]

The above default case was followed by the default of the Golden Belt *Ṣukūk*. On 14 November 2009, the originator announced that the issuer would not be able to make periodic payments on the *ṣukūk*.[135] Part of the blame for this default has been placed on a lack of due diligence by the transaction arranger as well as the auditors' narrow views on the Saad Group activities.[136] The originator had no funds available to meet its financial obligations, especially after the global financial crisis. Actually, the reason for the liquidity crisis of the Group is not limited to the financial crisis worldwide, warranting further analysis. According to the originator, '[f]reezing orders in Saudi Arabia and other jurisdictions have rendered impossible the ability of Saad Trading, Contracting & Financial Services to perform its payment obligations'.[137] In May 2009, the Saudi Arabian

[131] H Anwar and M Patterson, 'Aston Martin Owner Is First to Default on Gulf Sukuk (Update3)' (*Bloomberg*, 12 May 2009). http://www.bloomberg.com/apps/news?pid=newsarchive&sid=aiqILW051D9c. Accessed 21 December 2013.

[132] El Gamal; Anwar and Patterson.

[133] The Investment Dar, 'Our History-Milestones' (*TID*, undated). http://www.inv-dar.com/En_OurHistory.cms?ActiveID=1083. Accessed 21 December 2013.

[134] M Morris, 'Dar Gets Ratings Downgrade' (*Arabian Business*, 19 May 2009). http://www.arabianbusiness.com/dar-gets-ratings-downgrade-18605.html. Accessed 24 December 2013.

[135] Sukuk, 'Saad Unit Defaults on Sukuk' (*Sukuk*, 15 November 2009). http://www.sukuk.com/news/articles/72/Sukukme-Saad-unit-defaults-on-sukuk.html. Accessed 22 December 2013.

[136] R Wilson, 'Sukuk Defaults: Islamic Debt Investors Need Better Data' (*World Economics*, February 2013). http://www.world-economics-journal.com/Papers/Sukuk%20Defaults%20Islamic%20Debt%20Investors%20Need%20Better%20Data_435d6ca7-d1ab-4ab1-afe1-b108784cc835.paper?PaperID=435D6CA7-D1AB-4AB1-AFE1-B108784CC835. Accessed 22 December 2013.

[137] Sukuk, *supra* note 135.

Monetary Agency (SAMA), Saudi Arabia's Central Bank, froze the bank accounts of Al-Sanea, the Chairman of the Saad Group, and his family members.[138] Although no official reason was given by the SAMA, it is anticipated that the dispute between the Saad Group and Ahmad Hamad Al Gosaibi & Brothers (AHAB), two Saudi business families, was the reason behind the freezing order.[139] Later in July 2009, Al-Sanea was accused of the fraud of approximately USD 10 billion in New York by AHAB.[140] In September 2009, the governor of SAMA announced that the Saad Group has settled unpaid amounts with its creditors in the KSA with no mention of a debt settlement with international creditors.[141] A Royal Committee established in 2009 to resolve the dispute between the two families viewed this dispute as a private affair, consequently allowing only creditors in the KSA to take legal action against the two families.[142]

Following SAMA's actions, several steps have been taken by the Group in order to remedy its financial problems. On 2 June 2009, the Group sought financial advice from BDO Capital Finance related to its restructuring plans.[143] The Group sold several of its assets to raise funds during the same month, including a USD 50 billion stake in 3i Infrastructure and GBP 144 million of holdings in Berkeley Group Holdings Plc (a UK homebuilder).[144] The SAMA action against the Group and subsequent remedies caused distress in the market: a court in the Cayman Islands froze USD 10 billion of Saad Group's assets in the same year.[145] In November 2009, an Abu Dhabi court also put the Group's assets in the

[138] H Anwar, 'Saad's Islamic Bonds Priced for 'Default,' ING Says (Update2)' (*Bloomberg*, 11 June 2009). http://www.bloomberg.com/apps/news?pid=newsarchive&sid=akDBpOPBtkkg. Accessed 21 December 2013.

[139] B Sturgess, 'Sukuk Defaults in the Kingdom: A Case Study in Saudi Arabia's Opaque Bankruptcy Process' (*World Economics*, March 2013). http://www.worldeconomics.com/Papers/Sukuk%20Defaults%20in%20the%20Kingdom%20A%20Case%20Study%20in%20Saudi%20Arabia%E2%80%99s%20Opaque%20Bankruptcy%20Process_d7d209a1-a644-4568-9d43-cca1f82ec535.paper?PaperID=D7D209A1-A644-4568-9D43-CCA1F82EC535. Accessed 2 January 2014.

[140] Ibid.

[141] Ibid.

[142] F Kane, 'Saudis Wash Their Hands of The Al Gosaibi Affair' (*The National*, 30 May 2011). http://www.thenational.ae/business/industry-insights/finance/saudis-wash-their-hands-of-the-al-gosaibi-affair. Accessed 22 June 2015.

[143] H Anwar, *supra* note 138.

[144] Ibid.

[145] Sukuk, *supra* note 135.

UAE on hold due to unpaid debts.[146] Furthermore, banks in the UAE have been instructed by the UAE Central Bank not to lend the Group.[147] Following the default, the *ṣukūk* holders agreed to dissolve the trust in April 2010, according to the Citicorp Trustee Co. Ltd. (the trustee).[148] Although 25% of *ṣukūk* holders voted for the dissolution of the trust in May 2010, the trustee subsequently decided not to dissolve the trust until receiving payments for this service from the originator.[149] Settlement of the Group's financial obligations is however problematic due to the freezing orders placed on its assets worldwide. Despite Société Générale, a French Bank, being entitled to USD 50 million in accordance to a High Court ruling in London, the enforcement of this ruling is impossible due to assets being frozen.[150]

5.5.3.3 Bailout

Nakheel *Ṣukūk* was on the verge of default, following the Golden Belt *Ṣukūk* case. On 25 November 2009, the market received a shocking announcement made by Nakheel PJSC regarding its restructuring plan for the Nakheel *Ṣukūk* due in December 2009.[151] The Dubai Department of Finance said that Dubai World (a global holding company wholly owned by the Government of Dubai) is asking all its investors, including the investors of Nakheel PJSC, for standstill agreements on its debt and longer maturity dates by at least 30 May 2010.[152] Dubai World held USD 26 billion of outstanding debt, including Nakheel's USD 4.1 billion *ṣukūk* obligation, which would go under the restructuring process as announced on 1 December

[146] Ibid.

[147] The Economist, 'The Fallout From A Falling Out' (*The Economist*, 9 July 2009). http://www.economist.com/node/13998715. Accessed 21 December 2013.

[148] A Sharif and H Anwar, 'Saad Investors Agree to Dissolve Islamic Bond Trust' (*Bloomberg*, 28 April 2010). http://www.bloomberg.com/news/2010-04-28/saad-trading-bondholders-approve-dissolution-of-650-million-sukuk-trust.html. Accessed 22 December 2013.

[149] Sukuk, 'Golden Belt Sukuk Holders Approve Dissolution' (*Sukuk*, 18 May 2010). http://www.sukuk.com/news/articles/28/Golden-Belt-sukuk-holders-approve-dissolution.html. Accessed 22 December 2013.

[150] R Wilson, *supra* note 136.

[151] M Johnson and J Hughes, 'Markets Reel Over Nakheel Default Fears' (*The Financial Times*, 25 November 2009). http://www.ft.com/cms/s/0/d1b1f72e-d9f6-11de-b2d5-00144feabdc0.html#axzz2o7OB9wYp. Accessed 22 December 2013.

[152] Ibid.

2009.[153] A default event has not been recorded for this case, owing to the USD 10 billion funds injection and bailout by Emirate of Abu Dhabi commenced on 14 December 2009.[154] Dubai World has received USD 4.1 billion from the bailout amount to pay its upcoming obligations, including Nakheel *Ṣukūk* due on the same day of the bailout announcement.[155]

5.5.4 Role of the Rating Agencies

Rating agencies play a vital role in efficient and fair Islamic financial markets as they facilitate adequate, true, and timely information. A rating agency provides a credit rating, an opinion about the creditworthiness of the entity, financial instruments, or issuer of such financial instruments according to a pre-defined rating ranking system.[156] The rating on *ṣukūk* plays a vital function in predicting the probability of default, identifying the stability of the issuance, and informing *ṣukūk* holders about the issuer's status. A rating on *ṣukūk*, however, does not mean evaluation or verification of the adherence of individual *ṣukūk* arrangements to Islamic law.[157] Further, the credit rating does not constitute a recommendation to purchase, sell, or hold the certificates.[158]

There are several international rating agencies that provide ratings on *ṣukūk*, such as S&P, Moody's, and Fitch Ratings. S&P assigns their rating dependent on (1) the creditworthiness of the entity providing credit-

[153] Fitch Ratings, 'Fitch Maintains Five Dubai-Based Banks' Individual Ratings on Watch Negative' (*Fitch Ratings*, 16 December 2009). https://www.fitchratings.com/creditdesk/press_releases/detail.cfm?pr_id=545097. Accessed 24 December 2013.

[154] B Thompson, 'Abu Dhabi Gives Dubai $10bn to Help Pay Debts' (*BBC*, 14 December 2009). http://news.bbc.co.uk/1/hi/8411215.stm. Accessed 22 December 2013.

[155] Ibid.

[156] Moody's Investros Service, 'Code of Proressional Conduct' (*Moody's Investros Service*, Decemebr 2013). https://www.moodys.com/uploadpage/Mco%20Documents/Documents_professional_conduct.pdf. Accessed 25 Decemebr 2013.

[157] L Noor, 'Sukuk Rating-General Approach, Criteria and Methodology' in Berhad RRS (ed), *Malaysian Sukuk Market Handbook: Your Guide to the Malaysian Islamic Capital Market* (RAM Rating Services Berhad undated) 159; S&P, *supra* note 83, 4.

[158] The offering circular of *ṣukūk* often contains the following statement: 'A credit rating is not a recommendation to buy, sell or hold securities, does not address the likelihood or timing of prepayment and may be subject to suspension, revision, or withdrawal at any time by the assigning rating organisation. A suspension, reduction or withdrawal of the ratings assigned to the Certificates may adversely affect the market price of the Certificates'. See, for example, Offering Circular of Tamweel *Ṣukūk* Limited 9; Offering Circular of Golden Belt 1 *Ṣukūk* Company B.S.C.(c)17.

enhancement mechanisms and the ranking of *ṣukūk* compared to other entity's financial obligations in a structure called '*ṣukūk* with full credit-enhancement mechanisms'; (2) performance of the underlying asset in a category called '*ṣukūk* with no credit-enhancement mechanisms'; (3) a combination of the above approaches known as '*ṣukūk* with partial credit-enhancement mechanisms'.[159] Moody's and Fitch Ratings analyses are dependent on whether the structure is asset based or asset backed.[160] In brief, they employ a very similar rating methodology that reflects the returns and risk of the underlying structure.

We now look at the role played by the rating agencies when the above *ṣukūk* experienced default and financial problems. S&P had initially assigned a CCC+ rating to East Cameron *Ṣukūk*.[161] The issuance was poorly rated, owing to undeveloped amounts of energy deposits used to collateralise the transaction at the time of issuance.[162] As a result of the shortfall on the ORRI, S&P downgraded the rating of the issuance from CCC+ to CC on 14 January 2009.[163] Then, the agency further lowered the rating from CC to D due to not receiving a servicer report.[164] Here, the rating of an asset-backed *ṣukūk* is seen to be downgraded because of the low performance of the underlying asset.

In the case of TID's default on USD 100 million *ṣukūk* (TID *Ṣukūk* 2005), Capital Intelligence (an international credit rating agency—CRA) downgraded TID from BB rating to selective default (SD) with a negative outlook in February 2009.[165] If it was an asset-backed structure, TID's rating would not have been affected by the default on its *ṣukūk*. In another problematic *ṣukūk*, S&P assigned A+ rating to the Nakheel *ṣukūk*

[159] S&P, *supra* note 83, 5.

[160] A Hassoune, K Howladar and S Harris, 'The Meaning of Ratings for Islamic Financial Institutions and Sharīʿah -Compliant Instruments' in IFSB (ed), *The Changing Landscape of Islamic Finance: Imminent Challenges and Future Directions* (IFSB 2010) 148; Fitch Ratings, 'Rating Sukuk: Cross-Sector Criteria' (*Fitch Ratings*, 9 August 2013). https://www.fitchratings.com/creditdesk/reports/report_frame.cfm?rpt_id=715279. Accessed 25 December 2013.

[161] S Sapp, *supra* note 88, 4.

[162] M Khnifer, *supra* note 33, 13.

[163] S&P, 'TEXT-S&P on East Cameron Gas Co (Sukuk) 2006' (*Reuters*, 14 Junuary 2009). http://uk.reuters.com/article/2009/01/14/idUKN1447583720090114. Accessed 11 December 2013.

[164] Ibid.

[165] M Morris, *supra* note 134.

on the grounds that the *ṣukūk* would benefit from government support.[166] It seems, however, that the assumptions under which the A+ rating was provided were inappropriate and misleading, particularly after the announcement of a six-month standstill.[167] Golden Belt *Ṣukūk* was initially given a rating of BBB+ by S&P and baa1 by Moody's.[168] On 2 June 2008, the rating of the originator was downgraded by Moody's from baa1 to B1, following the announcement of asset freezing undertaken by SAMA against the Saad Group.[169] Due to inadequate information about the development of the Group's restructuring plan, Moody's has withdrawn all ratings from 2 June 2009.[170]

There was uncertainty surrounding the rating of Tamweel Limited *Ṣukūk*, particularly triggered by the merger plan announcement previously discussed. On 27 November 2008, Moody's announced that its A3 rating of Tamweel Limited *Ṣukūk* was on review with direction uncertain.[171] However, no rating action has been taken against Tamweel Residential *Ṣukūk*. According to the Moody's index, the rating remains unchanged in this case because the initial rating was given independently of the credit rating of Tamweel PJSC.[172] In this regard, RAM Rating stated '[i]t is possible for different *ṣukūk* issues from the same obligor to carry different ratings'.[173]

5.6 Consequences of *Ṣukūk* Defaults

After presenting *ṣukūk* issues that have been subject to default and financial difficulty, it is worth highlighting the consequences of such problematic *ṣukūk* in the wider market. Ahmad and Wahab note that the '[increasing

[166] S Zaheer and S Wijnbergen, *supra* note 96, 30.

[167] Ibid.

[168] Offering Circular of Golden Belt 1 *Ṣukūk* Company B.S.C.(c)16, 17.

[169] P Lotter and C Kypreos, 'Moody's Downgrades Saad Group Entities to B1; On Review For Further Downgrade' (*Moody's* 2 June 2009). https://www.moodys.com/research/Moodys-downgrades-Saad-Group-entities-to-B1-on-review-for%2D%2DPR_180145. Accessed 24 December 2013.

[170] P Lotter and C Kypreos, 'Moody's Withdraw's Ratings On Saad Group Entities' (*Moody's*, 2 June 2009). https://www.moodys.com/research/Moodys-withdraws-ratings-on-Saad-Group-entities%2D%2DPR_180316. Accessed 24 December 2013.

[171] A Hassoune and M Haladjian, 'Moody's Reviews Tamweel's A3/P-2 Ratings, Direction Uncertain' (*Moody's*, 27 November 2008). https://www.moodys.com/research/Moodys-reviews-Tamweels-A3P-2-ratings-direction-uncertain%2D%2DPR_168275. Accessed 24 December 2013.

[172] Ibid.

[173] L Noor, *supra* note 157, 157.

number of defaulting *ṣukūk*] raises some concerns over the legal aspects and the operations of *ṣukūk* as an alternative financing instrument, besides affecting the welfare of its stakeholders'.[174] Detailed below are the three types of default consequences: market responses, legal consequences, and economic consequences.

Market responses refer to how the public and *ṣukūk* stakeholders react in the occurrence of default event. Defaults on *ṣukūk* payments came as a great shock for all concerned. An illustrative example of this is Nakheel *Ṣukūk* which was not predicted to fail in offering the level of protection expected for the *ṣukūk* holders, owing to the credit-enhancement mechanisms involved in the structure, namely a co-obligor guarantee, the Dubai World guarantee, and purchase undertaking.[175] Market investors have become much more aware about potential effects of default in the IFSI. There was previously an assumption that Islamic financial instruments are not subject to default or are default-free products on the grounds that their backing principles would prevent such behaviours, as opposed to other markets.[176] Investors have more recently begun to doubt that *ṣukūk* is more secured than its conventional counterpart. Moreover, it has been argued that default cases seriously reduced the credibility and viability of *ṣukūk*.[177]

Legal consequences refer to a number of issues found to be controversial and uncertain at the time of default from a legal point of view. *Ṣukūk* defaults have shown the weaknesses of certain legal systems, particularly how the KSA legal framework resolved the Golden Belt *Ṣukūk* failure.[178] There was obvious preferential treatment in relation to debt settlement given by the KSA legal system to Saudi creditors over foreign creditors.[179] Also, the issue of treatment of *ṣukūk* holders compared with conventional creditors in restructuring and bankruptcy has gained more attention forming a significant precedent.[180] Another concern raised by default cases is

[174] N Ahmad and N Wahab, *supra* note 4, 2635.

[175] O Salah, *supra* note 113, 1 27.

[176] N Muhamed and R Radzi, *supra* note 22, 24.

[177] R Abdul Aziz, 'Sukuk Have Lost A Lot Of Credibility Of Late. Is This Justified? Did We Get It Wrong? How Do We Fix It? What Are The Alternatives To Sukuk?' (2010) 1 So Far: The Journal Of Strategic Thinking In Islamic Finance 6, 7.

[178] Wilson, 'Sukuk Defaults: Islamic Debt Investors Need Better Data'.

[179] B Sturgess, *supra* note 39.

[180] R Wigglesworth, 'Sukuk: Defaults Destabilise A Reviving Market' (*Financial Times*, 7 December 2009). http://www.ft.com/cms/s/0/90e4c3d6-e2be-11de-b028-00144feab49a.html#axzz2p9f6MCpA. Accessed 1 January 2014.

related to investor protection; to what extent has the default case diminished the rights of investors. Indeed there were instances where lawyers and bankers were digging into *ṣukūk* legal documents to ensure whether the structure was secured by the underlying assets.[181] Liquidation has become a major concern in default scenarios. To illustrate, there was uncertainty about the court ruling in such an event, given that the structure is designed using UK law.[182] This is compounded by the ongoing confusion between asset-backed and asset-based structures and the lack of distinction between beneficial rights and legal right over the asset.[183] In fact, every default case was accompanied by discussion of asset-backed versus asset-based structures in order to find out whether *ṣukūk* holders had recourse to the asset. Default in the *ṣukūk* market also called for careful consideration of the implications of restructuring issues, arising from principle differences in *ṣukūk* structuring.[184] The issue of recognition of a credit rating agency (CRA) for *ṣukūk* issuance and whether this is required by the local authorities is uncertain in several jurisdictions. According to Majid, Shahimi, and Abdullah 'Malaysia is one of the first few countries in the world to require the recognition of CRAs for the purpose of rating a bond or *ṣukūk* issue'.[185]

The economic consequences are concerned with how far *ṣukūk* defaults impacted market growth and stability. The soundness of the defaulting party will be highly affected since such events cause hardship to employees and shareholders, risk of bankruptcy proceedings, and the danger of creditors being quickly forced to ask for their debts. As mentioned earlier, less growth in *ṣukūk* market has been recorded as a direct result of such defaults. Concerns have been raised about the future success of ICMs in some jurisdictions, including Malaysia, due to *ṣukūk* defaults.[186] Furthermore, the financial reputation of some jurisdictions claiming to be international hub for Islamic finance has been largely affected and tested following default events such as Malaysia and Dubai. However, it has been argued that Malaysia has received less criticism compared to the Middle East due to its effective investor protection mechanisms—namely legal framework, disclosure standards, and governance structure.[187]

[181] R Wigglesworth, *supra* note 9.
[182] Ibid.
[183] Ibid.
[184] N Ahmad and N Wahab, *supra* note 4, 2643.
[185] H Majid, S Shahimi and M Abdullah, *supra* note 20, 6.
[186] Ibid. 2.
[187] Ibid. 10.

5.7 Conclusion

The wave of *ṣukūk* defaults across several countries has posed an important question for the IFSI, concerning the integrity of its instruments. Although *ṣukūk* failures have been occurring for more than a decade, the literature has not yet tackled adequately the question of why defaults happened. Furthermore, a concrete concept of default has not been well established nor standardised in the context of different Islamic finance instruments and regions. Neither has the resolution of such scenarios been well expounded. When discussing the reasons for defaults in the *ṣukūk* market, one should be conceptually clear that credit risk and *ṣukūk* structural shortcomings are of course interrelated. The default case studies reveal that several legal resolutions have been taken by local authorities as well as *ṣukūk* holders in order to resolve the implications of such defaults. These actions include undergoing formal bankruptcy procedures, restructuring plans, bailout by third party, dissolving *ṣukūk* assets, postponement of cash flows, standstill announcement, and freezing of defaulting party's assets. The implications of default of asset-backed vis-à-vis asset-based structure entail particular consideration in terms of recourse to the asset, investors risk exposures, default procedures, and credit rating.

This chapter looked at a number of problematic *ṣukūk*. East Cameron *Ṣukūk* defaulted in 2008 because of the hurricane in the area of the underlying asset. The originator tried to claw back the underlying asset by filing a petition for bankruptcy protection under Chapter 11 of the Bankruptcy Code. The court found that the *ṣukūk* in question was an asset-backed *ṣukūk*, and not secured loans. East Cameron *Ṣukūk* would be unimportant if not for the fact that it illustrates how *ṣukūk* holders' rights are affected by the originator's default. It provides an important precedent for how Western courts look at the concept of *ṣukūk* as an asset-backed structure and the legal consequences of *ṣukūk* default. The Investment Dar *Ṣukūk* and Golden Belt *Ṣukūk* proved that asset-based structures cannot protect investors once a default event is triggered. Although Nakheel *Ṣukūk* was not a real default case, it illustrates the legal uncertainty that exists in many *ṣukūk* markets in near-default situations in regard to the treatment of *ṣukūk* holders and recourse to the asset. Tamweel PJSC *Ṣukūk* provides an illustration of how asset-backed and asset-based structures are viewed differently from a rating agency perspective once a financial uncertainty event is triggered.

There are some common issues that can be understood from this series of *ṣukūk* defaults and financial difficulties. In this context, understanding the division of *ṣukūk* into asset-backed and asset-based structures is of paramount importance. First, there is a concern about the position of *ṣukūk* holders and their rights following a default: *ṣukūk* holders of asset-backed *ṣukūk* are legal owners and thus have full recourse to the underlying asset. *Ṣukūk* holders of asset-based *ṣukūk* conversely are beneficial owners and have recourse to the originator. While *ṣukūk* holders in asset-backed structures have the status of secured creditors, *ṣukūk* holders in asset-based structures rank *pari passu* with unsecured creditors. Second, the default cases analysed have proven that *ṣukūk* holders face different types of risks: while they face asset risk in asset-backed structure, they face credit risk or originator risk in an asset-based structure. Third, managing default cases has raised questions about 'resolving the claims of foreign creditors in accordance with international standards and best practices'.[188] In particular, it has been argued that the principles of international insolvency law such as the transparency in all aspects of the resolution process and equal treatment for all creditors have been violated in some *ṣukūk* defaults.[189] Fourth, in the light of the dominance of asset-based *ṣukūk*, the primary source of repayment for *ṣukūk* holders is future financial receivables and purchase obligations. However, the defaulted originator will not be able to make periodic payments and exercise purchase undertaking. Even if the *ṣukūk* is structured as asset backed, the ability of *ṣukūk* holders to have recourse to the underlying asset is uncertain. This is of particular significance for sovereign *ṣukūk* wherein the relevant legal environment inhibits taking possession of the state's assets. Finally, the application of the Islamic law of insolvency following a default is problematic. Problems that arise in the event of the insolvency of originators are due, to some extent, to the underdeveloped state of Islamic law of corporate insolvency. However, the precedent set by the ruling in the case of East Cameron *Ṣukūk* shows that the substance of the transaction will be considered over its form.

After understanding how *ṣukūk* structures work and how they respond to financial distress, the next chapter shall focus on issues warranting a discussion from a legal point of view.

[188] R Shapiro, 'The Importance of International Standards in Managing Defaults in Islamic Finance: Saudi Arabia and the Saad Group's Sukuk Default' (*Sonecon*, May 2013) 1. http://www.sonecon.com/docs/studies/Shapiro_Paper_Sukuk_Default_new.pdf. Accessed 6 September 2015.

[189] Ibid. 4–5.

CHAPTER 6

Legal Issues Surrounding *Ṣukūk* Structures

6.1 Introduction

This chapter discusses eight legal issues surrounding the applications of contemporary *ṣukūk* (trust investment certificates). As discussed in Chaps. 3 and 4, the majority of legal issues arise in asset-based *ṣukūk*. Such issues typically arise in practice due to contradictions between Islamic law and general laws and regulations imposed by the wider legal environment. The legality of *ṣukūk* structures has been in the spotlight due to the aforementioned defaults, among others, which sparked a wave of criticism.

It is important at the outset to explain why these issues require such discussion. The selection of legal issues in the chapter is motivated by three reasons: first, they are very relevant to the discussion of asset-backed *ṣukūk* versus asset-based *ṣukūk*. Second, it is believed that issues listed in this chapter threaten the development of the *ṣukūk* market. While some issues cast doubt on the legitimacy of *ṣukūk* structures from a sharia point view, others are considered to be problematic from the view of legislators in some jurisdictions. Third, this debate lacks a deeper and holistic analysis; although some issues have been already pointed out by sharia scholars, legal practitioners, and Islamic finance-supporting institutions,[1] the need for further discussion remains.

[1] See generally M Al-ʿuthmānī, 'Sukuk and Their Contemporary Applications' (*Islamic Economics and Finance Pedia*, Undated). http://www.iefpedia.com/english/wp-content/uploads/2009/11/Sukuk-and-their-Contemporary-Applications.pdf. Accessed 15 February 2012; M Laldin, 'Sukuk in Various Juridictions: Shariah and Legal Issues' (2012) 2 Journal of Islamic Business and Management 15. AAOIFI issued a short and special document as a

S. Al-Ali, *Raising Capital on* Ṣukūk *Markets*,
https://doi.org/10.1007/978-3-030-14536-1_6

Another significant question that needs to be raised before moving into the main discussion is: how have such worrying issues arisen in the *ṣukūk* market? One should understand that the notion that *ṣukūk* are required to be structured in accordance with Islamic law does not mean they are always sharia-compliant structures from a practical perspective. Further, there has generally been a market shift in *ṣukūk* structuring from an idealist approach to a more pragmatic approach, and this deviation has caused some problematic issues. Whether this market shift is viewed as obligatory or optional depends on several factors, including the existing legal system and compliance approach, whether strict or flexible. While an idealist approach follows literally the rules of Islamic law, a pragmatic approach takes into account practical impediments.[2] The latter approach has resulted in the attachment of financial innovations and mechanisms to *ṣukūk* structures, causing an ongoing debate in the industry.

6.2 Asset Suitability: The Concern over Intangibility Assets

There are two key factors affecting the choice of asset in individual *ṣukūk* structures; asset suitability from a commercial perspective and asset suitability from an Islamic perspective. The former refers to the profitability and productivity of the asset chosen to underlay the financial transaction, with the latter referring to the compliance of the asset selected with Islamic law. Choice of the underlying asset is not a worrying issue in conventional markets, as opposed to Islamic financial markets. Assets underlying *ṣukūk* structures need to be not only commercially viable, but also acceptable from an Islamic perspective. This drastically limits the choice of assets available for those seeking Islamic financial transactions. Despite the fact that the above two factors are interrelated, asset suitability from Islamic perspective will always dominate the process of asset selection.

Asset suitability remains a matter of concern from an Islamic law point of view because of the continued disagreement amongst sharia scholars over the permissibility of certain assets to underlay financial transactions.

response to observations raised about *ṣukūk*. See AAOIFI, 'AAOIFI Shari'ah Resolutions: Issues on Sukuk' (*AAOIFI*, February 2008). http://www.kantakji.com/media/7760/f173.pdf. Accessed 6 October 2014.

[2] See O Saeed and O Salah, 'Development of Sukuk: Pragmatic and Idealist Approaches to Sukuk Structures' (2014) 29 Journal of International Banking Law and Regulation 41.

It is helpful to look at the types of asset that can be used to underlay *ṣukūk* and Islamic law's position on suitability of such asset classes. There are three potential types of assets for *ṣukūk* structures: existing tangible assets (such as buildings, vehicles); future tangible assets (such as properties to be developed or under development); and intangible assets (such as shares, intellectual property rights, and debt).[3] The discussion of asset suitability in Islamic law falls under the general theory of contracts which determines the elements of a contract, particularly the subject matter. The issue of whether the above types of assets are suitable to underlay *ṣukūk* structures depends very much on the extent to which they are regarded as valid subject matter from an Islamic law standpoint. Considering a particular type of asset as suitable from an Islamic law point of view depends on meeting certain conditions of the contract subject matter, namely lawfulness, existence, deliverability, and precise determination.[4]

The sharia controversy regarding the lawfulness of the subject matter, and in some cases the existence of the subject matter, is the most important of the debates surrounding asset suitability in the *ṣukūk* structures. Lawfulness in this context implies, among other things, that the subject matter must be a property of value (*māl mutaqawam*) in the view of Islamic law.[5] There is consensus among sharia scholars regarding certain assets that are not considered property of value, such as wine and pork. The sharia definition of property of value becomes very challenging in view of existing financial innovations and advanced financial instruments. As for the existence condition, this presupposes that the subject matter of a contract must exist at the time the contract is made according to the view of majority of jurists.[6] In this respect, many financial transactions have been prohibited under Islamic law because they fall within the topic of *bayʿ al-maʿdūm* (sale of non-existent asset). Exceptions to this principle, allowing for non-existent assets to underlay contracts are allowed in the case of *salam* (a forward sale (fungible commodity)) and *istiṣnāʿ* (contract of manufacture) contracts.[7]

[3] E Ali, 'Issues in Islamic Debt Securitisation' in M Bakar and E Ali (eds), *Essential Readings in Islamic Finance* (CERT Publications 2008) 462–463.

[4] M Bakar, 'Contract in Islamic Commercial Law and Their Application in Modren Islamic Financial System' in Bakar M and Ali E (eds), *Essential Readings in Islamic Finance* (CERT Publications 2008) 51. See also Ayub 108.

[5] E Ali, *supra* note 3, 461; Nawawi 99.

[6] M Bakar, *supra* note 4, 51; E Ali, *supra* note 3, 463–464.

[7] In this regard, SC's Sharia Advisory Council (SAC) departs from the majority view. It has ruled that the trading of non-existent asset is permissible. Its ruling is based on the *ḥanbalī*

From the prior discussion, one can state that existing tangible assets and future tangible assets (according to *salam* and *istiṣnāʿ*) are accepted to underlay *ṣukūk* structures from Islamic law perspective. However, intangible assets prompt a sharia issue due to their lack of physical existence. The concern over intangible assets is related to the concept of property of value in Islamic law as defined above. The issue mainly arises because of the unsettled definition of property (*māl*) in Islamic law. While the majority of jurists include corporeal matter, usufructs, and rights in the definition of property, the minority of jurists (primarily of the *ḥanafi* view) limit the definition of property to corporeal matters.[8] This dispute over what constitutes property makes *ṣukūk* structures using intangible assets acceptable in the view of the majority, and not acceptable according to the minority. Adopting the majority view on the rule of intangible assets in *ṣukūk* inevitably provides more flexibility in the selection of the underlying asset. In this regard, IIFA's Resolution No. 43[9] and AAOIFI's Sharia Standard No. 42[10] recognise property rights arising from intangible matters as valid such as business name, corporate name, trade mark, literary production, invention, and discovery. Therefore, it can be concluded that they have adopted the majority opinion that considers intangible assets as a form of property capable of ownership.

Caution must be exercised when discerning the suitability of certain intangible assets from an Islamic law viewpoint. A good illustration of this is the selection of financial receivables to underlay *ṣukūk* structures. The acceptance and application of such assets throughout the IFSI are far from straightforward, despite the opinion of the majority of jurists regarding legality of intangible assets. The following section is devoted to this issue.

view which does not stipulate the existence of the object but rather its certainty when the contract is being made. See SC, *Resolutions of The Securities Commission Shariah Advisory Council* (2 edn, Securities Commission 2007) 23.

[8] For more discussion, see E Ali, *supra* note 3, 461–462; S Bouheraoua and others, 'Shariah Issues in Intangible Assets' (Innovation and Financial Engineering Products and Applications: Between the Conventional and Islamic Finance Industries, Algeria, May 2014) 4.

[9] IIFA, *Resolutions and Recommendations of the Council of Islamic Fiqh Academy* (1 edn, IDB 2000) 89.

[10] AAOIFI, 'Al-Ḥuqūq Al-Māliah Wa Al-Taṣaruf Fīhā' (*AAOIFI*, undated). http://www.kantakji.com/media/9219/42ife.pdf. Accessed 7 Novermber 2014.

6.3 *BAYᶜ AL-DAYN* (SALE OF DEBT)

Bayᶜ al-dayn (sale of debt) is defined as 'the sale of payable right either to the debtor himself, or any third party'.[11] Identifying the instances in which *bayᶜ al-dayn* occurs in the *ṣukūk* market is significant. *Bayᶜ al-dayn* typically takes place in four situations: (1) securitisation of debts, (2) securitisation of asset pools that include receivables, (3) in trading *ṣukūk* certificates in the secondary market, and (4) the restructuring process. *Bayᶜ al-dayn* as it occurs in the restructuring scenario will be discussed later.

The main debate on *bayᶜ al-dayn* in *ṣukūk* is not about whether debt is a recognised legal asset in the view of sharia. Payable right is intangible in nature and therefore falls under the broader definition of asset held by the majority of jurists, as discussed above. Rather, the practice of *bayᶜ al-dayn* in *ṣukūk* markets is mainly questioned because of the sharia controversy about the permissibility of the sale of debt. The issue of sale of debt has been subject to great debate among past scholars, particularly the sale of debt to a third party.[12] *Ribā* (usury) and *gharar* (uncertainty) have been always central points for discussing the sale of debt in Islamic law. While the element of uncertainty arises from the inability of the seller to deliver the sold item to the purchaser, the interest element arises when the rules of *sarf* (exchange of money), parity and spot transaction, are not followed. Therefore, it is argued that the practice of *bayᶜ al-dayn* in *ṣukūk* also brings the issue of *ribā al-buyūᶜ* (*ribā* occurring through sale of *ribawi* (*Ribā*-based) products), particularly when the rules of *sarf* are violated.

Debts securitisation exists when future payments created from an underlying deferred payment sale transaction are sold and then used as a subject matter in the *ṣukūk* structure.[13] To be more specific, financial

[11] S Rosly and M Sanusi, 'The Application of Bay Al-Inah and Bay Al-Dayn in Malaysian Islamic Bonds: An Islamic Analysis' (1999) 1 International Journal of Islamic Financial Services 1, 8.

[12] Sharia scholars generally tend to differentiate between the sale of debt to the debtor and the sale of debt to the third party. There is less controversy in Islamic law about selling the debt to the debtor which is regarded permissible according to dominant juristic view. However, the point of contention seems to be the selling of debt to a third party. The majority view considers the sale of debt to a third party is prohibited because it involves uncertainty. The minority view allows it subject to certain conditions. See H Amin, 'An Analysis of the Classical and Contemporary Juristic Opinions on Bay Al-Dayn' (2007) 1 Labuan e-Journal of Muamalat and Society 31.

[13] E Ali, *supra* note 3, 478.

receivables constitute the whole part of the *ṣukūk* pool in this case. In this case, issuance of *ṣukūk* essentially means sale of debt to a third party (*ṣukūk* holders). AAOIFI's Sharia Standard No. 17[14] and IIFA's Resolution No. 178[15] have addressed this matter, and ruled that such practice is not permissible. They here adopt the view of majority of jurists who prohibit the sale of debt to a third party. IIFA, however, has allowed structures with this functionality only when debt securitisation falls within the principles of *ḥiwālah* (transfer of debt or assignment of debt).[16] This exception is irrelevant from a practical point of view because debt trading involves a discounting practice which contradicts *ḥiwālah*. The SAC of SC has come up with a general resolution concerning the practice of debt sale in the ICM, stating that the sale of debt is permissible with emphasis on its validity for the development of the ICM.[17]

The second situation of sale of debt in *ṣukūk* refers to inclusion of receivables into the pool of the *ṣukūk* assets. While in the first situation the *ṣukūk* pool consisted entirely of debts, debts along with other assets, such as tangible assets and usufructs, form the *ṣukūk* pool in the second situation. Sharia scholars have questioned not only the securitisation of debt, but also the inclusion of debts in the *ṣukūk* pool. For instance, Al-ʿuthmānī states that '[t]he inclusion of *murābaḥah* contracts into such *ṣukūk* … cannot but bring into question the issue of the sale of debt, even if the percentage of the *murābaḥah* contracts may be considerably less than that of the *ijārah*, *mushārakah* and *istiṣnāʿ* contracts'.[18] According to the general view of SC's SAC on the sale of debt as mentioned above, such practice should not be problematic in Islamic law. IIFA's Resolution No. 188 has differentiated between two situations when looking at the permissibility of securitising and trading of *ṣukūk* pool that includes debts, that is, dependent

[14] AAOIFI's Sharia Standards states '[a]s for debts owed as a liability, it is not permissible to securitize them for the purpose of trading'. See AAOIFI, *Shari'a Standards for Islamic Financial Institutions* (AAOIFI 2010) 310.

[15] IIFA, 'Al-Qarārāt Wa Al-Tawṣiyāt: Al-Dawrah Al-Tāsiʿah ʿashrah' (*Fiqhacademy*, 2009). http://www.fiqhacademy.org.sa/. Accessed 7 November 2014.

[16] Ibid.

[17] SC, *supra* note 7, 16.

[18] M Al-ʿuthmānī, 'Sukuk and Their Contemporary Applications' (*Islamic Economics and Finance Pedia*, Undated). http://www.iefpedia.com/english/wp-content/uploads/2009/11/Sukuk-and-their-Contemporary-Applications.pdf. Accessed 15 February 2012, 3–4.

debts and independent debts.[19] While trading of asset pool that includes dependent debts is permissible without any size consideration, the permissibility ruling in case of asset pool that includes debts which are independent is subject to the majority standard.[20] The application of IIFA's view is subject to difficulty in practice, given the absence of a collective definition of majority standard (*miʿyār al-aghlabiah*)[21] and dependency standard (*miʿyār al-tabaʿiah*).[22] AAOIFI discusses the inclusion of debts in the *ṣukūk* pool based on the objectives of the corporation in question and its usual activity (primary asset) as provided by its Sharia Standard No. 21. To be more specific, trading of asset pools that include debt is permissible when the primary asset for the corporation is trading in tangible assets, benefits, and rights, with the condition that the total value of debt is not more that 70%.[23] When the primary asset for the corporation is trading in gold, silver, or currencies, and trading in debts, the rules of *sarf* and rules of debt must be followed, respectively.[24]

The third situation refers to the selling and trading of *ṣukūk* in secondary markets in the following circumstances: the trading of *ṣukūk* before the beginning of the *ṣukūk* activity; completion of liquidation; and *ṣukūk* representing receivables (i.e. *ṣukūk* representing assets that are sold for a deferred price).[25] In short, it refers to *ṣukūk* representing cash or debts when *ṣukūk* trading is taking place. While debt securitisation and the inclusion of debts in the asset pool attract attention before a *ṣukūk* is issued, this third situation is concerned with *ṣukūk* that have already been sold to *ṣukūk* holders. In this situation, sale of *ṣukūk* may fall under the sale of debt between the creditor and debtor or to a third party. *Ṣukūk* representing ownership of tangible assets, usufruct, or services after the beginning of the underlying *ṣukūk* activity do not come under this category, and

[19] IIFA, *supra* note 15.

[20] IIFA, 'Al-Qarārāt Wa Al-Tawṣiyāt: Al-Dawrah Al-ʿishrīn' (*Fiqhacademy*, 2012). http://www.fiqhacademy.org.sa/. Accessed 9 November 2014.

[21] This refers to the percentage and size of debts allowed to be included in the *ṣukūk* pool. This issue remains unsettled in Islamic law.

[22] This refers to the meaning of dependent or independent debts and in which instances debt can be described as dependent or independent. Although IIFA describes debt as dependent or independent based on its relation with the underlying *ṣukūk* project, there is no explanation of how this occurs in practice.

[23] AAOIFI, *supra* note 14, 382.

[24] Ibid.

[25] Ibid. 315.

therefore it is permissible to trade in them.[26] As for SC's SAC, trading *ṣukūk* representing cash or debts in secondary markets is considered permissible and in accordance with its general permissibility ruling regarding the sale of debt, mentioned above. In addition, BNM's SAC ruled that the IIFS is allowed to repurchase the Negotiable Islamic Debt Certificate (NIDC) before maturity.[27] AAOIFI, on the other hand, is of the view that such practice of *ṣukūk* trading is not permissible. Several instances in which *ṣukūk* trading raises the issue of sale of debt have been identified, including *ṣukūk* representing subleased assets, parallel *istiṣnāʿ* arrangements, *ṣukūk* representing *istiṣnāʿ* when the purchaser has received the manufactured item, and *ṣukūk* representing *murābaḥah* (a sale with a mark-up) when the purchaser has received the item.[28] Here, one must add that the motive for the prohibition of trading the above-mentioned *ṣukūk* should not be confused with the reason for prohibition of *salam ṣukūk* trading; while the issue of sale of debt is reason for the prohibition in the former, uncertainty justifies the prohibition of the latter.

6.4 Ownership

Another argument against the legitimacy of *ṣukūk* in practice is premised on *ṣukūk* ownership. Before presenting the issues related to ownership in *ṣukūk*, it is worth defining briefly the concept of ownership in Islamic law, given the sharia-compliant nature of *ṣukūk* transactions. As a general principal, Islamic law places great emphasis on the ownership of the subject matter in a financial transaction, considered an essential element of the contract under Islamic law. Bakar states that 'inherent in the lawfulness of the object is the condition that the object must be legally owned (or authorised) by the parties to a contract'.[29] An ownership requirement implies that the person in question must own the asset in order to enjoy total freedom to transect with the asset. In the general context of *ṣukūk*, AAOIFI has stressed the requirement of ownership representation in

[26] Ibid.

[27] The reason for the NIDC to be discussed under sale of debt is that they are in the form of *bayʿ al-ʿīnah ṣukūk* and thus repurchase of such instruments by the originator amounts to the sale of debt. See BNM, *Shariah Resolutions in Islamic Finance* (BNM 2010) 106.

[28] AAOIFI, *supra* note 14, 315.

[29] M Bakar, *supra* note 4, 51.

ṣukūk in its Sharia Standards.[30] According to ownership concept in the *ṣukūk*, the holders of *ṣukūk* are considered the owners of the underlying *ṣukūk* project and asset.

However, there have been some concerns related to the ownership concept in *ṣukūk*. In this regard, Al-ʿuthmānī has criticised a number of *ṣukūk* in the market because 'there is doubt regarding their representation of ownership'.[31] The main concerns about ownership in *ṣukūk* have centred on beneficial ownership and registration, as elaborated below.

6.4.1 Beneficial Ownership

The concept of ownership in relation to investment has changed and evolved over the years. The basic implication of the legal nature of investment is that 'investors have "ownership" rather than just contractual rights'.[32] Consequently, contractual rights have been allowed to become property, namely 'a thing [that] can be owned and transferred to another person'.[33] This has been done by way of partitioning the rights associated with a thing or property. English law has come up with the notion of division of property rights and interests over property. While 'ownership of an asset suggests that the owner has all rights relating to a particular asset',[34] the trust concept partitions these rights between the trustee and the beneficiaries. Trust is an English legal concept that originated in the thirteenth century[35]; it is defined as 'a relationship recognised by equity which arises where property is vested in (a person or) persons called the trustee, which those trustees are obliged to hold for the benefit of other persons called cestuis que trust or beneficiaries'.[36] Two main features distinguish trust from other legal concepts, namely the holding of property rights for other people, and the obligations imposed upon the trustee.[37] Several functions of trust generally make it attractive and useful to be included in

[30] AAOIFI Sharia Standard No. 17 states: 'Investment *ṣukūk* represent a common share in the ownership of the assets made available for investors'. See AAOIFI, *supra* note 14, 309.

[31] M Al-ʿuthmānī, *supra* note 18, 3.

[32] I MacNeil, *An Introduction to the Law on Financial Investment* (2nd edn, Hart Publishing Ltd 2012) 9.

[33] Ibid.

[34] G Virgo, *The Principles of Equity & Trusts* (Oxford University Press 2012) 47.

[35] Ibid. 40.

[36] J Martin and H Hanbury, *Modern Equity* (Sweet & Maxwell 2012) 49.

[37] G Virgo, *supra* note 34, 42.

ṣukūk which are the segregation of assets, asset partitioning, management of property, convenient property holding, and tax avoidance.[38] As a result of creation of a trust, several rights and interests arise. Trust law divides ownership into legal and beneficial ownership.[39] This has allowed for a legal title of a property to remain with the original owner while transferring the benefits associated with the property to the beneficiaries.

Trust concepts have been used in *ṣukūk* as a way of transferring the beneficial interest in relation to the underlying asset to *ṣukūk* holders. *Ṣukūk* that represent beneficial ownership are known as asset-based *ṣukūk*. The essence and nature of ownership differs between asset-backed *ṣukūk* and asset-based *ṣukūk*. While the asset is transferred by way of true sale in the former, beneficial ownership related to the asset is transferred to *ṣukūk* holders in the latter.

There are various reasons for importing the notion of beneficial ownership into *ṣukūk*. Beneficial ownership has been regarded as a solution in the case of sovereign issues or issues involving foreign investors in which the government does not want to sell national assets for public policy reasons.[40] The choice of beneficial ownership has been also motivated by that fact that true sale is not suitable for fast-moving *ṣukūk* issuances since the achievement of true sale requires detailed information and efforts.[41] Further, beneficial ownership is preferred to avoid sales taxes, property gains taxes, and stamp duty.[42]

Despite these advantages, issue of beneficial ownership remains problematic in Islamic law. Whether beneficial ownership is recognised in Islamic law is a matter of debate. Al-Amine notes that there is a pressing need to look at the permissibility and scope of beneficial ownership under Islamic law.[43] In 2014, the International Sharia Research Academy for Islamic Finance (ISRA) and the Islamic Research and Training Institute (IRTI) organised an International Sharia Scholars Forum where sharia

[38] Ibid. 46.

[39] See ibid. 48.

[40] M Kamali and A Abdullah, 'Preface' in M Kamali and A Abdullah (eds), *Islamic Finance: Issues in Sukuk and Proposals for Reform* (International Institute of Advance Islamic Studies and Islamic Foundation 2014) vii.

[41] Ibid. viii.

[42] Ibid.

[43] M Al-Amine, 'Unresolved Sharīʿah Issues in Ṣukūk' in Kamali M and Abdullah A (eds), *Islamic Finance: Issues in Ṣukūk and Proposals for Reform* (International Intitute of Advanced Islamic Studies and Islamic Foundation 2014) 30.

scholars, senior industry practitioners, and academicians gathered to discuss the status of legal ownership vis-à-vis beneficial ownership in the IFSI.[44] In the case of *Dato' Hj Nik Mahmud bin Daud v. Bank Islam Malaysia Bhd*,[45] the Court of Appeal had to consider the distinction between legal and beneficial ownership to address Dato' Hj Nik's (the appellant) argument that the BBA transaction is void because it contravenes the Kelantan Malay Reservations Enactment 1930 and the National Land Code 1965, which prohibit the sale of Malay reserve land to non-Malay.[46] The court rejected the appellant's argument because what has been transferred is the beneficial ownership, and the legal owner has not been changed in the land records. There are four constraints and challenges in defining beneficial ownership under Islamic law: (1) it falls short of a true sale; (2) it provides the buyer with only some rights, namely the right to use an asset and to receive returns from it; (3) it does not give the buyer the right to sell the asset or dispose of it; and (4) the legal title remains with the seller.[47] However, the focus shall be on the challenges 1–3, since the last challenge is less problematic, as explained below.

The prevailing view suggests that beneficial ownership is not recognised in the classical Islamic law, and there has been no attempt by past sharia scholars to divide ownership into legal and beneficial.[48] For a sharia ruling on beneficial ownership, one refers to the following statement by the AAOIFI: 'The Manager issuing the *ṣukūk* must clarify the transfer of ownership of such assets in its (*ṣukūk*) books, and must not keep them as his own assets'.[49] This statement clearly shows that AAOIFI considers beneficial ownership as not sharia-compliant. Beneficial ownership implies that

[44] ISRA, '9th International Shari'ah Scholars Forum' (*ISRA*, 2014). http://ifikr.isra.my/event-articles/-/eventArticles/browseArticles?_7013_WAR_fatwaportlet_eventCode=ISSF2014. Accessed 19 September 2015.

[45] [1998] 3 CLJ 605.

[46] Ibid.

[47] See M Kamali and A Abdullah, *supra* note 40, vii; M Kamali and A Abdullah, 'Introduction' in M Kamali and A Abdullah (eds), *Islamic Finance: Issues in Sukuk and Proposals for Reform* (International Institute of Advanced Islamic Studies and Islamic Foundation 2014) 4; M Al-Amine, *supra* note 43, 40.

[48] E Ali, *supra* note 3, 476; R Haneef, 'Second Keynote: Legal Ownership and Benefical Ownership From Sharia and Legal Perspective: General Scope and Main Challenges' (Contemporary Issues in the Application of Islamic Finance: Benefical and Legal Ownership and Takaful in Light of the Islamic Concept of Cooperation, November 2014, Malalysia); M Kamali and A Abdullah, *supra* note 40, vii.

[49] AAOIFI, *supra* note 1, 1.

only certain rights related to the asset in question are transferred to *ṣukūk* holders. This harks back to the definition of ownership as 'a set of legal rights held by an owner in respect of a thing'.[50] AAOIFI has insisted on the point that all rights of ownership must be given to *ṣukūk* holders. AAOIFI states '[*ṣ*]*ukūk*, to be tradable, must be owned by the *ṣukūk* holders, with all the rights and obligations of ownership, in real assets, whether tangible, usufructs or services, capable of being owned and sold legally'.[51] This makes structures missing any of ownership rights questionable from Islamic law standpoint.

However, proponents of beneficial ownership argue that it does not contradict Islamic law because the conditions of sale transaction are met.[52] Another argument that has been put forward to justify importing the notion of beneficial ownership into *ṣukūk* is the necessity (*ḍarūrah*).[53] Ali has attempted to analyse the concept of legal interest vis-à-vis beneficial interest in comparison with several concepts in Islamic law, including ownership and possession.[54] The division of ownership into complete and incomplete in Islamic law offers, to some extent, grounds for partitioning the rights related to property. It is argued that incomplete ownership corresponds with beneficial interest because the owner in both scenarios lacks full control over the asset and is entitled only to the benefit. Ali states 'the position of a beneficial interest may be argued to be analogous to the concept of incomplete ownership (*milk naqis*), because the beneficial owner's rights over the property are normally made subject to the fulfilment of the rights of the legal owner'.[55] While in complete ownership the owner enjoys total freedom to transact with the asset, the owner has limited freedom to deal with the asset in incomplete ownership.[56] For example, complete ownership applies to the buyer in the sale contract, and incomplete ownership applies to the tenant in the tenancy agreement and to the owner in an

[50] I MacNeil, *supra* note 32, 9.

[51] AAOIFI, *supra* note 1, 1.

[52] R Haneef, 'The Case for Receivables-Based Ṣukūk: A Convergence between the Malaysian and Global Shariah Standards on Bay al-Dayn?' in M Kamali and A Abdullah (eds), *Islamic Finance: Issues in Sukuk and Proposals for Reform* (International Institute of Advanced Islamic Studies and Islamic Foundation 2014) 146.

[53] M Kamali and A Abdullah, *supra* note 40, vii.

[54] E Ali, *supra* note 3, 475.

[55] Ibid.

[56] Ibid.

insolvency situation.[57] With regard to the concept of possession, Ali argues that a beneficial owner can be recognised in Islamic law in a situation whereby the buyer is not fully enjoying the asset because the buyer has not possessed the asset yet (constructive possession).[58] In this particular scenario, Islamic law recognises the buyer as de jure owner, although there is lack of the buyer's full enjoyment of the asset.

However, these Islamic law concepts do not create equitable interest in the asset. Thus, one may find that the concept of *waqf* (charitable endowment) in Islamic law provided the most appropriate legal grounds for the separation of rights related to the asset including equitable interest because trust concept is very similar to the *waqf* concept.

6.4.2 *Registration of Ownership Transfer*

This subsection questions whether the registration of transfer of legal ownership is required from an Islamic law perspective. As a matter of practice, originators tend to avoid registering the transfer of legal ownership because this leads to increased transaction costs. This is compounded by the fact that a similar transaction cost will be incurred when the asset in question is transferred to the originator on maturity of the *ṣukūk*. As far as sharia compliance is concerned, Islamic law does not require registration to take place in the sale contract. In Islamic law, the legal ownership is transferred automatically when the sale contracts are completed. As Al-Amine states:

> Registration of ownership transfer in the Land Register, for instance, is not a pre-condition for the compliance and validity of a sale and purchase contract under Islamic law. A sale-and-purchase contract is valid through offer and acceptance and there is no sharia requirement that this must be registered. Registration is just a modern legal formality.[59]

Therefore, the absence of registration of ownership transfer does not affect the validity of a transaction under Islamic law. The buyer is thus entitled to all ownership rights related to the asset in question, although the registration has not taken place.

[57] Ibid.
[58] Ibid. 477.
[59] M Al-Amine, *supra* note 43, 39.

Based on the above, it can be seen that the absence of registration in beneficial ownership is not a worrying issue. Algari[60] and Haneef[61] argue that the issue of whether asset transfer is registered or not is merely procedural and legal requirement. Al-Amine also notes that the reliance on the issue of registration to differentiate between legal ownership and benefice ownership is misleading.[62] From an Islamic law perspective, the absence of registration does not make the buyer as beneficial owner.

6.5 *Bayʿ al-ʿĪnah*

It is evident from established market practice that certain *ṣukūk* structures have involved *bayʿ al-ʿīnah* (sale and buy-back). The issue of *bayʿ al-ʿīnah* is relevant to asset-based *ṣukūk*. A fundamental feature of *bayʿ al-ʿīnah* is the sell and buy-back transaction between the two parties involved regardless of other names given in the arrangement.[63] This is of particular significance in the context of the Malaysian *ṣukūk* market where *bayʿ al-ʿīnah* has been most widely applied, as opposed to in the GCC. Some examples of Malaysian *ṣukūk* instruments based on *bayʿ al-ʿīnah* are the GII, the Sale and Buy Back Agreement, the NIDC, and the *Murābaḥah* Notes Issuance Facility.[64]

There are several situations in which *bayʿ al-ʿīnah* occurs in *ṣukūk* which include *bayʿ al-ʿīnah ṣukūk*, *murābaḥah ṣukūk*, BBA *ṣukūk*, *istiṣnāʿ ṣukūk*, and *ijārah ṣukūk*. Before discussing the application of *bayʿ al-ʿīnah* in these mentioned structures, two important remarks need to be made. While the presence of *bayʿ al-ʿīnah* in *bayʿ al-ʿīnah ṣukūk* is straightforward, its existence in the remaining structures requires careful attention. Also, not all *murābaḥah ṣukūk*, BBA *ṣukūk*, *istiṣnāʿ ṣukūk*, and *ijārah ṣukūk* involve *bayʿ al-ʿīnah* because each one of them has a different form in practice.

In relation to *bayʿ al-ʿīnah ṣukūk*,[65] this structure starts by the investors providing the asset that they own to the SPV who will sell it to the

[60] M Algari, 'Taṭbīq Al-Mulkiyyah Al-Nafʿiyyah Wa Al-Mulkiyyah Al-Qānūniyyah Fī Al-Tamwīl Al-Islāmī' (Contemporary Issues in the Application of Islamic Finance: Benefical and Legal Ownership and Takaful in Light of the Islamic Concept of Cooperation, Malalysia, November 2014).

[61] R Haneef, *supra* note 48.

[62] M Al-Amine, *supra* note 43, 40.

[63] E Ali, *supra* note 3, 455.

[64] A Thomas and S Mokhtar, 'Debt-Based Sukuk: Murabahah, Istisna' and Istithmar (Tawarruq) Sukuk' in Thomas A (ed), *Sukuk* (Sweet & Maxwell Asia 2009) 127–128.

[65] E Ali, *supra* note 3, 454.

originator for a deferred payment. The SPV then buys back the asset from the originator for a cash price that is less than the deferred price. In order to buy back the asset, the SPV issues *ṣukūk* to the investors to raise funds. The structure of *murābaḥah ṣukūk* and BBA *ṣukūk* is basically similar in the Malaysian context, and the term 'BBA *ṣukūk*' actually refers to *murābaḥah ṣukūk* in other jurisdictions, particularly the GCC. The Malaysians distinguish between these structures in terms of duration, that is, *murābaḥah ṣukūk* is used for short- and medium-term periods with a lump sum feature, and BBA is used for long periods with an instalment payment feature.[66] Therefore, *murābaḥah ṣukūk* and BBA *ṣukūk* behave the same when it comes to *bayʿ al-ʿīnah* application. *Bayʿ al-ʿīnah* exists in specific *murābaḥah ṣukūk* arrangement known sometimes as 'two-party *murābaḥah ṣukūk*'.[67] This structure starts with assets provided by the originator to the SPV, as opposed to *bayʿ al-ʿīnah ṣukūk*. The originator sells the asset that it owns to the SPV for a cash price which is paid through issuance of *ṣukūk* to investors. The originator then buys back the asset from the SPV for a deferred price that is higher than the cash price. With regard to *istiṣnāʿ ṣukūk*,[68] *bayʿ al-ʿīnah* occurs when the structure involves a sell and buy-back transaction between the originator and SPV, that is, first *istiṣnāʿ* and second *istiṣnāʿ* agreements. Such structures start with selling sale of an asset to be constructed by the SPV to the originator for a deferred price. The SPV then buys back the asset in question from the originator and the payment is made in stages. The SPV raises funds to make these progress payments via issuance of *ṣukūk*. As for *ijārah ṣukūk*, the presence of *bayʿ al-ʿīnah* in it is debatable, owing to the controversy among sharia scholars regarding whether sale and leaseback in *ijārah ṣukūk* is regarded as a form of *bayʿ al-ʿīnah*.[69] According to *ijārah ṣukūk* using sale and leaseback mechanisms,[70] the SPV first purchases originator's

[66] Ibid.

[67] A Thomas and S Mokhtar, *supra* note 64, 131.

[68] Ibid. 138.

[69] This structure has been considered as a form of *bayʿ al-ʿīnah* by some scholars for two reasons: purchase undertaking at a pre-agreed price and the asset goes back to the original seller eventually. However, AAOIFI holds the view that it is permitted provided that the lease is not conditional. For further information, see M Al-Amine, *Global Sukuk and Islamic Securitization Market: Financial Engineering and Product Innovation* (Brill 2012) 148.

[70] S Mokhtar and A Thomas, 'Ijarah Sukuk' in Thomas A (ed), *Sukuk* (Sweet & Maxwell Asia 2009) 153.

asset for the cash price which is paid by issuance of *ṣukūk*; the SPV then leases back the asset to the originator.

The *bayʿ al-ʿīnah* in *ṣukūk* is of a sharia concern due to the well-established controversy about the legality of such structures in Islamic law. While *bayʿ al-ʿīnah* is allowed according to the *shāafiʿı* (school of Islamic Law founded by Muḥammad Al-Shāfiʿi in the eighth century in Iraq and Egypt) and *ẓāhirī* (school of Islamic law founded by Dāwūd al-Ẓāhiri in the ninth century) schools, it has been prohibited by the *mālikī* and the *ḥanbalī* schools.[71] This has resulted in divergent opinions regarding its permissibility in the IFSI. Malaysia has followed the permissibility view as provided by the SAC of BNM[72] and SAC of SC.[73] However, the GCC region considers the prohibition view as provided by different SSBs in the region including AAOIFI.[74] In fact, AAOIFI states that *bayʿ al-ʿīnah* transactions are 'strictly prohibited'.[75]

6.6 Methods of *Ṣukūk* Restructuring

The need for *ṣukūk* restructuring typically arises in two situations: in the event of default and a corporation's voluntary restructuring, that is, merger, acquisition, and reorganisation of its structure.[76] The first event causes potential problems regarding the method chosen for restructuring the *ṣukūk*. The second event is less a matter of concern since such restructuring will not affect *ṣukūk* transactions and the *ṣukūk* holders' position but rather the organisation structure. The main question in the case of restructuring *ṣukūk* post-default event is the suitability of the chosen restructuring method from a sharia point of view. Before discussing sharia issues related to *ṣukūk* restructuring methods, it is important to highlight that Islamic law generally encourages restructuring as a method of relief when the debtor is in difficulty. The principles of forgiveness and time extension in Islamic bankruptcy law arguably legitimise *ṣukūk* restructuring from an Islamic viewpoint. However, the question of what methods of

[71] For more discussion about legality of *bayʿ al-ʿīnah* in Islamic law, see SC, *supra* note 7, 20. See also S Rosly and M Sanusi, 'Some Issues of Bay' Al-'Inah in Malaysian Islamic Financial Markets' (2001) 16 Arab Law Quarterly 263.

[72] BNM, *supra* note 27, 109.

[73] SC, *supra* note 7, 20.

[74] See A Shaharuddin and others, *Fatwas on Islamic Capital Markets: A Comparative Study between Malaysia and Gulf Co-Operation Council (GCC) Countries* (ISRA 2014) 18.

[75] AAOIFI, *supra* note 14, 526.

[76] H Dar and T Azmi (eds), *Global Islamic Finance Report 2011* (BMB Islamic UK Ltd 2011) 232.

ṣukūk restructuring are considered sharia-compliant remains a matter of concern.

The application of debt restructuring methods from the conventional market on *ṣukūk* is not suitable from an Islamic law perspective owing mainly to the fact that *ṣukūk* fundamentally differ from conventional bonds. Rankin states that '[d]ue to the nature of Islamic finance structures, careful consideration must be given to the timing and structure of any refinancing or restructuring of *ṣukūk*'.[77] The issue of *ṣukūk* restructuring methods lacks attention not only theoretically, but also in practice. Bakar argues that most *ṣukūk* prospectuses, if not all, lack instructions and guidance about the mode of *ṣukūk* restructuring assumed for the event of default.[78] Following is a list of four potential modes of *ṣukūk* restructuring with evaluation of their suitability from an Islamic law perspective:

1. Cash injection: this method refers to the practice of injecting funds into the originator in the event of financial difficulty by the *ṣukūk* holders or a third party (usually financial institutions or governments). From an Islamic law perspective, such capital injections should be in form of *qarḍ ḥasan* (an interest-free loan) or a gift. The legality of cash injection is subject to further debate when it is conditional or pre-agreed among related parties. Cash injection is considered as a sort of guarantee, an issue requiring particular attention as shall be discussed later. The application of cash injection is straightforward in practice since it only requires the approval of the party injecting its capital. Further, it can be applied to all *ṣukūk* structures and types. The effectiveness of cash injection can be seen when it is used by the originator to remove or reduce the number of parties ahead of *ṣukūk* holders, such as senior lenders.[79] However, the exercise of this option by the originator is subject to the availability of capital and willingness of the party injecting its capital in this situation. It is likely that *ṣukūk* holders might be reluctant to

[77] D Rankin, 'Restructuring and Buy-Back of Sukuk' in R Ali (ed), *Sukuk and Islamic Capital Markets* (Global Business Publishing Ltd 2011) 163.

[78] M Bakar, 'Restructuring Of Sukuk: A Shariah Perspective' (*Amanie i-Connect*, 16 May 2012). http://www.amanie-iconnect.com/component/k2/item/10-restructuring-of-sukuk-a-shariah-perspective. Accessed 10 November 2014.

[79] D Rankin, *supra* note 77, 163.

inject further money into the same originator after being exposed to default risk.

2. Rescheduling financial obligations: this approach involves extending the duration of existing *ṣukūk* so as to provide more time for the originator to meet payment obligations. The process of rescheduling financial obligations in Islamic law becomes a worrying issue when it involves any change in the amount of the payment obligation. In this case, the sharia ruling varies depending on the underlying *ṣukūk* structure. With regard to *ijārah ṣukūk*, any decrease or increase in the future payment obligations is permissible according to the principles of *ijārah* (lease). However, increase in the financial obligations from any previous periods which have not yet been made is not permissible because such financial obligations are debts owed to the lessor by the lessee.[80] As for *istiṣnāʿ ṣukūk* and *murābaḥah ṣukūk*, the debt nature of their financial obligations means only the discount practice is allowed. Neither the reduction nor the increase of payment obligations is permitted in the context of *mushārakah* (participation financing) and *muḍārabah ṣukūk*. Bakar notes that 'a *ṣukūk* haircut will not be possible on general principles of *muḍārabah* (investment partnership)/*mushārakah* as the haircut would imply the capital guarantee for the *ṣukūk* investors'.[81] In practice, this option requires the approval of the *ṣukūk* holders and amendments to the existing *ṣukūk* documents and terms. This option does not look appealing for either the originator or *ṣukūk* holders. From the originator's perspective, this method does not remove the default transaction from its books or replace it with a new transaction.[82] As for *ṣukūk* holders, this option does not change their risk exposure since they would most likely want to change the current underlying structure.[83]
3. Exchange of the existing *ṣukūk* with a new *ṣukūk*: this refers to retiring the existing *ṣukūk* and off-setting outstanding financial obligations by creating a new set of financial obligations at a new rate and duration. The sharia rules concerning the exchange process are as follows: the new *ṣukūk* offered must represent ownership at the time of exchange; ownership transfer should take place directly after the

[80] See AAOIFI, *supra* note 14, 145.
[81] M Bakar, *supra* note 78.
[82] H Dar and T Azmi, *supra* note 76, 234.
[83] Ibid.

exchange; the independence of the new *ṣukūk* (in the case of investment-based structures) from the payment obligations related to existing *istiṣnāʿ ṣukūk* and *murābaḥah ṣukūk*; debt or receivables cannot form the required capital in the case of issuing of new investment-based structures.[84] Some of these rules present real practical challenges for the originators as they are in a default situation and restructuring process.[85] For example, issuing new certificates based on investment structures is nearly impossible because these require new capital.

Having pointed out the sharia observations related to the exchange process, the exchange of existing *istiṣnāʿ ṣukūk* and *murābaḥah ṣukūk* with the same type of certificates brings back the issue of sale of debt as discussed above. Therefore, the exchange of such certificates with investment-based *ṣukūk* structures is a suitable method to avoid the controversy about the legality of selling debt in Islamic law. With regard to investment-based *ṣukūk* structures, this exchange is accomplished either by issuing new investment-based *ṣukūk* structures (using the same underlying assets) or *ijārah ṣukūk* (using different assets), or a combination of both.[86] As for *ijārah ṣukūk*, the exchange is also made using the same underlying assets, new assets, or a combination thereof.[87] In practice, the exchange process typically involves several steps, including circulation of the exchange offer by the new issuer (i.e. selling the existing certificates of *ṣukūk* holders to the new issuer), the new issuer's promise to issue new *ṣukūk*, appointment of different dealers and agents, suspension of existing *ṣukūk* trading, ownership transfer between existing issuer and new issuer, and formal entrance into the new arrangement with *ṣukūk* holders after the acquisition of the asset.[88]

4. Exchange of the existing *ṣukūk* with shares of the originator: for the purpose of the exchange with shares, the differences between equity-based *ṣukūk* and debt-based *ṣukūk* should be established. In the case of equity-based *ṣukūk*, the exchange means an equity-for-equity

[84] Ibid. 233.
[85] Ibid.
[86] Ibid. 234.
[87] Ibid. 235.
[88] Ibid. 234.

> swap which is acceptable in Islamic law due to their equity nature.[89] In the case of debt-based *ṣukūk*, the exchange is effectively a debt-for-equity swap which brings back the discussion of the permissibility of sale of debt under Islamic law due to their debt nature.

As seen above, the choice of restructuring mode of *ṣukūk* in a default situation varies depending on several factors including the underlying *ṣukūk* structure and the approval of *ṣukūk* holders. *Ṣukūk* restructuring requires great input from the SSB, and therefore the importance of another stage of sharia scrutiny cannot be overlooked. In this context, Bakar states 'the restructuring modes must be equally endorsed by relevant sharia board or advisor to be compliant to ensure that Islamic based investors are not victimized in the process of restructuring the *ṣukūk*'.[90]

6.7 Undertaking

Undertaking has become a major component of a number of contemporary *ṣukūk*. While there is some discussion about the application of undertaking in different Islamic financial transactions, there is less discussion about it in *ṣukūk*, particularly from a sharia standpoint. For example, AAOIFI's sharia standards refer to the practice of undertaking as part of several financial transactions but offer no mention of undertaking as practised in *ṣukūk*.[91] There are three key concerns that can be elaborated from analysis of the current undertaking practices in *ṣukūk*. The first issue is concerned with the legality of undertaking as practised in *ṣukūk* structure. The second concern is related to the bindingness and enforceability of undertaking. In other words: will the party providing purchase undertaking be obliged to buy back the *ṣukūk* asset from *ṣukūk* holders? The third concern is whether purchase undertaking is a guarantee. This issue will be discussed in the following section.

The first concern entails identification of the undertaking forms present in *ṣukūk* in order to examine their legal status under Islamic law. Looking at the practice of *ṣukūk*, it can be said that there are two relevant forms of undertaking, namely *waʿd* (unilateral undertaking or promise) and *muwāʿadah*

[89] M Bakar, *supra* note 78.

[90] Ibid.

[91] S Osman and A Jalil, 'An Islamic Perspective of Promise and Its Relationship with the Islamic Law of Contract' (International Seminar on Usul Fiqh, Nilai, October 2013) 7.

(bilateral undertaking). The practice of *waʿd* refers to unilateral undertaking provided by the originator to buy the asset back from the SPV. This form of undertaking can be seen in '*ijārah ṣukūk* for asset acquisition',[92] and 'sale and leaseback *ijārah ṣukūk*'.[93] *Muwāʿadah* refers to 'a mutual promise between two parties with intention to conclude a contract in future'.[94] This form of undertaking can be found in *istiṣnāʿ ṣukūk* as practised in Malaysia in which the structure involves purchase undertaking and sale undertaking.[95] *Muwāʿadah* generally differs from *waʿd* in terms of parties and the number of promises involved.

Having identified *waʿd* and *muwāʿadah* as relevant undertaking applications in *ṣukūk*, we will discuss their legality and binding nature, respectively. As a general rule, the practice of *waʿd* is permissible provided that the subject matter is not prohibited, and there is no intention to break the promise in the future.[96] However, sharia scholars disagree on the binding nature of a unilateral undertaking.[97] The reason for this is the issue of religiously (morally) binding (*mulzim diyānah*) vis-à-vis legally binding (*mulzim qaḍāʾ*). Majority of jurists hold the 'not binding view' meaning a unilateral undertaking is considered religiously binding, but not legally binding.[98] This view implies that a unilateral undertaking is not enforceable in court. Other scholars hold the 'binding view' which means undertaking is binding religiously and legally and therefore is enforceable in the court.[99] An analysis of contemporary resolutions of a unilateral undertaking nature related to several financial transactions shows that the binding view has been typically held by IIFA, AAOIFI, and SAC's BNM.[100] Moreover, the SAC of BNM has a specific resolution in the context of *ṣukūk* as follows:

[92] S Mokhtar and A Thomas, *supra* note 70, 147.

[93] Ibid. 153.

[94] K Saripudin and others, 'Application of Promise in Sukuk Musharakah Structure' (2012) 12 Middle-East Journal of Scientific Research 160, 161.

[95] A Thomas and S Mokhtar, *supra* note 64, 138.

[96] M Muhammad, H Yaacob and S Hasan, *The Bindingness and Enforceability of A Unilateral Promise (Wa'd): An Analysis From Islamic Law and Legal Perspectives* (ISRA 2011) 5–6.

[97] Some researchers have identified six opinions held by past jurists on this matter. See ibid. 7. However, these opinions can be reduced and summarised in two opinions as shall be explained.

[98] See K Saripudin and others, *supra* note 94, 162.

[99] See ibid.

[100] See M Muhammad, H Yaacob and S Hasan, *supra* note 96, 12–16.

> [T]he obligation of purchase undertaking in *ṣukūk* is valid and acknowledged by sharia. This is because such obligation is derived from a binding promise (*waʿad mulzim*) by the *ṣukūk* issue to purchase an underlying asset of the *ṣukūk* based on agreed terms and conditions.[101]

IIFA has provided certain cases where a legally binding view should be considered including when it is made conditional upon a cause and when the promisee has incurred expenses due to the promise.[102]

As for *muwāʿadah*, its legal status varies depending on type, whether binding *muwāʿadah* or non-binding *muwāʿadah*. While in the former none of the parties have an option whether to or not to perform the undertaking in the future,[103] in the latter both parties have a choice whether or not to exercise the undertaking in future. The prevailing opinion of sharia scholars holds that non-binding *muwāʿadah* is permissible.[104] But the question arises as to whether binding *muwāʿadah* is permissible or not. This is a matter of controversy and the central theme and rationale of the prohibition of binding *muwāʿadah* is that it is actually a contract.[105] AAOIFI states, in the general context of *murābaḥah* transactions, that '[a] bilateral promise between the customer and the institution is permissible only if there is an option to cancel the promise which may be exercised either by both promisors or by either one of them'.[106] The position of IIFA regarding the legality of *muwāʿadah* needs careful consideration. On the one hand, IIFA's ruling No. 40–41 considers binding *muwāʿadah* as not permissible, that is, in the context of *murābaḥah*.[107] On the other hand, IIFA's ruling No. 157 generally allows for binding *muwāʿadah* to take place in certain cases:

> [W]here it is impossible to conclude a sales agreement due to the commodity not being in the possession of the seller while a general need exists to oblige both parties to implement a contract in the future, either by legislation or some other means, such as the recognized practices of international commerce.[108]

[101] BNM, *supra* note 27, 171.
[102] M Muhammad, H Yaacob and S Hasan, *supra* note 96, 13.
[103] Ibid. 26.
[104] See K Saripudin and others, *supra* note 94, 163.
[105] AAOIFI, *supra* note 14, 130.
[106] Ibid. 117.
[107] IIFA, *supra* note 9, 91–92.
[108] M Muhammad, H Yaacob and S Hasan, *supra* note 96, 28.

Pertaining to its binding nature, IIFA is of the view that *muwāʿadah* is religiously binding, and not legally binding according to its ruling No. 157.[109] The IIFA's position on the binding nature of *muwāʿadah* seems confused: while IIFA states that bilateral promises are religiously binding only as a basic rule in the first section of ruling No. 157, it allows for bilateral promises to be considered legally binding in certain cases in the third section of the same ruling.[110]

6.8 Guarantee

It is evidenced that some *ṣukūk* arrangements involve a guarantee of capital and return. In most cases, capital is guaranteed by the exercise of asset purchase undertaking, and the return is guaranteed by offering loans to *ṣukūk* holders in the event of an earnings shortfall. Looking at the typical *ṣukūk* arrangement, two potential parties could provide a guarantee, namely the *ṣukūk* manager and the third party (such as sovereigns). Regardless of how the guarantee is formed which may vary in practice, it is generally 'intended to secure obligations and protect amount of debts, either from being uncollectible or from being in default'.[111] Understanding the concept of guarantee is significant because of the ambiguity about some practices in the market and whether they fall under guarantee or not. The literature is vague in determining the exact connotation of guarantee practice in *ṣukūk*. A good illustration of this point is the exercise of purchase undertaking, explored below.

6.8.1 Is Purchase Undertaking a Guarantee?

One might wonder why it is important to know whether purchase undertaking functions as a guarantee or not. If purchase undertaking is considered a form of guarantee, this means that such practices would fall under the guarantee topic and therefore the Islamic law of guarantee would be applied to purchase undertaking. Although establishing a guarantee has

[109] IIFA, 'Al-Qarārāt Wa Al-Tawṣiyāt: Al-Dawrah Al-Sābiʿah ʿasharah' (*Fiqhacademy*, 2006). http://www.fiqhacademy.org.sa/. Accessed 13 November 2014.

[110] M Muhammad, H Yaacob and S Hasan, *supra* note 96, 28.

[111] AAOIFI, *supra* note 14, 59.

been identified as one of the top functions of the purchase undertaking,[112] this is not necessarily true in all situations. To be more specific, the practice of purchase undertaking functions as a guarantee when it is priced at the nominal value, and not at the market value. Looking at the effects of purchase undertaking priced at par, one finds that the capital would not be subject to market forces anymore and *ṣukūk* holders receive their capital regardless of the asset's market value.[113] However, purchase undertaking priced at market value would not minimise the risk of the transactions. In this respect, Laldin says '[*w*]*a'd* becomes problematic when it is in the form of purchase undertaking of *ṣukūk* certificate at face value because at this state, it becomes somewhat like a guarantee of the capital and such is not possible where *ṣukūk* is an investment instrument'.[114] AAOIFI and IIFA are among the leading proponents of this view.[115] However, Mokhtar suggests that distinction needs to be made between asset purchase undertakings in the context of *ṣukūk* since their functions and effects vary.[116] According to Mokhtar, unconditional purchase undertaking 'may play a role of guarantee in substance'[117] provided that it is priced at principal plus unpaid profit or at par and this 'unconditional obligation on one partner to pay means that the investor is not taking any liability on his capital'.[118] Mokhtar found that the existence of conditional purchase undertaking, although at par, 'does not take away the nature of profit-and-loss sharing in the equity-based instruments'.[119]

6.8.2 *The Ruling of Guarantee in Debt-Based* Ṣukūk*;* Ijārah Ṣukūk*; and* Mushārakah, Muḍārabah, *and* Wakālah Ṣukūk

If a guarantee is provided in debt-based *ṣukūk*, it is most likely to be for the deferred price payments (cost plus profit) as in the case of BBA,

[112] S Mokhtar, *Application of Wa'ad In Equity Based Sukuk: Empirical Evidence* (ISRA 2011) 53.

[113] Ibid. 54.

[114] M Laldin, *supra* note 1, 22.

[115] Although they do not explicitly mention the function of purchase undertaking, their positions can be understood by looking at their resolutions on the subject of *ṣukūk*. See AAOIFI, *supra* note 1; IIFA, *supra* note 20.

[116] S Mokhtar, *supra* note 112, 49.

[117] Ibid.

[118] Ibid. 54.

[119] Ibid. 49.

murābaḥah, *bayʿ al-ʿīnah*, *tawaruq*, and *istiṣnāʿ* structures. In such cases, *ṣukūk* represent receivables on the selling price. Guaranteeing the selling price under these transactions is permissible, whether the guarantee is provided by the originator or a third party. In contracts of exchange, AAOIFI's Sharia Standard No. 5 states '[a] contract of guarantee is permissible in contracts of exchange, e.g a contract of sale, or contract of rights, e.g. right of intellectual property. Such a guarantee contract does not affect the validity of the original contract in which it is required'.[120]

As for *ijārah ṣukūk*, purchase undertaking takes place at maturity for both asset acquisition and sale and leaseback *ijārah ṣukūk*. There is disagreement among sharia scholars regarding whether such practice falls under capital guarantee or not. It seems that the controversy centres on purchase undertaking priced at par rather than purchase undertaking priced at market value. According to the majority view, purchase undertaking amounts to a capital guarantee when it is priced at a nominal value and is therefore not permissible.[121] AAOIFI and IIFA are both proponents of this opinion.[122] It has been argued that in this case *ijārah ṣukūk* becomes similar to conventional bonds and the transaction objective becomes 'the exchange of spot cash for a greater amount of delayed cash'.[123] The minority view does not consider purchase undertaking priced at par a capital guarantee and therefore it is considered permissible on the grounds that it does not contradict the nature of the contracts and *ṣukūk*, which in this case, consists of contracts that meet all conditions of Islamic commercial law.[124] In regard to rental payments on *ijārah ṣukūk*, it is permitted to guarantee them as far as Islamic law is concerned. In the context of lease, AAOIFI's Sharia Standard No. 5 states '[p]ermissible security, of all kinds, may be taken to secure the rental payments'.[125]

As for *ṣukūk* based on *mushārakah*, *muḍārabah*, or *wakālah* (agency; investment contract in which agent represents investor(s)), one must look at the object of the guarantee, whether capital or returns, in order to address its legality from a sharia point of view. For returns guarantees, it has been argued that providing loans in the event of returns shortfall is not acceptable since such practice would make the whole arrangement of a sale

120 AAOIFI, *supra* note 14, 59.

121 S Bouheraoua, B Sairally and S Hasan, 'A Critical Appraisal of Sharīʿah Issues Related to Ṣukūk Al-Ijārah' (2012) 4 ISRA International Journal of Islamic Finance 167, 173.

122 Ibid.

123 Ibid. 174.

124 Ibid. 173.

125 AAOIFI, *supra* note 14, 145.

with credit transaction prohibited in Islamic law.[126] Even in certain cases where capital guarantee might be acceptable in *mushārakah*, *muḍārabah*, and *wakālah ṣukūk* as seen below, 'the partner that enjoyed the guarantee can only get back his principal and not any additional amount because any additional amount will be *ribā*'.[127] Therefore, AAOIFI's Sharia Board states:

> It is not permissible for the manager of *ṣukūk*, whether the manager acts as the *muḍārib* (investment manager), or *sharīk* (partner), or *wakīl* (agent) for investment, to undertake to offer loans to *ṣukūk* holders, when actual earnings fall short of expected earnings.[128]

Pertaining to the capital guarantee in *mushārakah*, *muḍārabah*, and *wakālah ṣukūk*, different rules apply depending on whether the guarantee is provided by the *ṣukūk* manager or the third party. For the *ṣukūk* manager, it is not permissible to include capital guarantee in *ṣukūk* based on *mushārakah*, *muḍārabah*, or *wakālah*. To illustrate, the Islamic law of guarantee does not permit stipulation of guarantee in the case of trust (fiduciary) contracts. In this respect, AAOIFI's Sharia Standard No. 5 states:

> The prohibition against seeking a guarantee in trust contracts is more stringent in *mushārakah* and *muḍārabah* contracts, since it is not permitted to require from a manager in the *muḍārabah* or the *mushārakah* contract or an investment agent or one of the partners in these contracts to guarantee the capital, or to promise a guaranteed profit. Moreover, it is not permissible for these contracts to be marketed or operated as a guaranteed investment.[129]

AAOIFI's Sharia Standard No. 17 prohibits the inclusion of any kind of guarantee statement in the prospectus.[130] To avoid any source of confusion, this statement should be linked to the *ṣukūk* manager's guarantee that is provided in *ṣukūk* based on *mushārakah*, *muḍārabah*, or *wakālah*. It should be noted that such prohibition does not include cases of negligent acts or omissions since such cases make the *ṣukūk* manager a guaran-

[126] M Al-ʿuthmānī, *supra* note 18, 7.
[127] S Mokhtar, *supra* note 112, 51.
[128] AAOIFI, *supra* note 1, 2.
[129] AAOIFI, *supra* note 14, 59.
[130] See ibid. 314.

tor of the capital at its nominal value.[131] There has been an attempt to validate capital guarantee provided by the *ṣukūk* manager in equity-based *ṣukūk* on the grounds that such *ṣukūk* are based on a partnership of property, and not on a partnership of contract.[132] While the former allows for capital guarantee, the latter does not.[133] Al-ʿuthmānī challenged this argument, and asserted that partnership of contract occurs in *ṣukūk*.[134]

The concept of a third-party guarantee has been subject to two opposing permissibility standards. Among the proponents of permissibility of the third party's guarantee is AAOIFI. AAOIFI's Sharia Standard No. 5 states:

> It is permissible for a third party, other than the *muḍārib* or investment agent or one of the partners, to undertake voluntarily that he will compensate the investment losses of the party to whom the undertaking is given, provided this guarantee is not linked in any manner to the *muḍārabah* financing contract or investment agency contract.[135]

According to this view, it is permitted to provide guarantees in *ṣukūk* based on *mushārakah*, *muḍārabah*, or *wakālah*, provided that the above conditions are met. In addition to these conditions, AAOIFI requires that the third party guarantees the net value of assets, market value of assets, fair value of assets, or a price to be agreed when the purchase is made.[136] Thus, AAOIFI is of the view that a third-party guarantee of the nominal value of the assets is not allowed.[137] The other view prohibits the concept of a third-party guarantee on the grounds that it opens the door to usury, and the prohibition of guarantee is well established in the case of equity-based *ṣukūk*.[138]

[131] AAOIFI, *supra* note 1, 2.
[132] M Al-ʿuthmānī, *supra* note 18, 10.
[133] Ibid.
[134] Ibid. 10–11.
[135] AAOIFI, *supra* note 14, 67.
[136] AAOIFI, *supra* note 1, 2.
[137] Ibid.
[138] M Al-Amine, *supra* note 69, 164.

6.9 Conclusion

This chapter shows that a solely theoretical investigation of *ṣukūk* is insufficient in order to understand their practical nature. Investigating *ṣukūk* as practised reveals that they are different from *ṣukūk* in theory. Some issues are not easily discovered due to the complexity of existing *ṣukūk* structures and large *ṣukūk* documents. In most cases, the *ṣukūk* circular is considered the primary source of information regarding each structure. This chapter demonstrates that one should carefully examine the *ṣukūk* circular in order to identify practices contradicting with Islamic law and the operating legal environment. The best illustrations of this point are issues such as *bayʿ al-dayn* and *bayʿ al-ʿīnah* which are not described or even mentioned in *ṣukūk* documents. Therefore, the examination process presupposes a proper understanding of both Islamic law and legal environment. Fresh thinking is not only required to address such issues, but also to explore legal tricks and issues that are to a large extent hidden. Nevertheless, the existence of several sharia issues in *ṣukūk* causes doubt about the role of the sharia advisors in protecting and promoting the integrity of the IFSI particularly after *ṣukūk* issuance has been endorsed.

The existence of such problems is, to some extent, justifiable, given that *ṣukūk* market is under development in most jurisdictions. The presence of such issues differs from one jurisdiction to another, and they are not necessarily of particular significance in all jurisdictions. For example, *bayʿ al-dayn* causes a sharia concern in the GCC region rather than Malaysia. One finds that Malaysia is more flexible and lenient than other jurisdictions when it comes to sharia concerns.

CHAPTER 7

Regulation of the *Ṣukūk* Market: Case of Malaysia, the UAE, and the KSA

7.1 Introduction

This chapter outlines how *ṣukūk* (trust investment certificates) is regulated in three key domestic markets. Regulation of *ṣukūk* markets is at the heart of the present discussion of asset-backed *ṣukūk* and asset-based *ṣukūk*; however, there has so far been little concrete discussion about the regulations concerning *ṣukūk*. *Ṣukūk* regulation refers to the formal regulations which are aimed specifically at offers of *ṣukūk* to the public, covering the buyers, sellers, and holders of *ṣukūk* engaging in different *ṣukūk* activities including issuance, offering, invitation to subscribe, and invitation to purchase. Beyond the scope of this definition is the complete range of financial regulations relating to *ṣukūk* activities in general such as regulations relating to conduct of business, market abuse, insider dealing, and fraud. This description also does not include general law or substantive law as it applies to the specific context of *ṣukūk* markets, including contract law, tort law, and company law. However, general reference needs to be made to several regulations developed outside the *ṣukūk* market but which have a considerable bearing on the regulation of *ṣukūk* activities. Identifying the regulations of particular importance to *ṣukūk* transactions in each country is the principal focus of this chapter. This chapter provides a legal framework for *ṣukūk* practice and the principal means of issuing *ṣukūk* to the public in these countries.

S. Al-Ali, *Raising Capital on* Ṣukūk *Markets*,
https://doi.org/10.1007/978-3-030-14536-1_7

For the purpose of this chapter, Malaysia,[1] the UAE,[2] and KSA[3] have been chosen as case studies. The discussion of *ṣukūk* regimes in this chapter is presented in this sequence because it begins with the most pioneering *ṣukūk* market worldwide first and then moves to the following market. Historically, these territories have been the most important locations for *ṣukūk* issuance and investment. Therefore, understanding regulations of *ṣukūk* in these countries provides the best illustration of the key *ṣukūk* practices worldwide.

Before discussing more detailed case studies, this chapter begins with a brief discussion of the regulation of the IFSI necessary before examining regulation in individual *ṣukūk* markets. The analysis of each country's *ṣukūk* regime begins with the general regulatory and legal structure concerning *ṣukūk* transactions. The discussion of each *ṣukūk* regime then examines the two basic elements of any of *ṣukūk* market: the regulation of offers of *ṣukūk* (governing *ṣukūk* issuance and *ṣukūk* prospectus) and regulation of *ṣukūk* listing (governing the admission of *ṣukūk* on the official list and authorised market). However, this chapter does not intend to present a comprehensive account of every regulatory position concerning *ṣukūk*. The discussion and analysis in this chapter seek to answer the following questions: what is the regulatory approach adopted in the *ṣukūk* market across these countries? Are there specific rules concerning *ṣukūk* passed by regulatory authorities in these countries? Does *ṣukūk* market regime differ significantly between these jurisdictions? How does *ṣukūk* fit within the country's general legal framework, especially in the absence of special rules regarding *ṣukūk*?

7.2 Regulation of the IFSI

Any discussion of *ṣukūk* market regimes would be incomplete without understanding of the regulation of the IFSI. In particular, there is need to appreciate the relevance of financial regulation to Islamic financial markets, including *ṣukūk* markets, and to determine whether *ṣukūk* markets require special regulations due to the sharia-compliant nature of such.

[1] Malaysia is a federation consisting of 13 states and three federal territories, founded in 1957.

[2] The UAE is a federation of seven emirates, founded in 1971.

[3] The KSA was founded in 1932.

Regulating the financial services sector is an important contributing factor for the development of sound market operation. Regulation is defined as 'body of statutory and governmental or public agency rules that govern social and economic life in the modern world'.[4] It is believed that financial markets are among the most regulated sectors[5] due to the long history and recent expansion in the financial regulation. Trading in the securities market, for instance, received regulatory attention from City of London as early as 1697 when an Act was enacted.[6] It has been said that the level of regulations and governance in the City of London during the eighteenth century was, to some extent, similar to our present regulations.[7] This shows that administering and governing financial markets was an early historical concern. Although the general commercial law, namely contract and property law, is considered to be the basic legal framework for market operation, it does not however offer sufficient coverage for the modern investments, which establishes the reasoning for statutory regulation to be introduced.[8]

The role and function of the law in ensuring the soundness of financial markets cannot be overlooked. The importance and need for a well-regulated financial environment can be witnessed in the government interventions to reform their financial systems after the global recession.[9] Although the law has only a limited role in the creation and early foundation of a financial market, it plays a far more vital role in facilitating ongoing growth.[10] Therefore, there are many laws and regulations that have been enacted in both developed and developing economies.

In the common and civil law jurisdictions, there has been increasingly significant activity in developing the body of regulatory law pertaining to

[4] E Avgouleas, *The Mechanics and Regulation of Market Abuse: a Legal and Economic Analysis* (Oxford University Press 2005) 172.

[5] D Gowland, *The Regulation of Financial Markets in the 1990s* (Edward Elgar Publishing Limited 1990) 1.

[6] I MacNeil, *An Introduction to the Law on Financial Investment* (2nd edn, Hart Publishing Ltd. 2012) 39.

[7] B Rider, C Abrams and M Ashe, *Guide to Financial Services Regulation* (3rd edn, CCH Editions 1997) 1.

[8] I MacNeil, *supra* note 6, 17, 20.

[9] B Grewal, 'Constraints on Growth in Islamic Finance' (IFSB 4th Public Lecture on Financial Policy and Stability, Jordan, 2011) 14, 15.

[10] B Rider, 'Legal Aspects of Islamic Asset Securitisation' in IFSB (ed), *Strategies for the Development of Islamic Capital Markets: Infrastructures and Legal Aspects of Islamic Asset Securitisation* (IFSB 2011) 50.

financial markets in the last century.[11] Important elements that greatly contributed to the phenomenon of regulation development include globalisation, cross-border investments, and advancements in technology. The major effort and research in the field of regulation have focused on identifying regulation objectives and issues concerning efficient regulation.[12] Whether it is a statutory regulation model, a self-regulation model, or a hybrid, different models have been developed to meet individual country's preferences, based on its market history and local conditions.[13] In fact, the adoption of a particular regulation system often varies within the jurisdiction; the UK is a good illustration of this as it moved from self-regulation to statutory regulation in 1986.[14] Further, operational concepts and forms have been structured in the area of financial regulation, such as the choice between functional regulation and institutional regulation, the choice between single regulators and multiple regulators, and legal separation of different financial activities.[15] Moreover, a range of regulatory instruments have been drawn up by primary regulators and specialised authorities. These include disclosure, authorisation, prudential regulation, conduct of business regulation, portfolio regulation, intervention, crisis management power, deposit guarantee, and compensation schemes.[16] To tackle uncertainties and fill unpredicted gaps which exist within hard law and common law systems, soft law has been developed by various institutions and bodies, for example, Basel II and papers of the Financial Markets Law Committee (FMLC).[17] Financial regulation architecture has been developed with the dynamic nature of financial markets and to deal with sophisticated financial structures.

It is essential to appreciate the rationality of existing laws and regulations in ensuring a supportive legal environment for financial markets. Financial regulation manages a number of separate financial risks that arise in the modern financial markets by imposing adequate obligations on

[11] Ibid. 52.

[12] C Goodhart and others, *Financial Regulation: Why, How and Where Now?* (Routldge 1998) 142.

[13] I MacNeil, *supra* note 6, 32, 33.

[14] Ibid. 32.

[15] Ibid. 33.

[16] Ibid. 34–39.

[17] R McCormick, *Legal Risk in the Financial Markets* (2nd edn, Oxford University Press 2010) 307–308.

financial institutions.[18] As regulated institutions operate within changeable marketplaces, the main concern of regulatory authorities is changing their behaviour so as to effectively and efficiently respond to new variables and challenges.[19] This can be viewed in light of the fact that financial regulators around the world became more interested in risk-based regulation post global meltdown and recession.[20] Given the complexity of financial markets, selected and restricted regulation objectives should be adopted by regulators.[21] It is well established that financial regulation is primarily concerned with investor protection and ensuring the soundness and stability of financial markets.[22] For instance, issuers of securities are obliged by securities regulation to disclose all relevant information related to the issuance or investment to the new buyers in order to avoid information asymmetry.[23] This particular rule is aimed to offer protection to prospective investors by facilitating access to the information required for investment decisions. As mentioned earlier, regulations are very much concerned about changing the behaviour of financial institutions. Thus, in the event of financial failure and crisis, the bailing out of financial institutions, (i.e. the concept of too big to fail) has been criticised and replaced by another technique, namely taking over the failing institutions and restructuring them, so as to reduce moral hazard in financial markets and encourage a more risk-taking attitude.[24] While regulation may impose certain costs on regulators,[25] an unregulated market will facilitate inefficient and high-cost services and products, leading to an uncompetitive market.[26] In the absence of market regulations, there is a high potential for market imperfections

[18] G Walker, 'Financial Markets and Exchanges' in M Blair, G Walker and S Willey (eds), *Financial Markets and Exchanges Law* (2nd edn, Oxford University Press 2012) 10–11.

[19] C Goodhart and others, *supra* note 12, 191.

[20] I MacNeil, *supra* note 6, 20.

[21] C Goodhart and others, *supra* note 12, 192.

[22] F Mishkin and S Eakins, *Financial Markets and Institutions* (6th edn, Pearson Prentice Hall 2009) 33; C Goodhart and others, *supra* note 12, 192; E Ferran and C Goodhart (eds), *Regulating Financial Services and Markets in the Twenty First Century* (Hart Publishing 2001) 8.

[23] E Avgouleas, *supra* note 4, 169.

[24] I MacNeil, *supra* note 6, 31–32.

[25] C Goodhart and others, *supra* note 12, 190.

[26] F Fabozzi and F Modigliani, *Capital Markets: Institutions and Instruments* (2nd edn, Prentic Hall 1996) 28.

and failures.[27] Failure to meet financial regulations may result in a criminal offence and questioning of the lawfulness of the rights and transactions.[28] Adequate market regulations minimise the possibility of moral hazard, fraud, conflict of interest and duties, insider dealing, money laundering, and other forms of market misconduct and abuse.

Therefore, it is argued that laws and regulations are necessary not only to the successful development of the conventional financial services industry, but also to its Islamic counterpart. This stems from the fact that both operate within the global economic system. Although the IFSI forms only a very small part of the international financial system, compared to its conventional counterpart, the necessity of regulating the IFSI, its products, and its institutions cannot be ignored. As a prerequisite for the listing and trading of Islamic financial products, laws should exist to create tradable obligations and facilitate an effective transfer of rights.[29] Moreover, the failure of any of IIFS resulting from lack of efficient regulations at this particular stage of operation may cause more reputation damage and prove a systemic risk to the development of the industry compared to similar failures in conventional financial institutions.[30]

The need for laws and regulations to address the Islamic financial markets is vital. An effective legal framework for the IFSI would be a legal framework that accommodates the intricacies of, and specific services provided in, the IFSI.[31] Although the IFSI has existed for almost four decades, there are few states that promulgated special legislation governing Islamic banking, *takāful* (Islamic insurance) system, and ICM.[32] Malaysia has thus far the most effective and sound regulatory framework for the IFSI, especially after passing the Islamic Financial Services Act 2013. Unlike the former legislation such as the Islamic Banking Act 1983 and the *Takaful*

[27] D Llewellyn, *The Economic Rationale for Financial Regulation* (Financial Services Authority 1999) 21.

[28] B Rider, *supra* note 10, 50.

[29] Ibid. 47.

[30] A Mirakhor and N Krichene, 'The Recent Crisis: Lessons for Islamic Finance' (IFSB 2dn Public Lecture on Financial Policy and Stability, Kuala Lumpur, 2009) 3, 71.

[31] N Thani and A Othman, 'The Effective of the Legal and Regulatory Framework for Islamic Financial Services' in IFSB (ed), *Islamic Finance: Global Legal Issues and Challenges* (IFSB 2008) 3.

[32] R Wilson, 'Sharīʿah Governance for Islamic Financial Instituions' (2009) 1 ISRA International Journal of Islamic Finance 59, 61.

Act 1984, the Islamic Financial Services Act 2013 regulates all IIFS including Islamic banks and *takāful* operators.[33]

Having outlined the importance of financial regulations that address the special needs of the IFSI, the discussion below looks at the specifics of regulation in the *ṣukūk* markets of Malaysia, the UAE, and the KSA.

7.3 Malaysian *Ṣukūk* Regime

Malaysia, in practical terms, has two separate financial regulatory schemes: 'the Labuan regulatory scheme' and 'the rest of Malaysia'. Labuan is an offshore financial centre inside Malaysia,[34] with its own financial services regulator, Labuan Financial Services Authority (Labuan FSA)[35] and its own financial exchange, Labuan International Financial Exchange (LFX).[36] The rest of Malaysia retains its own independent financial regulatory system, with its own capital market regulator, SC[37]; a central bank with

[33] For more discussions about Islamic Financial Services Act 2013, see Z Hasan, 'An Overview of the Recent Malaysian Islamic Financial Stability Act' (2013) 8 Journal of International Banking Law and Regulation 297.

[34] Labuan, a federal territory in east Malaysia, was declared as an international centre for business and finance in 1990 by the Government of Malaysia. This was accompanied by the establishment of Labuan International Business and Financial Centre (Labuan IBFC). For more information about the launch of Labuan IBFC, see BNM, 'Speeches and Interviews' (*BNM*, 10 March 2009). http://www.bnm.gov.my/index.php?ch=9&pg=15&ac=268. Accessed 6 June 2014.

[35] Labuan FSA was established in 1996. According to Section 3 (2) of Labuan Financial Services Authority Act 1996, it aims at achieving the following: (1) promoting Labuan as an international centre for business and financial services; (2) developing national policies and objectives for the development of financial services in Labuan; (3) acting as the central regulatory, supervisory, and enforcement authority of financial services in Labuan.

[36] LFX, one of the Bursa Malaysia subsidiaries, was established in 2000. It mainly offers listing and trading facilities for all financial instruments traded in Labuan.

[37] SC was established in 1993. According to Section 15 (1) of Securities Commission Act 1993, its functions, among others, include: (1) regulating all matters pertaining to securities and derivatives; (2) regulating takeovers and mergers of companies; (3) maintaining the investors' confidence in the securities and derivatives markets; (4) licensing and supervising all licensed persons; and (5) promoting and developing securities market in Malaysia. Prior to its establishment, Malaysian capital market was overseen by six public bodies: (1) Capital Issues Committee, Ministry of Finance; (2) Panel on Takeovers and Mergers, Prime Minister's Department; (3) Foreign Investment Committee, Prime Minister's Department; (4) Companies Commission of Malaysia; (5) Ministry of International Trade and Industry (MITI); and (6) BNM. See M Omar, M Abduh and S Raditya, *Fundamentals of Islamic Money and Capital Markets* (John Wiley & Sons 2013) 42.

particular approval power of securities, BNM,[38] and its own stock exchange, Bursa Malaysia.[39]

Each regulatory scheme maintains its own laws and regulations relating to financial services and products. In Labuan, the Labuan Islamic Financial Services and Securities Act 2010[40] and LFX Rules[41] govern *ṣukūk* activities. In the rest of Malaysia, regulations established through Guidelines on *Ṣukūk*,[42] Guidelines on Prospectus,[43] and Main Market

[38] BNM was established in 1959. According to Section 5 (2) of the Central Bank of Malaysia Act 2009, it aims, among others, at achieving the following: (1) formulating monetary policy in Malaysia; (2) issuing currency in Malaysia; (3) regulating and supervising financial institutions which are subject to the BNM's laws, and (4) promoting a sound financial system. Financial institutions licensed under the Banking and Financial Institutions Act 1989 are required to seek an approval from BNM for the issuance of securities. See SC, *Regulatory Requirement, Legal Documentation, Accounting, Auditing and Taxation in the Islamic Capital Market* (LexisNesis 2009) 26.

[39] Established in 1973, Bursa Malaysia (previously known as Kuala Lumpur Stock Exchange) is an exchange holding company consisting of ten subsidiaries. Bursa Malaysia Securities Bhd and LFX are the relevant financial exchanges for the *ṣukūk* market in Malaysia. While the former provides and maintains securities exchange under the wider Malaysia regulatory scheme, the latter provides and maintains offshore financial exchange under the Labuan regulatory scheme. See M Omar, M Abduh and S Raditya, *supra* note 37, 45.

[40] This Act comprises 12 Parts accounting for 161 Sections. It provides a comprehensive legal framework for licensing and regulating sharia-compliant financial activities in Labuan. It forms a one-stop reference for conducting Islamic finance services in Labuan.

[41] These Rules, which are issued by LFX, comprises eight Chapters.

[42] These Guidelines, which are issued by SC, comprise 21 Chapters. These Guidelines are the first of its kind in the world, which was known as Guidelines on the Offering of Islamic Securities, which came into effect on 26 July 2004. Previously, Islamic securities including *ṣukūk* were subject to the Guidelines on the Offering of Private Debt Securities (PDS) which are equally applicable to conventional securities. This was an obstacle for Malaysian *ṣukūk* market since the PDS Guidelines recognise only issuance of *ṣukūk* representing debt obligation such as *ijara*, BBA, and *Murābaḥah* (a sale with a mark-up), and not equity-based *ṣukūk*. Guidelines on *Ṣukūk* discuss different aspects of *ṣukūk* in detail and provide a comprehensive guide covering one-off *ṣukūk* issuance, *ṣukūk* programme, ringgit currency-denominated *ṣukūk*, and foreign currency-denominated *ṣukūk*. The bulk of the Guidelines on *Ṣukūk* is made up of the provisions fleshing out the details of four main parts: requirements for *ṣukūk* issuance and trading, approval for *ṣukūk* issuance and trading, requirements for retail *ṣukūk* issuance, and trading and approved sharia rulings, principles, and concepts. See A Mutalip, 'Guidelines on Offering Islamic Securities' (*Azmi & Associates*, 2005). http://www.azmilaw.com.my/archives/Article_outside_publications_asian_counsel/Guidelines_on_offering_islamic_securities_%2800124292%29.PDF. Accessed 17 March 2014.

[43] These Guidelines, which are issued by SC, comprise four Parts.

Listing Requirements[44] govern *ṣukūk* activities. There is other legislation relevant to the *ṣukūk* market in wider Malaysia,[45] including the Capital Market Services Act 2007 (CMSA)[46] and Companies Act 1965,[47] which are equally applicable to conventional securities.[48] Both regulatory schemes provide special regulations and rules concerning *ṣukūk* offering and listing, excepting the listing requirements in Labuan, which are applicable to all financial instruments, whether conventional or Islamic.

7.3.1 Regulation of the Offer of Sukūk

In the wider Malaysian regulatory scheme, the regulation of offers of *ṣukūk* is set out in the Guidelines on *Ṣukūk*, Capital Market Services Act 2007, and Guidelines on Prospectus. The most important aspects relating to the offer of *ṣukūk* are provided by Paragraphs 3.01–3.02 as follows:

> 3.01 A corporation within the meaning of sub-section 2(1) of the CMSA and a foreign government are eligible to issue, offer or make an invitation to subscribe or purchase *ṣukūk*.
>
> 3.02 Any person who is eligible to issue, offer or make an invitation to subscribe or purchase *ṣukūk* can only do so upon obtaining the SC's approval under these Guidelines.[49]

The above two paragraphs contain some key terms relating to the offer of *ṣukūk* in Malaysia—'*ṣukūk*', 'corporation', and 'approval'. The SC's regulatory definition of the term *ṣukūk* is contained in Chapter 1 of the Guidelines on *Ṣukūk*. Three features relating to ringgit-denominated

[44] These Listing Requirements, which are issued by the Main Market of Bursa Malaysia Securities Berhad, comprise 16 Chapters.

[45] Paragraph 11.03 of the Guidelines on *Ṣukūk* says '[a]n issuer and its principal adviser must ensure that the issue, offer or invitation to subscribe or purchase *ṣukūk* has complied with all the relevant laws which govern the proposal, including:

(a) the CMSA;
(b) the Companies Act 1965; and
(c) all other relevant SC guidelines'.

[46] This Act comprises 394 Sections.

[47] This Act comprises 374 Sections.

[48] See generally L Keong, *Securities Regulation in Malaysia* (Butterworths 1997).

[49] Guidelines on *Ṣukūk*, Paragraphs 3.01–3.02.

ṣukūk arise from this definition: first, they are certificates of equal value; second, they represent undivided ownership or investment in the underlying assets; third, they are structured in accordance with sharia principles and concepts as approved by the SC's SAC. While the first and second features constitute common features of most *ṣukūk* worldwide, the third feature distinguishes ringgit-denominated *ṣukūk* from other *ṣukūk* structures elsewhere. Therefore, the issuer of ringgit-denominated *ṣukūk* is required to comply with the sharia principles endorsed by the SC's SAC. Another related aspect here is the required appointment of a sharia advisor imposed upon the *ṣukūk* issuer to carry out certain responsibilities.[50] This is an area where the agreement of the principal advisor is required.[51]

Of particular importance here is the definition of a corporation, mentioned as one of the eligible persons for issuing, offering, or making an invitation to subscribe or purchase *ṣukūk*. Paragraph 3.01 of the Guidelines on *Ṣukūk* makes clear reference to the Capital Market Services Act 2007 pertaining to the meaning of the term corporation. Section 2 (1) of Capital Market Services Act 2007 defines a corporation as 'any body corporate formed or incorporated or existing within or outside Malaysia and includes any foreign company'. However, this definition excludes some corporate bodies including bodies' corporate incorporated in Malaysia which are declared to be a public authority or agent of the Malaysian government or of any State, any corporation sole, any society, or trade union.[52] Therefore, local and foreign companies are eligible to engage in *ṣukūk* activities in Malaysia. In this respect, there is another regulatory term used by the Guidelines on *Ṣukūk* relating specifically to the issuance of *ṣukūk* by a foreign company: 'foreign currency-denominated *ṣukūk*'. This term refers to *ṣukūk* that are '(a) issued by a foreign issuer; (b) not originated in Malaysia; and (c) issued or offered to investors in Malaysia and at least one another country; or (d) an invitation to subscribe or purchase made to investors in Malaysia and at least one another country'.[53] Distinguishing between

[50] Ibid., Paragraph 5.01.

[51] Ibid. According to Principal Advisor Guidelines, the term principal advisor refers to 'the corporate finance advisor responsible for making submissions to the SC for corporate proposals'. Principal advisor plays several roles in the process of *ṣukūk* issuance as provided by Guidelines on *Ṣukūk*.

[52] For more information, see Capital Market Services Act 2007, Section 2 (1).

[53] Guidelines on *Ṣukūk*, Paragraph 2.01.

ringgit-denominated *ṣukūk* and foreign currency-denominated *ṣukūk* is significant due to the different regulatory requirements applicable.[54]

The regulatory definition of the term approval is provided by Chapter 1 of the Guidelines on *Ṣukūk* in which 'approval means an approval, authorisation or recognition under Part VI of the CMSA as the case may be'.[55] Section 212 (2) states:

> A person who proposes to undertake a proposal, scheme, transaction, an arrangement or activity, or issue securities or offer for subscription or purchase securities, or issue an invitation to subscribe for or purchase securities, in relation to ... shall seek the approval of the Commission under Division A.[56]

This section mentions four cases for seeking an approval from SC which include the listing and quotation of securities of a corporation or Islamic securities on a stock exchange. Another important requirement during the documentation process for *ṣukūk* is related to *ṣukūk* trust deed. Paragraph 10.01 states 'an issuer of *ṣukūk* must enter into a trust deed, appoint a *ṣukūk* trustee and comply with the requirements of Division 4 of Part VI of the CMSA, unless the issue is exempted under Schedule 8 of the CMSA'.[57]

However, the picture of the *ṣukūk* offerings is not completed without a reference to other regulatory factors. There are other important aspects and terms relating to the offer of *ṣukūk* which are not defined in the Guidelines on *Ṣukūk*—these include 'issue', 'invitation', and 'prospectus'. The term 'issue' in relation to securities typically means 'to bring or cause to be brought into existence those securities' pursuant to section 2 (1) of the Capital Market Services Act 2007. In the context of capital market, the term invitation refers to 'an invitation to make an offer or application'.[58] In this respect, the offer of *ṣukūk* to the public is facilitated by means of prospectus according to section 37 (1) of the Companies Act 1965. However, this is only applicable to public companies since private

[54] See ibid., Paragraph 5.04. It excludes foreign currency-denominated *ṣukūk* from the requirement to comply with sharia principles endorsed by SAC.

[55] Ibid., Paragraph 2.01.

[56] Capital Market Services Act 2007, Section 212 (2).

[57] Guidelines on *Ṣukūk*, Paragraph 10.01. See also Capital Market Services Act 2007, Section 258.

[58] Capital Market Services Act 2007, Section 227.

companies are prohibited from offering their securities to the public according to section 15 (1) (c) of the Companies Act 1965.

The term prospectus is defined as follows:

> [A] notice, circular, advertisement or document inviting applications or offers to subscribe for or purchase securities, or offering any securities for subscription or purchase and, unless expressly specified, includes a supplementary prospectus, replacement prospectus, shelf prospectus, short form prospectus, profile statement, supplementary shelf prospectus and abridged prospectus.[59]

The regulation of prospectus is set out in the Guidelines on Prospectus and Division 3 of Part VI of the Capital Market Services Act 2007. Special regulations regarding the contents of *ṣukūk* prospectus is contained in Division 2 of Part 1 of the Guidelines on Prospectus.[60] According to Section 232 (1), issuing, offering, or making an invitation to subscribe or purchase *ṣukūk* shall not be made without registration of the prospectus with SC and compliance with the Capital Market Services Act 2007 provisions.[61] However, prospectus requirements under Capital Market Services Act 2007 do not apply to an excluded offer, an excluded invitation, or an excluded issue.[62]

There are additional requirements in the case of the offer of retail *ṣukūk*. Paragraph 2.01 of the Guidelines on *Ṣukūk* defines the term 'retail *ṣukūk*' as '*ṣukūk* that are proposed to be issued or offered to retail investors and include an invitation to subscribe or purchase *ṣukūk* that are made to retail investors'.[63] In general, all requirements under the Guidelines on *Ṣukūk* are applicable to retail *ṣukūk* unless otherwise specified.[64] Detailed information and requirements relating to retail *ṣukūk* are set out in Part D of the Guidelines on *Ṣukūk*. The following general conditions regarding the offer of *ṣukūk* in the wider Malaysian scheme can be drawn from the above

[59] Ibid., Section 226.

[60] This Division, which entirely focuses on the information to be disclosed in the *ṣukūk* prospectus, comprises 16 Chapters.

[61] Capital Market Services Act 2007, Section 232 (1).

[62] See ibid., Section 226 and Section 231 (1).

[63] The term 'retail investors' means 'any person who is not a high net-worth individual, a high net-worth entity or is an accredited investor as specified in these Guidelines'. The term accredited investor includes BNM, Labuan bank, *takāful* operator, and others. See Guidelines on Sales Practices of Unlisted Capital Market Products.

[64] Guidelines on *Ṣukūk*, Paragraph 21.02.

discussion: obtaining approval from SC; appointment of a sharia advisor; appointment of a principal advisor; appointment of a *ṣukūk* trustee; compliance with the Guidelines on *Ṣukūk*; and reference to other relevant laws. One also must realise the regulatory implications and requirements of different types of *ṣukūk*.

With regard to the Labuan regulatory scheme, offers of *ṣukūk* are regulated under Chapter 1 (Offer of Securities) and Chapter 2 (*Ṣukūk*) of Part III of the Labuan Islamic Financial Services and Securities Act 2010. Section 13 (1) provides for the offer of *ṣukūk* in Labuan as follows:

> Subject to subsections (2) to (7), a person, its officers, directors, agent or any other person on its behalf, shall not make an offer for subscription or purchase, or issue an invitation to subscribe for or purchase securities in or from within Labuan without
>
> (a) the prior written approval of the Authority; and
> (b) in relation to *ṣukūk*, the endorsement from a sharia advisor under subsection (9).[65]

The above provides that offering *ṣukūk* in Labuan is generally subject to two conditions: an approval from the Labuan FSA and an endorsement from a sharia advisor. However, these two requirements do not apply to certain types of *ṣukūk*.[66] According to Section 16, no offer of *ṣukūk* in or from within Labuan should be made without a prospectus being registered with the Labuan FSA.[67] The regulation of prospectus in relation to the offer of securities in general is contained in Sections 16–20.[68] The key terms relating to the offer of *ṣukūk*, contained in Labuan Islamic Financial Services and Securities Act 2010, include 'securities', '*ṣukūk*', and 'prospectus'. Whereas the term 'securities' refers generally to conventional security types, it is used here to refer to securities issued in accordance with sharia principles which include *ṣukūk*.[69] The term '*ṣukūk*' and 'prospectus' are defined under Section 2 (1).[70] There is more flexibility in terms of the

[65] Labuan Islamic Financial Services and Securities Act 2010, Section 13 (1).
[66] See ibid., Section 13 (5) (b) and Section 13 (6).
[67] Ibid., Section 16.
[68] Ibid., Sections 16–20.
[69] Ibid., Section 2 (1).
[70] Ibid.

sharia principles applicable to *ṣukūk* in Labuan compared to wider Malaysia. *Ṣukūk* structures are not required to comply only with sharia principles approved by SAC of the Labuan FSA.[71]

7.3.2 Regulation of the Ṣukūk *Listing*

Regulating the wider Malaysian regulatory scheme, the official list is maintained by the Main Market of the Bursa Malaysia Securities Berhad. Chapter 4B (i.e. Listing of *Ṣukūk* and Debt Securities)[72] of the Main Market Listing Requirements sets out the requirements for listing *ṣukūk* and debt securities. The issuer of particular *ṣukūk* has an option to list such as 'Exchange Traded Bonds' or under the 'Exempt Regime'.[73] While the former refers to *ṣukūk* listed and quoted for trading, the latter refers to *ṣukūk* listed but not quoted for trading.[74] Part C and Part D of Chapter4B are concerned with Exchange Traded Bonds and the Exempt Regime, respectively. With regard to Exchange Traded Bonds, '[a]n issuer must first obtain approval(s) from SC and other relevant authorities (where applicable) before listing and quotation of any *ṣukūk* or debt securities'.[75] Paragraph 4B.04 sets out admission requirements for *ṣukūk* listed as Exchange Traded Bonds, which include submitting a listing application through a principal advisor.[76] Further, there are certain provisions required in the trust deed or any other document governing *ṣukūk* holders' rights for the purpose of listing *ṣukūk* as Exchange Traded Bonds.[77] Foreign issuers are required to appoint an agent in Malaysia, maintain a paying agent in Malaysia, and disclose all information and documents in English.[78] Continuing listing obligations relating to foreign issuers, convertible or exchangeable *ṣukūk* and the obligor are provided by Paragraph 4B.09.[79] Requirements regarding the disclosure of information and submission of financial statements are set out in Paragraphs 4B.10–4B.11.[80] For the

[71] For the definition of sharia principles, see ibid.

[72] This Chapter comprises 5 Parts.

[73] Main Market Listing Requirements, Chapter 4B, Paragraph 4B.01 (2).

[74] Ibid., Paragraph 4B.02. Exempt Regime includes *ṣukūk* which are excluded offers and excluded issues.

[75] Ibid., Paragraph 4B.04.

[76] Ibid.

[77] Ibid., Paragraph 4B.06. This requirement does not apply to *ṣukūk* issued by the Government of Malaysia and others.

[78] Ibid., Paragraph 4B.07.

[79] Ibid., Paragraph 4B.09.

[80] Ibid., Paragraphs 4B.10–4B.11.

Exempt Regime, Paragraph 4B.15 states 'an applicant seeking to list any *ṣukūk* or debt securities on the Exchange under the Exempt Regime needs to obtain the approval of the SC only if an approval under section 212(4) of the CMSA is required for the issue or offer of the *ṣukūk* or debt securities'.[81] It is to be noted that *ṣukūk* with less than one year maturity date cannot be listed under the Exempt Regime.[82] The admission procedures applicable to Exchange Traded Bonds are also applicable to *ṣukūk* under the Exempt Regime with some modifications.[83] Requirements relating to disclosure of information and submission of financial statements are provided by Paragraphs 4B.18–4B.19.[84] Part E is concerned with circumstances in which the issuer of *ṣukūk* or listed *ṣukūk* may be de-listed from the official list. These include, among others, maturity and full redemption of *ṣukūk*.[85]

For the Labuan regulatory scheme, Chapter 4 of the LFX Rules sets out the listing requirements for all financial instruments to be listed on the LFX.[86] As mentioned earlier, the LFX Rules do not provide special listing requirements regarding *ṣukūk*. Rules 1–5 set out listing criteria and qualifications for the financial instrument which include issuer compliance with relevant laws and regulations; financial instrument compliance with relevant rules and regulations; being denominated in any currencies allowed by the LFX; being freely transferable; and ability of the investors in obtaining necessary information in case it is a convertible instrument and an acceptable method of listing.[87] Rules 6–9 are concerned with secondary listing.[88] Rules 10–13 are concerned with the application procedure for listing and documents to be submitted.[89] Rule 10 provides that listing application must be submitted to the LFX by a listing sponsor.[90] Rules 14–19 explain the information in the listing document.[91] Rule 20 requires

[81] Ibid., Paragraph 4B.15.

[82] Ibid., Paragraph 4B.16 (2).

[83] Ibid.

[84] Ibid., Paragraphs 4B.18–4B.19.

[85] For more information, see ibid., Paragraph 4B.22.

[86] These Rules comprises 40 Rules.

[87] LFX Rules, Chapter 4, Rules 1–5.

[88] Ibid., Rules 6–9. In this case, the financial instrument is agreed to be listed on another exchange as the primary exchange.

[89] Ibid., Rules 10–13.

[90] Ibid., Rule 10. Listing sponsor, as the issuer's main channel of communication with LFX, is responsible for submission of complete and proper application to LFX.

[91] Ibid., Rules 14–19.

the appointment of a listing sponsor at all times.[92] Rule 26 demonstrates the listing fees.[93] Rules 27–35 provide post-listing obligations.[94] Censure, Suspension, and De-listing are presented in Rules 36–40.[95]

7.4 UAE *Ṣukūk* Regime

In general, there are two different financial regulatory jurisdictions in the UAE: 'the federal financial regulatory jurisdiction' and 'the Dubai International Financial Centre (DIFC) jurisdiction'.[96] The federal jurisdiction has its own financial regulatory system, with its own financial regulator for the capital markets, SCA[97]; another regulator with a specific securities regulation role—the Central Bank of the UAE[98]—and two stock

[92] Ibid., Rule 20.

[93] Ibid., Rule 26.

[94] Ibid., Rules 27–35.

[95] Ibid., Rules 36–40.

[96] DIFC is a financial free zone established in Dubai according to Federal Decree No. 35 of 2004 to Establish Financial Free Zone in Dubai. Federal Law No.8 of 2004 Regarding the Financial Free Zones laid the ground for establishing a financial free zone in any Emirate of the UAE. Having its own legal system and courts based on common law system, DIFC is a city within a city which is empowered to create its own laws regarding civil and commercial matters. However, UAE criminal law is still applicable in the DIFC. Article 3 (2) of Federal Law No.8 of 2004 Regarding the Financial Free Zones states: 'These Zones and Financial Activities shall also be subject to all Federal laws, with the exception of Federal civil and commercial laws'. For more information about the DIFC establishment, see Dubai Law No. 9 of 2004 in Respect of the Dubai International Financial Centre. For more information about DIFC legal system, see A Carballo, 'The Law of the Dubai International Financial Centre: Common Law Oasis or Mirage Within the UAE?' (2007) 21 Arab Law Quarterly 91.

[97] SCA is a public regulatory authority established in Abu Dhabi according to the Federal Law No. 4 of 2000 Concerning the Emirates Securities and Commodities Authority and Market. According to Article 4 of this Law, its functions and powers include (1) proposing regulations to the Council of Ministers; (2) making certain regulations; (3) forming specialist technical committees to perform a specific work; (4) being in touch with international markets; and (5) performing any acts according to its objectives.

[98] Union Law No. 10 of 1980 Concerning the Central Bank, the Monetary System, and Organisation of Banking laid the ground for its establishment. Article 5 of this Law provides the main functions of the Central Bank of the UAE which include (1) issuing and managing the UAE currency; (2) managing the credit policy of the UAE; (3) developing and overseeing the banking system in the UAE; (4) acting as the Government's banker; (5) providing financial assistance to the Government; (6) maintaining UAE's gold and currency reserves; and (7) acting as the lender of last resort to banks operating in the UAE.

exchanges—Abu Dhabi Securities Exchange (ADX)[99] and Dubai Financial Market (DFM).[100] DIFC retains its own independent financial regulatory system, with its own financial services regulator, the Dubai Financial Services Authority (DFSA)[101] and an international financial exchange, NASDAQ Dubai.[102]

Both jurisdictions have their own laws and regulations regarding the general practice of financial services and businesses.[103] Under the federal jurisdiction, Decision No. 16 of 2014 Concerning the Regulation of *Ṣukūk*[104] governs *ṣukūk* activities. For the DIFC jurisdiction, DIFC Law No.13 of 2004 Law Regulating Islamic Financial Business,[105] DIFC Law No. 1 of 2012 Markets Law,[106] DFSA Rulebook[107]: Markets Rules (MKT),[108] DFSA Rulebook: Islamic Financial Rules (IFR)[109] and NASDAQ Dubai Business Rules: Rulebook 3–Admission and Disclosure Standards (ADS)[110] regulate *ṣukūk* activities. While federal jurisdiction has enacted special regulations relating to *ṣukūk* activities, DIFC jurisdiction has no special rules concerning *ṣukūk* with partial exception of IFR, which covers all types of Islamic securities.

[99] ADX is a stock exchange established in Abu Dhabi according to Local Law No. 3 of 2000.

[100] DFM is a stock exchange established in Dubai according to Local Decree No. 14 of 2000.

[101] Dubai Law No. 9 of 2004 in respect of the Dubai International Financial Centre laid the ground for the establishment of various bodies within DIFC including DFSA.

[102] NASDAQ Dubai is a stock exchange located in DIFC which started its operation in 2005. It is regulated and licensed by the DFSA according to DIFC Law No.1 of 2004 Regulatory Law. For the purpose of DIFC laws and regulations, it refers to an authorised market institution since it is the only one existing in the DIFC jurisdiction.

[103] See generally G Mayew, 'Securities Regulation in the UAE' (*International Financial Law Review* October 2010). http://www.iflr.com/Article/2680248/Securities-regulation-in-the-UAE.html. Accessed 8 May 2014.

[104] This Decision, which is issued by SCA Board, comprises 28 Articles. Prior to this Decision, *ṣukūk* activities were governed by Decision No. (93/r) of 2005 Concerning the Listing of Islamic Bonds. This Decision, which is issued by SCA Board, comprises 37 Articles.

[105] This Law, which is one of the DFSA Administrated Laws, comprises two Parts.

[106] This Law, which is one of the DFSA Administrated Laws, comprises nine Parts.

[107] DFSA Rulebook is made up of 15 modules by the Board of Directors of the DFSA according to DIFC Law No.1 of 2004 Regulatory Law.

[108] MKT, which is part of DFSA Rulebook, comprises ten Chapters.

[109] IFR, which is part of DFSA Rulebook, comprises eight Chapters.

[110] NASDAQ Dubai has issued four Rulebooks comprising NASDAQ Dubai Business Rules which are approved by DFSA. Rulebook 3 is ADS which comprises five Standards.

7.4.1 *Regulation of the Offer of* Ṣukūk

For the federal regulatory jurisdiction, regulation of the offer of *ṣukūk* generally is contained in the Decision No. 16 of 2014 Concerning the Regulation of *Ṣukūk*. Article 1 provides some key terms and regulatory definitions which are relevant to the offer of *ṣukūk* including securities, *ṣukūk*, government *ṣukūk*, obligor, issuer, and sharia committee.[111] Article 2 (2) excludes government *ṣukūk* from the application of this decision.[112] However, the governmental nature of such *ṣukūk* shall be considered in case they are listed in the market.[113] According to Article 2 (3), this decision is not applicable to *ṣukūk* not offered through a public subscription and *ṣukūk* not listed in the market.[114] Retail *ṣukūk* must be offered through a public subscription and listed in the market pursuant to Article 3 (1).[115] Article 3 (2) requires the obligor to obtain SCA's approval before offering or listing *ṣukūk* in the market.[116] According to Article 4, the obligor must not be prevented from involvement in *ṣukūk* by its constitutional documents.[117] Article 5 provides that any *ṣukūk* issuance must be approved by a sharia committee and concern no less than AED 10 million.[118] For the purpose of *ṣukūk* issuance, Article 6 provides that the obligor must sign a trust agreement and appoint a licensed bank in the UAE as a paying agent.[119] The returns on *ṣukūk* shall be used in accordance with Islamic law pursuant to Article 11.[120] These above conditions and regulatory definitions form together the most important dictates concerned with making an offer of *ṣukūk* under the federal regulatory jurisdiction.

Within the DIFC jurisdiction, the DIFC Law No.13 of 2004 Law Regulating Islamic Financial Business is concerned with all types of Islamic financial business conducted in the DIFC. According to Article 9 (1), an endorsed licence to conduct Islamic financial business in the DIFC needs to be taken out by authorised firms or market institutions that perform

[111] Decision No. 16 of 2014 Concerning the Regulation of *Ṣukūk*, Article 1.
[112] Ibid., Article 2 (2).
[113] Ibid.
[114] Ibid., Article 2 (3).
[115] Ibid., Article 3 (1).
[116] Ibid., Article 3 (2).
[117] Ibid., Article 4.
[118] Ibid., Article 5.
[119] Ibid., Article 6.
[120] Ibid., Article 11.

Islamic financial business.[121] An offer of *ṣukūk* is subject to regulations set out in DIFC Law No. 1 of 2012 Markets Law, MKT, and IFR. According to IFR 7.1.1 (2), '[a] Person making Offers of Islamic Securities in or from the DIFC must comply with the requirements in the Markets Law 2012 and the MKT module except to the extent otherwise provided in this chapter'.[122] IFR is considered, to some extent, the only special regulations concerning the offer of *ṣukūk* in the DIFC. IFR makes it clear that one must refer to the Markets Law 2012 and the MKT in matters relating to the offer of Islamic securities.[123] IFR does not include detailed information about the offer of Islamic securities. It defines Islamic securities as '[a]ny Security Offered, or held out expressly or implicitly, as Islamic or sharia compliant'.[124] DIFC legislation does not use the term *ṣukūk*, but it does use the term Islamic securities, which includes *ṣukūk* and others. Most of the requirements applicable to an offer of *ṣukūk* in or from DIFC are set out in Part 2 (Offer of Securities)[125] of DIFC Law No. 1 of 2012 Markets Law and Chapter 2 (Offer of Securities)[126] of MKT. The most important regulatory aspect regarding the offer of *ṣukūk* in DIFC jurisdiction is described by Article 11 (1) of the DIFC Law No. 1 of 2012 Markets Law as follows:

> 'A person shall not:
>
> (a) make an Offer of Securities to the Public in or from the DIFC: or
> (b) have Securities admitted to trading on an Authorised Market Institution, except as provided in this Law and the Rules made for the purposes of this Law'.

The above Article forms a general prohibition regarding the offer of securities in DIFC. However, Article 13 (1) excludes exempt offerors (including securities of an exempt offeror[127] and securities unconditionally

[121] DIFC Law No.13 of 2004 Law Regulating Islamic Financial Business, Article 9 (1).

[122] DFSA Rulebook: Islamic Financial Rules, Rule 7.1.1.

[123] Ibid.

[124] DFSA Rulebook: Glossary Module (GLO).

[125] This Part comprises 4 Chapters.

[126] This Chapter comprises 13 Rules.

[127] Article 13 (2) of the DIFC Law No. 1 of 2012 Markets Law defines an exempt offeror as 'a recognised government or other person included in the list of Exempt Offerors maintained by the DFSA in the Rules'.

guaranteed by said exempt offeror) from the prohibition provided by Article 11 (1).[128] Article 12 defines the term offer of securities to the public.[129] Article 14 (1) requires obtaining an approved prospectus in order to make an offer of securities to the public in or from the DIFC.[130] The prospectus is considered an approved prospectus if it is approved by the DFSA.[131] However, exempt offers and exempt securities are excluded from the requirement to obtain an approved prospectus.[132] Prospectus content requirements are presented in Article 15.[133] Information about the offer of securities is set out in Chapter 2 of MKT, including structure, content, approval, and publication of prospectus. IFR 7.2.3 contains certain requirements applicable to the contents of a prospectus of Islamic securities. These form the only provisions in the DIFC jurisdiction which relate to the offer of *ṣukūk*.

7.4.2 Regulation of Ṣukūk *Listing*

For the federal regulatory regime, the listing of *ṣukūk* offered through a public subscription is regulated by the Decision No. 16 of 2014 Concerning the Regulation of *Ṣukūk*. This decision provides special rules relating to the listing of *ṣukūk* in the UAE. The SCA's approval is required before listing any *ṣukūk* in the market as provided by Article 3 (2).[134] In the case of primary listing of retail *ṣukūk*, the obligor is required to be incorporated in the UAE and outside financial free zone.[135] Article 7 provides the conditions and documents concerning the approval of primary listing of *ṣukūk*.[136] Joint listing of *ṣukūk* in the market is allowed subject to certain conditions and submission of documents pursuant to Article 8.[137] Article 17 imposes six continuing obligations on the obligor with regard to primary listing of *ṣukūk*.[138] Retail *ṣukūk* listed in the market are required to

[128] Ibid., Article 13 (1).
[129] Ibid., Article 12.
[130] Ibid., Article 14 (1).
[131] Ibid., Article 14 (2) (a).
[132] Ibid., Article 14 (3).
[133] Ibid., Article 15.
[134] Decision No. 16 of 2014 Concerning the Regulation of *Ṣukūk*, Article 3 (2).
[135] Ibid., Article 4 (2).
[136] Ibid., Article 7.
[137] Ibid., Article 8.
[138] Ibid., Article 17.

comply with additional conditions as provided by Article 18.[139] Articles 19–23 are concerned with the suspension and cancellation of *ṣukūk* listing.[140] Articles 24–28 deal with penalties and the obligation to publish information.[141]

Within the DIFC jurisdiction, there are two types of regulations which need to be considered by the issuer for the purpose of *ṣukūk* listing. The first category is concerned with admission of *ṣukūk* to the official list of securities, namely DIFC Law No. 1 of 2012 Markets Law, MKT, and IFR. The second category is concerned with the admission to trading of *ṣukūk* on the NASDAQ Dubai, and includes ADS. This forms a two-stage admission process applicable to *ṣukūk* issuers seeking an admission of *ṣukūk* to trading in the DIFC jurisdiction: an admission to the official list of securities maintained by the DFSA and an admission to trading on NASDAQ Dubai. On the subject of admission of *ṣukūk* to the official list,[142] Article 33 (1) provides that DFSA grants admission of *ṣukūk* to the official list only when such admission meets all requirements under DIFC Law No. 1 of 2012 Markets Law and rules made for the application of such law.[143] *Ṣukūk* included in the official list of securities must be admitted to trading on NASDAQ Dubai.[144] Chapter 2 under Part 3 of the DIFC Law No. 1 of 2012 Markets Law is concerned with the official list of securities. More detailed information is contained in the rules made for the purpose of DIFC Law No. 1 of 2012 Markets Law, which are MKT and IFR. Chapter 9 of the MKT outlines the listing rules[145]; an applicant seeking to list *ṣukūk* must meet general eligibility requirements, including incorporation, submission of financial statements, availability of working capital, general suitability, and management experience, among others.[146] Rule 9.4 of MKT provides requirements for the listing application. Circumstances of suspension, de-listing, and restoration are presented in rule 9.6 of MKT. While the above-mentioned rules are applicable to all

[139] Ibid., Article 18.

[140] Ibid., Articles 19–23.

[141] Ibid., Articles 24–28.

[142] See Article 29 of the DIFC Law No. 1 of 2012 Markets Law relating to maintaining an official list of securities. Guidance 6 under Chapter 9 of the MKT states: 'The DFSA will maintain the List on the DFSA website'.

[143] DIFC Law No. 1 of 2012 Markets Law, Article 33 (1).

[144] See ibid., Article 33 (3) and Article 33 (5).

[145] This Chapter comprises eight Rules.

[146] DFSA Rulebook: Markets Rules, Rule 9.3.

financial instruments (whether Islamic or conventional), IFR contains two rules relating to Islamic securities only: continuing disclosure relating to Islamic securities and admission of Islamic securities to an official list of securities.[147] Rule 7.4 of IFR stipulates that an applicant seeking listing of sharia-compliant securities on the official list of securities must submit a sharia pronouncement, any details about declaration of trust, and any documents concerning the sharia nature of the proposed security. This forms a special rule within DIFC jurisdiction regarding the admission of *ṣukūk* to the DFSA's official list of securities. To admit *ṣukūk* for trading on NASDAQ Dubai, an applicant is required to fulfil all requirements set out in the ADS as a second stage of compliance. ADS comprises five standards: ADS1 provides requirements which are applicable to all securities seeking admission to trading on the NASDAQ Dubai. ADS2 provides requirements which are applicable to specific types of securities including sharia-compliant securities. According to ADS 2.5.1, an issuer of such security is required to publish a sharia pronouncement on its website and submit a copy to NASDAQ Dubai. ADS3 presents the ongoing obligations for the issuer required to maintain eligibility for such admission on the NASDAQ Dubai. ADS4 and ADS5 detail corporate actions and NASDAQ Dubai's powers and requirements, respectively.

7.5 Kingdom of Saudi Arabia *Ṣukūk* Regime

The financial regulation regime in the KSA comprises an independent capital market regulator, the Capital Markets Authority (CMA),[148] and a sole stock exchange, the Saudi Stock Exchange (known as Tadawul).[149] The regulations governing *ṣukūk* activities in the KSA include Offers of Securities Regulations[150] and Listing Rules[151] which are issued by

[147] See DFSA Rulebook: Islamic Financial Rules, Rules 7.3–7.4.

[148] CMA is a government organisation established by Capital Market Law. This Law, which was issued by Royal Decree No. (M/30) dated 2/6/1424 H. (2 July 2003), comprises ten Chapters. Prior to 2003, capital market activities were regulated by two authorities: Ministry of Commerce and SAMA, the central bank. For more information, see J Beach, 'The Saudi Arabian Capital Market Law: A Practical Study of the Creation of Law in Developing Markets' (2005) 41 Stanford Journal of International Law 307, 311.

[149] Established as a joint stock company in 2007, Saudi Stock Exchange constitutes the sole market for the trading in securities in Saudi Arabia. Chapter 3 of the Capital Market Law laid the grounds for its establishment.

[150] These Regulations comprise six Parts accounting for 19 Articles.

[151] These Rules comprise nine Parts accounting for 53 Articles.

CMA. However, these do not provide special rules regarding *ṣukūk* activities in the KSA; rather, they are equally applicable to all capital market securities, whether conventional or Islamic.

7.5.1 Regulation of the Offer of **Ṣukūk**

In general, the offer of *ṣukūk* in the KSA is subject to the Offers of Securities Regulations and Listing Rules (containing the conditions of a public offer and information about prospectus contents for debt instruments and convertible debt instruments).[152] Article 1 defines offering securities as:

> [I]ssuing securities, inviting the public to subscribe therefor or the direct or indirect marketing thereof; or any statement, announcement or communication that has the effect of selling, issuing or offering securities, but does not include preliminary negotiations or contracts entered into with or among underwriters.[153]

According to Article 6, an offer of *ṣukūk* is either a public offer or a private placement.[154] Broadly defined, any offer which does not fall under the categories of a private placement is considered a public offer.[155] A public offer must meet all requirements and conditions stated by the Listing Rules.[156] One of the most important conditions regarding a public offer of *ṣukūk* in the KSA is that the issuer of *ṣukūk* must be a Saudi joint stock company[157]; therefore, other forms of companies in the KSA are prohibited from offering *ṣukūk* to the public. In this respect, Articles 116–122 of the Companies Law of 1965 concerning bonds issued by a joint stock company will be applied. Other conditions of a public offering of *ṣukūk* include approval of the issuer's board; submission of an application for registration and admission to listing to CMA; appointment of the issuer's representatives (a director and a senior executive); and providing contact

[152] Although it is called Listing Rules, it sets out some requirements regarding the public offer. Article 2 (a) of the Listing Rules states: 'The purpose of these Rules is to regulate the public offering, registration and admission to listing of securities in the Kingdom'.

[153] Offers of Securities Regulations, Article 1.

[154] Ibid., Article 6.

[155] Ibid., Article 7.

[156] Ibid., Article 8.

[157] Listing Rules, Article 11 (a).

details for these representatives.[158] Instances of a private placement include *ṣukūk* issued by the government or a supranational authority recognised by the CMA; *ṣukūk* strictly offered to sophisticated investors; and a limited *ṣukūk* offer.[159] In addition to these circumstances, CMA may treat a particular offer of *ṣukūk* as a private offer.[160] Regulatory definitions of the relevant key terms relating to an offer of *ṣukūk* in the KSA are significant, particularly the terms 'sophisticated investors' and a 'limited *ṣukūk*' offer. Pursuant to Article 10, sophisticated investors include the government; supranational authorities recognised by the CMA; the Saudi Stock Exchange or any stock exchange recognised by the CMA; the Depository Centre; professional investors; authorised persons and institutions acting on their own account; and others.[161] A *ṣukūk* offer is regarded a limited offer when it is offered for no more than 60, excluding sophisticated investors, with the amount paid (for each *ṣukūk* holder) no less than SAR 1 million or equivalent amount[162]; offered for the issuer's employee or affiliate; and any other requirements specified by the CMA.[163]

With regard to the *ṣukūk* prospectus, one should refer to Articles 21–25 of the Listing Rules. Approval of the prospectus must be obtained from CMA before it is made available to the public.[164] Article 23 details situations in which a prospectus is not required.[165] Annex 5 provides information about the contents of prospectuses applicable to *ṣukūk* offers.[166]

7.5.2 Regulation of Ṣukūk *Listing*

Ṣukūk and securities in general are listed in the Tadawul whereby the Listing Rules must be met by all types of securities for the purpose of registration and admission to list securities in the KSA. Article 2 (b) states '[s]ecurities may not be offered by way of a public offer unless all the requirements and conditions provided for in these Rules have been

[158] Ibid., Articles 2–4.

[159] Offers of Securities Regulations, Article 9 (a).

[160] Ibid., Article 9 (b).

[161] Ibid., Article 10.

[162] However, less than this amount is allowed when the *ṣukūk* total value does not exceed SAR 5 million or an equivalent amount. See ibid., Article 11 (b).

[163] Ibid., Article 11 (a).

[164] Listing Rules, Article 22 (a).

[165] Ibid., Article 23.

[166] Ibid., Annex 5.

fulfilled'.[167] Article 5 (a) requires the appointment of an independent financial advisor and an independent legal advisor when the production of a prospectus is required for registration and admission to listing.[168] In the case of a voluntary cancellation of listing by the issuer, appointment of financial and legal advisors is required according to Article 5 (b).[169] The CMA may request the appointment of a financial advisor and/or a legal advisor in situations where the appointment of them is not mandatory.[170] Articles 6–10 set out the requirements, obligations, and duties imposed on financial and legal advisor.[171] Conditions for registration and admission to listing relating to issuers, securities (in general), cross-listing, debt instruments, contractually based securities, and convertible debt securities are found in Part 3 of the Listing Rules. With regard to the issuer seeking registration and admission to listing on Tadawul, the issuer must be a Saudi stock company; carry out its business under the same management for at least three years; publish its audited financial statements for at least the last three years; submit the application after one year in cases of restructuring and alteration in capital; have senior executives with appropriate experience for the management of its activity; have adequate working capital for 12 months subsequent to prospectus publication; and CMA satisfaction regarding such listing.[172] For securities, in general, they must comply with statutory conditions in the KSA; be duly authorised by the issuer's constitutional documents; be freely transferable; and tradable and be registered under the Securities Depository Centre.[173] Article 19 sets out all documents required for submission of an application for registration and admission to listing.[174] Article 35 is concerned with circumstances of suspension and cancellation of listings.[175] Related matters to Article 35 are presented in the subsequent Articles.[176] Articles 40–52 are concerned with listing obligations.[177]

[167] Ibid., Article 2 (b).
[168] Ibid., Article 5 (a).
[169] Ibid., Article 5 (b).
[170] Ibid., Article 5 (c).
[171] Ibid., Articles 6–10.
[172] Ibid., Article 11.
[173] Ibid., Article 12.
[174] Ibid., Article 19.
[175] Ibid., Article 35.
[176] Ibid., Articles 36–39.
[177] Ibid., Articles 40–52.

7.6 Assessment of the *Ṣukūk* Regimes

It should be clear now how *ṣukūk* markets are regulated in Malaysia, the UAE, and the KSA, and which regulations deal specifically with *ṣukūk* in these countries. This discussion is important to remove any uncertainty as to how *ṣukūk* fit into the legal and regulatory frameworks of these countries. Haynes asserts that 'although regulators are recognising sharia bond issues there is not clear-cut recognition in every state as to where such bond issues fit in the regulatory structure'.[178] The underlying purpose of the above discussion is to ascertain whether *ṣukūk* markets are regulated effectively in these jurisdictions. When looking at the development of a *ṣukūk* market under the relevant legal system, one should look at the permissibility of conducting this particular kind of business by law and the presence of a supportive legal environment.[179] From discussion of the regulations concerning *ṣukūk* in Malaysia, the UAE, and the KSA, one can see that the law in these countries does not inhibit the existence of *ṣukūk* markets. However, the potential for issues to arise, in the context of *ṣukūk* markets, is greater when it comes to the presence of a supportive legal environment.

Identifying whether a particular country provides a legal environment supportive of a *ṣukūk* market is subject to great difficulty for several reasons. There are a host of issues determining the effectiveness of a *ṣukūk* market legal environment. Such issues in the context of *ṣukūk* markets are rarely perceived, let alone identified. In addition, the meaning of supportive or effective legal environment is challenging in the context of *ṣukūk* markets. There is uncertainty as to what constitutes an effective legal framework for *ṣukūk* markets. This is compounded by the fact that legal frameworks designed for conventional financial markets are not effective for Islamic financial markets. In this respect, Rider says:

> An effective legal and regulatory framework that caters for the growth and sustainability of Islamic financial markets actually needs to take into consideration various issues that may not be so relevant to its conventional counterpart, in addition to other similar concerns about the soundness and stability of the financial system.[180]

[178] A Haynes, 'New Sources of Finance' (2011) 2 Company Lawyer 33.
[179] B Rider, *supra* note 10, 49.
[180] Ibid.

There has been some discussion of the issue of an effective legal and regulatory framework in the context of business development. Shihata proposes three pillars for such a framework: (1) existence of legally binding rules; (2) presence of suitable measures for making, enforcing, and changing the law; and (3) existence of well-functioning public institutions.[181] It would not be prudent to exhaustively address every issue and element constituting an effective legal framework in the selected countries. Rather, the following discussion focuses on four issues that are relevant to the existence of an enabling legal and regulatory framework for *ṣukūk* markets, and looks at the extent to which Malaysia, the UAE, and the KSA consider them in their existing framework. These are regulatory approach, role of the institutions, disclosure of information, and sharia compliance.

7.6.1 Regulatory Authorities and Their Approach to the IFSI

The discussion of regulatory approach is concerned with the way a country regulates the *ṣukūk* market. There are two common approaches towards the regulation of the IFSI. The first approach differentiates between the IFSI and conventional finance in terms of the regulatory and legal framework. This approach intends to provide a level playing field for both the IFSI and its conventional counterpart, with varying degrees of implementation. The financial regulator adopts two tiers of regulation—the first tier is applicable to both the IFSI and its conventional counterpart and the second tier is applicable only to the IFSI, addressing its specific needs. Given the infancy of the IFSI in many countries, the incentives provided by regulatory authorities for the IFSI may go beyond the purpose of levelling the playing field.[182] Such an approach addresses legal characteristics of the IFSI, gives institutional support, and recognises the real economic risks of Islamic financial products.[183] The financial regulator adopting this approach requires a substantial knowledge and expertise in the area of the IFSI. The second approach does not consider the differences between the IFSI and its conventional counterpart, and thus applies the same legal and regulatory requirements. Given that such legal and regulatory requirements

[181] I Shihata, 'The Role of Law in Business Development' (1996) 20 Fordham International Law Journal 1577, 1782.

[182] IFSB, 'Appendix: Case Studies' in IFSB (ed), *Strategies for the Development of Islamic Capital Markets* (IFSB 2011) 247.

[183] J Ercanbrack, *The Transformation of Islamic Law in Global Financial Markets* (Cambridge University Press 2015) 293.

are conventional finance based in most cases, the specific features of the IFSI are ignored. This approach is currently operating in most jurisdictions hosting the IFSI. In such jurisdictions, the financial regulator is referred to as a risk-based regulator as its focus is on the substantive economic risks of financial institutions, and not on the legal form of the products and services provided by such institutions.[184] While Malaysia and the UAE are examples of the first approach, the KSA follows the second approach.

Malaysia has made it clear that it will take all measures to become an international Islamic financial centre.[185] It is a pioneer in the development of the IFSI, starting in 1963.[186] The significance of the Malaysian model can be seen in the fact that it has the biggest *ṣukūk* market in the world in terms of value and number of issuances for the period from January 1996 to September 2013, as demonstrated in Chap. 2. Key elements supporting the creation and operation of the IFSI in Malaysia include an effective legal and regulatory framework, a robust sharia governance framework, tax incentives, and liquidity management facilities.[187] As a leading jurisdiction in the IFSI, Malaysia introduced the first comprehensive legislation to regulate all IIFS, that is, the Islamic Financial Services Act 2013.

The general practice of the IFSI in the UAE was traditionally left to the market and is best described as a market-driven approach. However, this situation changed after the launch of the 'Dubai-Capital of Islamic Economy' Initiative in October 2013 which encompasses *ṣukūk* development as one of the main sectors.[188] This initiative has been followed by the establishment of the Dubai Islamic Economy Development Centre (DIEDC) on 18 December 2013 pursuant to Dubai Law No. 13 of 2013 Establishment of Dubai Islamic Economy Development Centre. Dubai's strategy towards becoming the capital of Islamic economy will provide the legal capacity necessary for the development of the IFSI, not only in Dubai

[184] Ibid.

[185] Central Bank of Malaysia Act 2009, Article 60.

[186] For more information about the development of the IFSI in Malaysia, see M Laldin, 'Islamic Financial System: The Malaysian Experience and the Way Forward' (2008) 24 Humanomics 217.

[187] IFSB, *supra* note 182, 245.

[188] E Chand and Wam, 'Dubai-World Capital of Islamic Economy: Initiative Unveiled' (*Emirates 24/7 News*, 5 October 2013). http://www.emirates247.com/news/dubai-world-capital-of-islamic-economy-initiative-unveiled-2013-10-05-1.523457. Accessed 16 August 2015.

but throughout the Emirates. The supporting role for the IFSI in Dubai can be traced back to the 1970s, when the first Islamic bank in the world—the Dubai Islamic Bank—still operating, was founded. The UAE includes specific provisions on the IFSI in its legislation, such as Federal Law No. 6 of 1985 regarding Islamic Banks, Financial Institutions and Investment Companies, and Decision No. 4 of 2010 Takaful Insurance Regulations. Apart from the rest of the UAE, the DIFC jurisdiction clearly supports the development of the IFSI as proven by the DIFC laws and rulebook concerning the IFSI.[189]

Although the KSA is considered a significant location for the growth in the IFSI, it lacks the enabling regulatory infrastructure. There are no laws and regulations concerning the general practice of the IFSI passed in the KSA as yet, let alone directly addressing the *ṣukūk* market. The absence of special laws regarding the *ṣukūk* market and the IFSI in the KSA was explained by the former governor of SAMA, Muḥammad al-Jāsir, who said:

> We have richness in diversity. The essence in Islam is permissibility. The genesis of things is permissibility. Everything is permissible unless it is shown to contravene Islamic tenets. Someone has to tell me if and how it contravenes explicitly. In fact, most conventional financial products are fine as long as they do not contravene Islamic tenets. Regulators and supervisors are not religious scholars. They are in charge of financial stability. The safety of the institution is paramount.[190]

The above statement raises some questions about the suitability of such regulatory treatment of the IFSI in the KSA. One cannot rely on the permissibility rule in Islamic law when it comes to the regulation of the IFSI in the very advanced and complex financial sector. Although financial regulators are not religious bodies, the creation and operation of a sound IFSI in a country require special regulatory treatment for the IFSI. The treatment by regulators in the KSA of *ṣukūk* as debt financial instruments is inappropriate since it causes confusion between Islamic financial

[189] See DFSA, 'The DFSA's Approach to Regulating Islamic Finance in the DIFC' (*DFSA*, undated). http://www.dfsa.ae/Documents/Islamic%20finance%20docs%20for%20upload/DFSA's%20approach%20to%20regulating%20Islamic%20finance.pdf. Accessed 17 August 2015.

[190] M Parker, 'Islamic Finance is Growing at a Phenomenal Pace: Al-Jasser' (*Arab News*, 30 November 2009). http://www.arabnews.com/node/330520. Accessed 31 July 2015.

instruments and their conventional counterparts. In this regard, some commentators state that 'the formally regulated *ṣukūk* market in the KSA is new and immature; companies' and financial regulations have not included specific rules and guidelines regarding *ṣukūk* issuances and listings'.[191] After studying the relevant regulatory and legal framework in the KSA, Al Elsheikh and Tanega concluded that its *ṣukūk* market suffers from heavy regulation and market drawbacks.[192]

7.6.2 Role of the Regulatory and Market Institutions

The role of the regulatory and market institutions is generally linked with the regulatory approaches to the IFSI as discussed in the earlier section. Said institutions are required to play an active role towards the development of the IFSI in jurisdictions that are interested in providing a level playing field for both the IFSI and its conventional counterpart. Such institutions need to address various issues that are relevant to the creation and operation of the IFSI, including authorisation of IIFS, capital adequacy standards to IIFS, risk management with respect to IIFS, governance standards for IIFS, strategies for the development of the IFSI, dispute resolutions for the IFSI, and establishment of capital and money markets.[193] Such areas do not come under functions of the regulatory and market institutions in jurisdictions wherein the legal form of the Islamic financial transactions is not a matter of regulation.

The Malaysian regime provides an excellent example of a supportive environment for *ṣukūk* practice, arising from the efficiency of its regulatory and market institutions. For example, SC has paid particular attention to ICM by setting up a special unit called Islamic Capital Market Department.[194] SC established its own SAC in order to advise on sharia issues relating to the practice of ICM in Malaysia. Furthermore, SC's great interest in enhancing the profile of the *ṣukūk* market can be found in its Capital Market Master Plan 1 (CMP1) 2001 and Capital Master Plan 2 (CMP2) 2011, which encourages the issuance of Islamic debt securities by

[191] A Al Elsheikh and J Tanega, 'Sukuk Structure and its Regulatory Environment in the Kingdom of Saudi Arabia' (2011) Law and Financial Markets Review 183,190.

[192] Ibid.

[193] B Rider, *supra* note 10, 193.

[194] SC, *Regulatory Requirement, Legal Documentation, Accounting, Auditing and Taxation in the Islamic Capital Market* 22.

government and government-related entities[195] in order to increase the scale of the *ṣukūk* segment.[196] The particular role of BNM in *ṣukūk* market includes approval power of securities issued by financial institutions working under the Banking and Financial Institutions Act 1989,[197] providing incentives to Islamic banking institutions structuring Islamic private debt securities,[198] and active participation in *ṣukūk* issuance by trading and facilitating regular issues of *ṣukūk* with the government and government-linked companies.[199] Bursa Malaysia is considered the largest *ṣukūk* listing exchange globally with a value of USD 27.7 billion in 2010.[200] Bursa Malaysia has also its own sharia committee, advising on sharia issues relating to its financial services.[201] An important initiative concerning the local *ṣukūk* market implemented by Bursa Malaysia is the establishment of Bloomberg-AIBIM-Bursa Malaysia Corporate *Ṣukūk* index in September 2012 with the aim of tracking the performance of Malaysian ringgit-denominated corporate *ṣukūk*.[202] Considering that Malaysia has strong credit rating frameworks as proven by establishing two local rating agencies, namely MARC and RAM Rating Services Berhad,[203] the Malaysian model will continue to attract attention of the international Islamic financial markets, due in part to its ongoing efforts placed in talent enrichment as proven by the establishment of several institutions such as the Islamic Banking and Finance Institute Malaysia (IBFIM), the International Centre for Leadership in Finance (ICLIF), the International Centre for Education in Islamic Finance (INCEIF) and the ISRA.[204] To add further legal

[195] Recommendation 75 of CMP1 says '[t]he government and government-related entities should consider issuing Islamic debt securities in the global market'. See SC, *Capital Market Masterplan* (SC 2001) 183.

[196] See SC, *Capital Market Masterplan 2* (SC 2011) 55.

[197] SC, *Regulatory Requirement, Legal Documentation, Accounting, Auditing and Taxation in the Islamic Capital Market* 26.

[198] BNM, *Financial Sector Masterplan* (BNM 2001) 81.

[199] BNM, *Financial Sector Blueprint 2011–2020* (BNM 2011) 110.

[200] BNM, 'Financial Stability and Payment Systems Report 2010' (*BNM*, 2011) 53. http://www.bnm.gov.my/files/publication/fsps/en/2010/fs2010_book.pdf. Accessed 30 January 2014.

[201] Bursa Malaysia, 'Shariah Committee' (*Bursa Malaysia*, 2014). http://www.bursamalaysia.com/market/islamic-markets/shariah-committee/. Accessed 17 February 2014.

[202] BNM, 'Financial Stability and Payment Systems Report 2012' (*BNM*, 2013) 79. http://www.bnm.gov.my/files/publication/fsps/en/2012/fs2012_book.pdf. Accessed 29 January 2014.

[203] B Rider, *supra* note 10, 197.

[204] For more information about the specific role of these institutions, see ibid. 198–199.

certainty in the market, the Kuala Lumpur Regional Centre for Arbitration (KLRCA) was established in 1978 in Malaysia to hear disputes concerning the IFSI.[205]

The UAE capital market authority is the first in the whole Gulf region to have issued specific regulations pertaining to *ṣukūk* practice. Another significant initiative regarding *ṣukūk* in the UAE is provided by Fatwa and the Sharia Supervisory Board of the DFM. In April 2014, it issued the 'DFM Standard for Issuing, Acquiring and Trading *Ṣukūk*'. It is a comprehensive standard covering important issues such as types of *ṣukūk*, issuance of *ṣukūk*, the general principles for issuance of *ṣukūk*, sharia rules for the issuance of *ṣukūk*, and *ṣukūk* guarantees.[206] However, this is a standard only, and not a formal regulation of *ṣukūk*. In addition, DIFC has published a comprehensive introduction about *ṣukūk* that covers *ṣukūk* structures and regulatory and legal requirements for *ṣukūk* issuance in the DIFC jurisdiction.[207] In Dubai, the DIEDC is an important institution that was established to promote Dubai as the global capital of Islamic economy. The DIEDC has seven areas of focus, namely finance, *ḥalāl* industry, family-friendly tourism, digital infrastructure, Islamic arts, knowledge, and standards.[208] Despite its recent establishment in 2013, the DIEDC has developed several initiatives including the Dubai Global *Ṣukūk* Centre, the Dubai Centre for Islamic Banking and Finance, the Halal Cluster, the Salam Project, the Dubai Technology Entrepreneurship Centre, the Islamic Economy Award, the Global Islamic Economy Summit, the Halal Expo, the Global Islamic Economy Portal, and the Executive Master's in Business Administration in Islamic Banking and Finance.[209] Commenting on the launch of the Global Islamic Economy Indicator in 2015 which describes the UAE as one of the healthiest environments for Islamic economy worldwide, Al Gergawi, Chairman of the Board of DIEDC, states:

[205] For more information, see J Colon, 'Choice of Law and Islamic Finance' (2011) 46 Texas International Law Journal 421.

[206] See DFM Fatwa and the Sharia Supervisory Board, 'DFM Standard for Issuing, Acquiring and Trading Ṣukūk' (*DFM*, 2014). http://www.dfm.ae/documents/sukuk/DFMSukukStandardFinalEn3032014.pdf. Accessed 28 September 2015.

[207] DIFC, Clifford Chance and Amani Consulting, *Dubai International Financial Centre: Sukuk Guidebook* (DIFC 2009).

[208] See DIEDC, 'DIEDC' (*DIEDC*, undated). http://www.iedcdubai.ae/index. Accessed 18 August 2015.

[209] See ibid.

> The UAE today is taking on greater global importance in the Islamic economy... Our strategy for developing the Islamic economy is not limited to Islamic banking and finance ... but spans seven key sectors forming the true pillars of an economy ... Studies are showing similar interest and solid growth in *ṣukūk*, with the UAE leading the way globally in this field thanks to its distinguished regulatory expertise in *ṣukūk* issuance.[210]

As a specific initiative with respect to *ṣukūk*, the Dubai Global *Ṣukūk* Centre 'aims at transforming Dubai into a leading global hub for the issuance, listing, and trading of *ṣukūk*',[211] and 'offers an integrated and leading platform, in addition to housing the world's leading financial institutions that operate regionally and globally from Dubai'.[212] To address the nature of disputes arising from Islamic financial transactions, three arbitration centres are established in the UAE, namely the Dubai International Arbitration Centre (DIAC), the Abu Dhabi Commercial Conciliation and Arbitration Centre (ADCCAC), and the International Islamic Centre for Reconciliation and Commercial Arbitration (IICRCA).[213]

As a result of the KSA regulatory approach to the IFSI, there has been no demonstrable effort provided by the regulatory authorities towards the development of the *ṣukūk* market. The launching of a *ṣukūk* and bond trading platform by Tadawul in June 2009 might be an exception, although not many trading and transactions have been recorded since.[214] In this regard, it is stated that '[f]urther development of the *ṣukūk* market in Saudi Arabia requires proactive involvement of the government authorities in addressing some of the key issues faced by the DCM issuers and investors'.[215] There is currently a lack of sovereign *ṣukūk* issuance in the KSA.[216] In addition, the current Companies Law of 1965 deters *ṣukūk* issuances in the KSA *ṣukūk* market in several ways[217]:

[210] T Fleihan, 'UAE top Arab Nation and Second Globally in 73-Country Islamic Economy Indicator' (*GIES*, 28 September 2015) accessed 29 September 2015.

[211] DIEDC, 'Dubai Global Sukuk Centre' (*DIEDC*, undated). http://www.iedcdubai.ae/initiatives/dubai_global_sukuk_centre. Accessed 18 August 2015.

[212] Ibid.

[213] See J Colon, *supra* note 205, 422.

[214] Saudi Hollandi Capital, *Sukuk Market in Saudi Arabia* (Saudi Hollandi Capital 2013) 12.

[215] V Rabindranath and P Gupta, *An Overview – Sukuk Market in Saudi Arabia* (Watheeqa Capital Company 2010) 1.

[216] Ibid.

[217] Ibid. 2. See also D Elshurafa, 'Project Finance and Sukuk in Saudi Arabia: An Ongoing Project?' Butterworths Journal of International Banking and Financial Law 99.

- It only allows issuance of *ṣukūk* by joint stock companies.
- It does not facilitate issuance of large *ṣukūk* since the *ṣukūk* value must not exceed the company's paid-up capital.
- It does not provide an efficient mechanism for setting up SPVs.
- Setting up joint stock companies takes from four to six months.
- Minimum capital of USD 500,000 is required to set up joint stock companies.

Therefore, efforts need to be focused on establishing local rating agencies in the KSA. Due to the absence of domestic rating agencies in the KSA, local companies need to approach foreign rating agencies to obtain ratings for their issuances.[218] From the perspective of local companies, this is unfavourable because of the high costs, considerable time sink, and because it places local companies on the same level with other companies in foreign markets.[219]

7.6.3 Disclosure of Information

Central to the entire discipline of securities law is the regulation of information.[220] The significance of disclosure of information as a tool for investor protection in the financial sector is well established. The above discussion presented some disclosure requirements regarding *ṣukūk* by the financial regulators in Malaysia, the UAE, and the KSA. There is often difficulty in understanding the disclosure regime in a particular country, owing to 'the overlapping diversity of disclosure laws'.[221] Therefore, it will be helpful to think of disclosure of information in these countries as being regulated by means of three types: first, the regulation of offer of *ṣukūk*; second, the regulation of *ṣukūk* listing, and third, disclosure and transparency rules. The following discussion outlines the current disclosure laws concerning *ṣukūk* that come under these three types of regulations in the countries in question. Then it looks at whether they included specific disclosure requirements regarding *ṣukūk* in its disclosure laws.

[218] V Rabindranath and P Gupta, *supra* note 215, 3.

[219] Ibid.

[220] See A Hudson, *Securities Law* (2nd edn, Sweet & Maxwell 2013) 226.

[221] P Latimer, 'How to Ensure Disclosure of Information in Securities Markets Post-GFC' (2013) 42 Common Law World Review 111, 136.

In the wider Malaysia, disclosure regime applicable to *ṣukūk* includes Chapter 16 of the Guidelines on *Ṣukūk* (Disclosure of Material Information); Division 2 of the Guidelines on Prospectus (Debenture and *Ṣukūk*); Chapter 9 of the Main Market Listing Requirements (Continuing Disclosure); and Paragraph 4B.10 (disclosure of information applicable to Exchange Traded Bonds) and 4B.18 (disclosure of information applicable to Exempt regime) under Chapter 4B of the Main Market Listing Requirements. For the Labuan regulatory regime, Rules 27–35 are concerned with post-listing obligations, including disclosure of information.[222]

In the UAE federal regulatory regime, Decision No. 3 of 2000 Concerning the Regulations as to Disclosure and Transparency, Decision No. 26 of 2015 Concerning the Amendment of Certain Rules of Disclosure and Transparency Regulation, and Decision No. 16 of 2014 Concerning the Regulation of *Ṣukūk* set out the disclosure of information requirements applicable to *ṣukūk*. Under DIFC jurisdiction, disclosure requirements are set out under Chapter 3 (Market Disclosure) of Part 4 (Obligations of Reporting Entities) of the DIFC Law No. 1 of 2012 Markets Law, Chapter 4 (Market Disclosure) of MKT, and Rule 7.3 of IFR.

In the KSA, disclosure requirements are set out in Chapter 7 of the Capital Markets Law,[223] and Part 4 (Registration and Listing) and Part 8 (Continuing Obligations) of the Listing Rules. In addition, Article 14 of the Offers of Securities Regulations sets out some disclosure requirements.

The issue of whether there are specific disclosure requirements for *ṣukūk* transactions in Malaysia, the UAE, and the KSA needs further attention. It is sufficient at this stage to see how the above-mentioned jurisdictions have dealt with disclosure requirements with respect to *ṣukūk*. As discussed in Chap. 8, there is a great need to put in place specific disclosure requirements for *ṣukūk*. While there are disclosure obligations precisely relating to *ṣukūk* in Malaysia and the UAE, this is not the case in the KSA. As considered above, this is naturally the result of the different approaches to regulation of the IFSI adopted in these countries.

In wider Malaysia, the disclosure of information regime provides specific requirements for *ṣukūk*. The special disclosure of information requirements concerning *ṣukūk* deal with issuing of sharia pronouncement and keeping the *ṣukūk* holders informed about the *ṣukūk* transaction. Examples

[222] LFX Rules, Chapter 4, Rules 27–35.

[223] For more information about this Law, see J Beach, *supra* note 148.

of situations in which disclosure of information in relation to *ṣukūk* is required are mentioned in Paragraph 4B.10:

1. An issuer must immediately announce to the Exchange any material information.
2. Without limiting the generality of subparagraph (1) above, an issuer must immediately announce to the Exchange the following:
   (a) any issuance of a new tranche or programme by the issuer;
   (b) any change in the terms of the *ṣukūk* or debt securities;
   (c) any redemption or cancellation of the *ṣukūk* or debt securities;
   (d) any amendment to the Trust Deed, if applicable;
   (e) any appointment or replacement of Trustee or paying agent, if applicable;
   (f) any change of its sharia advisor appointed by the issuer as required under the SC's Islamic Securities Guidelines (*Ṣukūk* Guidelines);
   (g) any occurrence of an event of default under the Trust Deed; and
   (h) credit rating of its *ṣukūk* or debt securities, including a summary of the rating report relevant to the *ṣukūk* or debt securities published by a credit rating agency, if available.[224]

The regulation of a *ṣukūk* prospectus also contains a number of requirements relating to disclosure of information. These include salient features of *ṣukūk* issuance, applicable sharia principles, summary of the rights of *ṣukūk* holders, recourse to *ṣukūk* holders in the event of default, sharia pronouncement, and a statement of consent from sharia advisors.[225]

In the wider UAE jurisdiction, the new regulation provides detailed disclosure obligations imposed on the obligor in case of primary listing of *ṣukūk* and retail *ṣukūk*, though they do not address special features of *ṣukūk*.[226] As for the former regulation, there were disclosure obligations in the prospectus which include general information about the sharia committee (members, names, and expertise) and general information about the *ṣukūk* issuance (description of the terms, the nature of issuance, a sum-

[224] Main Market Listing Requirements, Chapter 4B, Paragraph 4B.10.
[225] Guidelines on Prospectus, Division 2 (Debenture and *Ṣukūk*).
[226] See Decision No. 16 of 2014 Concerning the Regulation of *Ṣukūk*, Articles 17–18.

mary of the rights of *ṣukūk* holders, and expected profits).[227] In the DIFC jurisdiction, disclosure requirements in the prospectus include:

1. the opinion of the sharia Supervisory Board in respect of whether the Securities are sharia compliant;
2. a description of the structure of the underlying transaction and an explanation of the flow of funds; and
3. where applicable, the disclosures required by the Sharia Standards published from time to time by AAOIFI with respect to investment *ṣukūk*.[228]

As part of its continuous disclosure relating to Islamic securities, the DIFC jurisdiction also requires disclosing details of any changes in relation to the sharia advisory board, including any changes to the membership, identity, qualifications, and experience.[229] As seen above, the DIFC contains a unique obligation which is the requirement to comply with disclosure requirements as provided by AAOIFI.

7.6.4 Sharia Compliance: The Role of the Islamic Law in the Legal Systems and Sharia Governance Framework

Ensuring sharia compliance of *ṣukūk* transactions is not only the responsibility of sharia scholars, but also the relevant legal and regulatory framework in which *ṣukūk* are issued and traded. Sharia scholars will not be able to faithfully perform their duties without regulatory and legal measures that facilitate their key functions in accordance with high-quality standards. From a legal and regulatory perspective, there are two ways to ensure the sharia-compliant nature of *ṣukūk* transactions: a strong presence of Islamic law in the legal system and specific regulations for dealing with the sharia compliance issue. While the first is concerned with the role of Islamic law in the legal system of the country, the second way is concerned with the measures that are taken by the relevant legal and regulatory authorities to ensure a robust sharia governance framework.

Having said this, the following discussion looks at the position of Islamic law in the legal systems of Malaysia, the UAE, and the KSA, with

[227] See Decision No (93/r) of 2005 Concerning the Listing of Islamic Bonds, Article 10.
[228] See DFSA Rulebook: Islamic Financial Rules, Rule 7.2.3 (c).
[229] See ibid., Rule 7.3.

particular focus on the IFSI. It attempts to clarify the position of Islamic law in the constitution and the judicial system of the said countries. It does not intend to investigate only the position of Islamic law as a constitutional source, although there is a tendency in related literature to discuss the role of Islamic law as a constitutional source in order to decide whether the relevant legal framework offers a supportive environment for the IFSI. However, this is not necessarily helpful for three reasons. First, the discussion of the position of Islamic law as a constitutional source is subject to difficulty and complexity.[230] The best illustration of this is the existence of different categories of Islamic law as a constitutional source in the Muslim world. Second, it is inaccurate to state that 'the sharia is no longer the sovereign law of most countries in the Muslim world'[231] because the sharia or Islamic law has not been referred to as an overall constitutional source, nor the principal source of legislation or a legislative source in the constitution of these countries. Third, the most important aspect in the constitution—when it comes to the practice of the IFSI—is not having any provision that inhibits the existence of the IFSI. Other aspects that are important to the development of the IFSI are dealt with by the secondary law. In this regard, Rider asserts that 'in most developed economies the bulk of the relevant law relating to the creation and operation of financial markets will consist of regulations promulgated directly or derivatively under the authority of primary legislation'.[232] In addition, the following discussion looks at the key regulations concerning the sharia compliance issue in particular countries, or what has been referred to earlier as a sharia governance framework. In this respect, reference is made to sharia governance framework concerning other sectors such as Islamic banking and *takāful* since the *ṣukūk* sector cannot stand alone. The main purpose is to show how the sharia compliance issue has been dealt with in said countries, and whether or not they offer a robust sharia governance framework.

In Malaysia, there is reference to sharia in its Federal Constitution of 1957. The Malaysian legal system was influenced by British colonisation, and it is currently based on the English common law system and Islamic law. The role of Islamic law in the Malaysian legal system can be inferred

[230] For specific discussion on sharia as a constitutional source, see L Al-Rimawi, *Raising Capital on Arab Equity Markets: Legal and Juridical Aspects of Arab Securities Regulation* (Kluwer Law International 2012) 101–133.

[231] J Ercanbrack, *supra* note 183, 1.

[232] B Rider, *supra* note 10, 53.

from the Articles 3 (1), 4 (1), 74 (2), and 121 (1A) of the Federal Constitution of 1957. Article 3 (1) states that 'Islam is the religion of the Federation'.[233] Some extended the interpretation of this provision and used it to prove that Islamic law is the law of the land.[234] Such positive approach towards this provision is not surprising, given that Article 4 (1) seems to limit the role of sharia in Malaysia. It states that '[t]his Constitution is the supreme law of the Federation'.[235] The advocates of the limited role of sharia in Malaysia base their argument on this provision in particular.[236] It is obvious that the different interpretations of these two provisions have caused confusion about the position of Islamic law in Malaysia, but understanding how laws are enacted under the Malaysian legal system also helps in this context. The Federal Constitution of 1957 empowers both the federal legislator (i.e. the Parliament) and the state legislator to enact laws.[237] Therefore, the authority to make laws in Malaysia is distributed between the federal legislator and state legislator. With regard to enacting Islamic laws, Article 74 (2) states that 'the Legislator of a State may make laws with respect to any of the matters enumerated in the State List'[238] which include 'Islamic law and personal and family law of persons professing the religion of Islam'.[239] This is a source of confusion. By referring only to this provision, one may include matters related to the IFSI under the State List because the IFSI is part and parcel of Islamic law. However, matters related to finance, trade, and insurance come under the Federal List.[240] The fact that the Islamic Financial Services Act 2013 was passed by the Parliament proves the jurisdiction of the Federal Legislator over matters related to the IFSI. The issue of how the Malaysian judicial system hears actions filed by IIFS is of particular significance. Although the

[233] Federal Constitution 1957, Article 3 (1).

[234] Z Hasan, 'The Position of Al-Quran As a Source of Law Under the Malaysian Legal System' (*Zulkiflihasan*, undated) 7. https://zulkiflihasan.files.wordpress.com/2008/06/jurnal-quran.pdf. Accessed 23 August 2015.

[235] Federal Constitution 1957, Article 4 (1).

[236] For more discussion, see S Ahmad and R Rajasingham, 'IDE Asian Law Series No. 4: The Malaysian Legal System, Legal Practice and Legal Education' (*Institute of Developing Economies*, 2001) 23. http://www.ide-jetro.jp/English/Publish/Download/Als/pdf/04.pdf. Accessed 23 August 2015.

[237] Federal Constitution 1957, Articles 74 (1) and 74 (2).

[238] Ibid., Article 74 (2).

[239] Ibid., Ninth Schedule, List II–State List.

[240] Ibid., Ninth Schedue, List I–Federal List.

Malaysian judicial system consists of civil courts and sharia courts,[241] sharia courts cannot hear an action filed by IIFS. Article 121 (A1) disallows civil courts to decide on matters that come under the jurisdiction of sharia courts.[242] List II-State List states that sharia courts 'shall have jurisdiction only over persons professing the religion of Islam and in respect only of any of the matters included in this paragraph'.[243] While civil courts have jurisdiction over matters that come under the Federal List, sharia courts have jurisdiction over matters that come under the State List. As a result, civil courts have a constitutional authority to decide upon matters related to the IFSI. This is proven by the fact that all cases regarding Islamic banking in Malaysia have been decided by civil courts.[244] Naturally, this raises questions about the suitability of civil courts and the competency of civil judges to decide on matters related to the IFSI. The case of ***Bank Islam Malaysia Berhad v. Adnan Bin Omar***[245] questioned the jurisdiction of civil courts in Malaysia over matters related to the IFSI.[246] In this case, the defendant raised an unsuccessful challenge to the jurisdiction of the civil court over Bank Islam Berhad (the plaintiff) by virtue of Article 121 (1A) of the Federal Constitution.[247] The judge rejected such an argument: '[s]ince the plaintiff is a corporation, it cannot have a religion and, as such, will not be subject to the jurisdiction of the sharia courts'.[248] However, the issue of suitability of civil courts to hear cases against IIFS in Malaysia was remedied by the Central Bank of Malaysia Act 2009. Article 56 provides that civil courts and arbitration centres in Malaysia shall refer to the published rulings of the SAC or refer to SAC in case of any disputes in relation to IFSI.[249] This provision addresses, to a large extent, the concern about the competency of civil courts and civil judges in Malaysia to decide on disputes related to the IFSI.

[241] Ibid., Articles 121 (1) and 121 (1A).

[242] Ibid., Article 121 (1A).

[243] Ibid., Ninth Schedule, List II–State List.

[244] For more discussion of these cases, see Z Hasan and M Asutay, 'An Analysis of the Courts' Decisions on Islamic Finance Disputes' (2011) 3 ISRA International Journal of Islamic Finance 41.

[245] Kuala Lumpur High Court, Unreported Civil Suit No. S3-22-101-91.

[246] M Ibrahim, 'The Regulatory Framework and Legal Aspects of Islamic Banking and Finance in Malaysia' in M Bakar and E Ali (eds), *Essential Readings in Islamic Finance* (CERT Publications 2008) 272.

[247] Ibid. 277.

[248] Ibid. 278.

[249] Central Bank of Malaysia Act 2009, Article 56.

Malaysia has paid great attention to the unique features of the IFSI and the significance of sharia compliance. In this regard, its legal system has given Islamic law a strong position by promulgating regulations that are concerned with ensuring the sharia-complaint nature of Islamic financial transactions. These regulations include: Capital Market and Services Act 2007, Central Bank of Malaysia Act 2009, Islamic Financial Services Act 2013, Sharia Governance Framework for Islamic Financial Institutions, and Guidelines on *Ṣukūk*. Article 316A of the Capital Market and Services Act 2007 provides for the establishment of SC's SAC that is responsible for the sharia compliance within ICM. Part VII of the Central Bank of Malaysia Act 2009 deals with the Islamic financial business. Article 51 states that '[t]he Bank may establish a Sharia Advisory Council on Islamic Finance which shall be the authority for the ascertainment of Islamic law for the purposes of Islamic financial business'.[250] Part IV of the Islamic Financial Services Act 2013 deals with sharia requirements. Article 30 (1) states that '[a] licensed person shall establish a sharia committee for purposes of advising the licensed person in ensuring its business, affairs and activities comply with sharia'.[251] Thus, the sharia-compliant nature of Islamic financial transactions is ensured by establishing SAC at the regulatory level and internal sharia committees at the industry level. Sharia Governance Framework for Islamic Financial Institutions is introduced by the BNM to provide 'a comprehensive guidance to the board, Sharia Committee and management of the IFI [Islamic financial institution] in discharging its duties in matters relating to sharia'. Paragraph 3.1 asserts that '[t]he Framework shall be applicable to all IFIs regulated and supervised by the Bank'.[252] While the above regulations are concerned with sharia-compliant nature of all Islamic financial transactions, Guidelines on *Ṣukūk* provide a specific focus on the sharia-compliant nature of *ṣukūk* transaction. In particular, it has dealt with the appointment of a sharia advisor, duties of the sharia advisor, issuance of the sharia pronouncement, and the requirement to comply with sharia principles endorsed by SAC.[253] Paragraph 5.01 asks the *ṣukūk* issuer to appoint a sharia advisor carrying out the following responsibilities: providing advice regarding all aspects of *ṣukūk*, issuing a sharia pronouncement, ensuring compliance with sharia

[250] Ibid., Article 51.

[251] Islamic Financial Services Act 2013, Article 30 (1).

[252] Sharia Governance Framework for Islamic Financial Institutions, Paragraph 3.1.

[253] Guidelines on *Ṣukūk*, Chapters 5 and 6.

rulings and concepts endorsed by SAC, and applying *ijtihād* (scholarly endeavour) in the absence of SAC's rulings and concepts.[254] It provides for specific contents that must be covered by the sharia pronouncement as follows:

1. Basis and rationale of the pronouncement, structure, and mechanism of the *ṣukūk* issue
2. The applicable sharia rulings, principles, and concepts used in the *ṣukūk* issue
3. The relevant sharia matters relating to the documentation of the *ṣukūk* issue.[255]

Moreover, the Guidelines on *Ṣukūk* provide detailed information about sharia rulings applicable to all types of ringgit-denominated *ṣukūk* and specific types of *ṣukūk*. Examples of the issues that have been given attention are the underlying asset, asset pricing, rebate, and compensation.[256] For instance, Paragraph 7.01 provides for three requirements with regard to the underlying asset used in BBA *ṣukūk*, *murābaḥah ṣukūk*, *istiṣnā*ʿ *ṣukūk*, and *ijārah ṣukūk*: (1) meeting the sharia requirements in terms of the nature and usage of the asset, (2) obtaining consent from the chargee or joint owner if the asset is jointly owned, and (3) receivables must be certain and transacted on spot basis.[257] With regard to the compensation issue, Paragraph 7.05 states that '*[t]a'widh* is permissible under *ṣukūk bay*ʿ *bithaman ājil*, *ṣukūk murābaḥah*, *ṣukūk istiṣnā*ʿ and *ṣukūk ijārah* only if the issuer/obligor delays the payment of any amount due and payable to the investors'.[258] There is also clarity on the sharia principles that are acceptable in Malaysia. These principles are well described and identified in the Guidelines on *Ṣukūk*.[259] With regard to the Labuan regulatory scheme, it provides that the endorsement from a sharia advisor is required for offering *ṣukūk*.[260] Apart from this, there is no more information and requirements in relation to sharia-compliant nature of the *ṣukūk* in Labuan.

[254] Ibid., Paragraph 5.01.
[255] Ibid., Paragraph 5.01 (b).
[256] Ibid., Chapters 7 and 8.
[257] Ibid., Paragraph 7.01.
[258] Ibid., Paragraph 7.05.
[259] Ibid., Appendix 1.
[260] Labuan Islamic Financial and Securities Act 2010, Part III, Chapter 1, Section 13, Paragraph 1 (b) and Subsection 9.

In the UAE, there is a strong commitment to the Islamic law constitutionally. Article 7 of the UAE Constitution 1971 states that 'Islam is the official religion of the Union. The Islamic sharia shall be a main source of legislation in the Union'.[261] The relationship between Islamic law and the UAE foundational laws is organic and cannot be overlooked. In this regard, Ercanbrack asserts that 'the UAE has reserved a much greater role for the sharia in its Civil Code and other foundational laws'.[262] Articles 1 and 2 of the UAE Civil Transactions Code give a prominent role for the Islamic law in the judicial system of the UAE. Article 1 states that:

> The legislative provisions shall apply to all matters dealt with by those provisions in the letter and in spirit. There shall be no innovative reasoning (Ijtihad) in the case of provisions of definitive import. If the judge finds no provision in this law, he has to pass judgment according to the Islamic sharia. If no provisions are found here either, he must appropriate solutions from the schools of *imam* Mālik or *imam* Aḥmad Bin Ḥanbal and if none is found there, then from the schools of *imam* al-Shāfiʿī and *imām* Abūḥanīfah as most befits. If the judge does not find the solution there, then he must render judgment in accordance with custom, provided that the custom is not in conflict with public order or morals, and if a custom is particular to a given Emirate, then his judgment will apply only to the Emirate.[263]

Article 2 provides that '[t]he rules and principles of Islamic jurisprudence shall be relied upon in the understanding, construction and interpretation of these provisions'.[264] The judicial system in the UAE is based on civil law and Islamic law and the court system consists of both civil courts and sharia courts.[265] As is the case in Malaysia, disputes related to commercial transactions, including the IFSI, come under the jurisdiction of civil courts.

[261] UAE Constitution, Article 7.

[262] J Ercanbrack, *supra* note 183, 264.

[263] UAE Civil Transactions Code, Article 1.

[264] Ibid., Article 2.

[265] The discussion of the UAE judicial system needs careful consideration because of the presence of four judicial systems in the UAE. These are the Federal judicial system, Abu Dhabi judicial system, Dubai judicial system, Ras al-Khaimah judicial system, and the DIFC judicial system. For more discussion on the UAE judicial system, see B Al-Muhairi, 'The Development of the UAE Legal System and Unification with the Judicial System' (1996) 11 Arab Law Quarterly 116. For more discussion on the DIFS judicial system, see A Campbell and E Campbell, 'The Courts of the Dubai International Financial Centre' (2012) 1 Journal of International Banking Law and Regulation 12.

In the UAE, the regulations concerning sharia compliance and governance are set out by Federal Law No. 14 of 2018 Regarding the Central Bank and Organization of Financial Institutions and Activities; Federal Law No. 6 of 1985 regarding Islamic Banks, Financial Institutions, and Investment Companies; Decision No. 4 of 2010 Takaful Insurance Regulations; and Decision No. 16 of 2014 Concerning the Regulation of *Ṣukūk*. Article 5 of the Federal Law No. 6 of 1985 regarding Islamic Banks, Financial Institutions, and Investment Companies provides for the establishment of a higher sharia authority to ensure sharia compliance within the IFSI and to offer binding opinions on matters related to the IFSI. However, this provision has not been put into effect and such authority has not taken place until 2018. Article 6 is concerned with the requirement to establish an internal sharia supervisory authority within IIFS.[266] In 2015, the board of directors of the Central Bank of the UAE has reviewed a plan for the establishment of a higher sharia authority for the IFSI in the UAE.[267] The higher sharia authority formed in 2018 after the new legislation issued by the Central Bank of the UAE. Article 17 is concerned with, among others, the establishment of the higher sharia authority; number of the members; qualification and experience of the members; and binding opinions of such authority.[268] Article 79 provides, among others, for the establishment of the internal sharia supervision committee within the financial institutions; membership conditions; and appointment of the committee members.[269] For the UAE *takāful* sector, Article 10 of the Decision No. 4 of 2010 Takaful Insurance Regulations requires *takāful* operators to set up internal sharia committees. Article 17 provides for the creation of a higher sharia authority within the Insurance Authority, the regulator of the UAE insurance sector.[270] However, such an authority does not appear in the current hierarchical structure of the Insurance Authority. Article 5 (1) of the Decision No. 16 of 2014 Concerning the Regulation of *ṣukūk* states that '[t]he *ṣukūk* must be

[266] Federal Law No. 6 of 1985 regarding Islamic Banks, Financial Institutions and Investment Companies, Article 6.

[267] H Haider, 'Shariah Authority on Cards' (Khaleej Times, 22 March 2015). http://www.khaleejtimes.com/article/20150322/ARTICLE/303229876/1037. Accessed 28 August 2015.

[268] Federal Law No. 14 of 2018 Regarding the Central Bank and Organization of Financial Institutions and Activities, Article 17.

[269] Ibid, Article 79.

[270] Decision No. 4 of 2010 Takaful Insurance Regulations, Article 17.

approved by the Sharia Committee of the Obligor. If the Obligor does not have a Sharia Committee, the *ṣukūk* must be approved by a Sharia Committee approved by the Arranger'. Apart from the requirement to appoint a sharia committee, the obligor is required to use the *ṣukūk* proceeds according to Islamic law.[271]

In the KSA, Islamic law is regarded as an overall constitutional source. Article 1 of the KSA Constitution 1992 considers 'the Holy Quran and the Prophet's Sunna (traditions)' as the constitution of the country. Apart from Islamic law, the law in the KSA is derived from various forms of enacted legislation which cannot conflict with Islamic law, such as Royal Orders, Royal Decrees, and Council of Ministers Resolutions.[272] With regard to the prominent role of Islamic law in the KSA judicial system, Article 84 states that:

> Courts shall apply the provisions of Islamic sharia to cases brought before them, according to the teachings of the Holy Quran and the Prophet's Sunna as well as other regulations issued by the Head of State in strict conformity with the Holy Quran and the Prophet's Sunna.[273]

The KSA judicial system consists of sharia courts, the Board of Grievances, and various specialised committees such as the Committee for the Settlement of Banking Disputes.[274] Sharia courts generally decide on all civil and criminal cases, except for matters that come under the jurisdiction of the adjudicatory bodies (the Board of Grievances and specialised committees).[275] In 2007, the new Law of Judiciary was enacted, which proposed reforms in relation to restructuring judiciary bodies in the KSA.[276] However, such reforms have yet to fully take place, and they are being considered in phases.[277] There have been some issues warranting considerable attention with regard to the KSA judicial system. For exam-

[271] Decision No. 16 of 2014 Concerning the Regulation of *Ṣukūk*, Article 1 and 11.

[272] Latham & Watkins, 'Doing Business in Saudi Arabia' (*Latham & Watkins*, May 2010) 2. http://www.lw.com/upload/pubContent/_pdf/pub3507_1.pdf. Accessed 28 August 2010.

[273] KSA Constitution 1992, Article 48.

[274] Latham & Watkins, *supra* note 270, 2.

[275] Ibid.

[276] See B Al Hamidani, 'The New Court System in Saudi Arabia' (*Al Tamimi & Co.*, May 2014). http://www.tamimi.com/en/magazine/law-update/section-8/may-7/the-new-court-system-in-saudi-arabia.html. Accessed 28 August 2015.

[277] Latham & Watkins, *supra* note 270, 2.

ple, there are no past court cases available to be viewed by the public because of the absence of an official recording system for legal precedents.[278] This is because the judge is at liberty to decide on the subject matter based on *ijtihād* and individual understanding. Therefore, predicting the interpretation of documents and enforceability of contracts or ascertaining the court's ruling is subject to difficulty.[279] There is no codified Islamic law of contract in the KSA, and prevailing legal opinion depends very much on each individual's legal practice.[280]

The regulatory approach taken by the KSA regime has resulted in the absence of any provisions addressing the sharia-compliant nature of *ṣukūk* transactions. The potential reason for the absence of any regulations related to the IFSI in the KSA is the legislator's concern about using Islamic law or the religion of Islam as a marking tool for financial transactions. Another possible reason is that the judge under the KSA judicial system is authorised to decide on all matters based on *ijtihād*, and therefore there was no need to enact special laws about the IFSI. This also applies to sharia scholars sitting on the sharia supervisory board of the IIFS. Although the IIFS in the KSA have established internal sharia boards, it is uncertain whether such practice is mandatory from a legal and regulatory point of view. The presence of the 'KSA Leading Scholars Authority', founded in 1971, justifies, to some extent, the absence of regulations concerning the sharia compliance issue within the IFSI since it issues rulings about all matters related to Islamic law. Nonetheless, the significant role of the regulations and laws in the financial sector has been already emphasised. Regulations concerning the sharia governance contribute to the soundness and stability of the IFSI. Thus, issues relating to soundness of the IFSI should be addressed by regulations, and not by sharia rulings alone.

7.7 Conclusion

This chapter has identified regulations which are of particular importance to *ṣukūk* markets in Malaysia, the UAE, and the KSA, as administrated by their financial and regulatory authorities. The investigation of the *ṣukūk*

[278] Dhabaan & Partners, 'Report to Cambridge Regional College on Legal Issues Around Operating in Saudi Arabia' (*Cambridge Regional College*, 8 November 2013) 3. http://www.camre.ac.uk/wp-content/uploads/2013/12/Eversheds-advice-on-Saudi-Arabia.pdf. Accessed 28 August 2015.

[279] Ibid.

[280] Ibid. 3–4.

regimes has shown that there is a significant difference between these countries in terms of the sufficiency of regulations relating to *ṣukūk*. Returning to the questions posed at the beginning of this chapter, it is now possible to state that the regulatory approach towards *ṣukūk* differs from one country to another. While there are special regulations on *ṣukūk* in Malaysia and the UAE, the KSA has not issued any special rules for such instrumentation of *ṣukūk*. The most obvious finding to emerge from this study is that Malaysia and the UAE have addressed a wide range of *ṣukūk* aspects in their regulations. The chapter also elaborated on why some jurisdictions have not paid any attention to *ṣukūk* from a regulatory or legal point of view.

Malaysia is a role model for all countries when it comes to the regulatory treatment of the IFSI. In the context of *ṣukūk*, it issued special regulation that takes into consideration the main features of such instrument. The sharia non-compliance risk in the context of the IFSI has been dealt with, to a large extent, by a set of legal and regulatory measures. The UAE is the top Arab nation and second only to Malaysia in terms of presence of a supportive Islamic economic environment. The new regulation passed in 2014 concerning *ṣukūk* proves strong interest in the development of *ṣukūk* market by the UAE capital market regulator. The presence of the DIFC is a key element attracting foreign investors to tap the UAE *ṣukūk* market. The establishment of the DIEDC constitutes a major step with regard to the development of the IFSI in the UAE. Despite some drawbacks regarding the regulation of the KSA *ṣukūk* market, the KSA has a great potential to be the leading jurisdiction in the IFSI, given its location, reputation, human resources, and liquidity. There are three factors that need to be considered in order to develop further the KSA *ṣukūk* market: enacting special regulations concerning *ṣukūk*, establishing a higher sharia supervisory body for the IFSI, and setting up local rating agencies.[281]

The UAE and KSA are considered the most important and promising markets in the whole Middle East. Both jurisdictions have taken serious actions in order to further attract local and foreign investments and diversify the economic sector. In 2018, the UAE issued new regulations and laws including Decretal Federal Law No. (14) of 2018 Regarding the Central Bank and Organization of Financial Institutions and Activities, the Federal Decree Law No. 9 of 2018 on Public Debt, Federal Decree No. 20 of 2018 on anti-money laundering and countering the financing of

[281] A Al Elsheikh and J Tanega, *supra* note 191, 195–196.

terrorism and Federal Law by Decree No. 9 of 2016 on Bankruptcy. KSA also witnessed recently new regulations including the Bankruptcy Law 2018 and Companies law 2016.

The issues listed in this chapter and the previous chapter seem to deter the development of ***ṣukūk*** market, and therefore they entail a comprehensive response to overcome some, if not all, of the issues. The next chapter addresses potential short- and long-term solutions so as to ensure the soundness of ***ṣukūk*** markets in the future.

CHAPTER 8

Proposed Approaches for the Development of Sound *Ṣukūk* Markets

8.1 Introduction

This chapter will set out six approaches for the creation and operation of a sound *ṣukūk* (trust investment certificates) market. Together, they form a development framework that can be applied to all *ṣukūk* markets. This suggests that the industry stakeholders have the option of adopting the proposed remedies or developing other approaches, following the development framework proposed in this chapter.

Having highlighted several structural, legal, and regulatory hurdles that *ṣukūk* market expansion encounters at both national and international levels, the necessity to deal with such hurdles and recommend best *ṣukūk* practice cannot be overstated. The remedies proposed in this chapter aim to ensure that the different problems and challenges facing *ṣukūk* are overcome at an early stage. However, the task of proposing sound practices for *ṣukūk* is complicated by the fact that *ṣukūk* markets differ from one jurisdiction to another in terms of the current level of development.

This chapter intends to find answers to important questions about contemporary *ṣukūk* practices and proposes six solutions that address the most pressing *ṣukūk* problems from a broader perspective. They need to be considered collectively, and thus the reliance on a single remedy is not sufficient in the process of *ṣukūk* enhancement. The nature of *ṣukūk* problems invites several parties to be involved in the process of *ṣukūk* development, including sharia advisors, investors, *ṣukūk* issuers, and regulatory authorities. By the end of this chapter, it is hoped that industry stakeholders will

S. Al-Ali, *Raising Capital on* Ṣukūk *Markets*,
https://doi.org/10.1007/978-3-030-14536-1_8

find some answers for unresolved issues facing the *ṣukūk* industry and will be able to develop better *ṣukūk* practices in accordance with the general development requirements put forth in this chapter.

8.2 Product Enhancement

An important way to improve a *ṣukūk* market is through product enhancement, that is, adding 'more value to an existing product so that it becomes more viable and appealing'.[1] Product enhancement is not meant to change the form or substance of *ṣukūk* products but rather to bring additional features to such products for different purposes.[2] This approach is of great significance, particularly as several structural deficiencies have been identified in *ṣukūk* products. Product enhancement in a *ṣukūk* market is a continuing process, mainly triggered by three factors: meeting the requirements of Islamic law, complying with national laws, and fulfilling the needs of *ṣukūk* stakeholders. Methods utilised for the purpose of product enhancement are the same ones used to develop the product in the first place, namely reverse engineering (begins with conventional products), innovative engineering (begins with Islamic contracts), or the functional approach (begins with actual customers' needs).[3]

There are many examples of the necessity of such improvements. In the case of equity-based *ṣukūk*, the often-quoted problem is the possibility of actual earnings falling short of expected earnings. Obviously, a manager of *ṣukūk* cannot offer loans to *ṣukūk* holders since this practice goes against the concept of equity-based *ṣukūk*. Given this scenario, there has been much debate on the possibility of creating a reserve account in equity-based *ṣukūk*, and a resolution issued by AAOIFI seems to support the notion of establishing such a reserve account.[4] In the case of *ṣukūk* issuance

[1] M Bakar, 'Shari'ah Approaches to Product Development and Product Enhancement in Islamic Banking and Finance: An Appraisal' in Bakar M and Ali E (eds), *Essential Readings in Islamic Finance* (CERT Publications 2008) 126.

[2] Ibid.

[3] For more discussion on the difference between these methods, see S Al-Suwailem, *Hedging in Islamic Finance* (Islamic Development Bank 2006) 104–109; Z Iqbal and A Mirakhor, *An Introduction to Islamic Finance* (2 edn, John Wiley & Sons 2011) 250–251; H Ahmad, *Products Development in Islamic Finance* (Edinburgh University Press 2011) 209–212.

[4] AAOIFI, 'AAOIFI Shari'ah Resolutions: Issues on Sukuk' (*AAOIFI*, February 2008) 2. http://www.kantakji.com/media/7760/f173.pdf. Accessed 6 October 2014.

and trading, it is felt that there is a need to introduce *ṣukūk* at the retail level and enable individuals to participate in major *ṣukūk* issuances for the purpose of expanding the *ṣukūk* trading platform and *ṣukūk* secondary market.[5] This goal can be achieved by allocating tranches to the retail sector and private individuals.[6] In addition, there is a tendency by financial regulators to enforce particular *ṣukūk* structures based on their risk profile, for example, asset-backed structures versus asset-based structures. There have been many discussions on the possibility of requiring asset-backed structure and discouraging asset-based structure. The prevailing view seems to support the notion of asset-backed *ṣukūk*, particularly in jurisdictions where such a structure is not impossible.[7] Another common problem is the absence of a *ṣukūk* secondary market or *ṣukūk* illiquidity in some jurisdictions. A secondary market can be expanded via several steps, for example, increasing the issuance of larger *ṣukūk* and encouraging *ṣukūk* for short and medium terms.[8] While the former step would address the volume concern, the latter step would increase the diversity of *ṣukūk*.[9] Furthermore, more long-term *ṣukūk* should be issued, offering an attractive investment opportunity for long-term investors, such as sovereign wealth funds, pension funds, and *takāful* (Islamic insurance) operators.[10] Another aspect of product enhancement in *ṣukūk* is concerned with the *ṣukūk* types. There have been many discussions of the possibility of going beyond the 14 *ṣukūk* types of AAOIFI[11]; structuring convertible *ṣukūk*, exchangeable *ṣukūk*, and hybrid *ṣukūk* appears to encourage the idea of exploring new types and structures. Another concern is the complexity of *ṣukūk* structures; the fact that one may need to read a number of separate documents, sometimes 17 separate documents, in order to understand the whole *ṣukūk* structure renders this product undesirable from many international investors' perspective.[12] Therefore, there is a need to reduce such complexity. Also, in the case of the assets consisting *ṣukūk* portfolio, there

[5] C Nethercott, H Rai and L Irvine, 'Sukuk: Rethinking Sukuk While Leaping Forward' in Edbiz Consulting (ed), *Global Islamic Finance Report 2014* (Edbiz Consulting Publication 2014) 130.

[6] Ibid.

[7] Ibid.

[8] Ibid.

[9] Ibid.

[10] Ibid.

[11] Ibid.

[12] P Casey, 'Emerging Issues From Inadequate Disclosure Requirements for Islamic Capital Market Products' in IFSB, IOSCO and SC (eds), *Disclosure Requirements for Islamic Capital Market Products* (IFSB, IOSCO, SC 2013) 36.

is a need to go beyond the traditional assets and move towards new asset classes so as to widen the risk profile for *ṣukūk*.[13] With the help of sharia advisors, blended asset structure and asset-light structures have been launched to cater for different investors' needs and circumstances.[14] In this respect, the sharia resolutions on several new assets appear to support the introduction of new underlying assets for *ṣukūk* products. These include shares, intellectual property rights, and government awards (such as concession, construction, supply, and services contracts).[15] Further to this is the aspect of *ṣukūk* product enhancement related to risk mitigation. Different types of risk arise from *ṣukūk*, and therefore there have been many debates on the possibility of minimising these risks via derivatives such as hedging instruments.[16]

8.3 Juristic Differences and Legal Certainty: Finding Possibilities to Marry Up?

Another initiative to develop sound *ṣukūk* practices lies in exploring the possibility of marrying up juristic differences and legal certainty, instead of putting the blame for lack of legal certainty in the *ṣukūk* market and the IFSI in general on the existence of divergent opinions in Islamic law. This section explains how juristic differences in the IFSI have been dealt with so far and how these can be used effectively to increase legal certainty in the *ṣukūk* market.

8.3.1 Examining the Existing Perception About Juristic Difference in Islamic Law: Sharia Non-compliance Risk

A strong correlation between the disagreement among sharia scholars and legal uncertainty has been established in recent Islamic finance debate. The existing literature has widely criticised the existence of disagreements

[13] C Nethercott, H Rai and L Irvine, 'Sukuk: Rethinking Sukuk While Leaping Forward' in Consulting E (ed), *Global Islamic Finance Report 2014* (Edbiz Consulting Publication 2014).

[14] See R Haneef, 'From Asset-Backed to Asset-Light Structures: The Intricate History of Sukuk' (2009) 1 ISRA International Journal of Islamic Finance 103.

[15] For more discussion on the legality of such assets to underlay *ṣukūk*, see E Ali, 'Issues in Islamic Debt Securitisation' in Bakar M and Ali E (eds), *Essential Readings in Islamic Finance* (CERT Publications 2008) 466–474.

[16] See M Al-Sheaibi, 'Derivatives and Sukuk in the Islamic Capital Market' in A Thomas (ed), *Sukuk* (Sweet & Maxwell Asia 2009).

in Islamic law and emphasised their direct effect on investor protection, invalidation of contractual obligations, and the reputation of the IFSI. For instance, Casey states the following:

> [I]t is frustratingly common for an instrument that has been approved by a group of well-reputed scholars then to be regarded as unacceptable on sharia grounds by major investors – whose Sharia Supervisory Boards may even contain some of the same scholars.[17]

The tendency of some writers to use terms such as 'sharia risk'[18] and 'sharia compliance risk'[19] to reflect the potential risk arising from disagreement in Islamic law shows how such disagreement is highly undesirable. IFSB has also used the term 'sharia non-compliance risk'[20] to refer to the 'risk that arises from IIFSs' failure to comply with the sharia rules and principles determined by the Sharia Board of the IIFS or the relevant body in the jurisdiction in which the IIFS operate'.[21] Lahsasna argues that while IFSB's definition recognises the risk arising from failure of the IIFS to comply with resolutions of the relevant sharia board, it does not address the risk arising from cases in which the sharia board changes its stance on the sharia-compliant nature of the transaction.[22] The dangers and consequences of sharia non-compliance risk cannot be ignored. Failure to comply with Islamic law jeopardises market participants' confidence in the market, damages the reputation of the IFSI, and questions the validity of

[17] P Casey, *supra* note 12, 38–39.

[18] See Todd Schmid, 'The Real Shariah Risk: Why The United States Cannot Afford To Miss The Islamic Finance Moment' (2013) 3 University of Illinois Law Review 1293.

[19] See Yusuf DeLorenzo, 'Shari'ah Compliance Risk' (2007) 7 Chicago Journal of International Law 397.

[20] IFSB, 'Guiding Principles on Liquidity Risk Management for Institutions Offering Islamic Financial Services [Excluding Islamic Insurance (*Takāful*) Institutions And Islamic Collective Investment Schemes]' (*IFSB*, March 2012) 5. http://www.ifsb.org/standard/eng_IFSB-12%20Guiding%20Principles%20on%20Liquidity%20Risk%20Mgmt%20_(March2012).pdf. Accessed 23 January 2015, IFSB, 'Guiding Principles of Risk Management for Institutions (Other Than Insurance Institutions) Offering Only Islamic Financial Services' (*IFSB*, December 2005) 26. http://www.ifsb.org/standard/ifsb1.pdf. Accessed 9 April 2015.

[21] IFSB, 'Guiding Principles of Risk Management for Institutions (Other Than Insurance Institutions) Offering Only Islamic Financial Services' (*IFSB*, December 2005) 26. http://www.ifsb.org/standard/ifsb1.pdf. Accessed 9 April 2015.

[22] A Lahsasna, *Sharīʿah Non-Compliance Risk Management and Legal Documentation in Islamic Finance* (Wiley 2014) 17.

Islamic financial transactions. Events causing sharia non-compliance risk might constitute breach of laws, impose civil and criminal sanctions against IIFS, and result in suspension of their licences[23] in jurisdictions where compliance with Islamic law is a regulatory requirement.

A good illustration of the risks of sharia non-compliance is the case of *The Investment Dar Company KSCC v. Blom Developments Bank SAL.*[24] In this case, the issue of sharia non-compliance was used as grounds by the TID to not pay profits to the Blom Development Bank. Initially, both parties entered into a 'Master Wakala Agreement' under which Blom Development Bank placed sums of money with TID.[25] According to the agreement, TID was obliged to pay the capital amount and fixed returns to Blom Development Bank.[26] However, TID was not able to pay the fixed returns as it faced financial difficulties by the end of 2008.[27] TID's lawyers and legal consultants in London successfully convinced the court that the transaction was not sharia-compliant and ultra vires to TID's memorandum of association.[28] In spite of the fact that the transaction was initially approved by TID's sharia council, TID challenged the sharia-compliance decision provided by its own appointed sharia scholars. In addition, the case of *National Ṣukūk Company v. Al-Madina Finance and Investment Company*[29] illustrates the issue of sharia non-compliance risk in the IFSI. In 2008, the National *Ṣukūk* Company (the Principal) entered into a *wakālah* (agency; investment contract in which agent represents investor(s)) agreement with the Al-Madina Finance and Investment Company (the Investment Agent), based on which the Investment Agent received KWD 11 million.[30] In 2009, the Principal filed a civil claim against the Investment Agent under the Kuwaiti court system since the latter had failed to repay the agreed amount (original facility amount plus a predefined profit).[31] The judgment provided by the Kuwait

[23] Ibid. 7.

[24] [2009] EWHC 3545 (Ch).

[25] Ibid.

[26] Ibid.

[27] Norton Rose, 'The Implications for the Islamic Finance Market of The Investment Dar Company KSCC v Blom Developments Bank Sal [2009] EWHC 3545 (Ch)' (*Norton Rose*, March 2010). http://www.nortonrosefulbright.com/knowledge/publications/27334/the-implications-for-the-islamic-finance-market-of-the-investment-dar-company-kscc-v-blom-developments-bank-sa. Accessed 5 August 2015.

[28] J Ercanbrack, *The Transformation of Islamic Law in Global Financial Markets* (Cambridge University Press 2015) 233.

[29] Kuwaiti Court of Cassation, petition no 1895,1932,1933,1937/2011, judgment dated 19 June 2012.

[30] Ibid.

[31] Ibid.

Court of First Instance requested the Investment Agent to pay the agreed amount based on expert's opinion.[32] The payment amount had been slightly reduced after the appeal by the Investment Agent.[33] A second appeal filed by the Investment Agent on the grounds that, among others, the expert's opinion failed to apply Islamic law of *wakālah*.[34] The court found the defences of the Investment Agent would influence the court's decision and therefore asked a panel of three experts to look at, among others, whether the *wakālah* agreement was sharia-compliant.[35] In this regard, some commentators said 'the credibility of [IIFS] may be negatively impacted if such as affirmative defence would allow nullification of these arrangements'.[36] The existence of disagreement in Islamic law has been regarded as a negative aspect of the IFSI and an issue that has posed great difficulty for its application not only by Western courts but also by most players in the IFSI. Further, the inappropriateness of divergent views of sharia scholars was clearly expressed in *Beximco Pharmaceuticals Ltd and others v. Shamil Bank of Bahrain*.[37]

Another recent example of the sharia non-compliance risk is Dana Gas *Ṣukūk*. The case *Dana Gas PJSC v Dana Gas Sukuk Limited* looks at the validity and enforceability of the different contracts governed by different jurisdictions under a single *ṣukūk* transaction.[38] In particular, this case raises the issue of whether sharia non-compliance risk would have effect on the legal enforceability of the *ṣukūk* structure.[39] Dana Gas *Ṣukūk* sent reverberations throughout the industry after announcing that it is no longer sharia-compliant, and therefore no periodic distribution amount will be paid to the *ṣukūk* holders. Due to the importance of this case, the following paragraphs elaborate on how the case evolved over a period of almost ten years.

[32] Ibid.

[33] Ibid.

[34] Ibid.

[35] Ibid.

[36] P Saba and F Fathnezhad, 'Implications of the Kuwait TID V. Blom Judgment on Wakala Contracts' (*Al Tamimi & Co.*, 2013). http://www.tamimi.com/en/magazine/law-update/section-5/january-2/implications-of-the-kuwait-tid-v-blom-judgment-on-wakala-contracts.html. Accessed 30 September 2015.

[37] [2004] EWCA Civ 19. For more discussion, see Chapter 1.

[38] [2017] EWHC 2340 Comm.

[39] See generally D Dey and Others, 'Dana Gas Sukuk: A red Herring or Cause for Concern' (*White & Case*, 2017). https://www.whitecase.com/publications/alert/dana-gas-sukuk-red-herring-or-cause-concern. Accessed 4 January 2019.

Incorporated in the UAE in 2005 as a public joint stock company, Dana Gas PJSC is known as a regional private sector gas company. In October 2007, Dana Gas PJSC issued USD 1 billion *muḍārabah ṣukūk*, due to mature in December 2012.[40] The *muḍārabah* (investment partnership) deal was governed by the UAE law and the purchase undertaking contract was governed by the English law.[41] In October 2012, Dana Gas PJSC was unable to repay its USD 920 million *ṣukūk* that were outstanding, and therefore reached standstill with its *ṣukūk* holders including BlackRock, Ashmore Group, and Spinnaker Capital.[42] In November 2012, Dana Gas PJSC agreed with its *ṣukūk* holders to restructure its USD 920 million *ṣukūk* and convert the outstanding *ṣukūk* into ordinary and convertible *ṣukūk*.[43] In December 2012, Dana Gas PJSC proposed new *ṣukūk* plan which included payment of USD 70 million for *ṣukūk* holders, average coupon rate of 8% on the remaining notes, extending the restructuring process till the second quarter of 2013 and converting the remaining *ṣukūk* into two equal tranches.[44] In April 2013, Dana Gas PJSC shareholders approved the *ṣukūk* restructuring plan.[45] In May 2013, the restructuring had been completed and new *ṣukūk* worth USD 850 million had been issued comprising USD 425 million ordinary *ṣukūk* and USD 425 million convertible *ṣukūk*.[46] In April 2017, Dana Gas PJSC started renegotiation with its *ṣukūk* holders in order to reach a standstill agreement for its USD 700 million outstanding *ṣukūk* that were due in October 2017.[47] In June 2017, Dana Gas PJSC declared that its USD 700 million outstanding *ṣukūk* was no longer sharia-compliant and

[40] For more information: see Offering Circular of Dana Gas Sukuk Limited (2007).

[41] Ibid. 25.

[42] Islamic Finance News, 'Dana Gaz Defaults on Sukuk' (*Islamic Finance News*, 2012). https://www.islamicfinancenews.com/the-dana-gas-case-timeline. Accessed 4 January 2019.

[43] Islamic Finance News, 'Dana Gas in Agreement with Sukukholders' (*Islamic Finance News*, 2012). https://www.islamicfinancenews.com/the-dana-gas-case-timeline. Accessed 4 January 2019.

[44] Islamic Finance News, 'Dana Gas Proposes New Sukuk Plan' (*Islamic Finance News*, 2012). https://www.islamicfinancenews.com/the-dana-gas-case-timeline. Accessed 4 January 2019.

[45] Islamic Finance News, 'Dana Gas Good to Go' (*Islamic Finance News*, 2013). https://www.islamicfinancenews.com/the-dana-gas-case-timeline. Accessed 4 January 2019.

[46] Islamic Finance News, 'Dana Gas Completes Restructuring' (*Islamic Finance News*, 2013). https://www.islamicfinancenews.com/the-dana-gas-case-timeline. Accessed 4 January 2019. For more information: see Offering Circular of Dana Gas Sukuk Limited (2013).

[47] Islamic Finance News, 'Dana Gas Renegotiates with Sukukholders' (*Islamic Finance News*, 2017). https://www.islamicfinancenews.com/the-dana-gas-case-timeline. Accessed 4 January 2019.

therefore proposed a new sharia-compliant structure with a four-year maturity at less than half of the current profit rates without a conversion feature.[48] It also secured injunctions from Sharjah Federal Court, High Court of Justice in the British Virgin Islands, and English High Court of Justice in London restraining *ṣukūk* holders from taking any actions against Dana Gas PJSC.[49] In July 2017, Dana Gas PJSC failed to reach a consensus with the ad hoc committee of the *ṣukūk* holders in relation to restructuring of the *ṣukūk* arrangement.[50] In August 2017, Dana Gas PJSC withdrew its restructuring plan of the outstanding *ṣukūk*.[51] In the same month, the UK High Court announced that the UK injunction on Dana Gas *ṣukūk* will remain and rejected the delegate's request to impose in advance the legal costs on the Dana Gas PJSC.[52] Dana Gas PJSC also applied to the Sharjah Court to discharge the injunction given by the court on the *ṣukūk*.[53] In September 2017, Dana Gas PJSC refused the proposal of its *ṣukūk* holders which included a three-year maturity extension and settlement of all periodic distributions.[54] In the same month, the London High Court started looking at the trial on Dana Gas *Ṣukūk* despite the injunction by the Sharjah Court restraining the Dana Gas PJSC and its creditors from initiating any proceedings.[55] In November 2017, the UK High Court announced that the purchase undertaking exercised by the issuer of Dana Gas *Ṣukūk* was valid and enforceable.[56] Following the decision of the English High Court, Dana Gas PJSC filed an appeal to the English Court of Appeal on the ground that the trial was

[48] Islamic Finance News, 'Dana Gas to Replace Unlawful Sukuk' (*Islamic Finance News*, 2017). https://www.islamicfinancenews.com/the-dana-gas-case-timeline. Accessed 4 January 2019.

[49] Ibid.

[50] Islamic Finance News, 'Dana Gas Rejects Deutsches's Sukuk Payment Request' (*Islamic Finance News*, 2017). https://www.islamicfinancenews.com/the-dana-gas-case-timeline. Accessed 4 January 2019.

[51] Islamic Finance News, 'Dana Gas Withdraws Swap Offer' (*Islamic Finance News*, 2017). https://www.islamicfinancenews.com/the-dana-gas-case-timeline. Accessed 4 January 2019.

[52] Ibid.

[53] Ibid.

[54] Islamic Finance News, 'Dana Gas Says No to Sukukholders Proposal' (*Islamic Finance News*, 2017). https://www.islamicfinancenews.com/the-dana-gas-case-timeline. Accessed 4 January 2019.

[55] [2017] EWHC 2340 Comm.

[56] *Dana Gas PJSC v Dana Gas Sukuk Limited and Others* [2017] EWHC 2928 Comm.

done in its absence.[57] In November 2017, the Court of Appeal in the UAE allowed Dana Gas PJSC to take part in the proceedings of the UK High Court on its disputed *ṣukūk*.[58] In February 2018, Judge George Leggatt of London High Court refused the attempt made by the Dana Gas PJSC in December 2017 to overturn his decision.[59] The court also issued an injunction asking Dana Gas PJSC to withdraw its proceedings and injunctions in the UAE.[60] In March 2018, Sharjah Court of First Instance, among others, suspended the enforcement of judgments made by the English High Court of Justice in the UAE.[61] In April 2018, the English High Court issued an injunction preventing Dana Gas PJSC from distributing dividends or raising any more debt.[62] In May 2018, an agreement was reached between Dana Gas PJSC and the *ṣukūk* holders to restructure the *ṣukūk* facility that was outstanding.[63]

The Dana Gas case is often cited to demonstrate the issue of sharia compliance versus legal enforceability.[64] In general, the industry has not welcomed the declaration made by the Dana Gas PJSC that the *ṣukūk* arrangement is no longer sharia-compliant. Regardless of the actual sharia rule for the *ṣukūk* in question, the industry questioned the sharia concern raised over the *ṣukūk* particularly in the event of default or financial difficulty. Such claim might be used by others in order to run away from their financial obligations. The case became complicated because of the issue of conflict of laws over the *ṣukūk* facility. While the *ṣukūk* is sharia-compliant at the time of issuance, the same structure issued becomes non-sharia-

[57] Islamic Finance News, 'UK High Court declares Purchase Undertaking Enforceable' (*Islamic Finance News*, 2017). https://www.islamicfinancenews.com/the-dana-gas-case-timeline. Accessed 4 January 2019.

[58] *Dana Gas PJSC v Dana Gas Sukuk Limited and Others* [2018] EWHC 278 Comm.

[59] Ibid.

[60] *Dana Gas PJSC v. Dana Gas Sukuk Limited and Others* [2018] EWHC 277 Comm.

[61] Islamic Finance News, 'Dana Gas Receives Orders From Sharjah Court' (*Islamic Finance News*, 2018). https://www.islamicfinancenews.com/the-dana-gas-case-timeline. Accessed 4 January 2019.

[62] Islamic Finance News, 'Court Restricts Dana Gas From Paying Dividends' (*Islamic Finance News*, 2018). https://www.islamicfinancenews.com/the-dana-gas-case-timeline. Accessed 4 January 2019.

[63] Islamic Finance News, 'Dana Gas Reaches Agreement' (*Islamic Finance News*, 2018). https://www.islamicfinancenews.com/the-dana-gas-case-timeline. Accessed 4 January 2019.

[64] For more discussion on this case, see D Ogali, 'Lady Justice Cannot Hear Your Prayers' (2018) 3 Fordham Law Review 1293; M Hekmatyar and E Parkar 'An Evaluation of Dana Gas's Mudarabah Sukuk From Shariah and Legal Perspectives' (2018) 9 European Journal of Islamic Finance 1.

compliant at the time of financial difficulty. However, it should be noted that obliging the obligor to purchase the *muḍārabah* asset by a way of purchase undertaking exercised by the issuer is not acceptable from a sharia point of view because this goes against the profit and loss sharing principle of *muḍārabah*.

8.3.2 The Role of Juristic Differences Rules

It is hoped that the following discussion will render the dominant perception of juristic differences inaccurate and will demonstrate how disagreements in Islamic law can provide legal certainty. Before several ways are addressed to marry up the disagreement in Islamic law and legal certainty, one should look at the factors driving the negative perception about disagreement in Islamic law, namely (1) a lack of knowledge on Islamic law and particularly on this so-called juristic difference and (2) inaccurate comparison of Islamic law with common law.

Juristic difference (*khilāf fiqhī*) refers to particular situations in which sharia scholars have different views over certain issues that are subject to disagreement. This definition suggests that Islamic law is built not only on disagreement among sharia scholars but also on agreement among them. The latter is known in Islamic law as consensus (*ijmāᶜ*) which constitutes a significant part of the body of Islamic law. In this respect, sharia scholars have already made a list of issues and interpretations they have agreed upon and indeed there is a significant record and work proving their agreements under various fields of Islamic law.[65] The definition also indicates that both agreement and disagreement exist in Islamic law, although the latter constitutes a large part of it. In relation to the IFSI, there are some areas which are subject to agreement, such as prohibition of interest, and other issues which are subject to disagreement such as sale of debt. Further, the definition implies that juristic difference in Islamic law is generally acceptable and tolerated. Juristic difference is one of its unique features that considerably contributed to its growth and development. Indeed, Kamali says that '[*i*]*khtilāf* has played an evidently important role in the development of the rich legacy of *fiqh* and sharia that will continue to provide a lasting source of influence'.[66] Earlier sharia scholars wrote

[65] See, for example, M Bin Al-Mundhir, *Al-Ijmāᶜ* (Dār Al-Muslim Lil-Nashr Wa Al-Tawziᶜ 2004).

[66] M Kamali, *Shari'ah Law: An Introduction* (Oneworld Publications 2008) 118.

extensively about the reasons for existence of juristic difference in Islamic law.[67] Knowledge of Sunna, methodology and principles of jurisprudence, and knowledge of Arabic language are some of the subjects that have caused disagreements in Islamic law.

Pertaining to the second factor, comparing Islamic law with common law has contributed to an inaccurate perception being formed about the juristic differences in Islamic law. In this respect, it has been said that common law has more legal certainty than Islamic law because the former does not allow for different interpretations. However, the nature of both laws is completely different. While the former is ready-made for application and self-evident, the latter is humanly conceived. A critical point to make, however, is in relation to the role of interpretation under Islamic law as opposed to under common law. In this context, Bakar says 'interpretation is necessary in Islamic law because the law is not self-evident. If all law were self-evident, there would be nothing to interpret'.[68] The ability and possibility to interpret sharia are what has produced such divergent opinions regarding Islamic law. However, the interpretation process plays a far smaller role in the case of modern statutes.[69] The nature of the English legal system, which is a system based on precedent, means its primary legal principles are presaged, and therefore the room for different interpretations is much smaller.[70] This is also justified by the principle of stare decisis in the common law which means that once a superior court has declared what the law is, all other inferior courts must subsequently follow that precedent.

However, Islamic law has not simply left the door open for confusion and uncertainty coming from different interpretations but rather put in place rules governing juristic differences. In this respect, Kamali states that '[*i*]*khtilāf* is a well-developed area of *fiqh* and works of scholarship on it date as far back as those of the *fiqh* itself'.[71] Therefore, efforts need to be focused on revisiting work on regulation of juristic differences so as to apply them to current juristic disagreements in the IFSI. The problem of

[67] See, for example, A Bin Taymiyah, *Raf' Al-Malām ʿan Al-Aʾimmah Al-Aʿlām* (Al-Riʾāsah Al-ʿāmmah Liidārāt Al-Buḥūth Al-ʿilmiyyah Wa-Al-Iftā Wa-Al-Daʿwah Wa-Al-Irshād 1992).

[68] M Bakar, 'The Shari'a Supervisory Board and Issues of Shari'a Rulings and their Harmonisation in Islamic Banking and Finance' in S Archer and R Abdel Karim (eds), *Islamic Finance: Innovation and Growth* (Euromoeny and AAOIFI 2002) 83.

[69] Ibid.

[70] See M Balala, *Islamic Finance and Law: Theory and Practice in Globalized World* (I.B. Tauris 2015) 8.

[71] M Kamali, *supra* note 66, 110.

legal uncertainty in the IFSI arising from divergent opinions would be resolved by adopting 'juristic difference rules' to help achieve legal certainty. These rules would help in closing or at least reducing the gap between divergent opinions under Islamic law and legal uncertainty in the contemporary IFSI. The following discussion attempts to explore the possibility of marrying up both of them based on juristic differences rules.

The first possibility that would help in increasing the level of legal certainty is that financial authorities could select a particular opinion and interpretation in Islamic law for the purpose of enforcement. This possibility is in accordance with the legal maxim saying that 'command of the ruler puts an end to disagreement'.[72] This is also supported by another legal maxim which states that 'command of the ruler is enforceable'.[73] These legal maxims leave no space for another opposing opinion to take place. The second proposal for dealing with divergent opinions is that financial authorities and regulators should take into account public interest in the process of selecting a single opinion to be applied in the IFSI. This suggestion follows the legal maxim, the 'affair of the ruler are determined by reference to public interest'.[74] The third possible initiative is that financial institutions and product developers should adopt an alternative product or structure when the existing one is causing dispute. This is supported by the legal maxim which states that, 'getting out of the disagreement is recommended'.[75] For instance, financial regulators could ban or discourage issuing *ṣukūk* based on *bayʿ al-ʿīnah* due to the continuing controversy about its permissibility. The fourth proposed solution is that a sharia scholar can consider the opposing view, particularly in cases concerning basic needs of the customers or when a juristic view can be applied along with the opposing view without compromise. This is based on the legal maxim which says 'exigencies are ranked as necessities'.[76] A good illustration of such a case is *ṣukūk* based on *tawarruq* (sale and resale transaction used to generate cash); although such a transaction has been prohibited by the IIFA, its usage might be considered in limited situations. An example of two different views working together is the practice of bilateral undertaking in *ṣukūk*. In order to solve it, it has been suggested that one undertaking should be non-binding, and this will ensure

[72] Ibid. 119.

[73] Ibid.

[74] Ibid. 60–61.

[75] See Y Soualhi, 'Bridging Islamic Juristic Differences in Contemporary Islamic Finance' (2012) 26 Arab Law Quarterly 313, 318.

[76] Ibid. 326.

the applicability of both opinions.[77] The fifth recommended practice is that sharia scholars, financial institutions, and regulators should ignore weak opinions in Islamic law.[78] This generally refers to an opinion based on weak evidence, misinterpretation of the text, or misunderstanding the actual case. In some cases, the definition of weak opinion covers an opinion that is against the majority view. The sixth recommendation is that there is a need for proper understanding of Islamic financial instruments because '[p]ast experience has shown that many juristic disputes arose because of different perceptions and weak understanding of the new product'.[79] Seventh is finding a balance between *maqāṣid* (objectives) and textual approaches in the process of understanding sharia.[80] The *Maqāṣid* approach in practice has been used to stretch the limits of Islamic finance and adopt controversial sharia-compliant products.[81] The textual approach relies only on the texts of sharia sources in deciding upon the legality of a certain product.[82]

8.4 Groping Towards Consistency: Standardisation and Harmonisation

Another suggested approach to enhance *ṣukūk* is to promote consistency in the *ṣukūk* market. In its literal meaning, the term consistency refers to a 'quality of achieving a level of performance which does not vary greatly in quality over time'.[83] From a technical perspective, a consistent *ṣukūk* market refers to a market in which the process of *ṣukūk* issuance and investment do not vary significantly from one jurisdiction to another or at least within one jurisdiction. Consistency in *ṣukūk* is needed not only to enable prospective investors to make informed investment decisions, but also to increase *ṣukūk* marketability and cross-border transactions. Malim asserts that achieving consensus on core issues related to the *ṣukūk* market facili-

[77] Ibid. 328.
[78] Ibid.
[79] Ibid. 330.
[80] Ibid. 332.
[81] Ibid. 333.
[82] Ibid.
[83] C Soanes and A Stevenson (eds), *Oxford Dictionary of English* (Oxford University Press 2006) 369.

tates a refined use of *ṣukūk* structures and creates a healthy market at both the national and international levels.[84]

A good example of the significance of *ṣukūk* consistency is the Jaban Bank for International Cooperation's (JBIC) plan for *ṣukūk* issuance in May 2008.[85] This issuance was subject to delay due to disagreement on its sharia compliance between the sharia boards of the deal's arrangers, namely Citibank of Dubai and CIMB.[86] This disagreement resulted in change of the proposed *ṣukūk* structure from *murābaḥah* (a sale with a mark-up) to *mushārakah* (participation financing).[87] It has been argued that if *ṣukūk* structures had been standardised in the first place, such disagreements among sharia boards and issuance postponement would have been avoided. In this scenario, consistent *ṣukūk* practice would have definitely reduced transaction costs and ensured sharia compliance.

Perhaps a rather more important point in regard to *ṣukūk* consistency is the identification of areas which lack consistency. These include regulations concerning *ṣukūk*, the *ṣukūk* structuring process, *ṣukūk* types, and remedies for *ṣukūk* defaults. So far, there has been no collective definition for *ṣukūk* adopted by all industry stakeholders. Although many theoretical works have attempted to describe *ṣukūk* structures and types, they have not succeeded in providing a common understanding for such structures due to different structuring processes taking place in various jurisdictions. In addition, sharia criticism of some *ṣukūk* structures shows that *ṣukūk* products are still not standardised. There is a need to list all *ṣukūk* types and structures that are acceptable and agreed upon in all jurisdictions to avoid situations such as the existence of some *ṣukūk* structures that are acceptable in Malaysia but are not necessarily acceptable in the Middle East, for example, two-party *murābaḥah ṣukūk* that is based on *bayʿ al-ʿīnah* sale and buy-back. In other words, the aim is to reach a level where there is a common understanding and agreed quality for *ṣukūk* structures in all jurisdictions. Another area that lacks consistency is *ṣukūk* legal documentation. Ali is of the view that the failure to achieve consistency in *ṣukūk* documentation is to be expected, owing to the smaller consideration given to *ṣukūk*

[84] M Malim, 'The Future of Sukuk: Islamic Capital Markets' in R Ali (ed), *Sukuk and Islamic Capital Markets* (Globe Business Publishing 2011) 169–170.

[85] H Yaacob, M Mohammad and E Smolo, *International Convention for Islamic Finance: Towards Standardisation* (ISRA 2011) 21.

[86] Ibid.

[87] Ibid.

as a structured product.[88] *Ṣukūk* documentation consists of two types: 'sharia transaction documents' and 'capital markets documents'.[89] While the consistency of the former will be affected by divergent sharia views, the consistency of the latter will be affected by various capital market regulations concerning *ṣukūk*.

With this in mind, two tools can be suggested to increase the level of consistency in the *ṣukūk* market. The first tool is standardisation—a term used to denote 'a required level or agreed level of quality'[90] or 'something used as a measure, norm, or model in comparative evaluation'.[91] Standardisation of *ṣukūk* means putting in place agreed norms and measures concerning *ṣukūk* practice for the purpose of adoption and application by all *ṣukūk* stakeholders. The second tool is harmonisation—a term which refers to making a thing consistent or compatible.[92] Harmonising *ṣukūk* means moving towards agreement on the most important matters pertaining to *ṣukūk* for the purpose of adoption and application by all *ṣukūk* stakeholders. While the former does not allow for any inconsistency to take place, the latter provides little room for differences to appear in the *ṣukūk* market.

However, in practice, there is great difficulty in achieving standardisation and harmonisation in the *ṣukūk* market in practice, particularly at the international level. This is compounded by the fact that there are opponents of the standardisation practice in the IFSI who argued that the existence of different opinions and practices is acceptable in Islamic law, and that such variety is part of its uniqueness and should remain.[93] Further, it is claimed that standardisation hinders further innovation and competition in the IFSI as it implies unified practices at all levels.[94] Nevertheless, the IFSI should strive to achieve a high level of consistency in the *ṣukūk* market via standardisation, harmonisation, or other suggested tools. Its conventional counterpart has reached an agreed level of practice and produced standards for its financial products and services. Important steps that

[88] R Ali, 'An Overview of the Sukuk Market' in Ali R (ed), *Sukuk and Islamic Capital Markets: A Practical Guide* (Globe Business Publishing 2011) 9.

[89] Ibid. 8.

[90] C Soanes and A Stevenson (eds), *Oxford Dictionary of English* (Oxford University Press 2006) 1723.

[91] Ibid.

[92] Ibid. 793.

[93] H Yaacob, M Mohammad and E Smolo, *International Convention for Islamic Finance: Towards Standardisation* (ISRA 2011) 20.

[94] W Ghoul, 'The Standardization Debate in Islamic Finance: A Case Study' (8 International Conference on Islamic Economics and Finance, Doha, December 2011) 4.

would facilitate standardisation or harmonisation in the IFSI include applying juristic differences rules to reduce the level of sharia inconsistency in practice, increasing the level of cooperation between all *ṣukūk* industry stakeholders and increasing the efficiency of Islamic finance standard-setting bodies.

8.5 Application of Islamic Finance-Supporting Institutions' Work on *Ṣukūk*

Effort needs to be focused on several initiatives and the work on the *ṣukūk* sector carried out by the international Islamic finance-supporting institutions. This has already been recognised in order to put in place minimum international standards and guiding principles pertaining to the *ṣukūk* market. Such work is expected to enhance *ṣukūk* practices by assisting local authorities in finding the gaps that exist in their jurisdictions, identifying applicable principles for identified gaps, and addressing specificities of *ṣukūk* products. In this respect, four major organisations—IIFA, AAOIFI, IFSB, and IIFM—have developed essential content related to the *ṣukūk* market in the form of resolutions, sharia standards, guidelines, reports, and evaluation.[95] An attempt is made here to list their efforts and evaluate their contributions to the *ṣukūk* sector.

IIFA, which is based in the KSA, was established in 1981 and started operations in 1983. It is an international body consisting of sharia scholars, experts, and thinkers from 43 countries who have been brought together to answer inquiries related to all aspects of Muslims' lives. In relation to *ṣukūk*, there are ten resolutions passed separately in different sessions for the period 1986–2013. Three out of the ten resolutions have recommended conducting further research on the subject matter to discuss in the subsequent session, and therefore do not contain specific rules on *ṣukūk*.[96] Resolutions that contain rules on *ṣukūk* are as follows:

[95] There are other institutions that have work relevant to *ṣukūk* sector such as the WB, IMF, IDB, and IRTI. However, the nature of their work is different from IIFA, AAOIFI, IFSB and IIFM. The focus here is on work that offers guidance and rules for *ṣukūk* sector rather than general discussion and debate about the IFSI.

[96] These are: resolution no 22 (10/3), entitled '*Muqaradha* Bonds and Development and Investments Certificates'; resolution no 110 (4/12), entitled 'Lease Ending with Ownership and Leasing Bonds'; resolution no 156 (5/17), entitled '*mushārakah ṣukūk*'. See IIFA, *Resolutions and Recommendations of the Council of Islamic Fiqh Academy* (1 edn, IDB 2000) 35, 253. See also IIFA, 'Qarār Raqam 156 (5/17) Bisha'an Astikmāl- Ṣukūk Al-Mushārakat:

- Resolution No. 30 (4/5) entitled 'Muqaradha Bonds and Investments Certificates' has defined *muqāraḍah* certificates and identified four elements underlying such certificates.[97]
- Resolution No. 60 (11/6) entitled 'Bonds' has prohibited conventional bonds and recommended *muḍārabah ṣukūk* as an alternative.[98]
- Resolution No. 101 (4/11) entitled 'Debt Sale and Loan Debentures and their Islamic Substitutes in Public and Private Sectors' has emphasised the prohibition of conventional bonds.[99]
- Resolution No. 137 (3/15) entitled '*Ijārah Ṣukūk*' has provided certain rules concerning *ijārah ṣukūk*.[100]
- Resolution No. 178 (4/19) entitled (*Al-Ṣukūk Al-Islāmiyya-H (Al-Tawrīq) Wa-Taṭbīqāatuh Al-Muʿāṣirah*) has defined Islamic securitisation and provided certain rules concerning *ṣukūk*.[101]
- Resolution No. 188 (3/20) entitled 'Completion of the Issue of Islamic Bonds (*Ṣukūk*)' has provided general rules on *ṣukūk* and specific rules on *ṣukūk* in relation to undertaking, leasing an asset to the seller, lease based on description and *ṣukūk* dealings.[102]
- Resolution No. 196 (2/21) entitled '*Astikmāl- Mawḍūʿ Al-Ṣukūk Al-Islāmiyyah*' has provided rules on *ijārah ṣukūk* based on description and *ṣukūk* issuance.[103]

AAOIFI, which is based in Bahrain, was inaugurated in 1990 and started operations in 1991. It is an international organisation consisting of 200 institutions from 40 countries, including central banks and Islamic financial institutions. It provides the IFSI with accounting, auditing, governance, ethics, and sharia standards. Among its publications on the IFSI,

Mukawināt Mawjūdātihā' (*IIFA*, undated). http://www.fiqhacademy.org.sa/qrarat/17-5.htm. Accessed 8 July 2015.

[97] IIFA, *Resolutions and Recommendations of the Council of Islamic Fiqh Academy*, *supra* note 96, 55.

[98] Ibid. 119.

[99] Ibid. 234.

[100] IIFA, 'Resolution no 137 (3/15) concerning Ijārah Ṣukūk' (*Fiqhacademy*, 2004). http://www.fiqhacademy.org.sa/qrarat/15-3.htm. Accessed 3 March 2015.

[101] IIFA, 'Al-Qarārāt Wa Al-Tawṣiyāt: Al-Dawrah Al-Tāsiʿah ʿashrah' (*Fiqhacademy*, 2009). http://www.fiqhacademy.org.sa/. Accessed 7 November 2014.

[102] IIFA, 'Resolution of OIC Fiqh Academy (related to Islamic Economic and Finance)' (2014) 22 Islamic Economic Studies 265.

[103] IIFA, 'Al-Qarārāt Wa Al-Tawṣiyāt: Al-Dawrah Al-Wāḥidah Wālʿishrīn' (*fiqhacademy*, 2013). http://www.fiqhacademy.org.sa/. Accessed 3 March 2015.

there are two works focusing on *ṣukūk*. The first work is called 'Sharia Standard no (17) on Investment *Ṣukūk*.[104] This standard provides a definition for *ṣukūk*, *ṣukūk* types, *ṣukūk* features, and rules concerning *ṣukūk* issuance and trading. The second work is called 'AAOIFI *Sharīʿah* Resolutions: Issues on *Ṣukūk*' which is a short and specialised document issued as a response to observations related to *ṣukūk*.[105] The document advises IIFS and SSB on six matters in relation to *ṣukūk* issuance including ownership, *ṣukūk* tradability, offering loans to *ṣukūk* holders in equity-based *ṣukūk*, purchase undertaking in equity-based *ṣukūk*, purchase undertaking in *ijārah ṣukūk*, and the role of SSB.

IFSB, which is based in Malaysia, was established in 2002 and commenced operations in 2003. It is an international organisation comprising 184 members, including regulatory authorities, international intergovernmental organisations, financial institutions, professional firms, and self-regulatory organisations. IFSB has issued four standards which include *ṣukūk* under their scope as follows:

- IFSB Standard no. 2—'Capital Adequacy Standard for Institutions (other than Insurance Institutions) offering only Islamic Financial Services (IIFS)' issued in December 2005 which defined *ṣukūk* and its types and provided minimum capital requirements for *ṣukūk* held by IIFS.[106]
- IFSB Standard no. 7—'Capital Adequacy Requirements for *Ṣukūk*, Securitisations and Real Estate investment' issued in January 2009 which deals with *ṣukūk* and securitisation definition, *ṣukūk* structures and some regulatory capital requirements for IIFS in relation to *ṣukūk* not covered in the previous standard.[107]
- IFSB Standard no. 15—'Revised Capital Adequacy Standard for Institutions Offering Islamic Financial Services (Excluding Islamic

[104] AAOIFI, *Shari'a Standards for Islamic Financial Institutions* (AAOIFI 2010) 303–323.

[105] AAOIFI, *supra* note 4.

[106] IFSB, 'Capital Adequacy Standard for Institutions (other than Insurance Institutions) Offering Only Islamic Financial Services (IIFS)' (*IFSB*, December 2005). http://www.ifsb.org/standard/ifsb2.pdf. Accessed 4 March 2015.

[107] IFSB, 'Capital Adequacy Requirements for Ṣukūk, Securitisations and Real Estate investment' (*IFSB*, January 2009). http://www.ifsb.org/standard/eng_%20IFSB-7%20Capital%20Adequacy%20Requirements%20for%20Sukuk,%20Securitasations%20and%20Real%20Estate%20investment%20(Jan2009).pdf. Accessed 4 March 2015.

Insurance (Takaful) Institutions and Islamic Collective Investment Schemes)' issued in December 2013, which includes a section on *ṣukūk* and securitisation.[108]

- IFSB Standard no. 16 – 'Revised Guidance on Key Elements in the Supervisory Review Process of Institutions Offering Islamic Financial Services (Excluding Islamic Insurance (Takaful) Institutions and Islamic Collective Investment Schemes)' issued in March 2014, which provides guidance on securitisation risk and related off-balance sheet exposures for IIFS and supervisory authorities.[109]

IIFM, which is based in Bahrain, was set up by IDB and the central banks of Bahrain, Brunei Darussalam, Indonesia, Sudan, and Malaysia. It is an international organisation which addresses the standardisation needs of products and documentations in the IFSI. Its primary works on *ṣukūk* are in the form of *ṣukūk* market research and analysis. These are as follows:

- IIFM *Ṣukūk* Analysis (as of December 2009)[110]
- IIFM *Ṣukūk* Report 1st Edition: A Comprehensive Study of the International *Ṣukūk* Market[111]
- IIFM Study on Indonesian *Ṣukūk* Market & Global *Ṣukūk* Issuances[112]
- IIFM *Ṣukūk* Report 2nd Edition: A Comprehensive Study of the Global *Ṣukūk* Market.[113]

[108] IFSB, 'Revised Capital Adequacy Standard for Institutions Offering Islamic Financial Services (Excluding Islamic Insurance (Takaful) Institutions and Islamic Collective Investment Schemes)' (*IFSB*, December 2013). http://www.ifsb.org/standard/2014-01-28_eng_IFSB15%20Revised%20Capital%20Adequacy_(Jan%202014).pdf. Accessed 4 March 2015.

[109] IFSB, 'Revised Guidance on Key Elements in the Supervisory Review Process of Institutions Offering Islamic Financial Services (Excluding Islamic Insurance (Takaful) Institutions and Islamic Collective Investment Schemes)' (*IFSB*, March 2014). http://www.ifsb.org/standard/IFSB-16%20Revised%20Supervisory%20Review%20Process_March%202014%20(final-clean).pdf. Accessed 4 March 2014.

[110] IIFM, 'IIFM Sukuk Analysis (as of December 2009)' (*IIFM*, December 2009). http://www.iifm.net/documents/iifm-sukuk-analysis-december-2009. Accessed 4 March 2015.

[111] IIFM, 'IIFM Ṣukūk Report 1st Edition' (*IIFM*, 2010). http://www.iifm.net/documents/iifm-sukuk-report-1st-edition. Accessed 4 March 2015.

[112] IIFM, 'IIFM Study on Indonesian Sukuk Market & Global Sukuk Issuances' (*IIFM*, August 2010). http://www.iifm.net/documents/iifm-study-indonesian-sukuk-market-global-sukuk-issuances. Accessed 4 March 2015.

[113] IIFM, 'IIFM Ṣukūk Report 2nd Edition: A Comprehensive Study of the Global Sukuk Market' (*IIFM*, 2011). http://www.iifm.net/documents/iifm-sukuk-report-2nd-edition-comprehensive-study-global-sukuk-market. Accessed 4 March 2015.

- IIFM *Ṣukūk* Report 3rd Edition: A Comprehensive Study of the Global *Ṣukūk* Market[114]
- IIFM *Ṣukūk* Report 4th Edition: A Comprehensive Study of the Global *Ṣukūk* Market.[115]

The above efforts form to a large extent a reliable source of information about the *ṣukūk* market, especially for regulatory authorities new to the area. However, an often-cited problem regarding the above-mentioned resolutions and standards is that they are adopted voluntarily. For example, AAOIFI's standards are adopted in limited jurisdictions only, namely Bahrain, DIFC, Jordan, Lebanon, Qatar, Sudan, and Syria.[116] Another point relates to the nature of their work and its suitability to the contemporary IFSI. The work of the AAOIFI and IFSB seems to receive more consideration from the industry stakeholders because it is drafted in a similar way to conventional financial standards. However, at the same time, one can see that some work is not up to date and do not cover issues of recent concerns. For example, AAOIFI's sharia standard on *ṣukūk* was issued in 2003 and many issues have emerged following this date. Indeed, there are some areas which have not yet been covered by these authorities such as core principles for effective *ṣukūk* regulations. Another point relates to their essential function and whether in reality they play the role of standard setters. For instance, IIFA is neither a body with a special focus on the IFSI nor a standard-setting body. Although IIFM claims to play a standard-setting function, it has not yet issued any standards in relation to *ṣukūk*. Nevertheless, there is a great need for financial regulators to consider the efforts made by Islamic finance-supporting institutions, whether by way of implementation or consultation. Such institutions should also play a more active role in the *ṣukūk* market by addressing recent *ṣukūk* concerns and cooperating with local financial authorities.

[114] IIFM, 'IIFM Ṣukūk Report 3rd Edition: A Comprehensive Study of the Global Sukuk Market' (*IIFM*, April 2013). http://www.iifm.net/documents/iifm-sukuk-report. Accessed 4 March 2015.

[115] IIFM, 'IIFM Ṣukūk Report 4th Edition: A Comprehensive Study of the Global Sukuk Market' (*IIFM*, November 2014). http://www.iifm.net/documents/iifm-sukuk-report-4th-edition. Accessed 4 March 2015.

[116] AAOIFI, 'About AAOIFI' (*AAOIFI*, undated). http://www.aaoifi.com/en/about-aaoifi/about-aaoifi.html. Accessed 30 September 2015.

8.6 Application of Conventional Standards for Securities Regulation

Application of conventional standards for securities regulation is another recommended method to improve the *ṣukūk* market. It has been argued that the conventional financial industry has more expertise than the IFSI in terms of market experience and finance knowledge which has enabled it to introduce core principles for effective regulation in all financial sectors, namely banking, securities, and insurance. Therefore, considering its effort in developing securities regulation might be of great help in the area of *ṣukūk* regulation. Furthermore, this would possibly be a starting point to stimulate international Islamic finance standard setters to put in place core principles for effective *ṣukūk* regulation that are internationally recognised. This is of particular significance because the *ṣukūk* market lacks international core principles for effective *ṣukūk* regulation that would assist local financial authorities in developing their own *ṣukūk* regimes.

In the context of the conventional financial industry, a major organisation created for the propose of developing and promoting international standards for securities regulation is the International Organization of Securities Commissions (IOSCO), which was established in 1983. Prime IOSCO work on the securities sector include the 'Objectives and Principles of Securities Regulation' (hereafter IOSCO Principles) issued in 1998, which was revised in 2003 and 2010,[117] and the 'Methodology for Assessing Implementation

[117] IOSCO Principles document consists of 38 principles of securities regulation which are grouped into nine categories as follows:

- Principles Relating to the Regulator
- Principles for Self-Regulation
- Principles for the Enforcement of Securities Regulation
- Principles for Cooperation in Regulation
- Principles for Issuers
- Principles for Auditors, Credit Ratings Agencies, and other information service providers
- Principles for Collective Investment Schemes
- Principles for Market Intermediaries
- Principles for Secondary Markets

These principles are based on three objectives of securities regulation which are (1) protecting investors; (2) ensuring markets fairness, efficiency, and transparency, and (3) reducing systemic risk. See IOSCO, 'Objectives and Principles of Securities Regulation' (*IOSCO*, June 2010). http://www.iosco.org/library/pubdocs/pdf/IOSCOPD323.pdf. Accessed 10 February 2015.

of the IOSCO Objectives and Principles of Securities Regulation' released in 2011 (hereafter IOSCO Assessment Methodology).[118]

Having presented the primary sources of conventional standards for securities regulation, a critical question arises: is it possible to apply IOSCO's work to *ṣukūk*? The notion of applying of conventional standards for securities regulation might seem at the outset problematic because such standards have not been issued with *ṣukūk* in mind. To answer this question properly, an assessment needs to be made of IOSCO's work in order to identify the possibility of their application to the *ṣukūk* sector and find any gaps that may arise due to the difference between conventional securities and *ṣukūk*.

Three crucial assessments of IOSCO's work are worth mentioning. The first review is made by IOSCO which released a report called 'Islamic Capital Market Fact Finding Report' in 2004 (hereafter IOSCO's Report 2004).[119] The IOSCO's Report 2004 has assessed the applicability of IOSCO Principles (2003 version) by (1) conducting a survey questionnaire that was distributed to selected IOSCO members and external parties and (2) discussing some of the IOSCO Principles in the context of the ICM. According to its key findings, 'the IOSCO Principles can and should apply equally to the Islamic capital market',[120] and therefore separate regulatory principles are not needed. Indeed, most countries' responses imply that IOSCO's work is applicable to their ICMs.[121] Moreover, IOSCO's Report 2004 asserts that the regulation of the ICM should comply with the IOSCO Principles.[122] However, it acknowledges the need for some jurisdictions in certain instances to develop their own guidelines so as to address the specificities of ICM products while applying conventional principles of securities regulation to the ICM.[123] IOSCO's Report 2004

[118] The IOSCO Assessment Methodology is designed to provide interpretation for the IOSCO Principles and give guidance for self-assessment or third-party assessment of the implementation of the IOSCO Principles. The IOSCO Assessment Methodology does not alter the IOSCO Principles or introduce new principles. See IOSCO, 'Methodology for Assessing Implementation of the IOSCO Objectives and Principles of Securities Regulation' (*IOSCO*, February 2008). www.iosco.org/library/pubdocs/pdf/IOSCOPD226.pdf. Accessed 10 February 2015.

[119] IOSCO, 'Islamic Capital Market Fact Finding Report' (*IOSCO*, July 2004). http://www.iosco.org/library/pubdocs/pdf/IOSCOPD170.pdf. Accessed 10 February 2015.

[120] Ibid. 52.

[121] Ibid. 50.

[122] Ibid. 72.

[123] Ibid.

also recognises the benefit of IOSCO Principles to any international debate on issues concerning ICM.[124]

The second review was also made by IOSCO which issued a report in 2008 called 'Analysis of the Application of IOSCO's Objectives and Principles of Securities Regulation for Islamic Securities Products' (hereafter IOSCO's Analysis 2008).[125] IOSCO's Analysis 2008 starts by confirming that the findings of this report do not differ from the findings of IOSCO's Report 2004.[126] It also clearly states that '[t]he analysis of this report has not identified any concerns with respect to the compatibility of the IOSCO Core Principles with the Islamic securities market'.[127] However, IOSCO's Analysis 2008 highlights certain areas that need to be considered to increase the benefit of implementing IOSCO Principles in the context of the ICM.[128]

The third review was a working paper called 'Evaluation of Core Principles Relevant to Islamic Finance Regulation' issued by the IFSB in

[124] Ibid. 74.

[125] IOSCO, 'Analysis of the Application of IOSCO's Objectives and Principles of Securities Regulation for Islamic Securities Products' (*IOSCO*, September 2008). http://www.iosco.org/library/pubdocs/pdf/IOSCOPD280.pdf. Accessed 10 February 2015.

[126] Ibid. 4.

[127] Ibid.

[128] The report has listed the issues in the implementation related to the IOSCO Principles as follows:

- Principle 1: For the sake of clarity it would be beneficial for securities regulators to have a stated position on their regulatory responsibilities with respect to Islamic securities.
- Principle 3: Where regulators have responsibility for Shariah compliance, it is important to ensure that they possess the necessary powers and resources to regulate this in accordance with their remit.
- Principle 4: Regulators should ensure that processes are applied in a consistent, transparent and fair manner. In particular, where the regulator is directly involved in giving rulings on Shariah issues, it should consider disclosing key decisions, and the reasoning behind them.
- Principle 14: Regulators may wish to consider the relevant disclosure standards for *ṣukūk* within their jurisdiction.
- Principle 16: Accounting disclosures should be based on internationally acceptable standards (such as IFRS). Regulators, in considering their accounting requirements, should give due regard to the specific characteristics of Islamic securities. Standard-setting agencies such as the IASB may wish to consider the application of IFRS with regard to Islamic financial instruments with other bodies (such as AAOIFI).
- Principle 19: Regulators may wish to consider relevant disclosure standards for Islamic funds within their jurisdiction.

2014 (hereafter IFSB Working Paper).[129] The IFSB Working Paper covers both the IOSCO Principles and IOSCO Assessment Methodology to explore their applicability to the ICM. As a key finding, it states that '[i]n general, all 38 principles are applicable to ICM. However, in practice, in order to establish a more effective regulatory system, certain specific characteristics of ICM need to be considered by regulators or reflected in the regulatory system'.[130] As a significant contribution of the IFSB Working Paper, it has provided a table of the gap assessment which clearly demonstrates all IOSCO Principles and any specific characteristics of the ICM related to each principle. A very specific comment related to *ṣukūk*, and in particular the need for additional disclosures in *ṣukūk*, is made under IOSCO Principle 16.

The above-mentioned assessments agreed on two points: (1) the possibility of application of IOSCO Principles within the general context of the ICM and (2) the need to address unique aspects of ICM products in the implementation. The third review, the IFSB Working Paper, is more beneficial and informative because it provides a detailed description in relation to IOSCO Principles' application to *ṣukūk*.

- Principle 21: Where regulators have responsibility for regulating sharia compliance, they may wish to consider establishing criteria to ensure the intermediary has the relevant competencies
- Principle 22: Regulators should define their regulatory approach to determining the capital adequacy and prudential requirements for Islamic securities.
- Principle 23: Regulators who are responsible for sharia compliance may wish to require that Islamic financial institutions use sharia-compliant risk management techniques
- Principle 27: Exchanges which regulate the sharia compliance of a security may wish to tag them with a recognised marker and update this as appropriate.
- Principle 30: Regulators who are responsible for sharia compliance and/or market practitioners may wish to consider developing alternative mechanisms to Securities Borrowing and Lending which are consistent with sharia principles.

[129] The IFSB Working Paper is neither a guiding principle nor an exposure draft prepared by IFSB on the area of Islamic capital market regulation. It is a principle-by-principle gap analysis discussing the core principles provided by Basel Committee on Banking Supervision (BCBS), IOSCO, and International Association of Insurance Supervisors (IAIS) and their applicability to supervision of the various sectors of the IFSI. In the area of Islamic capital market, it has reviewed IOSCO's work and more particularly it has looked at whether the existing IOSCO's work is applicable to IFSI; requires adjustments; or new principles are required. See IFSB, 'Evaluation of Core Principles Relevant to Islamic Finance Regulation' (*IFSB*, November 2014). http://www.ifsb.org/docs/WP-02_CPIFR%20%28Nov%20 2014%29.pdf. Accessed 10 February 2015.

[130] Ibid. 95.

8.7 Effective Disclosure Regime for *Ṣukūk*

The next requirement to increase the soundness of the *ṣukūk* market is putting in place an effective disclosure regime for *ṣukūk*. Disclosure generally refers to the act of making 'information available so as to allow investors to make informed choices'.[131] The need for regulation in financial markets has been well recognised, and therefore several regulatory techniques have been developed to ensure effective regulation in the financial sector. In the context of securities market, the substance of the disclosure regime or so-called disclosure law consists of different parts and in reality it is a mix of 'legislation, common law and commission and stock exchange regulatory materials'.[132] It seems clear that disclosure has been over-relied upon as a regulatory device by financial regulators. Consequently, several devices supporting disclosure in the financial sector have been designed such as registration, audit, risk warnings, and cooling-off periods.[133]

Ṣukūk is generally perceived as a class of products within the broader securities market and therefore its need for a disclosure regime cannot be overemphasised. Islamic law places great importance on disclosure in financial transactions as can be inferred from several concepts under the Islamic law of contracts such as prohibition of uncertainty, prohibition of lies, and hiding facts in a transaction, the seller's obligation to disclose to the buyer all relevant information related to the goods, and option of defect (*khiyār al-ʿayb*) in sale contracts.[134] In addition, failure of disclosure, among others, has been regarded as a factor contributing to company failures and financial crises,[135] which 'can arise from non-disclosure, limited disclosure, false disclosure, misrepresentation or failure to disclose within the time limit set be the relevant obligation'.[136] In order to properly realise the significance of disclosure to *ṣukūk*, one should look at insufficient disclosure on the level of sharia compliance which 'may result in the introduction of non-sharia-compliant structures branded as sharia-compliant products, the utilisation of proceeds for non-compliant activities, legal misinterpretation and disputes'.[137]

[131] I MacNeil, *An Introduction to the Law on Financial Investment* (2 nd edn, Hart Publishing Ltd. 2012) 35.

[132] P Latimer, 'How to Ensure Disclosure of Information in Securities Markets Post-GFC' (2013) 42 Common Law World Review 111, 136.

[133] I MacNeil, *supra* note 131, 36.

[134] See L Al-Rimawi, *Raising Capital on Arab Equity Markets: Legal and Juridical Aspects of Arab Securities Regulation* (Kluwer Law International 2012) 137.

[135] P Latimer, *supra* note 132, 111.

[136] I MacNeil, *supra* note 131, 300.

[137] T Singh, 'Opening Remarks to the Roundtable' in IFSB, IOSCO and SC (eds), *Disclosure Requirements for Islamic Capital Market Products* (IFSB, IOSCO and SC 2013) 11.

8.7.1 Current Status of Disclosure Regimes Applicable to Ṣukūk

The need for development of *ṣukūk* disclosure regime depends on whether the current approaches of disclosure are sufficient or not. The prevailing view is that it is insufficient and has failed to address disclosure issues related to *ṣukūk*. Having reviewed a number of *ṣukūk* prospectuses for the period 2006–2010, IFSB concluded that 'there is no international standard in respect of specific disclosure requirements on *ṣukūk* issuance'.[138] It has been found that international *ṣukūk* feature more disclosure requirements compared to domestic *ṣukūk*.[139] While *ṣukūk* issuers try to comply with relevant authorities in *ṣukūk* involving global investors, they are met with local regulations in *ṣukūk* that target domestic investors.[140] Therefore, the contents of *ṣukūk* prospectuses, especially in the area of disclosure, vary depending on the offering jurisdiction as well as target investors.

The insufficient disclosure regime in the *ṣukūk* market is justified by the fact that commercial customers as opposed to retail customers form the largest base of *ṣukūk* investors.[141] The former rely heavily on advisors and private information to make investment decisions.[142] Moreover, the shortcoming of the approach used so far to deal with insufficient disclosure cases in the *ṣukūk* market highlights the importance of greater clarity on *ṣukūk* disclosure. In this respect, Casey argues that '[a]lthough there have been claims that disclosure was inadequate in specific cases, few of them have been subject to rigorous testing, at least in any public forum'.[143] It has also been argued that the current disclosure approaches relating to *ṣukūk* do not achieve the aim of creating a fair, efficient, and transparent market, owing to the continuing confusion about issues such as dispute resolution mode, recourse nature, and enforcement mechanism.[144]

[138] IFSB, IOSCO and SC, 'Forward' in IFSB, IOSCO and SC (eds), *Disclosure Requirements for Islamic Capital Market Products* (IFSB, IOSCO, SC 2013) 1.

[139] Ibid.

[140] Ibid.

[141] M Azmi 'The Importance of Strong Disclosure Regime in Facilitating Cross-Boarder Investments and Development of Islamic Capital Market Products and Services' in IFSB, IOSCO and SC (eds), *Disclosure Requirements for Islamic Capital Market Products* (IFSB, IOSCO and SC 2013) 77.

[142] Ibid.

[143] P Casey, *supra* note 12, 31.

[144] H Sabeti-Rahmati, 'Commentary One' in IFSB, IOSCO and SC (eds), *Disclosure Requirements of Islamic Capital Market Products* (IFSB, IOSCO, SC 2013) 84.

In contrast, Lee is satisfied with the current approaches of disclosure applied to the *ṣukūk* market and argues that there is no need for enhanced or additional disclosures for *ṣukūk*.[145] Lee's argument is based on two main points: the sufficiency of conventional disclosure principles to be applied to most existing *ṣukūk* products that mimic conventional products, and that the sharia-compliant nature of *ṣukūk* does not require additional disclosures. As for the first point, Lee says 'it is not a question of a failure of the IOSCO principles to specify what to disclose, but the manner of drafting of the disclosure'.[146] Pertaining to the second point, Lee states 'the sharia-compliant nature of the product in these cases does not drive the requirement of additional or enhanced disclosures'.[147] Further, Lee claims that the idea of advocating additional disclosures is 'speculation as to what is required with regards to sharia-compliance'.[148] Lee continues by arguing that the market does not demand additional disclosure implementation since it has been functioning successfully within the existing level of disclosures.[149] To make the idea of enhanced *ṣukūk* disclosure is less effective, Lee mentions some disadvantages of such an approach, including the ambiguity concerning what should be enhanced or added in the area of *ṣukūk* disclosure, the additional costs which will most likely be associated with it, and added risk factors.[150]

The following discussion will elaborate on the international standards of disclosure and additional disclosures on *ṣukūk* as significant parts of formulating an effective disclosure regime for the *ṣukūk* market.

8.7.2 International Standards of Disclosure Requirements

There has not yet been an international standard regarding *ṣukūk* disclosure. Despite the issuance of IFSB Standard no. 4—Disclosures to Promote Transparency and Market Discipline for Institutions offering Islamic Financial Services (excluding Islamic Insurance (*Takāful*) Institutions and Islamic Mutual Funds)—ICM products including *ṣukūk*

[145] See generally C Lee, 'Commentary Three' in IFSB, IOSCO and SC (eds), *Disclosure Requirements of Islamic Capital Market Products* (IFSB, IOSCO and SC 2013).

[146] Ibid. 60.

[147] Ibid.

[148] Ibid. 65.

[149] Ibid.

[150] Ibid.

are not under its scope.[151] This harks back to the possibility of applying conventional standards to securities regulation and the issue of whether such standards are sufficient in the area of *ṣukūk* disclosures. The need for development of specific disclosure requirements for *ṣukūk* depends on whether there are gaps between disclosure requirements within conventional securities and *ṣukūk*.

One can speak of two disclosure frameworks operating at an international level that may be relevant to *ṣukūk*: regulatory disclosure and accounting disclosure. Issues related to regulatory disclosure have been covered by IOSCO Principles and 'International Disclosure Principles for Cross-Border Offerings and Listings of Debt Securities by Foreign Issuers' issued by IOSCO in 2007 (hereafter IOSCO Disclosure Principles).[152] IOSCO Principles include general disclosure requirements. In particular, 3 of the 38 IOSCO Principles directly refer to disclosure issues that are relevant to *ṣukūk*.[153] IOSCO Disclosure Principles provide guidance to securities regulators on different areas of disclosure.[154]

As for accounting disclosures, there are two frameworks which are written with different products in mind: Financial Accounting Standards issued by AAOIFI (hereinafter AAOIFI's FAS) deals with accounting dis-

[151] See IFSB, 'Disclosures to Promote Transparency and Market Discipline for Institutions offering Islamic Financial Services (excluding Islamic Insurance (*Takâful*) Institutions and Islamic Mutual Funds)' (*IFSB*, December 2007). http://www.ifsb.org/standard/ifsb4.pdf. Accessed 5 March 2015.

[152] IOSCO, 'International Disclosure Principles for Cross-Border Offerings and Listings of Debt Securities by Foreign Issuers' (*IOSCO*, March 2007). https://www.iosco.org/library/pubdocs/pdf/IOSCOPD242.pdf. Accessed 5 March 2015.

[153] These are as follows:

- Principle 16: There should be full, accurate, and timely disclosure of financial results, risk, and other information, which are material to investors' decisions.
- Principle 18: Accounting standards used by issuers to prepare financial statements should be of a high and internationally acceptable quality.
- Principle 35: Regulation should promote transparency of trading.

[154] There are as follows: Identities of parties responsible for the document; Description of the debt securities; Risk factors; Markets; Information about the public offering; Taxation; Selected financial information; Information about the Issuer; Operating and financial review and prospects; Directors, senior management, and employees; Major shareholders and related party transactions; Interests of experts and counsel; Financial information. See IOSCO, 'International Disclosure Principles for Cross-Border Offerings and Listings of Debt Securities by Foreign Issuers' (*IOSCO*, March 2007). https://www.iosco.org/library/pubdocs/pdf/IOSCOPD242.pdf. Accessed 5 March 2015.

closure issues in the IFSI.[155] General issues related to accounting disclosure have been covered by International Financial Reporting Standards (IFRS) issued by International Accounting Standards Board (IASB).

Having identified the existing international disclosure frameworks, one may wonder whether they are sufficient to address disclosure issues in relation to *ṣukūk*. As for the regulatory disclosure requirements provided by IOSCO Principles, the key findings of IOSCO's Report 2004, IOSCO's Analysis 2008, and IFSB Working Paper confirm the applicability of IOSCO Principles and require additional disclosures in certain areas. On IOSCO Disclosure Principles, Wico states 'there are a few key areas of focus that could advance the development of disclosure standards for international Islamic capital market instruments'.[156] Sabeti-Rahmati holds that conventional disclosure standards are inadequate to address disclosure issues related to *ṣukūk*.[157] While they are mainly concerned with credit quality of the obligor in case of a plain vanilla bond, there is much to disclose in case of *ṣukūk*.[158]

After assessing the suitability of regulatory disclosure frameworks, the next step is to assess the accounting disclosure frameworks. According to Asian-Oceanian Standards-Setters Group (AOSSG) Survey November 2013, 64% of respondents believe that entities involved in the IFSI in their jurisdictions regard AAOIFI's FAS as the accounting framework of choice.[159] The AOSSG Survey November 2013 indicates that some jurisdictions requiring AAOIFI's FAS allow the application of IFRS when AAOIFI's FAS is absent.[160] Also, it highlights that some jurisdictions in which IFRS is a general requirement may allow

[155] See AAOIFI, *Accounting, Auditing and Governance Standards for Islamic Financial Institutions 1432H-2010* (AAOIFI 2004).

[156] Y Wico, 'Comparative Evaluation of Regulatory and Best Practices on Disclosure of Islamic Capital Market Products' in IFSB, IOSCO and SC (eds), *Disclosure Requirements for Islamic Capital Market Products* (IFSB, IOSCO and SC 2013) 27.

[157] C Lee, *supra* note 145, 85.

[158] Ibid.

[159] This is a survey undertaken by the AOSSG Islamic Finance Working Group, and it aims to understand the views of many countries in the Middle East and North Africa (MENA) about accounting for Islamic financial transactions. The survey has been distributed to accounting and auditing practitioners in 24 countries in MENA. See AOSSG, 'AOSSG Survey: Accounting and Islamic Finance in the Middle East and North Africa' (*AOSSG*, November 2013). http://aossg.org/docs/Publications/AOSSG_MENA_Islamic_Finance_Survey%20Findings_Nov_2013.pdf. Accessed 6 March 2015.

[160] Ibid. 4.

applying AAOIFI's FAS as an exception.[161] Given the above coexistence scenarios, a question arises as to whether IFRS are sufficient to address accounting disclosure issues related to *ṣukūk*. This is a significant concern because IFRS were not developed with Islamic finance principles in mind, as opposed to AAOIFI's FAS which are written to address disclosure issues related to the IFSI. On the one hand, the AOSSG Survey states that 'there may be aspects of reporting Islamic financial transactions and the statements of Islamic entities that are not thought to be adequately addressed by IFRS'.[162] On the other hand, Azmi argues that 'IFRS' does already require disclosures that may address some of these sharia compliance needs'.[163] This debate about IFRS applicability in the context of the IFSI explains the following statement in IOSCO's Report 2004:

> Accounting disclosures should be based on internationally acceptable standards (such as IFRS). Regulators, in considering their accounting requirements, should give due regard to the specific characteristics of Islamic securities. Standard setting bodies such as IASB may wish to consider the application of IFRS with regard to Islamic financial instruments with other bodies (such as AAOIFI).[164]

The following section will attempt to facilitate a better understanding of additional requirements that should be considered in developing a disclosure regime for *ṣukūk*.

8.7.3 Specific Disclosure Requirements of Ṣukūk Issuance

After observing the conventional disclosure requirements that are relevant to *ṣukūk*, it is equally important to look at special disclosure requirements in relation to *ṣukūk*. The rationale for enhanced *ṣukūk* disclosures is that specificities of *ṣukūk* demand additional disclosure requirements on top of the existing conventional disclosure requirements. Enhanced *ṣukūk* disclo-

[161] Ibid.

[162] AOSSG, 'AOSSG Survey: Accounting for Islamic Financial Transactions and Entities' (*ASB*, December 2011) 6. https://www.asb.or.jp/asb/asb_e/aossg/pressrelease_20120110_01_e.pdf. Accessed 6 March 2015.

[163] M Azmi, *supra* note 141, 74.

[164] IOSCO, 'Analysis of the Application of IOSCO's Objectives and Principles of Securities Regulation for Islamic Securities Products' (*IOSCO*, September 2008) 5. http://www.iosco.org/library/pubdocs/pdf/IOSCOPD280.pdf. Accessed 10 February 2015.

sures can be divided into two broad categories: structural disclosures and sharia-compliance disclosures.[165] The importance of this distinction can be seen when a claim has been made that a particular *ṣukūk* arrangement is sharia-compliant.[166] *Ṣukūk* issued without such a claim will raise disclosure issues that fall into the first category only.[167]

As for structural disclosure requirements, one of the issues that should be considered in enhancing *ṣukūk* disclosure is related to the form and substance of individual *ṣukūk* arrangements. *Ṣukūk* structures vary widely and therefore the information disclosed to investors should reflect such variations. This is best illustrated by the comment in the IFSB Working Paper on the applicability of IOSCO Principle 16 to the ICM products:

> As with conventional securities, the disclosure regime for ICM products should reflect the economic substance and risk profile of the product. For example, in the case of asset-based *ṣukūk*, relevant information focusing on the originator should be disclosed.[168]

This is also Casey's concern who says that 'to call an instrument a *sukūk* in fact says very little about its economic character, and even to name the contract on which it is based does not necessarily say much more'.[169] While information focusing on the originator is required in the case of asset-based *ṣukūk*, the information should focus on the underlying asset in case of asset-backed *ṣukūk*. In some cases, the prime focus of information should be on the business plan of the newly formed *ṣukūk* project rather than on the issuer, obligor, or the underlying asset.[170] This is of particular significance in the case of equity-based *ṣukūk* where rating methodology should clearly reflect risk-sharing elements.[171] In this respect, Nienhaus argues that 'the participatory *sukūk* have risk profiles very different from the asset-backed *sukūk*, and this raises new disclosure issues'.[172] Therefore,

[165] P Casey, *supra* note 12, 32.

[166] Ibid.

[167] Ibid.

[168] IFSB, 'Evaluation of Core Principles Relevant to Islamic Finance Regulation' (*IFSB*, November 2014) 103. http://www.ifsb.org/docs/WP-02_CPIFR%20%28Nov%20 2014%29.pdf. Accessed 10 February 2015.

[169] P Casey, *supra* note 12, 33.

[170] V Nienhaus, 'Commentary Two' in IFSB, IOSCO and SC (eds), *Disclosrue Requirements of Islamic Capital Market Products* (IFSB, IOSCO and SC 2013) 54.

[171] Ibid.

[172] Ibid.

risk profiles that vary from one structure to another raise different disclosure issues and require disclosure adjustments. In order to reflect the substance of *ṣukūk*, careful and accurate terminologies should be used to describe the nature of recourse in *ṣukūk*—whether the recourse is to the obligor, asset, or both.[173]

Another area of enhanced *ṣukūk* disclosures is related to *ṣukūk* documentation, in particular, the need for more simplicity in drafting *ṣukūk* related documents. It has been argued that the complexity surrounding the *ṣukūk* structure raises certain questions about disclosure in *ṣukūk*.[174] The complexity of *ṣukūk* exists because of the number of different transaction documents and the number of parties involved which can be as many as 16 and 6, respectively, in the case of Nakheel *Ṣukūk*.[175] It is uncertain whether less sophisticated investors are able to understand the separate *ṣukūk* documents working together seamlessly and the different types of risk related to them.[176]

Furthermore, disclosure is needed regarding the use of purchase undertakings, particularly in the case of equity-based *ṣukūk*.[177] Although they might be disclosed in some cases, the ways used to assess them do not necessarily offer proper disclosure. In this respect, Nienhaus states that '[p]urchase undertakings were disclosed in the *sukūk* documentations, but they were assessed by rating agencies and market players not from their sharia risk dimension, but as elements of the financial structure'.[178] A related aspect is the need for further disclosure in case of explicit versus implicit guarantee in incidents of quasi-sovereign *ṣukūk*.[179]

Another area to develop *ṣukūk* disclosure is related to continuous disclosure. The fact that most *ṣukūk* are traded OTC, including listed *ṣukūk*, raises a set of questions about disclosure[180]; there is less assurance that such traded instruments have met certain regulatory standards since it has been the practice of regulators to enforce continuous disclosure requirements

[173] H Sabeti-Rahmati, 'Commentary One' in IFSB, IOSCO and SC (eds), *Disclosure Requirements of Islamic Capital Market Products* (IFSB, IOSCO, SC 2013) 86.

[174] P Casey, *supra* note 12, 35.

[175] Ibid. 36.

[176] Ibid.

[177] L Alvi, 'Commentary One' in IFSB, IOSCO and SC (eds), *Disclosure Requirements of Islamic Capital Market Products* (IFSB, IOSCO and SC 2013) 46.

[178] V Nienhaus, *supra* note 170, 53.

[179] L Alvi, *supra* note 177, 48.

[180] P Casey, *supra* note 12, 38.

on instruments traded on the exchange.[181] Related to this issue is the requirement of continuous disclosure regarding the performance of the underlying asset of the *ṣukūk* structure, particularly in cases of asset-backed *ṣukūk*.

Having listed several areas of enhanced *ṣukūk* disclosure related to the structure, one moves to sharia compliance disclosures. In this respect, IFSB Working Paper has made the following statement assessing the applicability of IOSCO Principle 16 to ICM products: 'Additional disclosures might be relevant for investors in ICM products. These might include information on the sharia board, how the product meets sharia requirements, and details related to sharia compliance'.[182]

One can find a number of disclosure issues applicable to *ṣukūk* that follow from this general statement, for example, disclosing the names of sharia advisors who have approved the *ṣukūk* issuance.[183] This is helpful when the quality of the sharia advisors is subject to challenge.[184] Another aspect is related to disclosing the reasoning that leads to the sharia pronouncement. However, the issue of reasoning disclosure and its impact on investors' protection is a matter of debate. Proponents argue that disclosing the basis of a sharia pronouncement is helpful for institutional investors who have their own sharia advisors; furthermore, they hold that such disclosure is important for challenging the sharia pronouncement which may be required to ensure the right process is used to reach such an opinion.[185] The opponents of disclosing reasoning argue that it is irrelevant for less sophisticated investors because they lack the ability to understand the sharia interpretations.[186] Also, they argue that the requirement of disclosing the reasoning serves no purpose since investors make their own judgment as to sharia compliance according to the current market practice.[187]

Another area of sharia disclosures is whether a *ṣukūk* prospectus should explicitly disclose information as to whether the structure complies or deviates from sharia recommendations and resolutions of Islamic finance-supporting institutions such as AAOIFI.[188] Further, there are sharia dis-

[181] Ibid.
[182] IFSB, *supra* note 168, 103.
[183] P Casey, *supra* note 12, 39.
[184] M Azmi, *supra* note 141, 75.
[185] P Casey, *supra* note 12, 39.
[186] Ibid.
[187] C Lee, *supra* note 145, 62–63.
[188] V Nienhaus, *supra* note 170, 53–54.

closures related to continuous disclosure of the sharia compliance of a structure which should be made on a regular basis.[189] These include the activities of the originator and the use of *ṣukūk* proceeds, since such practices may change after the commencement of a *ṣukūk* project.[190]

8.8 Conclusion

This chapter has presented six approaches that will facilitate the creation of a sound *ṣukūk* market. These address the *ṣukūk* markets' needs from a macro-perspective. Developing a *ṣukūk* market is a long-term process, and there is great need for the involvement of all industry stakeholders. It is difficult to delegate the task of applying such recommendations to a single market stakeholder, such as financial regulators, and therefore all relevant parties have a vital role to play. Such approaches need to be implemented collectively, and reliance on one single approach will not serve the purpose of ensuring soundness in the *ṣukūk* market. They are not only helpful for new jurisdictions entering the *ṣukūk* market but also for those with established markets and experience. The door for new initiatives in the context of enhancing the *ṣukūk* market is always open and not restricted to those mentioned in this chapter.

Each approach serves a particular purpose and addresses certain difficulties within the wider context of the *ṣukūk* market. To illustrate, product enhancement aims to increase the marketability and attractiveness of *ṣukūk* products. The process of managing juristic differences attempts to provide more legal certainty to *ṣukūk* investors and issuers. As for standardisation and harmonisation in the *ṣukūk* market, they lead to consistency and promote cross-border transactions. Besides this, applying decisions and resolutions of the Islamic finance-supporting institutions ensures to a great extent the sharia compliance of *ṣukūk* products and reduces the level of disagreement over several sharia aspects of *ṣukūk* transactions. Last but not least, the application of conventional standards for securities regulation helps financial regulators and the Islamic finance-supporting institutions to develop guiding principles to supervise and regulate the *ṣukūk* market. Finally, an efficient *ṣukūk* disclosure regime assists investors in making an informed investment decision.

[189] H Sabeti-Rahmati, *supra* note 173, 86.
[190] P Casey, *supra* note 12, 39.

CHAPTER 9

Conclusion

This book has investigated the *ṣukūk* (trust investment certificates) market with a focus on the structural, legal, and regulatory concerns encountering such markets. Structural issues are related to the design and structure of *ṣukūk*. Legal issues are concerned with the sharia-compliant nature of *ṣukūk*. Regulatory issues relate to the regulation of *ṣukūk* markets in three jurisdictions, namely Malaysia, the UAE, and the KSA. After examining these different issues in relation to *ṣukūk*, the discussion moved into the issue of how the soundness of *ṣukūk* markets can be ensured and developed in the wider context.

Ṣukūk markets are ICMs in which *ṣukūk* are issued and traded. As the introduction of this book highlighted, *ṣukūk* is the second largest segment of the IFSI after Islamic banks. *Ṣukūk* in the current form dates from 1977, when the Ministry of Awqaf, Islamic Affairs and Holy Places in Jordan, wanted to issue *ṣukūk* in order to finance *waqf* (charitable endowment) properties. This is arguably the first *ṣukūk* issuance in our modern time. *Ṣukūk* markets have grown tremendously over the last three decades in terms of the total value, the sophistication of structures, and number of issuers. However, strong criticisms have been levelled against a number of *ṣukūk* practices. Although there has been discussion of the concerns surrounding *ṣukūk*, past studies on *ṣukūk* issues lack legal and regulatory perspectives. In addition, no study has provided a holistic analysis of *ṣukūk* issues. This book adopts this approach, and, in doing so, it fills the gaps in the knowledge by four main ways: first, it examines issues arising from *ṣukūk* structuring processes. Second, it discusses issues arising from the sharia-compliant nature

S. Al-Ali, *Raising Capital on* Ṣukūk *Markets*,
https://doi.org/10.1007/978-3-030-14536-1_9

of *ṣukūk* products. Third, it looks at the regulatory issues arising from the current regulations imposed on three *ṣukūk* markets which are Malaysia, the UAE, and the KSA. Fourth, it proposes six methods that would facilitate the establishment of sound *ṣukūk* markets.

Chapter 1 of this book provided an overview of the IFSI and the most pressing issues arising from its practices in the broader context. Understanding of such issues is vital before moving into the subject matter of this book. The first point deals with the soundness of the IFSI and explains how IFSI has been integrated within the global financial markets. The second issue is concerned with the definition of three terms that are relevant to the IFSI: sharia, Islamic law, and Islamic finance. The referent of these terms has been emphasised, particularly the distinction between sharia and Islamic law. The third issue is related to the basic features of the IFSI, namely prohibition of interest, uncertainty, gambling, and certain activities that contravene Islamic law. The fourth issue deals with the concept of sharia governance in the IFSI, particularly concerns casting doubt on the role of sharia boards in ensuring sharia compliance in the IFSI. The fifth issue is concerned with the governing law of the IFSI and applicability of Islamic law in disputes related to the IFSI. The sixth issue is related to liquidity in the IFSI; it was demonstrated that there are few instruments in the hands of the IIFS and regulatory authorities to facilitate effective liquidity management at national and international levels. The seventh issue is concerned with investor protection in the IFSI; the occurrence of *ṣukūk* defaults, among other issues, raised questions about the level of investor protection. Having elucidated how the IFSI currently works, the chapter clarified the purpose of this study. It was proven that *ṣukūk* markets face a number of concerns that are not well addressed from legal and regulatory perspectives.

Chapter 2 is aimed at introducing the reader to the fundamentals of *ṣukūk*. It was shown that there has been no collective or universally accepted definition of *ṣukūk*. In basic terms, *ṣukūk* are certificates which represent an undivided pro rata ownership interest in an underlying asset. In this regard, one suggests that the industry definition of *ṣukūk* should be more accurate. For example, the type of ownership should be clearly specified, whether legal ownership or beneficial ownership. This chapter also addressed the issue of whether *ṣukūk* is a traditional or new Islamic instrument; it was established that the current form of *ṣukūk* emerged in Jordan in 1977. This was arguably the first *ṣukūk* issuance after the birth of the IFSI in the late 1960s. However, the origins of *ṣukūk* can be traced back to the thirteenth, fifteenth, and eighteenth centuries. Such periods witnessed some practices by the Ottoman Empire that are found in modern *ṣukūk*. From its infancy stage, the *ṣukūk* industry has expanded greatly and become highly prominent in both Islamic and conventional jurisdictions. Malaysia, the UAE, and the KSA are the leading jurisdictions involved in *ṣukūk* issuance and investment. The USA and the UK are among the Western countries that have witnessed the issuance of *ṣukūk*. It was shown that *ṣukūk* markets have been subjected to decreased growth from 2008 to 2009. The main reasons for such a growth decline have been identified, including the impact of the global financial crisis and *ṣukūk* defaults. Chapter 2 discussed several economic advantages offered by *ṣukūk*; it was proven that *ṣukūk* serves the economy by providing funds for infrastructure projects and the avoiding speculative movement of funds. It was shown that *ṣukūk* is a permissible financial product under Islamic law, and it offers an alternative to conventional bonds. This chapter also presented different *ṣukūk* classifications and *ṣukūk* structures. The market has come up with different *ṣukūk* structures to meet different needs of all stakeholders, and therefore *ṣukūk* cannot be seen as one type. The final issue discussed in this chapter pertains to the pricing and valuation of *ṣukūk*; as a matter of practice, there are similarities between *ṣukūk* and conventional bonds with regard to the valuation method. This chapter intended to present some of the preliminary issues that form holistic understanding of the *ṣukūk* sector.

Chapter 3 discussed the first structural issue which is asset-backed *ṣukūk*. After addressing the division of *ṣukūk* into asset-backed and asset-based structures, the chapter focused in detail on the concept of asset-backed *ṣukūk*. The main factors that led to the birth of this new *ṣukūk* classification in the market were highlighted. One of the chapter's key arguments is that categorisation of *ṣukūk* to asset-backed and asset-based structures provides clear understanding of the current *ṣukūk* applications, as opposed to more traditional *ṣukūk* classifications. It was shown that while this type of *ṣukūk* is preferable from an Islamic law perspective, it constitutes only a minor part of the current *ṣukūk* market. The essential features of asset-backed *ṣukūk* include bankruptcy remoteness, true sale, enforceability of security, and generation of independent cash flows. Issuing entities are most likely to consider the choice of asset-backed *ṣukūk* where there are developed bankruptcy laws and legal environment. It was demonstrated that asset-backed *ṣukūk* are not affected by the insolvency of the originator. In addition, the holders of such *ṣukūk* assume all rights in relation to the asset backing the deal. In the event of insolvency of the originator, they thus enjoy the right of disposing of the asset. As a result, the insolvent originator is not able to claw back the asset in question.

Chapter 4 looked at the second new structural issue, asset-based *ṣukūk*. It was shown that asset-based *ṣukūk* is the most common type of *ṣukūk* in the market. The holders of asset-based *ṣukūk* do not assume all rights in relation to the underlying asset. The returns on asset-based *ṣukūk* depend on the credit ability of the originator, and not on the economic performance of the underlying asset. From the originator's perspective, the absence of developed bankruptcy laws and legal environment is one of the reasons for the choice of asset-based *ṣukūk*. *Ṣukūk* holders who do not want to take the risk of a *ṣukūk* asset or project tend to choose asset-based *ṣukūk*. This chapter argued that this particular type of *ṣukūk* triggers off issues in Islamic law. However, it further argued that it is inaccurate to assume that all asset-based *ṣukūk* are subject to criticism from an Islamic law point of view. It concluded that both asset-backed *ṣukūk* and asset-based *ṣukūk* are needed in the market because each form of *ṣukūk* serves different financial and investment needs. By the end of this chapter, one will be able to understand the ongoing debate about the issue of substance versus form in the IFSI. While asset-backed *ṣukūk* is an example of a transaction that meets the requirements of Islamic law in both substance and form, some asset-based *ṣukūk* provide illustration of transactions that meets requirements of Islamic law in form but not in substance.

Chapter 5 examined the third structural issue which is default in *ṣukūk* market. In doing so, it investigated the concept of default and Islamic law of insolvency; while the first issue is relevant to identify the event of default in *ṣukūk*, the second is relevant in understanding how the default event is dealt with under Islamic law. It was shown that the sharia-compliant nature of *ṣukūk* transaction necessitates understanding of default and insolvency law from an Islamic law point of view. Default in *ṣukūk* occurs when the originator is unable to make periodic payments on *ṣukūk*. While such practice can be called default in debt-based *ṣukūk*, there is no default in equity-based *ṣukūk* due to the principle of profit and loss sharing. It was shown that the global financial crisis and structural deficiencies are the key causes for *ṣukūk* defaults. The absence of the concept of a corporation in classical Islamic law raises questions about the suitability of the current state of the Islamic law of insolvency. The chapter then analysed some *ṣukūk* issuances that have been subject to financial difficulty, default, and near-default events. It was shown that asset-backed *ṣukūk* act differently from asset-based *ṣukūk* in the event of default. While the holders of asset-backed *ṣukūk* have full control over the asset backing the deal, the holders of asset-based *ṣukūk* join the list of the originator's unsecured creditors. The default of the East Cameron *Ṣukūk* provided the best illustration of the risk of re-categorisation in the *ṣukūk* market where the originator attempts to claw back the asset in question by claiming that the underlying transaction is merely a loan rather than asset-backed deal. It further showed how default events have been remedied. Of course, the default events came as a complete surprise to the industry for two main reasons. First, such *ṣukūk* were anticipated to be healthy. Second, market stakeholders were not satisfied with the way that default events had been tackled or remedied by the originators and regulatory authorities. The chapter also highlighted the consequences of default events in *ṣukūk* markets.

After discussing structural issues related to *ṣukūk* in Chaps. 3, 4, and 5, Chap. 6 focused on the legal issues surrounding *ṣukūk*. It analysed then the views of some organisations and authorities concerning *ṣukūk* legality, including the IIFA, AAOIFI, BNM's SAC, and SC's SAC. The first legal issue is concerned with the suitability of the underlying asset. It was shown that the choice of intangible assets is subject to disagreement in Islamic law. The current *ṣukūk* practices adopt the majority view, which allows intangible assets as the underlying assets in *ṣukūk*. The second legal issue is related to the sale of debt which occurs, for example, when debts or future cash flows are securitised in *ṣukūk*. This is an area where the Malaysians have departed from the view of many sharia boards in the GCC which tend to minimise or prohibit designing transactions involving sale of debt in the IFSI. The third issue deals with ownership, particularly the presence of beneficial ownership in asset-based *ṣukūk*. The debate over beneficial ownership is due to the fact that it is derived from the English trust concept. Therefore, there was no discussion about beneficial ownership per se by the earlier scholars. The main elements that trigger concern over beneficial ownership in Islamic law are; (1) the absence of a true sale, (2) the absence of a right to sell the asset, and (3) the presence of only some ownership rights. Providing sharia ruling on a beneficial ownership depends on how much Islamic law recognises the above three elements that constitute the notion of beneficial ownership. It was shown that the legal registration of the asset is not required under Islamic law, and therefore this issue should not be linked with the concern over beneficial ownership in *ṣukūk*. The fourth legal issue is related to *bayʿ al-ʿīnah* (sale and buy-back); it occurs when the originator sells its own asset to the SPV for cash price and then buys back the same asset at a deferred price. While the majority of scholars prohibit *bayʿ al-ʿīnah*, the minority of scholars permit it. The fifth issue is concerned with methods available for restructuring *ṣukūk* in the event of default. It was shown that a cause for concern is the application of the Western-style restructuring methods for defaults under *ṣukūk*. It further argued that conventional modes of debt restructuring are not equally compliant with the principles of Islamic law. The sixth issue is related to undertaking as included in many *ṣukūk* structures. It was shown that there are questions about the legality of incorporating undertaking into *ṣukūk*, the enforceability of undertaking, and whether undertaking is a form of guarantee. The seventh issue is concerned with the guarantee of capital amount or returns on *ṣukūk*. This is particularly relevant to equity-based *ṣukūk* that are based on profit and loss sharing. The common argument is that the guarantee of capital and returns destroys the concept of profit and loss sharing in equity-based *ṣukūk*.

Chapter 7 shifted focus to another set of issues surrounding *ṣukūk* which are regulatory issues. It illustrated how *ṣukūk* markets are regulated and supervised in three countries, namely Malaysia, the UAE, and the KSA. As was shown, these countries have adopted the multiple regulatory agencies approach, as opposed to the single regulatory agency approach. Malaysia is the most advanced market when it comes to regulation concerning *ṣukūk*. Malaysia has focused on the development of the IFSI as a priority sector. This is also true of the UAE, especially after the announcement of Dubai as the international capital for Islamic economy in 2013. While Malaysia and the UAE are examples of jurisdictions that promulgate special regulations concerning *ṣukūk*, the KSA is an example of a jurisdiction that has not issued any special regulations for *ṣukūk*.

Chapter 8 proposed six methods to be used to enhance the soundness of *ṣukūk* market. This chapter provides the framework upon which *ṣukūk* markets can be developed. The first method deals with product enhancement; this method suggests that there are many aspects of *ṣukūk* structure that need to be enhanced. The second method is concerned with juristic differences, proposing that juristic differences should not be seen as a reason for legal uncertainty in *ṣukūk* markets because Islamic law has existent juristic difference rules that manage disagreements in Islamic law. It was shown that sharia non-compliance risk arises not only from the failure of IIFS to comply with Islamic law or rules provided by the relevant higher sharia authority but also arises when the sharia board changes its stand on legality of products. The latter is best illustrated by the following cases: *Investment Dar Company KSCC v. Blom Developments Bank SAL*,[1]

[1] [2009] EWHC 3545 (Ch).

National Ṣukūk Company v. Al-Madina Finance and Investment Company,[2] and Dana *Gas PJSC v. Dana Gas Sukuk Limited*.[3] The third method is concerned with moving towards standardisation and harmonisation of *ṣukūk* structures and regulations. The fourth method is related to the application of the decisions and guidelines on *ṣukūk* provided by international Islamic finance-supporting institutions, namely IIFA, AAOIFI, IFSB, and IIFM. The fifth method is related to the application of the conventional standards for securities regulation provided by IOSCO. It was demonstrated that such standards are beneficial for the operation of *ṣukūk* markets. The sixth method is concerned with enhancement of *ṣukūk* disclosure requirements. This method suggests that the nature of *ṣukūk* transactions entails special disclosure requirements, for example, type of *ṣukūk* structure, whether asset-backed or asset-based, and the basis of sharia endorsement.

This book has shown that developing sound *ṣukūk* markets presents opportunities as well as challenges. However, this research has raised further concerns in need of careful examination. Liquidity remains one of the main concerns in many *ṣukūk* markets.[4] As of 2011, 70% or more of *ṣukūk* were not traded in the secondary market, and therefore illiquidity threatened the majority of *ṣukūk* markets.[5] This raises question as to how liquidity can be created or increased in *ṣukūk* markets. Governments and financial regulators can create liquidity in *ṣukūk* markets by encouraging corporations to issue more *ṣukūk*.[6] In Bahrain, for example, the Liquidity Management Centre (LMC) introduced an open ended short term *ṣukūk* programme in 2004 to provide liquidity.[7]

Another challenge to the development of *ṣukūk* markets is the marketability of *ṣukūk*. There are several factors affecting *ṣukūk* marketability;

[2] Kuwaiti Court of Cassation, petition no 1895,1932,1933,1937/2011, judgment dated 19 June 2012.

[3] [2017] EWHC 2340 Comm.

[4] See, for example, S Parasher, 'Sukuk Industry Development in the Bahrain Capital Market' in M Arrif, M Iqbal and S Mohamad (eds), *The Islamic Debt Market for Sukuk Securities: The Theory and Practice of Profit Sharing Investment* (Edward Elger Publishing Limited 2012) 161; IFSB (ed) *Strategies for the Development of Islamic Capital Markets: Infrastructures and Legal Aspects of Islamic Asset Securitisation* (IFSB 2011) 228.

[5] M Safari, M Ariff and S Mohamad, *Sukuk Securities: New Ways of Debt Contracting* (Wiley & Sons 2014) 190.

[6] IFSB (ed) *Strategies for the Development of Islamic Capital Markets: Infrastructures and Legal Aspects of Islamic Asset Securitisation* (IFSB 2011) 228.

[7] See S Parasher, *supra* note 4, 161.

there are wide variations in listing procedure and disclosure requirements on different stock exchanges.[8] Also, marketability of *ṣukūk* is affected by the fact that *ṣukūk* are traditionally designed as wholesale securities, and therefore retail investors have no access to *ṣukūk* market.[9] Further, most trades in *ṣukūk* currently take place OTC and thus such *ṣukūk* are not known to the public or other investors.[10]

The development of a retail *ṣukūk* market remains a big challenge in many jurisdictions.[11] Investors in retail markets are in need of greater disclosure compared to investors in an institutional market. Investors in retail markets do not have the resources to analyse lengthy *ṣukūk*-offering circular, and they cannot draw their own conclusions from the documents provided.[12] The absence of 'practical jurisprudence on areas affecting investor's rights'[13] in many countries deters the extension of *ṣukūk* to the retail market.

Another challenge to the enhancement of the *ṣukūk* market is related to *ṣukūk* trading. The oft-quoted problem is that '*ṣukūk* are traded to only a very limited extent'.[14] This is justified, to some extent, by the tendency of *ṣukūk* holders to keep *ṣukūk* until maturity.[15] The lack of *ṣukūk* trading will impact on some regulatory issues in *ṣukūk* markets such as clearing, settlement, and market manipulation. Such issues become irrelevant to the regulators of *ṣukūk* markets since most *ṣukūk* are traded OTC.[16]

An important aspect of *ṣukūk* market development is concerned with deepening the *ṣukūk* market. Three main activities are needed to deepen the market: issuing various types and new structures of *ṣukūk*, issuing larger sizes of *ṣukūk*, and issuing longer-dated *ṣukūk*.[17] The best illustration of this issue is that one type of *ṣukūk* constitutes 80% of issues in the Malaysian market.[18] There has been little discussion of the possibility of economic crimes in *ṣukūk* markets, such as manipulation and insider dealing. New *ṣukūk* structures and new bases for returns are situations in which

[8] R Frankhauser, 'Listing Sukuk' in R Ali (ed), *Sukuk and Islamic Capital Markets* (Globe Business Publishing 2011) 91.

[9] Ibid. 92.

[10] Ibid.

[11] M Safari, M Ariff and S Mohamad, *supra* note 5, 153.

[12] Ibid.

[13] Ibid.

[14] Ibid. 142.

[15] Ibid.

[16] Ibid.

[17] Ibid. 157, 191.

[18] Ibid. 191.

manipulation and insider dealing could potentially take place in a *ṣukūk* market.[19] Offering longer-dated *ṣukūk* poses some structural and regulatory considerations; finding suitable assets for longer-dated *ṣukūk* (such as airports and highways) is far easier for governments than commercial entities.[20] Continuing sharia compliance is a critical topic in case of longer-term *ṣukūk* as a sharia-compliant issue at the time of issuance might become non-compliant later.[21]

Another challenge to the development of *ṣukūk* market is concerned with market supervision, as opposed to market regulation.[22] Due to the fact that most *ṣukūk* trading takes place OTC, including listed *ṣukūk*, issues related to settlement, clearing, and market manipulation are minimal.[23] Issues related to market supervision are mostly dealt with by ensuring a sufficient continuing disclosure regime.[24] Given that *ṣukūk* are less traded, the need for continuing disclosures is less prominent in *ṣukūk* issuers' mind.[25] There is also a concern that the exchanges that list *ṣukūk* do not enforce adequate and proper disclosure requirements because they have little incentive to enforce such market requirements.[26] *Ṣukūk* that are listed but not traded on the exchange result in less income for the exchange.[27]

Ṣukūk market enhancement is also challenged by the issue of dispute resolution in *ṣukūk* transactions. In a developed ICM, the need has been already stressed for an effective dispute resolution framework that takes into account both legal principles and sharia requirements.[28] Although litigation has been seen as a traditional approach to dispute resolutions in *ṣukūk* transactions,[29] it has limitations arising from the role of Islamic law in the judicial system of states and the competence of civil courts and

[19] Ibid. 156.
[20] Ibid. 157.
[21] Ibid.
[22] Ibid. 151.
[23] Ibid.
[24] Ibid.
[25] Ibid.
[26] Ibid.
[27] Ibid.
[28] U Oseni and K Hassan, 'The Dispute Resolution Framework for the Islamic Capital Markets in Malaysia: Legal Obstacles and Options' in K Hassan and M Mahlknecht (eds), *Islamic Capital Markets: Products and Strategies* (John Wiley & Sons 2011) 106.
[29] U Oseni and K Hassan, 'The Regulation and Supervision of Sukuk in Global Capital Markets' in K Hassan and M Lewis (eds), *Handbook on Islam and Economic Life* (Edward Elgar 2014) 404.

judges to decide on matters related to the IFSI. Mention has been already made of the difficulty of Islamic law to be a governing law of the Islamic financial transactions under the judicial systems. Therefore, other dispute resolution options such as arbitration, mediation, and expert determination may better deal with disputes arising from *ṣukūk* transactions.[30]

Enforcement and recognition of foreign judgements and arbitral awards are other hurdles in the development of *ṣukūk* markets. This concern has been already expressed by a number of *ṣukūk*-offering circulars, particularly in the GCC region.[31] In fact, there have been some instances in which the enforcement and recognition of foreign judgements and arbitral awards in the GCC region were not supported by the relevant legal frameworks. The position of the GCC countries towards the enforcement of judgements and awards varies from one country to another.[32] The enforcement and recognition of foreign judgements and awards are subject to a set of multilateral treaties, bilateral treaties, and domestic laws.[33] The significance of international and regional conventions in this context cannot be ignored, including the New York Convention on the Recognition and Enforcement of Foreign Arbitral Awards of 1958 (New York Convention), the Convention of Judicial Cooperation between States of the Arab League of 1983 (Riyadh Convention), and the Convention on the Settlement of Investment Disputes between States and Nationals of Other States 1965 (ICSID Convention). The enforcement of foreign judgements and awards has continued to be an issue in the context of sovereign *ṣukūk* despite the international conventions that have been introduced to remove this legal uncertainty.

Product enhancement is a key factor in the development of *ṣukūk* markets. Several problems regarding the structure of *ṣukūk* can be overcome by continuous efforts on product enhancement. It is important to note that the sharia-compliant nature of *ṣukūk* transactions might be affected by product enhancement processes, and therefore any enhancement efforts must ensure to not compromise this. One of the common problems is related to sovereign assets being the underlying assets of *ṣukūk* transactions. The nature of sovereign assets has incentivised sovereign

[30] Ibid. 405.

[31] Ibid.

[32] For more discussion on the legal frameworks for the enforcement of foreign judgements and awards in the GCC countries with the exception of Oman, see ibid. 410–411.

[33] See generally H Al Mulla, 'Conventions of Enforcement of Foreign Judgment in the Arab States' (1999) 14 Arab Law Quarterly 33.

ṣukūk to move from an asset-backed to asset-based structure. This is because sovereign countries do not want foreign investors to own their assets. This problem can be addressed by adopting the right of pre-emption (*ḥaq al-shufʿah*) as provided by the Islamic law.[34] The right of pre-emption gives the government, as one of the *ṣukūk* holders, the priority to buy the underlying assets from its counterparties at maturity.[35] Based on the right of pre-emption, *ṣukūk* holders cannot sell the assets in question to whomever they want as long as the government is interested in purchasing them.[36] There should not be a problem with regard to recognition and documentation of *ḥaq al-shufʿah* under the English legal system because *ḥaq al-shufʿah* is recognised under 'the right of first refusal'.[37]

The compliance issue is another challenge to the development of *ṣukūk* markets. While the issue of compliance has been dealt with extensively in the conventional financial industry, it has received little discussion in the context of the IFSI. In its literal meaning, the word compliance refers to the state of complying with or meeting rules and principles. In the absence of codification of Islamic law and standardisation of financial products in the IFSI, it is uncertain what the IFSI needs to comply with. The technical meaning of compliance in the context of the IFSI provides that any activity is required to follow two different sets of rules. First, the IFSI is required to meet the rules provided by the relevant legal and regulatory framework. The creation and operation of a *ṣukūk* market in a country is subject to the rules provided by the relevant regulator since it does not operate in a vacuum. Second, the IFSI is required to comply with Islamic law because the credibility of its activities and products rests on meeting the rules of Islamic law. This is a unique burden on the IFSI which increases the cost of compliance. Unlike its conventional counterpart, the IFSI is required to comply with the rules provided by both the relevant market regulator and Islamic law. Of course, both sets of rules present challenges depending on the jurisdiction in which the IFSI operates. While the requirement to comply with the relevant legal framework raises the issue of enforceability and choice of law, the requirement to meet with Islamic law raises several issues such as lack of standardisation, sharia non-compliance risk, and creative sharia

[34] Al-Amine, 'Unresolved Sharīʿah Issues in Ṣukūk' in Kamali M and Abdullah A (eds), *Islamic Finance: Issues in Ṣukūk and Proposals for Reform* (International Intitute of Advanced Islamic Studies and Islamic Foundation 2014) 51.

[35] Ibid.

[36] Ibid.

[37] Ibid.

compliance. Such issues are of course interrelated and eventually they will impact the sharia-compliant nature of financial transactions.

The issue of creative sharia compliance is one of the challenges facing *ṣukūk* markets. 'Creative sharia compliance' is a relatively new term in the context of the IFSI. It refers to the state or fact of Islamic financial products that meet Islamic law requirements in form but not in substance.[38] The issue of creative sharia compliance cannot be understood without reference to the form and substance debate in the IFSI and in particular the practice of using *ḥīlah* (legal ruse) to design financial products.[39] This is of particular significance to *ṣukūk* markets as some regard asset-based *ṣukūk* as a good illustration of form over substance transactions in the IFSI. Nevertheless, the issue of meeting the form and substance of Islamic law in the *ṣukūk* market has continued to be a challenge. In this regard, AAOIFI puts more emphasis on the role of the sharia boards and in particular their role on advising IIFS 'to decrease their involvements in debt-related operations and to increase true partnerships based on profit and loss sharing, in order to achieve the objectives of the sharia'.[40] There is a general consensus in the IFSI that transactions based on profit and loss sharing better represent the spirit and objectives of Islamic law. This implies that there should be more issuance of *mushārakah* and *muḍārabah* *ṣukūk* in the market.

Another challenge is the development of a sharia-compliant rating methodology for *ṣukūk*. The current *ṣukūk* rating system has been criticised on the grounds that it 'replicates conventional securities rating methodology, where the main focus is on credit-rating of the instrument but lesser or no consideration is given to the value of the physical assets in terms of sharia credibility'.[41] As a result, *ṣukūk* holders are usually informed about the issuer's creditworthiness, and not about the quality of the underlying assets.[42]

[38] See generally A Alkhamees, 'A Critique of Creative Shari'ah Compliance in the Islamic Finance Industry with Reference to the Kingdom of Saudi Arabia and the United Kingdom' (PhD Thesis, The University of Warwick 2014).

[39] See ibid. 41–72.

[40] AAOIFI, 'AAOIFI Shari'ah Resolutions: Issues on Sukuk' (*AAOIFI*, February 2008) 4. http://www.kantakji.com/media/7760/f173.pdf. Accessed 6 October 2014.

[41] S Yussof, 'Measuring Sharīʿah Compliance in Ṣukūk Ratings: A Survey of Existing Methodologies' in M Kamali and A Abdullah (eds), *Islamic Finance: Issues in Sukuk and Proposals for Reform* (International Institute of Advanced Islamic Studies and Islamic Foundation 2014) 96.

[42] Ibid.

It is suggested that *ṣukūk* rating methodology should focus on two factors: profitability of the *ṣukūk* and sharia compliance of the *ṣukūk*.[43] Disclosures of sharia non-compliance risks have gained more attention, particularly after default and near-default cases and the involvement of international investors who lack knowledge about the nature of such risks.[44] Therefore, Yossof argues that '[r]ating agencies need to give an independent opinion on the existence of a potential sharia non-compliance risk that can transform the *ṣukūk* into an unsecured investment to the detriment of investor'.[45] The establishment of the Islamic International Rating Agency (IIRA) in 2005, a specialised body in the rating of IIFS and Islamic financial products, is a welcome initiative. However, issuers of *ṣukūk* might be reluctant to obtain rating from the IIRA due to its less experience and reputation compared to the international rating agencies such as S&P.

A supportive Islamic financial system is very important to a well-functioning domestic market for *ṣukūk*.[46] This means *ṣukūk* markets cannot stand alone and work independently.[47] Efforts should focus, among others, on encouraging domestic and other investors to raise funds using Islamic financial instruments including *ṣukūk*.[48] Further, the growth of a *ṣukūk* market is linked with the growth of other segments in the domestic market such as Islamic banking and *takāful* (Islamic insurance) since they ensure ongoing demand for *ṣukūk* and other instruments.[49]

Several attempts have already been made to develop a domestic market for *ṣukūk* in many countries. Although the different development approaches are acceptable to some degree,[50] there is need to put in place general requirements and building blocks for the development of domestic markets for *ṣukūk*. These include, among other things, (1) a legal and regulatory framework; (2) money markets; (3) primary markets; (4) investor base; and (5) market infrastructure for clearing, settlement, and secondary markets.[51] Legal and regulatory framework refers to an enabling

[43] Ibid.
[44] Ibid. 97.
[45] Ibid.
[46] K Kusuma and A Silva, 'Policy Research Working Paper 7133: Sukuk Markets-A Proposed Approach for Development' (*WB*, December 2014) 10. http://www-wds.worldbank.org/external/default/WDSContentServer/WDSP/IB/2014/12/04/000158349_20141204142423/Rendered/PDF/WPS7133.pdf. Accessed 26 July 2015.
[47] Ibid.
[48] Ibid.
[49] Ibid.
[50] Ibid.
[51] Ibid. 11.

environment for *ṣukūk* that encompasses a set of regulations concerning the creation and operation of SPVs, insolvency, collateral security laws, sharia governance, the creation and operation of rating agencies, investment policies of institutional investors, participation of foreign investors, market valuation, post-trading reporting, and secondary market architecture.[52] Money markets manage the short-term liquidity for financial institutions in which *ṣukūk* can be used.[53] As for the primary market, it should not have policies and procedures that do not place *ṣukūk* on a level playing field with other instruments.[54] Common concerns in the primary market are related to offering mechanisms, disclosure requirements, approval procedures, tax treatment, duration, and cost.[55] A diversified base of investors is required to provide sustainable demand for *ṣukūk* in the domestic market.[56] Advanced clearing and settlement procedures are essential to ensure effective participation of a wide range of investors and minimise the risk of settlement failures.[57]

The above-mentioned building blocks are of particular significance to countries that are considering or implementing legislative reforms to facilitate the issuance of *ṣukūk*. Such legislative reforms have taken place not only in Islamic jurisdictions, but also in conventional jurisdictions. The best example of this is the UK; in November 2007, HM Treasury and Debt Management Office published a feasibility study on the potential of the UK government to become an issuer of sovereign *ṣukūk*.[58] The study identified three main structuring issues that need to be looked at before issuing *ṣukūk* which are: (1) the need for primary legislation, (2) the identification of assets owned by the government, and (3) the taxation treatment of the assets transfer.[59] In response to the feasibility study, the UK

[52] Ibid. 11–12.

[53] Ibid. 12.

[54] Ibid. 13.

[55] Ibid. 13–14. For example, *ṣukūk* generally attracts more taxes compared to conventional bonds. The dual transfer of the underlying asset in *ijārah ṣukūk* attracts double property transfer tax. Without tax accommodation to *ṣukūk*, the cost of offering *ṣukūk* will be high. See, generally, B Rider, 'Legal Aspects of Islamic Asset Securitisation' in IFSB (ed), *Strategies for the Development of Islamic Capital Markets: Infrastructures and Legal Aspects of Islamic Asset Securitisation* (IFSB 2011) 177–181.

[56] K Kusuma and A Silva, *supra* note 46, 14.

[57] Ibid. 15.

[58] HM Treasury and Debt Management Office, 'Government Sterling Sukuk Issuance: A Consultation' (*HM Treasury*, November 2007). http://www.dmo.gov.uk/docs/publications/giltsmarket/consultationpapers/cons141107.pdf. Accessed 3 September 2015.

[59] Ibid. 4.

government issued a report in June 2008 which shows that the 'vast majority of responses to the consultation were supportive of the Government's feasibility study into potential *ṣukūk* issuance'.[60] The UK government's facilitation of *ṣukūk* issuances is best illustrated by a set of reforms to the taxation of *ṣukūk* introduced by the government after 2006.[61] For instance, the legislative reform excludes *ṣukūk* from the application of tax provisions related to trusts or collective investment schemes.[62]

Perhaps the most significant issue with regard to the development of *ṣukūk* markets is the role of international institutions. In this book, there has been discussion of the relevance of both international institutions supporting the IFSI such as AAOIFI and IFSB, and international institutions supporting the conventional financial industry such as IOSCO. However, the discussion has focused on the relevance of their standards and guiding principles to *ṣukūk* markets. There is need to focus on the role of the international institutions in promoting *ṣukūk* and setting new benchmarks for issuers around the world. In this respect, the important role of the IILM cannot be ignored. Established by central banks, monetary authorities, and multilateral organisations in 2010, IILM aims to facilitate cross-border Islamic liquidity management by creating and issuing sharia-compliant financial instruments that are short term in nature. In addition to hosting the IFSB, Malaysia hosts IILM. It is a unique institution in the IFSI and there is no institution equivalent to IILM in the conventional financial industry. The issuance of IILM's inaugural *ṣukūk* of USD 490 million in August 2013 has taken the market by surprise.[63] This issuance has been given an A-1 rating by S&P and was fully subscribed.[64] The 'IILM *Ṣukūk*' deserves special attention due to their unique features. These are: (1) tradable sharia-compliant financial instrument, (2) US dollar-denominated financial instrument, (3) short-term financial instrument (issued at maturities of up to one year), (4) money market instruments backed by sovereign assets, (5) distributed and tradable internationally by primary dealers,

[60] HM Treasury and Debt Management Office, 'Government Sterling Sukuk Issuance: A Response to the Consultation' (*HM Treasury*, June 2008) 5. http://webarchive.nationalarchives.gov.uk/+/http://www.hm-treasury.gov.uk/d/consult_sukukresponses020608.pdf. Accessed 3 September 2015.

[61] See ibid. 31–32.

[62] Ibid. 32.

[63] IILM, 'The Inaugural Issuance' (*IILM*, 2015). http://www.iilm.com/the-inaugural-issuance/. Accessed 14 September 2015.

[64] Ibid.

and (6) having strong global support since they result from a unique cooperation between central banks and multilateral development organisation.[65] The fact that IILM *Ṣukūk* are issued based on sovereign assets proves how such *ṣukūk* dealt with some issues in regard to the reluctance of governments to sell their assets to the SPV and foreign ownership. It seems that the beneficial ownership issue in *ṣukūk* is not problematic for the IILM sharia committee. The sale of sovereign assets to the SPV cannot be achieved without the notion of beneficial ownership. The IILM *Ṣukūk* are good illustrations of how the shortcomings of contemporary *ṣukūk* can be overcome, providing evidence of the continued evolution of Islamic financial instruments in an increasingly globalised IFSI.

[65] IILM, 'The Features of the IILM Sukūk' (*IILM*, 2015). http://www.iilm.com/the-features-of-the-iilm-suk%C5%ABk/. Accessed 14 September 2015.

GLOSSARY

For the sake of consistency, the process of transliterating the text from Arabic into English throughout the book has been undertaken by utilising ROTAS (Roman Transliteration of Arabic Script), a utility application that transliterates Arabic words into the Roman script. All Arabic words have been transliterated and italicised except those which have become part of the English language according to the *Oxford English Dictionary* such as sharia, Quran, and Sunna. Arabic words within titles of books, articles, and other types of sources have been kept as they are.[1]

A	
Aqwāl al-ṣaḥābah	sayings of the companions
B	
Bayʿ al-dayn	sale of debt
Buyʿ ul-ʿĪnuh	sale and buy-back
Bayʿal-maʿdūm	sale of non-existent asset
Bayʿ bithaman ʾājil	deferred payment sale
Baytu al-māl	State Treasury

(*continued*)

[1] Translation of the Quran into the English language provided by King Fahd Complex for the Printing of the Holy Quran has been used throughout this book. Some texts from *Ṣaḥīḥ Muslim* have been referred to in this book based on English translation provided by University of Sourthern California.

S. Al-Ali, *Raising Capital on* Ṣukūk *Markets*,
https://doi.org/10.1007/978-3-030-14536-1

(continued)

D	
Dhikru al-ḥaq	right mentioning
Ḍarūrah	necessity
F	
Fiqh	Literally understanding; Islamic law or Islamic jurisprudence
Fiqh al-muᶜāmalāt	Islamic financial law
G	
Gharar	uncertainty
H	
Hadith	report of the words and deeds of the Prophet Muḥammad (peace be upon him)
Ḥajr	interdiction
Halāk	damage
Ḥanafī school	school of Islamic law whose origins are attributed to Abū Ḥanīfah Al-Nuᶜmān in Kufa, Iraq, in eighth century.
Ḥanbali school	school of Islamic law whose origins are attributed to Aḥmad Bin Ḥanbal in ninth century.
Ḥaq al-shufᶜah	right of pre-emption
ḥīlah	legal ruse
Ḥiwālah	transfer of debt or assignment of debt
I	
Ijārah	lease
Ijārah muntahiyah biāltamlīk	operating lease of property
Ijmāᶜ	consensus
Ijtihād	scholarly endeavour
Ishām	securitisation of a ready stream of revenue
Istiḥsān	equity or juristic preference
Istighlāl	cash *waqf*
Istiṣḥāb	presumption of continuity
Istiṣnāᶜ	contract of manufacture
K	
Khasārah	loss
Khilāf fiqhī	juristic difference
Khiyār al-ᶜayb	option of defect
M	
Madhhab	legal school of Islamic law
Māl	property
Māl mutaqawam	property of value
Mālikī school	school of Islamic law attributed to Mālik Bin Anas in the eighth century in the Arabian Peninsula
Maqāṣid	objectives

(*continued*)

(continued)

Maṣlaḥah mursalah	considerations of public interest
Milk naqis	incomplete ownership
Miʿyār al-tabaʿiah	dependency standard
Miʿyār al-aghlabiah	majority standard
Muḍārabah	investment partnership
Muḍārib	investment manager
Mughārasah	agricultural
Mulzim diyānah	religiously (morally) binding
Mulzim qaḍāʾ	legally binding
Murābaḥah	a sale with a mark-up
Musāqāh	irrigation
Mushārakah	participation financing
Muwāʿadah	bilateral undertaking
Muzāraʿah	sharecropping
Q	
Qarḍ ḥasan	interest-free loan
Qimār	gambling
Qiyās	analogical reasoning
Quran	the book of Islamic revelation, scripture
R	
Ribā	usury
Ribā al-buyūʿ	*ribā* occurring through sale of *ribawi* products
Ribawi	*Ribā*-based
S	
Sad al-dhārāʾiʿ	blocking the means
Saḥīḥ Muslim	one of the six canonical collections of Hadith
Ṣaḥābi	companion
Salam	a forward sale (fungible commodity)
Sanadāt	bonds
ʿsār	difficulty
Sarf	exchange of money
Shāafiʿī school	school of Islamic Law founded by Muḥammad Al-Shāfiʿi in the eighth century in Iraq and Egypt
Sharikah al-ʿinān	contractual partnership
Sharʿ man qablanā	revealed laws preceding the sharia
Sharia	divine revelation found in the Quran and Sunna
Sharīk	partner
Shia	The followers, or party of Ali, believe that Muhammad's religious leadership and divine guidance were passed on his descendants, ʿalī Bin Abī Ṭālib, and his sons
Ṣukūk	trust investment certificates
Sunna	the sayings and doings of the Prophet Muḥammad (peace be upon him), the second source of Islamic law

(*continued*)

(continued)

Sunni	The largest branch of the Muslim community. The name derived from the Sunna, the exemplary behaviour of the Prophet
T	
Taflīs	insolvency
Takāful	Islamic insurance
Taṣfiyah	clearness
Tawarruq	sale and resale transaction used to generate cash
U	
ʿurf	custom
W	
Waʿd	unilateral undertaking or promise
Waʿad mulzim	binding promise
Wakālah	agency; investment contract in which agent represents investor(s)
Wakālah biālistithmār	investment agency
Wakīl	agent
Waqf	charitable endowment
Z	
Ẓāhirī school	school of Islamic law founded by Dāwūd al-Ẓāhiri in the ninth century

Bibliography

AAOIFI, 'AAOIFI Shari'ah Resolutions: Issues on Sukuk' (*AAOIFI*, February 2008). http://www.kantakji.com/media/7760/f173.pdf. Accessed 6 October 2014.

———, 'About AAOIFI' (*AAOIFI*, undated-a). http://www.aaoifi.com/en/about-aaoifi/about-aaoifi.html. Accessed 30 September 2015.

———, *Accounting, Auditing and Governance Standards for Islamic Financial Institutions 1432H-2010* (AAOIFI 2004).

———, 'Al-Ḥuqūq Al-Māliah Wa Al-Taṣaruf Fīhā' (*AAOIFI*, undated-b). http://www.kantakji.com/media/9219/42ife.pdf. Accessed 7 Novermber 2014.

———, *Shari'a Standards for Islamic Financial Institutions* (AAOIFI 2010).

Abbasi M, 'The Classical Islamic Law of Waqf: A Concise Introduction' (2012) 26 Arab Law Quarterly 121.

Abdel-Khaleq A and Richardson C, 'New Horizons for Islamic Securities: Emerging Trends in Sukuk Offerings' (2007) 7 Chicago Journal of International Law 409.

Abdelhady H, 'Islamic Law in Secular Courts (Agian)' (2010) 27 GPSOLO Magazine.

———, 'Islamic Law in Secular Courts (Agian): Teachable Moments from the Journey' (2009) 4 International Law News.

Abdul Aziz R, 'Sukuk Have Lost A Lot Of Credibility Of Late. Is This Justified? Did We Get It Wrong? How Do We Fix It? What Are The Alternatives To Sukuk?' (2010) 1 So Far: The Journal Of Strategic Thinking In Islamic Finance 6.

Abdul Jabbar S, 'Investor Protection in the Islamic Financial Services Industry' (PhD Thesis, University of London 2010).

S. Al-Ali, *Raising Capital on* Ṣukūk *Markets*,
https://doi.org/10.1007/978-3-030-14536-1

Abdullah D, 'Liquidity Management in Institutions Offering Islamic Financial Services' (Addressing Liquidity Management Challenges to Enhance the Financial Stability of the Islamic Financial Services Industry, KSA, December 2010).

Abdullah D and Chee K, *Islamic Finance: Why it Makes Sense* (Marshall Cavendish Business 2010).

Abdullah H and Ismail R, 'Sukuk under Development' (*IFLR*, 2009). http://www.iflr.com/Article/2283704/Sukuk-under-development.html. Accessed 6 January 2013.

Adam N and Thomas A (eds), *Islamic Bonds: Your Guide to Issuing, Structuring and Investing in Sukuk* (Euromoney Books 2004).

Admas J, 'Opening Remarks to the Roundtable Discussion' in IFSB and WB (eds), *Effective Insolvency Regimes: Institutional, Regulatory, and Legal Issues Relating to Islamic Finance* (IFSB and WB 2011).

Ahmad A, 'Islamic Modes of Finance and the Role of Sukuk' in Authority QFC (ed), *Islamic Finance: Instruments and Markets* (Bloomsbury Information Ltd 2010).

Ahmad H, *Products Development in Islamic Finance* (Edinburgh University Press 2011).

Ahmad N and Wahab N, 'Estimates of Distance-To-Default (DTD) Risk Indicator for Selected Sukuk in Malaysia' (3rd International Conference on Business and Economic Research, Indonesia, March 2012).

Ahmad S and Rajasingham R, 'IDE Asian Law Series No. 4: The Malaysian Legal System, Legal Practice and Legal Education' (*Institute of Developing Economies*, 2001). http://www.ide-jetro.jp/English/Publish/Download/Als/pdf/04.pdf. Accessed 23 August 2015.

Ahmed E, Islam A and Alabdullah T, 'Islamic Sukuk: Pricing Mechanism and Rating' (2014) 4 Journal of Asian Scientific Research 640.

Ahmed H, 'Islamic Finance at a Crossroads: The Dominance of the Asset-Based Sukuk' (2010) 6 Journal of International Banking and Financial Law 366.

———, 'Islamic Law, Investors' Rights and Corporate Finance' (2012) 12 Journal of Corporate Law Studies 367.

Ainley M and others, 'Islamic Finance in the UK: Regulation and Challenges' (*FSA*, 2007). http://www.fsa.gov.uk/pubs/other/islamic_finance.pdf. Accessed 7 April 2015.

Akhtar Z, 'Stakeholding in Sharia Compliant Assets and Investor Protection' (2011) 7 Journal of International Banking and Regulation 362.

Al-Amine M, *Global Sukuk and Islamic Securitization Market: Financial Engineering and Product Innovation* (Brill 2012).

Al Ansari R and Mohamed S, 'Thomson Reuters *Ṣukūk* Market Outlook 2018', (Thomson Reuters 2018) 2.

Al Ansari R and Others, 'Sukuk Perceptions & Forecast Study 2017', (Thomson Reuters 2017).

———, 'Unresolved Sharīʿah Issues in Ṣukūk' in Kamali M and Abdullah A (eds), *Islamic Finance: Issues in Ṣukūk and Proposals for Reform* (International Intitute of Advanced Islamic Studies and Islamic Foundation 2014).

Al-Damāgh Z, *Al-Ṣukūk Al-Islāmiah wa Dawrahā fī Al-Tanmiyah Al-Iqtiṣādiah* (Dār Al-Thaqāfah Lil-Nashr 2012).

Al-Manṣūr A, *Iflāsu Al-Sharikāti wa Atharuhu fī Al-Fiqhi wa Al-Niẓām*, vol 1 (1st edn, Dār Kunūz Ishbīlā Lil-Nashr Wa Al-Tawzīʿ 2012).

Al-Muhairi B, 'The Development of the UAE Legal System and Unification with the Judicial System' (1996) 11 Arab Law Quarterly 116.

Al-Nawawī Y, *Ṣaḥīḥ Muslim Bisharḥ Al-Nawawī*, vol 10 (Dār Iḥyā' Al-Turāth Al-ʿaraby 1392).

Al-Rimawi L, *Raising Capital on Arab Equity Markets: Legal and Juridical Aspects of Arab Securities Regulation* (Kluwer Law International 2012).

Al-Salem F, 'Islamic Financial Product Innovation' (2009) 2 International Journal of Islamic and Middle Eastern Finance and Management 187.

Al-Sheaibi M, 'Derivatives and Sukuk in the Islamic Capital Market' in Thomas A (ed), *Sukuk* (Sweet & Maxwell Asia 2009).

———, 'Insolvency Regimes: Regulatory, Institutional and Legal Challenges in Islamic Finance in Saudi Arabia' in IFSB and WB (eds), *Effective Insolvency Regimes: Institutional, Regulatory, and Legal Issues Relating to Islamic Finance* (IFSB and WB 2011).

Al-Suwailem S, *Hedging in Islamic Finance* (Islamic Development Bank 2006).

Al-ʿuthmānī M, 'Sukuk and Their Contemporary Applications' (*Islamic Economics and Finance Pedia*, Undated). http://www.iefpedia.com/english/wp-content/uploads/2009/11/Sukuk-and-their-Contemporary-Applications.pdf. Accessed 15 February 2012.

Al-Zuhayli W, *Financial Transactions in Islamic Jurisprudence* (El-Gamal M tr, 2nd edn, Dar Al-Fikr 2007).

Al Elsheikh A and Tanega J, 'Sukuk Structure and its Regulatory Environment in the Kingdom of Saudi Arabia' (2011) Law and Financial Markets Review 183.

Al Hamidani B, 'The New Court System in Saudi Arabia' (*Al Tamimi & Co.*, May 2014). http://www.tamimi.com/en/magazine/law-update/section-8/may-7/the-new-court-system-in-saudi-arabia.html. Accessed 28 August 2015.

Al Mulla H, 'Conventions of Enforcement of Foreign Judgment in the Arab States' (1999) 14 Arab Law Quarterly 33.

Alamsyah H, 'Lender of Last Resort in Islamic Banking' (Fourth Islamic Financial Stability Forum: Strengthening Financial Safety Nets in the Islamic Financial Services Industry, Malaysia, November 2011).

Alarabiya, 'Al-Sālim Yarud ʿalā Al-Muṣliḥ: Al-Ribā Lā Yajrī Fī Al-Wrāq Al-Naqdiyyah ʿind Al-Madhāhib Al-Arbaʿah' (*Alarabiya*, 2011). http://www.alarabiya.net/articles/2011/08/20/163226.html. Accessed 30 March 2015.

Aldohni A, 'The Challenge of Islamic Banking Disputes in the English Courts: The Applied Law' (2009) 24 Journal of International Banking & Financial Law 350.

Algari M, 'Taṭbīq Al-Mulkiyyah Al-Naf'iyyah Wa Al-Mulkiyyah Al-Qānūniyyah Fī Al-Tamwīl Al-Islāmī' (Contemporary Issues in the Application of Islamic Finance: Benefical and Legal Ownership and Takaful in Light of the Islamic Concept of Cooperation, Malalysia, November 2014).

Ali E, 'Issues in Islamic Debt Securitisation' in Bakar M and Ali E (eds), *Essential Readings in Islamic Finance* (CERT Publications 2008).

Ali M, 'Ṣukūk: Perception, Innovation and Challenges' in Kamali M and Abdullah A (eds), *Islamic Finance: Issues in Sukuk and Proposals for Reform* (International Institute of Advanced Islamic Studies and Islamic Foundation 2014).

Ali R, 'Legal Certainty for Sukuk' in Thomas A (ed), *Sukuk* (Sweet & Maxwell Asia 2009).

———, 'An Overview of the Sukuk Market' in Ali R (ed), *Sukuk and Islamic Capital Markets: A Practical Guide* (Globe Business Publishing 2011).

Ali R and Mufti I, 'Legal and Structural Anatomy of a Sukuk' in Ali R (ed), *Sukuk and Islamic Capital Markets* (Globe Business Publishing 2011).

Alim E (ed) *Ṣukūk Perceptions and Forecast Study 2014* (Thomson Reuters 2013).

Aljazeera, 'Majma' Al-Fiqh Al-Islāmī Yastankir Fatwā Jawāz Fawāid Al-Bunūk' (*Aljazeera*, 2003). www.aljazeera.net/News/archive/archive?ArchiveId=46677. Accessed 30 March 2015.

Alkhamees A, 'A Critique of Creative Shari'ah Compliance in the Islamic Finance Industry with Reference to the Kingdom of Saudi Arabia and the United Kingdom' (PhD Thesis, The University of Warwick 2014).

———, 'The Impact of Shari'ah Governance Practices on Shari'ah Compliance in Contemporary Islamic Finance' (2012) Journal of Banking Regulation 1.

Allen H, 'What is Financial Stability? The Need for Some Common Language in International Financial Regulation' (2014) 45 Georgetown Journal of International Law 929.

Allen W and Wood G, 'Special Paper No 160: Defining and Achieving Financial Stability' (*LSE*, April 2005). http://www.lse.ac.uk/fmg/documents/specialPapers/2005/sp160.pdf. Accessed 18 March 2015.

Alsaeed K, 'Sukuk Issuance in Saudi Arabia: Recent Trends and Positive Expectations' (PhD Thesis, Durham University 2012).

Alvi L, 'Commentary One' in IFSB, IOSCO and SC (eds), *Disclosure Requirements of Islamic Capital Market Products* (IFSB, IOSCO and SC 2013).

Amin H, 'An Analysis of the Classical and Contemporary Juristic Opinions on Bay Al-Dayn' (2007) 1 Labuan e-Journal of Muamalat and Society 31.

Amri M, 'Bond Pricing Practices in the Sukuk Market' in Arrif M, Iqbal M and Mohamad S (eds), *The Islamic Debt Market for Sukuk Securities: The Theory and Practice of Profit Sharing Investment* (Edward Elgar 2012).

Anwar H, 'Saad's Islamic Bonds Priced for 'Default,' ING Says (Update2)' (*Bloomberg*, 11 June 2009). http://www.bloomberg.com/apps/news?pid=newsarchive&sid=akDBpOPBtkkg. Accessed 21 December 2013.

Anwar H and Patterson M, 'Aston Martin Owner Is First to Default on Gulf Sukuk (Update3)' (*Bloomberg*, 12 May 2009). http://www.bloomberg.com/apps/news?pid=newsarchive&sid=aiqILW051D9c. Accessed 21 December 2013.

AOSSG, 'AOSSG Survey: Accounting and Islamic Finance in the Middle East and North Africa' (*AOSSG*, November 2013). http://aossg.org/docs/Publications/AOSSG_MENA_Islamic_Finance_Survey%20Findings_Nov_2013.pdf. Accessed 6 March 2015.

———, 'AOSSG Survey: Accounting for Islamic Financial Transactions and Entities' (*ASB*, December 2011). https://www.asb.or.jp/asb/asb_e/aossg/pressrelease_20120110_01_e.pdf. Accessed 6 March 2015.

Ariff M, Iqbal M and Mohamad S (eds), *The Islamic Debt Market for Sukuk Securities: The Theory and Practice of Profit Sharing Investment* (Edward Elgar 2012).

Arrif M, Iqbal M and Mohamad S, 'Introduction to Sukuk Debt Securities Markets' in Arrif M, Iqbal M and Mohamad S (eds), *The Islamic Debt Market for Sukuk Securities: The Theory and Practice of Profit Sharing Investment* (Edward Elgar 2012).

Askari H, Iqbal Z and Mirakhor A, *New Issues in Islamic Finance and Economics: Progress and Challenges* (John Wiley & Sons 2009).

Atkins T, 'Amlak, Tamweel to Merge into Real Estate Bank' (*Reuters*, 22 November 2008). http://www.reuters.com/article/2008/11/23/amlak-tamweel-idUSLN3963882008l123. Accessed 22 December 2013.

Avgouleas E, *The Mechanics and Regulation of Market Abuse: a Legal and Economic Analysis* (Oxford University Press 2005).

Awad A and Michael R, 'Iflas and Chapter 11: Classical Islamic Law and Modren Bankruptcy' (2010) 44 The International Lawyer 975.

Ayub M, *Understanding Islamic Finance* (John Wily & Sons Ltd 2007).

Azhar M and Haider J, 'Islamic Capital Market: Sukuk and its Risk Management in the Current Scenario' (Master Thesis, Umea University 2010).

Azmi M, 'The Importance of Strong Disclosure Regime in Facilitating Cross-Boarder Investments and Development of Islamic Capital Market Products and Services' in IFSB, IOSCO and SC (eds), *Disclosure Requirements for Islamic Capital Market Products* (IFSB, IOSCO and SC 2013).

Badr G, 'Islamic Law: Its Relation to Other Legal Systems' (1978) 26 The American Juornal of Comparative Law 187.

Bahrain Monetary Agency (ed) *Islamic Banking and Finance in the Kingdom of Bahrain* (Bahrain Monetary Agency 2002).

Bakar M, 'Contract in Islamic Commercial Law and Their Application in Modren Islamic Financial System' in Bakar M and Ali E (eds), *Essential Readings in Islamic Finance* (CERT Publications 2008a).

———, 'Developing Modern Islamic Financial System via Ijtihad: an Overview' in Bakar M and Ali E (eds), *Essential Readings in Islamic Finance* (CERT Publications 2008b).

———, 'Restructuring Of Sukuk: A Shariah Perspective' (*Amanie i-Connect*, 16 May 2012). http://www.amanie-iconnect.com/component/k2/item/10-restructuring-of-sukuk-a-shariah-perspective. Accessed 10 November 2014.

———, 'Riba and Islamic Banking and Finance' in Bakar M and Ali E (eds), *Essentail Readings in Islamic Finance* (CERT Publications 2008c).

———, 'The Shari'a Supervisory Board and Issues of Shari'a Rulings and their Harmonisation in Islamic Banking and Finance' in Archer S and Abdel Karim R (eds), *Islamic Finance: Innovation and Growth* (Euromoeny and AAOIFI 2002).

———, 'Shari'ah Approaches to Product Development and Product Enhancement in Islamic Banking and Finance: An Appraisal' in Bakar M and Ali E (eds), *Essential Readings in Islamic Finance* (CERT Publications 2008d).

Balala M, *Islamic Finance and Law: Theory and Practice in Globalized World* (I.B. Tauris 2015).

Barbour D, Norton J and Slover T, 'Asset Securitisation in Emerging Market Economics: Fundamentals Considerations' (1997) Yearbook of International Financial and Financial Law 281.

Basel Committee on Banking and Supervision, 'Asset Transfers and Securitisation' (*BIS*, 1992). http://www.bis.org/publ/bcbs10a.pdf. Accessed 14 May 2013.

Baudistel K, 'Bankruptcy-Remote Special Purpose Entities: An Opportunity for Investors to Maximize The Value of Their Returns While Undergoing More Careful dnd Realistic Risk Analysis' (2013) 86 Southern California Law Review 1309.

Beach J, 'The Saudi Arabian Capital Market Law: A Practical Study of the Creation of Law in Developing Markets' (2005) 41 Stanford Journal of International Law 307.

Bemo Securitisation SAL, 'East Cameron Gas Sukuk: A New Sukuk Innovation Comes to Market' (*Securitization*, 19 June 2006). http://www.securitization.net/pdf/content/BSEC_19Jun06.pdf. Accessed 9 December 2013.

Bennett M and Iqbal Z, 'The Role of Sukuk in Meeting Global Development Challenges' in Jaffer S (ed), *Global Growth, Opportunities and Challenges in the Sukuk Market* (1 edn, Euromoney Trading Inc 2011).

Bin Al-Mundhir M, *Al-Ijmāʿ* (Dār Al-Muslim Lil-Nashr Wa Al-Tawziʿ 2004).

Bin Manẓūr M, *Lisān Al-ʿarab*, vol 10 (1 edn, Dār Ṣādir Undated).

Bin Taymiyah A, *Raf Al-Malām ʿan Al-Aʾimmah Al-Aʿlām* (Al-Riʾāsah Al-ʿāmmah Liidārāt Al-Buḥūth Al-ʿilmiyyah Wa-Al-Iftā Wa-Al-Daʿwah Wa-Al-Irshād 1992).

BNM, *Financial Sector Blueprint 2011–2020* (BNM 2011a).

———, *Financial Sector Masterplan* (BNM 2001).

———, 'Financial Stability and Payment Systems Report 2010' (*BNM*, 2011b). http://www.bnm.gov.my/files/publication/fsps/en/2010/fs2010_book.pdf. Accessed 30 January 2014.

———, 'Financial Stability and Payment Systems Report 2012' (*BNM*, 2013). http://www.bnm.gov.my/files/publication/fsps/en/2012/fs2012_book.pdf. Accessed 29 January 2014.

———, 'Information: About IIMM' (*BNM*, Undated). http://iimm.bnm.gov.my/index.php?ch=4&pg=4&ac=22#3. Accessed 12 December 2012.

———, *Shariah Resolutions in Islamic Finance* (BNM 2010).

———, 'Speeches and Interviews' (*BNM*, 10 March 2009). http://www.bnm.gov.my/index.php?ch=9&pg=15&ac=268. Accessed 6 June 2014.

BNM and SC, *Malaysian Debt Securities and Sukuk Market: A Guide for Issuers and Investors* (BNM and SC 2009).

Board J, 'Development of Islamic Capital Markets' in IFSB (ed), *Strategies for the Development of Islamic Capital Markets: Infrastructures and Legal Aspects of Islamic Asset Securitisation* (IFSB 2011).

Bonderman D, 'Modernization and Changing Perceptions of Islamic law' (1968) 81 Harvard Law Review 1169.

Bouheraoua S and others, 'Shariah Issues in Intangible Assets' (Innovation and Financial Engineering Products and Applications: Between the Conventional and Islamic Finance Industries, Algeria, May 2014).

Bouheraoua S, Sairally B and Hasan S, 'A Critical Appraisal of Sharīʿah Issues Related to Ṣukūk Al-Ijārah' (2012) 4 ISRA International Journal of Islamic Finance 167.

Bursa Malaysia, 'Shariah Committee' (*Bursa Malaysia*, 2014). http://www.bursamalaysia.com/market/islamic-markets/shariah-committee/. Accessed 17 February 2014.

Cakir S and Raei F, 'IMF Working Paper WP/07/237: Sukuk vs. Eurobonds: Is There a Difference in Value-at-Risk?' (2007). https://www.imf.org/external/pubs/ft/wp/2007/wp07237.pdf. Accessed 1 December 2012.

Campbell A and Campbell E, 'The Courts of the Dubai International Financial Centre' (2012) 1 Journal of International Banking Law and Regulation 12.

Campbell A and Cartwright P, *Banks in Crisis: The Legal Response* (Ashgate Publishing 2002).

Carballo A, 'The Law of the Dubai International Financial Centre: Common Law Oasis or Mirage Within the UAE?' (2007) 21 Arab Law Quarterly 91.

Casey P, 'Emerging Issues From Inadequate Disclosure Requirements for Islamic Capital Market Products' in IFSB, IOSCO and SC (eds), *Disclosure Requirements for Islamic Capital Market Products* (IFSB, IOSCO, SC 2013).

Chand E, 'Islamic Banking: New Higher Sharia Authority set up' (emiratesnews247, 2018). http://www.emiratesnews247.com/islamic-banking-new-higher-sharia-authority-set/. Accessed 25 December 2018.

Chand E and Wam, 'Dubai-World Capital of Islamic Economy: Initiative Unveiled' (*Emirates 24/7 News*, 5 October 2013). http://www.emirates247.com/news/dubai-world-capital-of-islamic-economy-initiative-unveiled-2013-10-05-1.523457. Accessed 16 August 2015.

Čihák M, 'IMF Working Paper WP/06/163: How Do Central Banks Write on Financial Stability?' (*IMF*, June 2006). http://www.imf.org/external/pubs/ft/wp/2006/wp06163.pdf. Accessed 10 June 2012.

Cizakca M, 'Domestic Borrowing without the Rate of Interest: Gharar and the Origins of Sukuk' (Symposium on Sukuk Financial Instruments, Dubai, May 2010).

Colon J, 'Choice of Law and Islamic Finance' (2011) 46 Texas International Law Journal.

Cooch G and Williams M, *Oxford Dictionary of Law Enforcement* (Oxford University Press 2007).

Cosentino S, 'Swimming in New Waters-Bank Participation in Securitized Loan Pools' (1997) 65 UMKC Law Review 543.

Cox S, 'The Role of Capital Markets in Ensuring Islamic Financial Liquidity' in Archer S and Abdel Karim R (eds), *Islamic Finance: The Regulatory Challenge* (John Wiley & Sons 2007).

Crane R, 'The Essence of Islamic law' (1998) 3 The Journal of Islamic Law 185.

Dar H and Azmi T (eds), *Global Islamic Finance Report 2011* (BMB Islamic UK Ltd 2011).

Dar H, Rahman R and Malik R (eds), *Global Islamic Finance Report* (Ebdiz Consulting 2014).

DeLorenzo Y, 'Shari'ah Compliance Risk' (2007) 7 Chicago Journal of International Law 397.

Dey D and Others, 'Dana Gas Sukuk: A red Herring or Cause for Concern' (*White & Case*, 2017). https://www.whitecase.com/publications/alert/dana-gas-sukuk-red-herring-or-cause-concern. Accessed 4 January 2019.

Dey D and Ure S, 'Islamic Securitisation' in Ali R (ed), *Sukuk and Islamic Capital Markets* (Globe Business Publishing 2011).

DFM Fatwa and the Sharia Supervisory Board, 'DFM Standard for Issuing, Acquiring and Trading Ṣukūk' (*DFM*, 2014). http://www.dfm.ae/documents/sukuk/DFMSukukStandardFinalEn3032014.pdf. Accessed 28 September 2015.

DFSA, 'The DFSA's Approach to Regulating Islamic Finance in the DIFC' (*DFSA*, undated). http://www.dfsa.ae/Documents/Islamic%20finance%20docs%20for%20upload/DFSA's%20approach%20to%20regulating%20Islamic%20finance.pdf. Accessed 17 August 2015.

Dhabaan & Partners, 'Report to Cambridge Regional College on Legal Issues Around Operating in Saudi Arabia' (*Cambridge Regional College*, 8 November 2013). http://www.camre.ac.uk/wp-content/uploads/2013/12/Eversheds-advice-on-Saudi-Arabia.pdf. Accessed 28 August 2015.

Diaz-Granados R, 'A Comparative Approach to Securitization in the United States, Japan, Germany, and France' (1996) 4 Willamette Bulletin of International Law and Policy 1.

DIEDC, 'DIEDC' (*DIEDC*, undated-a). http://www.iedcdubai.ae/index. Accessed 18 August 2015.

———, 'Dubai Global Sukuk Centre' (*DIEDC*, undated-b). http://www.iedcdubai.ae/initiatives/dubai_global_sukuk_centre. Accessed 18 August 2015.

DIFC, Clifford Chance and Amani Consulting, *Dubai International Financial Centre: Sukuk Guidebook* (DIFC 2009).

Director TT, 'Circular of the Tax Director' (*Luxembourgforfinance*, 2010). http://www.luxembourgforfinance.lu/sites/luxembourgforfinance/files/taxcirc_2010_12jan_islamfin_en.pdf. Accessed 27 November 2012.

Djaraouane K and Serhal C, 'Choice of Governing Law in Islamic Finance Agreements' (2009) 2 International Business Law Journal 115.

Duns J, *Insolvecny: Law and Policy* (1st edn, Oxford University Press 2002).

Dusuki A, 'Challenges of Realizing Maqasid al-Shariah (Objectives of Shariah) in Islamic Capital Market: Special Focus on Equity-Based Sukuk' (International Islamic Management Conference on Islamic Capital Market, Penang, October 2009).

Dusuki A and Mokhtar S, *Critical Appraisal of Shariah Issues on Ownership in Asset-Based Sukuk as Implemented in the Islamic Debt Market* (ISRA 2010).

Edge I, 'Islamic finance, alternative dispute resolution and family law: developments towards legal pluralism?' in Griffith-Jones R (ed), *Islam and English Law: Rights, Responsibilities and the Place of Shari'a* (Cambridge University Press 2013).

El Gamal R, 'Update 1-Kuwait's Dar Defaults on $100 mln Sukuk' (*Reuters*, 12 May 2009). http://uk.reuters.com/article/2009/05/12/dar-sukuk-idUKLC28153620090512. Accessed 20 December 2013.

Elshurafa D, 'Project Finance and Sukuk in Saudi Arabia: An Ongoing Project?' (2013) Butterworths Journal of International Banking and Financial Law 99.

Ercanbrack J, *The Transformation of Islamic Law in Global Financial Markets* (Cambridge University Press 2015).

Fabozzi F and Modigliani F, *Capital Markets: Institutions and Instruments* (2 nd edn, Prentic Hall 1996).

Ferran E, *Mortgage Securitisation-Legal Aspects* (Butterworths 1992).

Ferran E and Goodhart C (eds), *Regulating Financial Services and Markets in the Twenty First Century* (Hart Publishing 2001).

Fisher J and Waters M, *The Law of Investor Protection* (2 edn, Sweet & Maxwell 2003).

Fitch Ratings, 'Fitch Maintains Five Dubai-Based Banks' Individual Ratings on Watch Negative' (*Fitch Ratings*, 16 December 2009). https://www.fitchratings.com/creditdesk/press_releases/detail.cfm?pr_id=545097. Accessed 24 December 2013.

———, 'Rating Sukuk: Cross-Sector Criteria' (*Fitch Ratings*, 9 August 2013). https://www.fitchratings.com/creditdesk/reports/report_frame.cfm?rpt_id=715279. Accessed 25 December 2013.

Fleihan T, 'UAE top Arab Nation and Second Globally in 73-Country Islamic Economy Indicator' (*GIES*, 28 September 2015) accessed 29 September 2015.

Foster N, 'Islamic Finance Law as an Emergent Legal System' (2007) 21 Arab Law Quarterly 170.

———, 'Islamic Perspectives on the Law of Business Organisations: Part 1: an Overview of the Classical Sharia and a Brief Comparison of the Sharia Regimes with Western-Style Law' (2010) 11 European Business Organization Law Review 3.

Frankhauser R, 'Listing Sukuk' in Ali R (ed), *Sukuk and Islamic Capital Markets* (Globe Business Publishing 2011).

Fuller G, *The Law and Practice of International Capital Markets* (3 edn, LexisNexis 2012).

Gaudiosi M, 'The Influence of the Islamic Law of Waqf on the Development of the Trust in England: The Case of Merton College' (1988) 136 University of Pennsylvania Law Review 1231.

Ghoul W, 'The Standardization Debate in Islamic Finance: A Case Study' (8 International Conference on Islamic Economics and Finance, Doha, December 2011).

Giglio G, 'Asset Securitisation in Argentina' (2005) 10 Journal of International Banking Law and Regulation 514.

Global Investment House, 'Sukuks – A New Dawn of Islamic Finance Era' (*Global Investment House*, January 2008). http://www.menafn.com/updates/research_center/regional/special_ed/gih0108.pdf. Accessed 12 December 2012.

Goode R, *Principles of Corporate Insolvency Law* (4th edn, Sweet & Maxwell 2011).

Goodhart C and others, *Financial Regulation: Why, How and Where Now?* (Routldge 1998).

Goud B, 'Description of a Sukuk Fatwa' (*Zawya*, 15 February 2009). http://www.zawya.com/blogs/blakegoud/090215215223/. Accessed 11 December 2013.

Gowland D, *The Regulation of Financial Markets in the 1990s* (Edward Elgar Publishing Limited 1990).

Graham M, 'Islamic Finance and the United States Bankruptcy Courts: The Future of Sukuk Certificate Holders' Rights and the Importance of Considering Shari'ah Precepts in the Bankruptcy Process' (2012) 20 Tulane Journal of International and Company Law 327.

Greuning H and Iqbal Z, *Risk Analysis for Islamic Banks* (The International Bank for Reconstruction and Development and the WB 2008).

Grewal B, 'Constraints on Growth in Islamic Finance' (IFSB 4th Public Lecture on Financial Policy and Stability, Jordan, 2011).

Haider H, 'Shariah Authority on Cards' (*Khaleej Times*, 22 March 2015). http://www.khaleejtimes.com/article/20150322/ARTICLE/303229876/1037. Accessed 28 August 2015.

Hallaq W, *The Origins and Evolution of Islamic Law* (Cambridge University Press 2005).

Hamoudi H, 'The Surprising Irrelevance of Islamic Bankruptcy' (2011) 19 American Bankruptcy Institute Law Review 505.

Haneef R, 'The Case for Receivables-Based Ṣukūk: A Convergence between the Malaysian and Global Shariah Standards on Bay al-Dayn?' in Kamali M and Abdullah A (eds), *Islamic Finance: Issues in Sukuk and Proposals for Reform* (International Institute of Advanced Islamic Studies and Islamic Foundation 2014a).

———, 'From Asset Backed to Asset Light Structures: The Intricate History of Sukuk' (2009) 1 ISRA International Journal of Islamic Finance 103.

———, 'Recent Trends and Innovations in Islamic Debt Securities: Prospects for Islamic Profit and Loss Sharing Securities' in Ali S (ed), *Islamic Finance: Current Legal and Regulatory Issues* (Islamic Finance Project 2005).

———, 'Second Keynote: Legal Ownership and Benefical Ownership From Sharia and Legal Perspective: General Scope and Main Challenges' (Contemporary Issues in the Application of Islamic Finance: Benefical and Legal Ownership and Takaful in Light of the Islamic Concept of Cooperation, November 2014b, Malalysia).

Hanif A and Johansen J, 'Sukuk' in Nethercott C and Eisenberg D (eds), *Finance: Law and Practice* (1 edn, Oxford University Press 2012).

Haqqi A, 'Shariah Governance in Islamic Financial Institution: An Appraisal' (2014) 11 US-China Law Review 112.

Hasan Z, 'An Overview of the Recent Malaysian Islamic Financial Stability Act' (2013) 8 Journal of International Banking Law and Regulation 297.

———, 'The Position of Al-Quran As a Source of Law Under the Malaysian Legal System' (*Zulkiflihasan*, undated). https://zulkiflihasan.files.wordpress.com/2008/06/jurnal-quran.pdf. Accessed 23 August 2015.

———, 'Shariah Governance in Islamic Financial Institutions in Malaysia, GCC Countries and the UK' (PhD Thesis, Durham University 2011).

Hasan Z and Asutay M, 'An Analysis of the Courts' Decisions on Islamic Finance Disputes' (2011) 3 ISRA International Journal of Islamic Finance 41.

Hassan A, *Sales and Contracts in Early Islamic Commerical Law* (The Other Press 2007).

Hassoune A and Haladjian M, 'Moody's Reviews Tamweel's A3/P-2 Ratings, Direction Uncertain' (*Moody's*, 27 November 2008). https://www.moodys.com/research/Moodys-reviews-Tamweels-A3P-2-ratings-direction-uncertain%2D%2DPR_168275. Accessed 24 December 2013.

Hassoune A, Howladar K and Harris S, 'The Meaning of Ratings for Islamic Financial Institutions and Sharīʿah-Compliant Instruments' in IFSB (ed), *The Changing Landscape of Islamic Finance: Imminent Challenges and Future Directions* (IFSB 2010).

Haynes A, 'New Sources of Finance' (2011) 2 Company Lawyer 33.

Hekmatyar M and Parkar E 'An Evaluation of Dana Gas's Mudarabah Sukuk From Shariah and Legal Perspectives' (2018) 9 European Journal of Islamic Finance 1.

HM Treasury and Debt Management Office, 'Government Sterling Sukuk Issuance: A Response to the Consultation' (*HM Treasury*, June 2008). http://webarchive.nationalarchives.gov.uk/+/http://www.hm-treasury.gov.uk/d/consult_sukukresponses020608.pdf. Accessed 3 September 2015.

HM Treasury and Office DM, 'Government Sterling Sukuk Issuance: A Consultation' (*HM Treasury*, November 2007). http://www.dmo.gov.uk/docs/publications/giltsmarket/consultationpapers/cons141107.pdf. Accessed 3 September 2015.

Howladar K, *The Future of Sukuk: Substance Over Form? Understanding Islamic Securitisation, Asset-Backed and AAOIFI Principles* (Moody's Investor Service 2009).

———, *Shari'ah and Sukuk: A Moody's Primer* (Moody's Investors Service 2006).

Hudson A, *Securities Law* (2nd edn, Sweet & Maxwell 2013).

Ibrahim M, 'The Regulatory Framework and Legal Aspects of Islamic Banking and Finance in Malaysia' in Bakar M and Ali E (eds), *Essential Readings in Islamic Finance* (CERT Publications 2008).

IDB, IFSB and IRTI, 'Islamic Financial Services Industry Development: Ten-Year Framework and Strategies' (*IFSB*, May 2007). http://www.ifsb.org/docs/10_yr_framework.pdf. Accessed 15 September 2012.

Idris U, 'Evaluation of Research Developments on the Islamic Securities (Sukuk)' (7th International Conference on Islamic Economics, Jeddah, March 2008).

IFIS, 'IFIS Global Sukuk Market H2-2010 Report' (*IFIS*, 2010). http://www.kantakji.com/media/8073/mn100.pdf. Accessed 17 January 2013.

IFSB, 'Appendix: Case Studies' in IFSB (ed), *Strategies for the Development of Islamic Capital Markets* (IFSB 2011a).

———, 'Capital Adequacy Requirements for Ṣukūk, Securitisations and Real Estate investment' (*IFSB*, January 2009a). http://www.ifsb.org/standard/eng_%20IFSB-7%20Capital%20Adequacy%20Requirements%20for%20Sukuk,%20Securitasations%20and%20Real%20Estate%20investment%20(Jan2009).pdf. Accessed 4 March 2015.

———, 'Capital Adequacy Standard for Institutions (other than Insurance Institutions) Offering Only Islamic Financial Services (IIFS)' (*IFSB*, December 2005a). http://www.ifsb.org/standard/ifsb2.pdf. Accessed 4 March 2015.

———, 'Disclosures to Promote Transparency and Market Discipline for Institutions offering Islamic Financial Services (excluding Islamic Insurance (*Takâful*) Institutions and Islamic Mutual Funds)' (*IFSB*, December 2007). http://www.ifsb.org/standard/ifsb4.pdf. Accessed 5 March 2015.

———, 'Evaluation of Core Principles Relevant to Islamic Finance Regulation' (*IFSB*, November 2014a). http://www.ifsb.org/docs/WP-02_CPIFR%20%28Nov%202014%29.pdf. Accessed 10 February 2015.

———, 'Guiding Principles of Risk Management for Institutions (Other Than Insurance Institutions) Offering Only Islamic Financial Services' (*IFSB*, December 2005b). http://www.ifsb.org/standard/ifsb1.pdf. Accessed 9 April 2015.

———, 'Guiding Principles on Liquidity Risk Management for Institutions Offering Islamic Financial Services [Excluding Islamic Insurance (*Takāful*) Institutions And Islamic Collective Investment Schemes]' (*IFSB*, March 2012). http://www.ifsb.org/standard/eng_IFSB-12%20Guiding%20Principles%20on%20Liquidity%20Risk%20Mgmt%20_(March2012).pdf. Accessed 23 January 2015.

———, 'Guiding Principles on Sharīʿah Governance Systems for Institutions offering Islamic Financial Services' (*IFSB*, December 2009b). http://www.ifsb.org/standard/IFSB-10%20Shariah%20Governance.pdf. Accessed 17 April 2015.

———, 'Islamic Financial Services Industry: Stability Report 2014' (*IFSB*, 2014b). http://www.ifsb.org/docs/2014-05-06_IFSI%20Stability%20Report%202014%20(Final).pdf. Accessed 22 March 2015.

———, 'Islamic Financial Services Industry: Stability Report 2017' (*IFSB*, 2017) 7. https://www.ifsb.org/docs/IFSB%20IFSI%20Stability%20Report%202017.pdf. Accessed 25 December 2018.

———, 'Revised Capital Adequacy Standard for Institutions Offering Islamic Financial Services (Excluding Islamic Insurance (Takaful) Institutions and Islamic Collective Investment Schemes)' (*IFSB*, December 2013). http://www.ifsb.org/standard/2014-01-28_eng_IFSB15%20Revised%20Capital%20Adequacy_(Jan%202014).pdf. Accessed 4 March 2015.

———, 'Revised Guidance on Key Elements in the Supervisory Review Process of Institutions Offering Islamic Financial Services (Excluding Islamic Insurance (Takaful) Institutions and Islamic Collective Investment Schemes)' (*IFSB*, March 2014c). http://www.ifsb.org/standard/IFSB-16%20Revised%20Supervisory%20Review%20Process_March%202014%20(final-clean).pdf. Accessed 4 March 2014.

———, 'Technical Note on Issues in Strengthening Liquidity Management of Institutions Offering Islamic Financial Services: The Development of Islamic Money Markets' (*IFSB*, March 2008). http://www.ifsb.org/docs/mar2008_liquidity.pdf. Accessed 10 April 2015.

——— (ed) *Strategies for the Development of Islamic Capital Markets: Infrastructures and Legal Aspects of Islamic Asset Securitisation* (IFSB 2011b).

IFSB, IDB and IRTI, 'Islamic Financial and Global Financial Stability' (*IFSB*, 2010). http://www.ifsb.org/docs/IFSB-IRTI-IDB2010.pdf. Accessed 10 April 2015.

IFSB, IOSCO and SC, 'Forward' in IFSB, IOSCO and SC (eds), *Disclosure Requirements for Islamic Capital Market Products* (IFSB, IOSCO, SC 2013).

IIFA, 'Al-Qarārāt Wa Al-Tawṣiyāt: Al-Dawrah Al-ʿishrīn' (*Fiqhacademy*, 2012). http://www.fiqhacademy.org.sa/. Accessed 9 November 2014.

———, 'Al-Qarārāt Wa Al-Tawṣiyāt: Al-Dawrah Al-Sābiʿah ʿasharah' (*Fiqhacademy*, 2006). http://www.fiqhacademy.org.sa/. Accessed 13 November 2014.

———, 'Al-Qarārāt Wa Al-Tawṣiyāt: Al-Dawrah Al-Tāsiʿah ʿashrah' (*Fiqhacademy*, 2009a). http://www.fiqhacademy.org.sa/. Accessed 7 November 2014.

———, 'Al-Qarārāt Wa Al-Tawṣiyāt: Al-Dawrah Al-Wāḥidah Wālʿishrīn' (*fiqhacademy*, 2013a). http://www.fiqhacademy.org.sa/. Accessed 3 March 2015.

———, 'Qarār Raqam 156 (5/17) Bishaʾan Astikmāl-Ṣukūk Al-Mushārakat: Mukawināt Mawjūdātihā' (*IIFA*, undated). http://www.fiqhacademy.org.sa/qrarat/17-5.htm. Accessed 8 July 2015.

———, 'Resolution no 137 (3/15) concerning Ijārah Ṣukūk' (*fiqhacademy*, 2004). http://www.fiqhacademy.org.sa/qrarat/15-3.htm. Accessed 3 March 2015.

———, 'Resolution of OIC Fiqh Academy (related to Islamic Economic and Finance)' (2014a) 22 Islamic Economic Studies 265.

———, *Resolutions and Recommendations of the Council of Islamic Fiqh Academy* (1 edn, IDB 2000).

IIFM, 'IIFM Study on Indonesian Sukuk Market & Global Sukuk Issuances' (*IIFM*, August 2010). http://www.iifm.net/documents/iifm-study-indonesian-sukuk-market-global-sukuk-issuances. Accessed 4 March 2015.

IIFA, 'IIFM Sukuk Analysis (as of December 2009)' (*IIFM*, December 2009b). http://www.iifm.net/documents/iifm-sukuk-analysis-december-2009. Accessed 4 March 2015.

———, 'IIFM Ṣukūk Report 1st Edition' (*IIFM*, 2010). http://www.iifm.net/documents/iifm-sukuk-report-1st-edition. Accessed 4 March 2015.

———, 'IIFM Ṣukūk Report 2nd Edition: A Comprehensive Study of the Global Sukuk Market' (*IIFM*, 2011). http://www.iifm.net/documents/iifm-sukuk-report-2nd-edition-comprehensive-study-global-sukuk-market. Accessed 4 March 2015.

———, 'IIFM Ṣukūk Report 3rd Edition: A Comprehensive Study of the Global Sukuk Market' (*IIFM*, April 2013b). http://www.iifm.net/documents/iifm-sukuk-report. Accessed 4 March 2015.

———, 'IIFM Ṣukūk Report 4th Edition: A Comprehensive Study of the Global Sukuk Market' (*IIFM*, November 2014b). http://www.iifm.net/documents/iifm-sukuk-report-4th-edition. Accessed 4 March 2015.

IIFM and ISDA, 'IFM and ISDA Launch Tahawwut (Hedging) Master Agreement' (*ISDA*, 2010a). http://www.isda.org/media/press/2010/press030110.html. Accessed 18 November 2013.

IIFM and ISDA, *ISDA/IIFM Tahawwut Master Agreement* (IIFM and ISDA 2010b).

IILM, 'The Features of the IILM Sukūk' (*IILM*, 2015a). http://www.iilm.com/the-features-of-the-iilm-suk%C5%ABk/. Accessed 14 September 2015.

———, 'The Inaugural Issuance' (*IILM*, 2015b). http://www.iilm.com/the-inaugural-issuance/. Accessed 14 September 2015.

IMF, 'The Financial Sector Assessment Program (FSAP)' (*IMF*, 2012). http://www.imf.org/external/np/exr/facts/pdf/fsap.pdf. Accessed 15 August 2012.

IOSCO, 'Analysis of the Application of IOSCO's Objectives and Principles of Securities Regulation for Islamic Securities Products' (*IOSCO*, September 2008a). http://www.iosco.org/library/pubdocs/pdf/IOSCOPD280.pdf. Accessed 10 February 2015.

———, 'International Disclosure Principles for Cross-Border Offerings and Listings of Debt Securities by Foreign Issuers' (*IOSCO*, March 2007). https://www.iosco.org/library/pubdocs/pdf/IOSCOPD242.pdf. Accessed 5 March 2015.

———, 'Islamic Capital Market Fact Finding Report' (*IOSCO*, July 2004). http://www.iosco.org/library/pubdocs/pdf/IOSCOPD170.pdf. Accessed 10 February 2015.

———, 'Methodology for Assessing Implementation of the IOSCO Objectives and Principles of Securities Regulation' (*IOSCO*, February 2008b). www.iosco.org/library/pubdocs/pdf/IOSCOPD226.pdf. Accessed 10 February 2015.

———, 'Objectives and Principles of Securities Regulation' (*IOSCO*, June 2010). http://www.iosco.org/library/pubdocs/pdf/IOSCOPD323.pdf. Accessed 10 February 2015.

Iqbal Z and Mirakhor A, *An Introduction to Islamic Finance* (2 edn, John Wiley & Sons 2011).

Islamic Development Bank Group, *Islamic Development Bank Group in Brief* (IDB 2013).

Islamic Finance News, 'Dana Gaz Defaults on Sukuk' (*Islamic Finance News*, 2012a). https://www.islamicfinancenews.com/the-dana-gas-case-timeline. Accessed 4 January 2019.

———, 'Dana Gas Receives Orders From Sharjah Court' (Islamic Finance News, 2018a). https://www.islamicfinancenews.com/the-dana-gas-case-timeline. Accessed 4 January 2019.

———, 'Court Restricts Dana Gas From Paying Dividends' (Islamic Finance News, 2018b). https://www.islamicfinancenews.com/the-dana-gas-case-timeline. Accessed 4 January 2019.

———, 'Dana Gas Reaches Agreement' (Islamic Finance News, 2018c). https://www.islamicfinancenews.com/the-dana-gas-case-timeline. Accessed 4 January 2019.

———, 'Dana Gas in Agreement with Sukukholders' (Islamic Finance News, 2012b). https://www.islamicfinancenews.com/the-dana-gas-case-timeline. Accessed 4 January 2019.

———, 'Dana Gas Proposes New Sukuk Plan' (Islamic Finance News, 2012c). https://www.islamicfinancenews.com/the-dana-gas-case-timeline. Accessed 4 January 2019.

———, 'Dana Gas Good to Go' (Islamic Finance News, 2013a). https://www.islamicfinancenews.com/the-dana-gas-case-timeline. Accessed 4 January 2019.

———, 'Dana Gas Completes Restructuring' (Islamic Finance News, 2013b). https://www.islamicfinancenews.com/the-dana-gas-case-timeline. Accessed 4 January 2019. For more information: see Offering Circular of Dana Gas Sukuk Limited (2013).

———, 'Dana Gas Renegotiates with Sukukholders' (Islamic Finance News, 2017a). https://www.islamicfinancenews.com/the-dana-gas-case-timeline. Accessed 4 January 2019.

———, 'Dana Gas to Replace Unlawful Sukuk' (Islamic Finance News, 2017b). https://www.islamicfinancenews.com/the-dana-gas-case-timeline. Accessed 4 January 2019.

———, 'Dana Gas Rejects Deutsches's Sukuk Payment Request' (Islamic Finance News, 2017c). https://www.islamicfinancenews.com/the-dana-gas-case-timeline. Accessed 4 January 2019.

ISRA, '9th International Shari'ah Scholars Forum' (*ISRA*, 2014). http://ifikr.isra.my/event-articles/-/eventArticles/browseArticles?_7013_WAR_fatwaportlet_eventCode=ISSF2014. Accessed 19 September 2015.

Jobst A, 'IMF Working Paper WP/07/117: The Economics of Islamic Finance and Securitization' (*IMF*, 2007). http://www.imf.org/external/pubs/ft/wp/2007/wp07117.pdf. Accessed 20 August 2013.

Jobst A and others, 'Islamic Bond Issuance: What Sovereign Debt Managers Need to Know' (2008) 1 International Journal of Islamic and Middle Eastern Finance and Management 330.

Johnson M and Hughes J, 'Markets Reel Over Nakheel Default Fears' (*The Financial Times*, 25 November 2009). http://www.ft.com/cms/s/0/d1b1f72e-d9f6-11de-b2d5-00144feabdc0.html#axzz2o7OB9wYp. Accessed 22 December 2013.

Junius A, 'Islamic Finance: Issues Surrounding Islamic Law as a Choice of Law under German Conflict of Laws Principles' (2007) 7 Chicago Journal of International Law 537.

Kadir Andri & Partners, 'Payment Default in Islamic Finance' (*IFLR*). http://www.iflr.com/Article/2452811/Payment-default-in-Islamic-finance.html. Accessed 18 November 2013.

Kamali M, *Principles of Islamic Jurisprudence* (3rd edn, The Islamic Texts Society 2003).

———, *Shari'ah Law: An Introduction* (Oneworld Publications 2008).

Kamali M and Abdullah A, 'Introduction' in Kamali M and Abdullah A (eds), *Islamic Finance: Issues in Sukuk and Proposals for Reform* (International Institute of Advanced Islamic Studies and Islamic Foundation 2014).

———, 'Preface' in Kamali M and Abdullah A (eds), *Islamic Finance: Issues in Sukuk and Proposals for Reform* (International Institute of Advance Islamic Studies and Islamic Foundation 2014).

Kamil W, 'Introduction to Sukuk' in Berhad RRS (ed), *Malaysian Sukuk Market Handbook: Your Guide to the Malaysian Islamic Capital Market* (RAM Rating Services Berhad undated).

Kane F, 'Saudis Wash Their Hands of The Al Gosaibi Affair' (*The National*, 30 May 2011). http://www.thenational.ae/business/industry-insights/finance/saudis-wash-their-hands-of-the-al-gosaibi-affair. Accessed 22 June 2015.

Keong L, *Securities Regulation in Malaysia* (Butterworths 1997).

Kettell B, *Islamic Capital Markets* (Brian Kettell 2009).

Khan I, 'Preface' in Thomas A (ed), *Sukuk* (Sweet & Maxwell Asia 2009).

Khayrullah W, 'Al-Muqaradah Bonds as the Basis of Profit Sharing' (*Irti*, Undated). http://www.irti.org/English/Research/Documents/IES/157.pdf. Accessed 30 April 2015.

Khnifer M, 'When Sukuk Default - Asset Priority of Certificate-holders vis a vis Creditors' (2010) 11 Opalesque Islamic Finance Intelligence 9.

Khorshid A, 'Sukuk and Securitization' in Khorshid A (ed), *Euromoney Encyclopedia of Islamic Finance* (Euromoney Institutional Investor PLC 2009).

Kilborn J, 'Foundations of Forgiveness in Islamic Bankruptcy Law: Sources, Methodology, Diversity' (*SSRN*, undated). http://papers.ssrn.com/sol3/papers.cfm?abstractid=1908896. Accessed 6 April 2013.

Klee K and Butler B, 'Asset-Backed Securitization, Special Purpose Vehicles and Other Securtization Issues' (2002) 35 Uniform Commercial Code Law Journal 23.

Kuran T, 'The Absence of the Corporation in Islamic Law: Origins and Persistence' (2005) 53 The American Juornal of Comparative Law 785.

Kusuma K and Silva A, 'Policy Research Working Paper 7133: Sukuk Markets-A Proposed Approach for Development' (*WB*, December 2014). http://www-wds.worldbank.org/external/default/WDSContentServer/WDSP/IB/2014/12/04/000158349_20141204142423/Rendered/PDF/WPS7133.pdf. Accessed 26 July 2015.

Kuwait Finance House Research, *Global Sukuk Report 3Q2011* (Kuwait Finance House Research 2011).

———, *Sukuk: Back on Track* (Kuwait Finance House Research 2010).

La Porta R and others, 'Investor Protection and Corporate Governance' (2000) 58 Journal of Financial Economics 3.

Lahsasna A, *Sharīʿah Non-Compliance Risk Management and Legal Documentation in Islamic Finance* (Wiley 2014).

Laldin M, *Introduction to Shari'ah & Islamic Juridprudence* (CERT Publications 2008a).

———, 'Islamic Financial System: The Malaysian Experience and the Way Forward' (2008b) 24 Humanomics 217.

———, 'Sukuk in Various Juridictions: Shariah and Legal Issues' (2012) 2 Journal of Islamic Business and Management 15.

Laldin M and Furqani H, 'Meeting Expectations: The Roles and Resposibilities of Sharia Scholars in Islamic Finance' in Hassan K and Lewis M (eds), *Handbook on Islam and Economic Life* (Edward Elgar 2014).

Lastra R, *International Financial and Monetary Law* (2nd edn, Oxford University Press 2015).

Latham & Watkins, 'Doing Business in Saudi Arabia' (*Latham & Watkins*, May 2010). http://www.lw.com/upload/pubContent/_pdf/pub3507_1.pdf. Accessed 28 August 2010.

Latimer P, 'How to Ensure Disclosure of Information in Securities Markets Post-GFC' (2013) 42 Common Law World Review 111.

Lee C, 'Commentary Three' in IFSB, IOSCO and SC (eds), *Disclosure Requirements of Islamic Capital Market Products* (IFSB, IOSCO and SC 2013).

Lew J, Mistelis L and Kroll S, *Comparative International Commercial Arbitration* (Kluwer Law International 2003).

Lin L, Lahsasna A and Ahmed R, 'Sharīʿah Issues in Islamic Capital Markets: Ṣukūk' (2013) 5 ISRA International Journal of Islamic Finance 99.

Llewellyn D, *The Economic Rationale for Financial Regulation* (Financial Services Authority 1999).

Lotter P, *Understanding Moody's Approach to Unsecured Corporate Sukuk* (Moody's Investors Service 2007).

Lotter P and Kypreos C, 'Moody's Downgrades Saad Group Entities to B1; On Review For Further Downgrade' (*Moody's* 2 June 2009). https://www.moodys.com/research/Moodys-downgrades-Saad-Group-entities-to-B1-on-review-for%2D%2DPR_180145. Accessed 24 December 2013.

———, 'Moody's Withdraw's Ratings On Saad Group Entities' (*Moody's*, 2 June 2009). https://www.moodys.com/research/Moodys-withdraws-ratings-on-Saad-Group-entities%2D%2DPR_180316. Accessed 24 December 2013.

MacNeil I, *An Introduction to the Law on Financial Investment* (2 nd edn, Hart Publishing Ltd 2012).

Mahmood N and Kamil W, 'Islamic Finance and the Impact of Insolvency' in *Effective Insolvency Regimes: Institutional, Regulatory, and Legal Issues Relating to Islamic Finance* (IFSB and WB 2011).

Majid H, Shahimi S and Abdullah M, 'Sukuk Defaults and Its Implication: A Case Study of Malaysian Capital Market' (8th International Conference on Islamic Economics and Finance, Qatar, December 2011).

Makdisi G, 'The Significance of the Sunni Schools of Law in Islamic Religious History' (1979) 10 International Journal of Middle East Studies 1.

Malim M, 'The Future of Sukuk: Islamic Capital Markets' in Ali R (ed), *Sukuk and Islamic Capital Markets* (Globe Business Publishing 2011).

MARC, 'Rating Approach to Sukuk: A Marc Perspective' (*MARC*, 2008). http://www.marc.com.my/home/userfiles/file/Methodologies/Rating%20Approach%20to%20Sukuk%20-%20A%20MARC%20Perspective.pdf. Accessed 18 March 2013.

Marinescs I, 'Where Does the Dirham Stop in a Sukuk Default?' (2012) 35 Hastings International and Comparative Law Review 451.

Martin J and Hanbury H, *Modern Equity* (Sweet & Maxwell 2012).

Maurer B, 'Form Versus Substance: AAOIFI Projects and Islamic Fundamentals in the Case of Sukuk' (2010) 1 Journal of Islamic Accounting and Business Research 32.

Mayew G, 'Securities Regulation in the UAE' (*International Financial Law Review* October 2010). http://www.iflr.com/Article/2680248/Securities-regulation-in-the-UAE.html. Accessed 8 May 2014.

McCormick R, *Legal Risk in the Financial Markets* (2 nd edn, Oxford University Press 2010).

Mcmillen M, 'Asset Securitisation Sukuk and Islamic Capital Markets: Structural Issues in these Formative Years' (2008) 25 Wisconsin International Law Journal 703.

———, 'Contractual Enforceability Issues: Sukuk and Capital Markets Development' (2007) 7 Chicago Journal of International Law 427.

———, 'Sharīʿah Considerations in The Bankruptcy Context and The First Bankruptcy (East Cameron)' in IFSB and WB (eds), *Effective Insolvecny Regimes: Institutional, Regulatory and Legal Issues Relating to Islamic Finance* (IFSB and WB 2011).

Melchert C, 'Traditionist-Jurisprudents and the Framing of Islamic Law' (2001) 8 Islamic Law and Society 383.

Mersch Y, 'About the Role of Central Banks in Financial Stability and Prudential Liquidity Supervision, and the Attractiveness of Islamic Finance' (IFSB 2nd Public Lecture on financial policy and Stability, Kuala Lumpur, 2009).

Mirakhor A and Krichene N, 'The Recent Crisis: Lessons for Islamic Finance' (IFSB 2dn Public Lecture on Financial Policy and Stability, Kuala Lumpur, 2009).

Mishkin F and Eakins S, *Financial Markets and Institutions* (6 th edn, Pearson Prentice Hall 2009).

Mohammad F, 'Greater Disclosure Required in the Sukuk Industry' (2010) Butterworths Journal of International Banking and Financial Law 258.

Mohsin M, 'The Practice of Islamic Banking System in Sudan' (2005) 26 Journal of Economic Coorperation 27.

Mokhtar S, *Application of Wa'ad In Equity Based Sukuk: Empirical Evidence* (ISRA 2011).

Mokhtar S and others, 'Sukuk and the Capital Markets' in Thomas A (ed), *Sukuk* (Sweet & Maxwell Asia 2009).

Mokhtar S and Thomas A, 'Ijarah Sukuk' in Thomas A (ed), *Sukuk* (Sweet & Maxwell Asia 2009).

Moody's Investros Service, 'Code of Proressional Conduct' (*Moody's Investros Service*, Decemebr 2013). https://www.moodys.com/uploadpage/Mco%20Documents/Documents_professional_conduct.pdf. Accessed 25 Decemebr 2013.

———, *Rating Symbols and Definitions* (Moody's Investors Service 2012).

Morris C and Murphy C, *Getting a PhD in Law* (Hart Publishing 2011).

Morris M, 'Dar Gets Ratings Downgrade' (*Arabian Business*, 19 May 2009). http://www.arabianbusiness.com/dar-gets-ratings-downgrade-18605.html. Accessed 24 December 2013.

Muhamed N and Radzi R, 'Implication of Sukuk Structuring: The Comparison on the Structure of Asset Based and Asset Backed Ijarah Sukuk' (2nd International Conference on Business and Economic Research, Malaysia, March 2011).

———, 'An International Comparative Study on Shariah Governance Supervision of Sukuk Defaults' (2012) 8 Journal of Islamic Economics, Banking and Finance 20.

Muhammad M, Yaacob H and Hasan S, *The Bindingness and Enforceability of A Unilateral Promise (Wa'd): An Analysis From Islamic Law and Legal Perspectives* (ISRA 2011).

Mutalip A, 'Guidelines on Offering Islamic Securities' (*Azmi & Associates*, 2005). http://www.azmilaw.com.my/archives/Article_outside_publications_asian_counsel/Guidelines_on_offering_islamic_securities_%2800124292%29.PDF. Accessed 17 March 2014.

Nadar A, 'Islamic Finance and Dispute Resolution: Part 1' (2009a) 23 Arab Law Quarterly 1.

———, 'Islamic Finance and Dispute Resolution: Part 2' (2009b) 23 Arab Law Quarterly 181.

Nawawi R, *Islamic law on Commercial Transaction* (CERT Publications 2009).

Nazar J, 'Regulatory and Financial Implications of Sukuk's Legal Challenges for Sustainable Sukuk Development in Islamic Capital Market' (8th International Conference on Islamic Economics and Finance, Qatar, December 2011).

Nethercott C, Rai H and Irvine L, 'Sukuk: Rethinking Sukuk While Leaping Forward' in Consulting E (ed), *Global Islamic Finance Report 2014* (Edbiz Consulting Publication 2014).

Nienhaus V, 'Capacity Building in the Financial Sector: Strategies for Strengthening Financial Institutions' (Inaugural Islamic Financial Stability Forum: Developing Capacity Building to Enhance Financial Stability in the Islamic Financial Services Industry, Sudan, April 2010).

———, 'Commentary Two' in IFSB, IOSCO and SC (eds), *Disclosrue Requirements of Islamic Capital Market Products* (IFSB, IOSCO and SC 2013).

Noor L, 'Sukuk Rating-General Approach, Criteria and Methodology' in Berhad RRS (ed), *Malaysian Sukuk Market Handbook: Your Guide to the Malaysian Islamic Capital Market* (RAM Rating Services Berhad undated).

Norton Rose, 'The Implications for the Islamic Finance Market of The Investment Dar Company KSCC v Blom Developments Bank Sal [2009] EWHC 3545 (Ch)' (*Norton Rose*, March 2010). http://www.nortonrosefulbright.com/knowledge/publications/27334/the-implications-for-the-islamic-finance-market-of-the-investment-dar-company-kscc-v-blom-developments-bank-sa. Accessed 5 August 2015.

O'Neill D, 'Sukuk Market on Trial as Islamic Bonds Default' (2009) 40 Euromoney 45.

Oditah F, 'Great Britain' in Baums T and Wymeersch E (eds), *Asset-Backed Securitization in Europe* (Kluwer Law International 1996).

Ogali D, 'Lady Justice Cannot Hear Your Prayers' (2018) 3 Fordham Law Review 1293.

Omar M, Abduh M and Raditya S, *Fundamentals of Islamic Money and Capital Markets* (John Wiley & Sons 2013).

Oseni U and Hassan K, 'The Dispute Resolution Framework for the Islamic Capital Markets in Malaysia: Legal Obstacles and Options' in Hassan K and Mahlknecht M (eds), *Islamic Capital Markets: Products and Strategies* (John Wiley & Sons 2011).

———, 'The Regulation and Supervision of Sukuk in Global Capital Markets' in Hassan K and Lewis M (eds), *Handbook on Islam and Economic Life* (Edward Elgar 2014).

Osman S and Jalil A, 'An Islamic Perspective of Promise and Its Relationship with the Islamic Law of Contract' (International Seminar on Usul Fiqh, Nilai, October 2013).

Ossa F, 'Sovereign Sukuk Are Back, but Asset-Backeds Still Sidelined' (*Structured Finance News*, 1 April 2011). http://www.structuredfinancenews.com/issues/11_4/sovereign-sukuk-are-back-but-asset-backeds-still-sidelined-218081-1.html. Accessed 11 December 2013.

Page A and Ferguson R, *Invetor Protection* (Weidenfeld and Nicolson 1992).

Parasher S, 'Sukuk Industry Development in the Bahrain Capital Market' in Arrif M, Iqbal M and Mohamad S (eds), *The Islamic Debt Market for Sukuk Securities: The Theory and Practice of Profit Sharing Investment* (Edward Elger Publishing Limited 2012).

Paris Europlace, 'French Sukuk Guidebook' (*Paris-europlace*, 2011). http://www.paris-europlace.net/files/French_Sukuk_Guidebook_Nov_2011.pdf. Accessed 18 March 2013.

Park E, 'Allowing Japanese Banks to Engage in Securitization: Potential Benefits, Regulatory Obstacles and Theories for Reform' (1996) 17 University of Pennsylvania Journal of International Economic Law 723.

Parker M, 'Islamic Finance is Growing at a Phenomenal Pace: Al-Jasser' (*Arab News*, 30 November 2009). http://www.arabnews.com/node/330520. Accessed 31 July 2015.

Pearce J and Lipin I, 'Special Purpose Vehicles in Bankruptcy Litigation' (2011) 44 Hofstra Law Review 177.

Rabindranath V and Gupta P, *An Overview – Sukuk Market in Saudi Arabia* (Watheeqa Capital Company 2010).

Rahman T, *Mudarabah and the Pakistan Perspective* (IDB 2000).

Rajapakse P, Copp R and Gardner J, 'Assessment of Insolvency Issues for the Mortgage Originator and Trustee-Issuer in Securitisation Programs' (2008) 34 Monash University Law Review 370.

RAM Rating Services Berhad, 'Dubai Sukuk Defaults: Does One Bad Apple Spoil the Entire Barrel' (2009) 26 Islamic Finance Bulletin 10.

———, *Sukuk Focus May 2010* (RAM Rating Services Berhad 2010).

Rankin D, 'Restructuring and Buy-Back of Sukuk' in Ali R (ed), *Sukuk and Islamic Capital Markets* (Global Business Publishing Ltd 2011).

Remo-Listana K, 'Market, Not Methodology, Drives Sukuk Defaults' (*Emirates 247*, 15 June 2010). http://www.emirates247.com/eb247/banking-finance/islamic-finance/market-not-methodology-drives-sukuk-defaults-2010-06-15-1.255596. Accessed 20 November 2013.

Reuters, 'Most Sukuk "not Islamic": Body Claims' (*Arabianbusiness*, 2007). http://www.arabianbusiness.com/most-sukuk-not-islamic-body-claims-197156.html#.VRm73fldXHU. Accessed 30 March 2015.

Rider B, 'Islamic Financial Law: Back to Basics' in IFSB (ed), *The Changing Landscape of Islamic Finance: Imminent Challenges and Future Directions* (IFSB 2010).

———, 'Legal Aspects of Islamic Asset Securitisation' in IFSB (ed), *Strategies for the Development of Islamic Capital Markets: Infrastructures and Legal Aspects of Islamic Asset Securitisation* (IFSB 2011).

Rider B, Abrams C and Ashe M, *Guide to Financial Services Regulation* (3rd edn, CCH Editions 1997).

Rifke I, 'The Management of Liquidity Risk in Islamic Banks: The Case of Indonesia' (PhD Thesis, Durham University 2010).

Robbins H, 'Soul Searching and Profit Seeking: Reconciling the Competing Goals of Islamic Finance' (2010) 88 Texas Law Review 1125.

Rosly S and Sanusi M, 'The Application of Bay Al-Inah and Bay Al-Dayn in Malaysian Islamic Bonds: An Islamic Analysis' (1999) 1 International Journal of Islamic Financial Services 1.

———, 'Some Issues of Bay' Al-'Inah in Malaysian Islamic Financial Markets' (2001) 16 Arab Law Quarterly 263.

S&P, 'Islamic Finance Outlook 2012' (*S&P*, September 2012). http://www.standardandpoors.com/spf/upload/Ratings_EMEA/2012-09-01_IslamicFinanceOutlook.pdf. Accessed 4 December 2013.

———, Global Ratings, 'Islamic Finance Outlook 2019 Edition', (S&P Global Ratings 2018) 13.

———, *Ratings Performance 2002: Default, Transition, Recovery, and Spreads* (S&P 2003).

———, 'TEXT-S&P on East Cameron Gas Co (Sukuk) 2006' (*Reuters*, 14 Junuary 2009). http://uk.reuters.com/article/2009/01/14/idUKN1447583720090114. Accessed 11 December 2013.

Saba P and Fathnezhad F, 'Implications of the Kuwait TID V. Blom Judgment on Wakala Contracts' (*Al Tamimi & Co.*, 2013). http://www.tamimi.com/en/magazine/law-update/section-5/january-2/implications-of-the-kuwait-tid-v-blom-judgment-on-wakala-contracts.html. Accessed 30 September 2015.

Sabeti-Rahmati H, 'Commentary One' in IFSB, IOSCO and SC (eds), *Disclosure Requirements of Islamic Capital Market Products* (IFSB, IOSCO, SC 2013).

Saeed A and Salah O, 'History of Sukuk: Pragmatic and Idealist Approaches to Structuring Sukuk' in Ariff M, Iqbal M and Mohamad S (eds), *The Islamic Debt Market for Sukuk Securities: The Theory and Practice of Profit Sharing Investment* (Edward Elgar 2012).

Saeed O and Salah O, 'Development of Sukuk: Pragmatic and Idealist Approaches to Sukuk Structures' (2014) 29 Journal of International Banking Law and Regulation 41.

Safari M, Ariff M and Mohamad S, 'Sukuk Securities, their Definitions, Classification and Pricing Issues' in Arrif M, Iqbal M and Mohamad S (eds), *The Islamic Debt Market for Sukuk Securities: The Theory and Practice of Profit Sharing Investment* (Edward Elgar 2012).

———, *Sukuk Securities: New Ways of Debt Contracting* (Wiley & Sons 2014).

Saidi N, 'Islamic Finance is Coming of Age: IFC Lists Sukuk on DIFC' (*Khaleej Times*, 2009). http://www.khaleejtimes.com/biz/inside.asp?xfile=/data/business/2009/November/business_November183.xml&section=business. Accessed 20 Junuary 2013.

Salah O, 'Dubai Debt Crisis: A Legal Analysis of the Nakheel Sukuk' (2010) 4 The Berkeley Journal of International Law 19.

Saleem M, 'Sukuk Default: Questions About Shari'ah Supervision' (2010) 174 NewHorizon.

Sapp S, *East Cameron Partners: The Sukuk Bond* (Ivey School of Business Foundation 2010).

Saripudin K and others, 'Application of Promise in Sukuk Musharakah Structure' (2012) 12 Middle-East Journal of Scientific Research 160.

Saudi Hollandi Capital, *Sukuk Market in Saudi Arabia* (Saudi Hollandi Capital 2013).

SC, *Capital Market Masterplan* (SC 2001).

———, *Capital Market Masterplan 2* (SC 2011).

———, *The Islamic Securities (Sukuk) Market* (LexisNexis Malaysia 2009a).

———, 'Mega Sukuk Defaults – Acid Test for Islamic Finance' (2009b) 4 Quarterly Bulletin of Malaysian Islamic Capital Market 1.

———, *Regulatory Requirement, Legal Documentation, Accounting, Auditing and Taxation in the Islamic Capital Market* (LexisNesis 2009c).

———, *Resolutions of The Secuities Commission Shariah Advisory Council* (2 edn, Securities Commission 2007).

Schacht J, *An Introduction to Islamic Law* (Oxford University Press 1982).

Schmid T, 'The Real Shariah Risk: Why The United States Cannot Afford To Miss The Islamic Finance Moment' (2013) 3 University of Illinois Law Review 1293.

Schwarcz S, 'The Alchemy of Asset Securitization' (1994) 1 Stanford Journal of Law, Business and Finance 133.

Shaharuddin A and others, *Fatwas on Islamic Capital Markets: A Comparative Study between Malaysia and Gulf Co-Operation Council (GCC) Countries* (ISRA 2014).

Shapiro R, 'The Importance of International Standards in Managing Defaults in Islamic Finance: Saudi Arabia and the Saad Group's Sukuk Default' (*Sonecon*, May 2013). http://www.sonecon.com/docs/studies/Shapiro_Paper_Sukuk_Default_new.pdf. Accessed 6 September 2015.

Sharif A and Anwar H, 'Saad Investors Agree to Dissolve Islamic Bond Trust' (*Bloomberg*, 28 April 2010). http://www.bloomberg.com/news/2010-04-28/saad-trading-bondholders-approve-dissolution-of-650-million-sukuk-trust.html. Accessed 22 December 2013.

Shenker J and Colletta A, 'Asset Securitiszation: Evolution, Current Issues and New Frontiers' (1991) 69 Texas Law Review 1369.

Shihata I, 'The Role of Law in Business Development' (1996) 20 Fordham International Law Journal 1577.

Singh T, 'Opening Remarks to the Roundtable' in IFSB, IOSCO and SC (eds), *Disclosure Requirements for Islamic Capital Market Products* (IFSB, IOSCO and SC 2013).

Siswantoro D, 'Analysis of the First Ijarah Sukuk Default In Indonesia: How Could It Be?' (2013) 3 International Journal of Islamic Banking & Finance 1.

Soanes C and Stevenson A (eds), *Oxford Dictionary of English* (Oxford University Press 2006).

Souaiaia A, 'On the Sources of Islamic Law and Practices' (2004–2005) 20 Journal of Law and Religion 123.

Soualhi Y, 'Bridging Islamic Juristic Differences in Contemporary Islamic Finance' (2012) 26 Arab Law Quarterly 313.

Sturgess B, 'Sukuk Defaults in the Kingdom: A Case Study in Saudi Arabia's Opaque Bankruptcy Process' (*World Economics*, March 2013). http://www.worldeconomics.com/Papers/Sukuk%20Defaults%20in%20the%20Kingdom%20A%20Case%20Study%20in%20Saudi%20Arabia%E2%80%99s%20Opaque%20Bankruptcy%20Process_d7d209a1-a644-4568-9d43-cca1f82ec535.paper?PaperID=D7D209A1-A644-4568-9D43-CCA1F82EC535. Accessed 2 January 2014.

Sukuk, 'Golden Belt Sukuk Holders Approve Dissolution' (*Sukuk*, 18 May 2010). http://www.sukuk.com/news/articles/28/Golden-Belt-sukuk-holders-approve-dissolution.html. Accessed 22 December 2013.

———, 'Saad Unit Defaults on Sukuk' (*Sukuk*, 15 November 2009). http://www.sukuk.com/news/articles/72/Sukukme-Saad-unit-defaults-on-sukuk.html. Accessed 22 December 2013.

Sundararajan V, 'Profit Sharing Investment Accounts: Measurement and Control of Displaced Commercial Risk (DCR) In Islamic Finance' (undated) 19 Islamic Economic Studies 41.

Tariq A, 'Managing Financial Risks of Sukuk Structures' (Master Thesis, Loughborough University 2004).

Tariq A and Dar H, 'Risks of Sukuk Structures: Implications for Resource Mobilization' (2007) 49 Thunderbrid International Business Review 203.

Thani N and Othman A, 'The Effective of the Legal and Regulatory Framework for Islamic Financial Services' in IFSB (ed), *Islamic Finance: Global Legal Issues and Challenges* (IFSB 2008).

The Board of Taxation, 'Review of the Taxation Treatment of Islamic Finance: Discussion Paper' (*Taxboard*, 2010). http://www.taxboard.gov.au/content/reviews_and_consultations/islamic_finance_products/discussion_paper/downloads/Islamic_Finance_Discussion_Paper.pdf. Accessed 23 April 2015.

The Economist, 'The Fallout From A Falling Out' (*The Economist*, 9 July 2009). http://www.economist.com/node/13998715. Accessed 21 December 2013.

The Investment Dar, 'About TID' (*TID*, 2013). http://www.inv-dar.com/En_AboutTID.cms. Accessed 17 December 2013.

———, 'Our History-Milestones' (*TID*, undated). http://www.inv-dar.com/En_OurHistory.cms?ActiveID=1083. Accessed 21 December 2013.

The United States Securities and Exchange Commission, 'Form 10-K' (*Wikinvest*, 31 December 2008). http://www.wikinvest.com/stock/TEL_Offshore_Trust_(TELOZ)/Filing/10-K/2009/F3243816. Accessed 11 December 2013.

Thomas A and Mokhtar S, 'Debt-Based Sukuk: Murabahah, Istisna' and Istithmar (Tawarruq) Sukuk' in Thomas A (ed), *Sukuk* (Sweet & Maxwell Asia 2009).

Thompson B, 'Abu Dhabi Gives Dubai $10bn to Help Pay Debts' (*BBC*, 14 December 2009). http://news.bbc.co.uk/1/hi/8411215.stm. Accessed 22 December 2013.

Virgo G, *The Principles of Equity & Trusts* (Oxford University Press 2012).

Vishwanath S and Azmi S, 'An Overview of Islamic Sukuk Bonds' (2009) The Journal of Structured Finance 58.

Vizcaino B, 'Oman sets up central Sharia Board in Move to Boost Islamic Finance' (*Reuters*, 2014). https://www.reuters.com/article/oman-islam-financing/oman-sets-up-central-sharia-board-in-move-to-boost-islamic-finance-idUSL6N0S305J20141008. Accessed 25 December 2018.

Walker G, 'Financial Markets and Exchanges' in Blair M, Walker G and Willey S (eds), *Financial Markets and Exchanges Law* (2nd edn, Oxford University Press 2012).

Wedderburn-Day R, 'Sovereign Sukuk: Adaption and Innovation' (2010) 73 Law and Contemporary Problems 325.

White & Case LLP, 'ISDA/IIFM Launch Tahawwut Master Agreement' (*White & Case LLP*, 2010). http://www.whitecase.com/files/Publication/9446775f-ab73-45e4-9431-fc8ca9765529/Presentation/PublicationAttachment/378e2415-b4ab-49c3-9c3f-02a221de1d18/alert_ISDAIIFM_Launch.pdf. Accessed 19 November 2013.

Wico Y, 'Comparative Evaluation of Regulatory and Best Practices on Disclosure of Islamic Capital Market Products' in IFSB, IOSCO and SC (eds), *Disclosure Requirements for Islamic Capital Market Products* (IFSB, IOSCO and SC 2013).

Wigglesworth R, 'Fears Rise Over Islamic Bonds' (*Financial Times*, 2009a). http://www.ft.com/cms/s/0/7e73fb0a-dac5-11de-933d-00144feabdc0.html#axzz2l0eYFI00. Accessed 18 November 2013.

———, 'Sukuk: Defaults Destabilise A Reviving Market' (*Financial Times*, 7 December 2009b). http://www.ft.com/cms/s/0/90e4c3d6-e2be-11de-b028-00144feab49a.html#axzz2p9f6MCpA. Accessed 1 January 2014.

Wilson R, 'How Expansive are the Frontiers' in Thomas A (ed), *Sukuk* (Sweet & Maxwell Asia 2009a).

———, 'Innovation in the Structuring of Islamic Sukuk Securities' (2008) 24 Humanomics 170.

———, 'Islamic Capital Markets: the Role of Sukuk' in Qatar Financial Center Authority (ed), (Bloomsbury Information Ltd 2010).

———, 'Sharīʿah Governance for Islamic Financial Instituions' (2009b) 1 ISRA International Journal of Islamic Finance 59.

———, 'Sukuk Defaults: Islamic Debt Investors Need Better Data' (*World Economics*, February 2013). http://www.world-economics-journal.com/Papers/Sukuk%20Defaults%20Islamic%20Debt%20Investors%20Need%20Better%20Data_435d6ca7-d1ab-4ab1-afe1-b108784cc835.paper?PaperID=435D6CA7-D1AB-4AB1-AFE1-B108784CC835. Accessed 22 December 2013.

Wong S and Seward J, 'Insolvency Regimes: Developing an Analytical Framework for Meeting Legal and Regulatory Challenges for Islamic Finance' in IFSB and WB (eds), *Effective Insolvency Regimes: Institutional, Regulatory, and Legal Issues Relating to Islamic Finance* (IFSB & WB 2011).

Wouters P, 'Asset-Backed Sukuk — Islamic Finance Going its Own Way' (*Islamic Finance News*, 2011). http://www.fimm.com.my/%5Cpdf%5CProduct%20Knowledge%5C30Mac11_Asset-backed%20Sukuk.pdf. Accessed 12 March 2013.

Yaacob H, Mohammad M and Smolo E, *International Convention for Islamic Finance: Towards Standardisation* (ISRA 2011).

Yunis H, 'Islamic Finance Transactions and the Impact of Insolvency' in IFSB and WB (eds), *Effective Insolvency Regimes: Institutional, Regulatory, and Legal Issues Relating to Islamic Finance* (IFSB and WB 2011).

Yussof S, 'Measuring Sharīʿah Compliance in Ṣukūk Ratings: A Survey of Existing Methodologies' in Kamali M and Abdullah A (eds), *Islamic Finance: Issues in Sukuk and Proposals for Reform* (International Institute of Advanced Islamic Studies and Islamic Foundation 2014).

Zacharias D, 'Fundamentals of the Sunnī Schools of Law' (2006) 66 ZaöRV 491.

Zaheer S and Wijnbergen S, 'Sukuk Defaults: on Distress Resolution in Islamic Finance' (*Tinbergen*, 2013). http://papers.tinbergen.nl/13087.pdf. Accessed 26 May 2015.

Zahid A and Ali H, 'Shari'ah as a Choice of Law in International Islamic Financial Contracts: Shamil Bank of Bahrain Case Revisited' (2013) 10 US-China Law Review 27.

Zahraa M, 'Characteristic Features of Islamic Law: Perceptions and Misconceptions' (2000) 15 Arab Law Quarterly 168.

Zaidi J, 'Nature of Risks Present in Sukuk Structures: Rating Agency Perspective' in Thomas A (ed), *Sukuk* (Sweet & Maxwell Asia 2009).

———, 'Overcoming Barriers to Liquidity: Commoditization, Sukuk, Promoting Issuance and a Secondary Market' (*Iirating*, 2007). http://www.iirating.com/Documents/PresentationSpeeches/speeches/Islamic%20Finance%20and%20Investment%20World%20Europe%202007.pdf. Accessed 11 May 2015.

Index[1]

A

[1] Note: Page numbers followed by 'n' refer to notes.

S. Al-Ali, *Raising Capital on* Ṣukūk *Markets*,
https://doi.org/10.1007/978-3-030-14536-1

GPSR Compliance

The European Union's (EU) General Product Safety Regulation (GPSR) is a set of rules that requires consumer products to be safe and our obligations to ensure this.

If you have any concerns about our products, you can contact us on ProductSafety@springernature.com

In case Publisher is established outside the EU, the EU authorized representative is:

Springer Nature Customer Service Center GmbH
Europaplatz 3
69115 Heidelberg, Germany

Batch number: 10837139

Printed by Printforce, the Netherlands